Legislative Oversight and Budgeting

WBI Development Studies

Legislative Oversight and Budgeting

A World Perspective

Rick Stapenhurst, Riccardo Pelizzo,
David M. Olson, *and* Lisa von Trapp,
Editors

THE WORLD BANK
Washington, DC

ISBN: 978-0-8213-7611-9
eISBN: 978-0-8213-7612-6
DOI: 10.1596/978-0-8213-7611-9

Library of Congress Cataloging-in-Publication Data
Legislative oversight and budgeting : a world perspective / edited Rick Stapenhurst ... [et al.].
   p. cm.
  Includes bibliographical references and index.
  ISBN 978-0-8213-7611-9—ISBN 978-0-8213-7612-6 (electronic)
  1. Budget. 2. Finance, Public—Accounting. 3. Legislative oversight. I. Stapenhurst, Rick.

HJ2005.L36 2008
328.3'456—dc22

2008021329

Contents

Foreword

Effective legislatures are fundamental to promoting good governance and are a critical component in a country's overall governance framework. Although differences exist across government systems, legislatures, through their constitutional mandates, fulfill three core functions: representation, lawmaking, and oversight. Governance goals of greater accountability, transparency, and participation are directly related to these three functions. Legislative oversight in particular seeks to ensure that the executive and its agencies, or those to whom authority is delegated, remain responsive and accountable.

This volume looks at oversight as a continuous and ongoing cycle. Legislatures may examine government policies as they are being developed or work to ensure that programs are implemented and administered efficiently, effectively, and in a manner consistent with legislative intent. In addition, this book highlights the important opportunities provided for oversight during the budget cycle. At the same time, the authors recognize the many factors and incentives legislators face that may assist or impede them in playing their oversight role.

The World Bank Institute's (WBI) parliamentary strengthening program, along with its main partners, seeks to strengthen legislatures' oversight capacity, particularly through the budget process. Specifically, WBI has developed workshops, seminars, and online courses that target members of public accounts committees and finance or budget committees and their staffs, as well as their different interlocutors—representatives from supreme audit institutions and other watchdog agencies, members of the executive branch, and civil society.

WBI also promotes applied research on legislative capacity building with regard to oversight. For example, WBI supported two roundtables during the annual meetings of the Southern Political Science Association: "Legislative Strengthening: Theories and Practices" (2004) and "The Role of Parliaments in the Budget Process" (cosponsored with Legislative Politics in 2005). More recently, WBI collaborated with the Research Committee of Legislative Specialists to facilitate a roundtable on "Recent Trends in Parliamentary Oversight" as part of the American Political Science Association's 2007 annual meeting. Several of the authors represented in this book, both academics and practitioners, presented versions of their chapters during these roundtables, and several other chapters were originally published as part of WBI's Working Papers Series on Contemporary Issues in Parliamentary Development.

Legislative oversight has often been lamented as understudied, but the chapters in this book are evidence of both a renewed interest and a growing body of literature on the topic. And although literature on legislative oversight has tended to be heavily weighted toward studies of established industrial democracies and the United States especially, the country case studies in this volume examine countries from around the world with diverse government systems, political contexts, histories, and cultures. Their various experiences and lessons learned are useful to legislators, legislative-strengthening practitioners, and other groups (such as civil society organizations) that work with legislatures, donors who support legislative strengthening work, and academics undertaking research in this field.

I would like to thank the Finnish Parliament and Ministry of Foreign Affairs, the Canadian International Development Agency, the Japanese Ministry of Finance, and the Norwegian Ministry of Foreign Affairs for their support of WBI's Parliamentary Strengthening Program and the publication of this book.

Roumeen Islam
Manager, Poverty Reduction & Economic Management
World Bank Institute

Introduction

Of the three core functions of legislatures—representation, lawmaking, and oversight—oversight is perhaps the least studied and practiced. Representation, however well or poorly it is done, has an impetus in the ambitions of organized parties, a periodic test in elections, and a performance standard in the correspondence between what people want and what they think they are getting. Lawmaking—which ranges from ritual legislative involvement to full participation in governing—is a constitutionally mandated event in almost any system even pretending to a rule of law. Oversight, by contrast, is not typically bolstered by the same order of external institutions or required events or with the same urgency and visibility. Moreover, oversight involves assessing the implementation process, and this generally occurs outside the public eye and in activities that are scattered in space and time.

Despite these conceptual and practical difficulties, this book demonstrates that legislative oversight does have scholars documenting its variety and effects, democratization proponents advocating its place among good governance practices, and elected officials in the countries promoting the legislative function of oversight through their activities.

My own perspective on legislative oversight comes from my scholarly interest in policy implementation and my interest in improving governance practices as a practitioner of democracy assistance. David Olson, in the concluding chapter of this book, observes that oversight occurs toward the end of the policy process, during the implementation of laws. In many systems, even those with a formal separation of legislative policy making and executive administrative powers, it is the opportunity for legislators to participate in implementation. Many of the evaluative standards that are applied in the implementation literature to measure how well a policy has been implemented have their parallels in the tasks of legislative oversight: fidelity to the law, probity in spending, efficiency in choices, effectiveness in producing the desired outcomes, and the acceptability and legitimacy of processes. Since it is the legislature that examines executive behavior, oversight is also a tool for checking the behavior of the system's single most powerful political actor. Many of the chapters in this book hit one or more of these different facets of critiquing how executives implement the law. Although policy making and lawmaking are often seen as the central legislative task, concern with the implementation of law is the realm of legislative oversight.

Just as a complete view of the policy process requires a concern with both policy making and implementation, a fuller involvement of the legislature in governing may be just what is needed to bring what people want closer into line with what they get. This lesson has been driven home to me during my recent experience directing a legislative assistance program in Nigeria. In 2008, a Nigeria House of Representatives committee investigation revealed that Nigeria had spent, under the former President Obasanjo, over US$10 billion for expanding power-generating capacity and received zero kilowatt hours in return. Many believe that the Nigerians already have many of the laws they need, they have the money thanks to oil, and they nominally spend it on many of the things people want, including power generation. The problem is that they are not receiving value for money spent when programs are not implemented by the executive (large sums are returned to the treasury because of the inability to spend the funds), resources are diverted through corruption, inefficient choices are made, and so many of the outcomes they seek worsen even as spending increases. The literature on democracy and economic growth stresses the democratic advantage of giving leaders feedback about how they are doing; legislative oversight is an important but underused means for giving them that information in a form that is typically hard to ignore.

This book originated in large part with the concern of practitioners about increasing and improving the part played by legislative oversight in governing developing democracies. As part of its governance program, the Poverty Reduction and Economic Reform Division of the World Bank Institute (WBIPR) seeks to strengthen parliamentary oversight to promote enhanced government accountability and transparency. WBI supported earlier work on the subject and, starting in 2004, collaborated with the Research Committee of Legislative Specialists (RCLS). Together they organized a series of roundtables, initially at the Southern Political Science Association's annual conference and, more recently, at the American Political Science Association's conference. Versions of many of the chapters in this book were originally presented during these roundtables.

The goal of this WBI-RCLS collaboration was to bring together scholars and practitioners working on oversight from many different perspectives and in many different legislative settings. Thus, this book is a truly eclectic compilation that samples worlds of practice and scholarship, both of which are in some flux.

The Distribution of Oversight Tools and Implications

The book begins with an inventory of oversight tools and powers and their distribution across different political systems. Riccardo Pelizzo and Rick

Stapenhurst, in chapter 1, present data on oversight tools collected from a survey of 83 countries by the Inter-Parliamentary Union in collaboration with the World Bank Institute. Data analysis reveals that legislatures in parliamentary systems are generally better equipped to oversee government activities than are legislatures in presidential and semipresidential systems. In the budget process of presidential systems, legislatures are generally the most active in the preparation of the budget, whereas legislatures in parliamentary systems are the most active in approving the budget. However, the tools alone cannot predict a legislature's oversight effectiveness, or the extent to which oversight potential is used in practice.

Pelizzo, in chapter 2 argues that a parliament's oversight potential, measured by the number of oversight tools available to a parliament in a given country, affects the probability that that country is formally democratic or a liberal democracy. Pelizzo supports this by statistical analysis. He also finds that the only oversight tool that is strongly and significantly related to a country's liberal-democratic status is the institutionalization of the ombudsman function.

Oversight and the Budget Process

"Deep Throat," an inside informant, advised reporters investigating wrongdoing in the Nixon Administration to "follow the money," and public policy scholar Eugene Bardach has argued that this is the best way to trace what is happening during implementation. The budget process provides critical opportunities for legislative oversight. As such, part two (chapters 3 through 10) examines budget oversight from the formulation and approval of the budget to the implementation and the ex post examination of the public accounts. In chapter 3, Stapenhurst describes legislatures' different roles in financial oversight and considers some of the lessons emerging from a decade of legislative development and reform. In chapter 4, Kerry Jacobs demonstrates, from an accountant's perspective, how the nature and role of budgets has a number of practical implications for those charged with exercising budgetary oversight. Then in chapter 5, Joachim Wehner constructs an index using data for 36 countries from a 2003 survey of budgeting procedures. The index captures six institutional prerequisites for legislative control, relating to amendment powers, reversionary budgets, executive flexibility during implementation, the timing of the budget, legislative committees, and budgetary information. The results reveal substantial variation in the level of legislatures' financial scrutiny of government among contemporary liberal democracies, suggesting that the power of the purse is a discrete and nonfundamental element of liberal-democratic governance.

Drawing on information from the World Bank–Organisation for Economic Co-operation and Development (OECD) budget procedures database and data from the Center for Budget and Policy Priorities' International Budget Project Open Budget Survey, Katherine Barraclough and Bill Dorotinsky, in chapter 6, examine legislatures' roles at the drafting stage of the budget and identify factors that influence different degrees of legislative involvement. The chapter also highlights some good practices for optimizing the role of the legislature in this phase to improve fiscal discipline, strategic allocation of resources, and operational efficiency.

In chapter 7 Dorotinsky again uses the World Bank-OECD budget procedures database to describe what happens if no budget is passed before the fiscal year begins and outlines the potential costs of failing to reach agreement. Data for OECD and non-OECD countries are compared, as well as parliamentary and presidential systems of government.

Specialized committees have emerged as fundamental tools for oversight in general and for the budget process and spending of public monies in particular. In many parliaments, the Public Accounts Committee (PAC) serves as the audit committee of parliament, making it a core institution of public financial accountability. PACs tend to be found in Westminster-model parliaments across the Commonwealth, although several other parliaments have adopted PACs, including Finland, Ethiopia, and Rwanda, among others. In chapter 8, Pelizzo and Stapenhurst look more closely at the specific oversight tool of PACs in national and subnational parliaments throughout the Commonwealth. Using a survey of 33 PAC chairs, they examine how PACs can contibute to effective oversight of government accounts and the conditions that promote a PAC's good functioning and success.

Effective oversight committees are most often those with supportive staff, useful partners, and allies from the bureaucracy and civil society. Legislatures and their committees are often assisted in their oversight function by extra-parliamentary accountability institutions, such as supreme audit institutions and ombudsmen. Parliamentary budget offices may also provide independent expertise and support to parliament. Barry Anderson, in chapter 9, discusses the potential value of such independent analytical budget units in putting the legislature on a more equal footing with the executive and in increasing the overall transparency, credibility, and accountability of the budget process. He concludes that such units must be nonpartisan, independent, and objective to successfully fulfill their core functions.

In chapter 10, John K. Johnson and Rick Stapenhurst examine the differences and similarities between six established and two planned budget offices. They argue that several more budget offices will appear over the next decade, particularly in countries with long-standing traditions of nonpartisan parliamentary services. Later in the book, Hon. Beatrice Kiraso Birungi provides an in-depth study of the Uganda Parliamentary Budget Office (PBO) alluded to in the Johnson and Stapenhurst piece. The Ugandan PBO was established by a private members bill, which also established a budget committee and redefined the way Uganda's Parliament participates in the budget process. It was passed despite government opposition. Kiraso demonstrates how parliaments can initiate their own legislation to ensure that they are able to participate fully and in a meaningful way in the budget process. Uganda's PBO, its successes, and the challenges it has faced offer many useful lessons for other parliaments.

A Study of Countries' Experiences

In the final section, attention turns to how oversight operates in the context of specific places. Chapters 11 through 22, in part three, present case studies that examine legislative oversight in regions and countries around the world. David Olson argues that the Polish Sejm is currently the most active post-communist parliament in terms of oversight and administrative review. He suggests that, in light of the Polish experience, postcommunist parliaments will have increasing capacity to be active in oversight as a result of both the budget process and the growing international influences on policy choices. In chapter 12, Thomas Remington examines the use of de facto oversight mechanisms by the Russian Federal Assembly and relates them to institutional performance in the postcommunist Russian state. He finds that, in contrast with the early 1990s, policy making has become much more efficient.

Mark Shephard, in chapter 13, contends that despite the House of Commons' awareness of its limitations in administrative review and oversight, change has been slow and hampered by the constitutional framework, executive hegemony, and strong partisanship within the United Kingdom's Parliament. Although some important concessions have been made recently, many of the successful reforms have focused on improving the efficiency of oversight rather than on ensuring the effectiveness of oversight. In chapter 14, Scott Desposato investigates how legislatures' ability to engage in effective oversight activities is related to both the formal institutional framework and informal institutional incentives. He demonstrates the impact of informal institutional incentives on the state assemblies' ability to oversee executive activities in Brazil.

Edward Schneier, in chapter 15, examines why the postreform Indonesian parliament has not put mechanisms of legislative oversight to effective use. Schneier cites endemic corruption and other political dynamics that diminish the legislature's incentives to perform an oversight role. In chapter 21, Vishnu Juwono and Sebastian Eckardt look more specifically at the role of the Indonesian parliament in budget oversight. They note that parliament now holds stronger powers with regard to the preparation of the state budget and oversight of its execution. However, they find, among other things, that excessively detailed legislative involvement in the current budget preparation process consumes considerable time and resources, and attention to detailed line items may distract from the focus on more aggregate spending priorities in the budget.

In chapter 16, Chen Friedberg examines parliamentary oversight in the Israeli parliament, the Knesset, through the lens of two committees, the State Control Committee and the Education and Culture Committee, during the 7th, 10th, and 13th Knessets. She focuses on the structural and procedural problems that characterize the Israeli parliamentary committee system and that may impair the effectiveness of its oversight.

In chapter 17 Robert J. Griffiths discusses parliamentary oversight of defense policy in postapartheid South Africa. Using the case study of the Strategic Defense Procurement Package, he provides insight into the development of transparency and accountability in defense policy, while highlighting the challenges to effective parliamentary oversight, such as party discipline, executive-legislative relations, and the capacity of parliamentary committees to adequately monitor the complexities of government policies.

While legislative budget institutions are being rediscovered as part of a second wave of reform in government financial administration, in chapter 18 Carlos Santiso finds that parliaments in Latin America are too often weak and discredited, with limited institutional capacity or political incentives to influence the budget. This situation is due to executive dominance as well as parliaments' own deficiencies. Ultimately Santiso argues that the governance of the budget must reflect a delicate balance between executive prerogatives and legislative oversight.

Carolyn Forestiere and Riccardo Pelizzo study how institutional and political conditions influence the Italian Parliament's power over the budget. Drawing on institutional and party system theories, they argue in chapter 19 that procedures and ideology provide the greatest incentives for parliamentarians to deviate from unilaterally supporting their governments during the passage of the national budget.

In chapter 20 Zdenka Mansfeldová and Petra Rakušanová analyze the bargaining process in the legislature of the Czech Republic. Over recent years, the budget process has undergone some great changes. Although the distribution of party power in the Parliament and the Budget Committee remains of crucial importance, joining the European Union has led the Parliament to seek a greater profile and strengthen its audit functions. At the same time professionalization of the deputies on the Budget Committee has greatly increased the committee's influence and prestige.

In his conclusions Olson notes that the chapters in this volume, written at various times, with different data, and for different purposes, are not the product of a single encompassing research design. To some degree the chapters in this book illustrate the difficulties in developing a limited and workable definition of legislative *oversight*. Moreover, while the policy implications of oversight are potentially important and deserve more research than reported in this book, the policy consequences of oversight need to be clearly distinguished from the oversight function itself. The case studies demonstrate the different means that legislatures have at their disposal for oversight, but also the different ways legislatures use these means. A variety of external and internal factors come into play, which may constrain or enable a given legislature's oversight capacity. In thinking about a given legislature's oversight function, it is important to examine time, societal context, and executive branches as both enabling and limiting oversight.

Robert T. Nakamura,
Resident Country Director, Nigeria
National Democratic Institute of International Affairs
Professor of Political Science, University at Albany, SUNY

I. OVERVIEW

CHAPTER 1

Tools for Legislative Oversight: An Empirical Investigation

Riccardo Pelizzo and Rick Stapenhurst

Roberta Maffio, in the journal *Quaderni di Scienza Politica* (2002), published a detailed and informative discussion of legislative oversight in comparative perspective. Her article testifies to the revived interest in the long-neglected study of legislative oversight of executive activity and provides a wealth of information with regard to the types, variety, and functioning of the instruments of legislative oversight.

Maffio developed a conceptual mapping of oversight tools, discussed their characteristics, and investigated whether the adoption of oversight tools by legislatures is related to a *model* of democracy (majoritarian, consensual, or mixed). She concluded that there is no correlation between the model of democracy and oversight potential. "There are some majoritarian democracies with strong oversight potential (such as Greece) and others with weak oversight potential (such as Ireland, New Zealand, and the United Kingdom). Similarly, among consensual democracies, she found cases characterized by both high oversight potential (such as Belgium, Germany, and the Netherlands) and by low oversight potential (for example, Japan)" (361).

This chapter builds upon and extends Mafio's analysis. Using data collected in 2001 by the Inter-Parliamentary Union (IPU) and the World Bank Institute (WBI) for 82 countries and the European Parliament (see table 1.1),[1] it investigates the relationship between legislatures' oversight potential and three variables: type of government (presidential, semipresidential, or parliamentary); gross national income level (low, middle, or high); and level of democracy (nondemocratic, quasi-democratic, or democratic) John Lees (1977) broadly defined legislative oversight as "the behavior by legislators and their staffs, individually or collectively, which results in an impact, intended or not, on bureaucratic behavior" (193).

In overseeing the executive, legislatures have many different tools at their disposal. Among the most common oversight tools are committee hearings, hearings in plenary sittings, commissions of inquiry, questions, question time,

Table 1.1. The Tools of Legislative Oversight

Country	Committee hearing	Hearing in plenary sitting	Commission of Inquiry	Questions	Question time	Interpellations	Ombudsman
Andorra	yes	yes	yes	yes	yes	n.a.	yes
Angola	yes	no	yes	yes	no	yes	no
Armenia	yes	yes	no	yes	yes	no	no
Australia	yes	no	yes	yes	yes	no	yes
Austria	yes	yes	yes	yes	yes	yes	yes
Azerbaijan	n.a.	n.a.	n.a.	no	n.a.	yes	yes
Belarus	yes	yes	yes	yes	yes	yes	n.a.
Belgium	yes	yes	yes	yes	yes	yes	yes
Benin	yes	yes	yes	yes	yes	yes	no
Brazil	yes	yes	yes	yes	no	yes	yes
Bulgaria	yes	yes	yes	yes	yes	n.a.	no
Cameroon	yes	yes	yes	yes	yes	no	no
Canada	yes	yes	yes	yes	yes	yes	no
Chad	yes	no	yes	yes	yes	yes	yes
China	yes	yes	yes	yes	n.a.	no	n.a.
Congo, Dem. Rep. of	n.a.	n.a.	n.a.	yes	no	yes	yes
Costa Rica	yes	yes	yes	yes	yes	yes	yes
Côte d'Ivoire	no	no	yes	yes	yes	no	yes
Croatia	yes	yes	yes	yes	yes	yes	yes
Cyprus	yes	yes	yes	yes	yes	no	yes
Czech Republic	yes	yes	yes	yes	yes	yes	yes
Estonia	yes	yes	yes	yes	yes	yes	yes
European Union	yes	yes	yes	yes	n.a.	yes	yes
France	yes	yes	yes	yes	yes	yes	yes
Gabon	yes	yes	yes	yes	yes	yes	yes
Germany	yes	yes	yes	yes	no	yes	yes
Greece	yes	yes	yes	yes	yes	yes	yes
Guatemala	yes	yes	yes	yes	yes	yes	n.a.

Country						
Guinea	yes	yes	yes	yes	yes	no
Guinea-Bissau	yes	yes	yes	yes	yes	no
Hungary	yes	yes	yes	yes	yes	yes
Iceland	yes	yes	yes	yes	n.a.	yes
Indonesia	yes	yes	yes	no	yes	yes
Iran, Islamic Rep. of	yes	yes	yes	yes	yes	n.a.
Ireland	yes	yes	yes	yes	n.a.	yes
Jamaica	yes	yes	yes	yes	no	yes
Japan	yes	yes	yes	yes	yes	yes
Jordan	yes	yes	yes	no	n.a.	yes
Kazakhstan	no	yes	yes	yes	no	no
Korea, Rep. Of	yes	yes	yes	yes	no	yes
Latvia	yes	yes	yes	n.a.	yes	yes
Lesotho	n.a.	n.a.	n.a.	n.a.	n.a.	n.a.
Liechtenstein	yes	no	no	no	yes	no
Lithuania	yes	yes	yes	yes	yes	yes
Luxem-bourg	yes	yes	yes	yes	yes	no
Macedonia	n.a.	n.a.	n.a.	no	yes	yes
Madagascar	yes	yes	yes	yes	yes	yes
Mali	yes	yes	yes	yes	yes	yes
Mexico	yes	no	yes	yes	n.a.	no
Mongolia	yes	yes	yes	yes	n.a.	yes
Namibia	yes	yes	yes	yes	n.a.	yes
Netherlands	yes	yes	yes	yes	n.a.	yes
Nicaragua	yes	yes	no	no	yes	yes
Niger	yes	yes	yes	yes	yes	no
Palau	no	yes	yes	yes	yes	yes
Philippines	n.a.	yes	yes	yes	n.a.	yes
Poland	yes	yes	yes	yes	n.a.	yes
Romania	yes	yes	yes	yes	yes	yes

(continued)

Table 1.1. (continued)

Country	Committee hearing	Hearing in plenary sitting	Commission of inquiry	Questions	Question time	Interpellations	Ombudsman
Russian Federation	n.a.	n.a.	n.a.	yes	n.a.	n.a.	yes
Rwanda	no	no	no	yes	yes	yes	yes
Samoa	n.a.	yes	yes	yes	yes	no	yes
Senegal	yes	yes	yes	yes	no	no	yes
Singapore	yes	yes	yes	yes	yes	n.a.	no
Slovak Republic	yes	yes	n.a.	yes	yes	yes	yes
Slovenia	yes	yes	n.a.	yes	yes	yes	yes
South Africa	yes	yes	n.a.	yes	yes	no	yes
Spain	yes	yes	yes	yes	yes	yes	yes
Sudan	yes	yes	yes	yes	yes	n.a.	no
Sweden	yes	yes	yes	yes	yes	yes	yes
Switzerland	yes	yes	yes	yes	yes	yes	no
Tajikistan	n.a.	n.a.	yes	yes	n.a.	yes	n.a.
Thailand	yes	yes	yes	yes	yes	n.a.	yes
Togo	yes	yes	yes	yes	yes	yes	no
Tunisia	yes	yes	yes	yes	yes	no	yes
Turkey	yes	yes	yes	yes	yes	no	no
Uganda	yes	yes	yes	yes	yes	n.a.	yes
Ukraine	n.a.	yes	n.a.	yes	yes	yes	yes
United Kingdom	yes	yes	yes	yes	yes	no	yes
Uruguay	yes	no	yes	yes	n.a.	yes	no
Yemen, Republic of	yes	yes	yes	yes	yes	no	no
Yugoslavia	yes	yes	yes	yes	yes	yes	no
Zambia	yes	yes	yes	yes	no	yes	yes
Zimbabwe	n.a.	n.a.	n.a.	yes	yes	n.a.	yes

Source: Authors' compilation from the IPU-WBI survey (Pelizzo and Stapenhurst, 2004a).
Note: n.a. = not applicable.

interpellations, the ombudsman, auditors general, committees (in general), and public accounts committees (more specifically).[2] These oversight tools can be grouped along two different dimensions: timing of the oversight activity (ex ante or ex post) and whether the activity is internal or external to the legislature. If legislative oversight is performed during policy formulation or before the government becomes engaged in a specific activity, then it is *ex ante*. Hearings in committees, hearings in the plenary, and requests for documentation are all tools that can be used ex ante. If legislative oversight is performed after the government has enacted a policy, to check whether that policy has been properly implemented, then it is *ex post*. Questions, interpellations, and committees of inquiry are examples of tools that are used ex post. Similarly, questions, question time, interpellations, hearings, and public account committees are *internal* tools, and ombudsmen and auditors general are *external* tools.

The IPU-WBI survey asked a variety of questions.[3] This chapter focuses only on questions and responses related to oversight of the government. Specifically, respondents were asked whether the government was considered an institution that must report to the legislature; how the legislature exercises oversight; whether the legislature can question government officials; whether the legislature holds question time; whether there are interpellations; and whether there is an ombudsman.[4] The resulting data indicate legislatures' potential for oversight (although not whether oversight is effective) by showing which institutional arrangements have been adopted to enhance oversight. The data can also be used to investigate whether the distribution of oversight tools is related to other variables, such as a country's system of government, its national income level, or the level of democracy as measured by the Gastil Index of Freedom.[5]

The Distribution of Oversight Tools and the Potential for Oversight

The data presented in tables 1.1 and 1.2 are interesting in at least three respects. First of all, the data indicate considerable variation in how common these various tools of legislative oversight are. For example, legislators can put oral or written questions to the government in 79 of the 82 countries (or 96 percent) for which data are available. Committees of inquiry and committee hearings are also common instruments of legislative control, used in more than 95 percent of the countries for which data are available. By contrast, interpellations and the ombudsman are considerably less common, with interpellations to the government used in about 75 percent of the countries and ombudsman offices instituted in less than 73 percent (see table 1.2).

Second, the analysis of the data indicates that all countries adopt some legislative oversight tools and that most use more than one tool. Complete information is available for only 49 of the 83 legislatures that were surveyed. In the remaining 34 legislatures information was incomplete or not provided at all (as in the case of Lesotho). In any case, more than 12 percent of the countries for which complete information is available use four legislative oversight tools, more than 14 percent use five tools, almost 33 percent use six tools, and the remaining 40 percent use seven tools (see table 1.3).

Table 1.2. Use of Oversight Tools, by Number of Respondents
(percent; N = 82)

Committee hearing	Hearing in plenary sitting	Committee of inquiry	Questions	Question time	Interpellations	Ombudsman
96	91	96	96	85	75	73

Source: Authors' compilation from the IPU-WBI survey (Pelizzo and Stapenhurst, 2004a).

Table 1.3. Number of Legislative Oversight Tools Used by Surveyed Countries

Zero	Two	Three	Four	Five	Six	Seven
Lesotho	Azerbaijan	Congo, Dem. Rep. of	Angola	Australia	Andorra	Austria
	Russian Federation	Macedonia	Armenia	Bulgaria	Belarus	Belgium
		Tajikistan	China	Cameroon	Benin	Costa Rica
		Zimbabwe	Côte d'Ivoire	Iran, Islamic Rep. of	Brazil	Croatia
			Kazakhstan	Jordan	Canada	Czech Republic
			Liechtenstein	Mexico	Chad	Estonia
			Rwanda	Mongolia	Cyprus	France
			Uruguay	Nicaragua	European Union	Gabon
				Palau	Germany	Greece
				Philippines	Guatemala	Hungary
				Samoa	Guinea	Indonesia
				Senegal	Guinea-Bissau	Japan
				Singapore	Iceland	Lithuania
				South Africa	Ireland	Madagascar
				Sudan	Korea, Rep. of	Mali
				Turkey	Jamaica	Romania
				Ukraine	Latvia	Spain
				Yemen, Rep. Of	Luxembourg	Sweden
					Namibia	Switzerland
					Netherlands	Zambia
					Niger	
					Poland	
					Slovakia	
					Slovenia	
					Thailand	
					Togo	
					Tunisia	
					Uganda	
					United Kingdom	

Source: Authors' compilation from the IPU-WBI survey (Pelizzo and Stapenhurst, 2004a).
Note: The scores of the countries in italics indicates that information concerning the presence or absence of some tools of legislative oversight was unavailable, as indicated in table 1.1.

Forms of Government and Oversight Tools

In addition to providing information concerning the distribution of oversight tools and the potential for legislative oversight, the IPU-WBI data shed some light on how tools and types of oversight are related to the form of government.[6] The analysis shows that the number of oversight tools available varies from one form of government to another. As shown in table 1.4, tools such as committee hearings, hearings in plenary sittings, question time, and interpellations are generally more common in parliamentary forms of government than in presidential and semipresidential systems. As a result, legislatures in parliamentary systems tend to have more oversight tools (and thus more oversight potential) at their disposal (see tables 1.5a and 1.5b).

However, these results do not allow one to make any inference as to the *effectiveness* of the oversight tools in question or *whether* legislatures in parliamentary systems are more effective than legislatures in either presidential or semipresidential systems in overseeing the executive.

Oversight Tools and Income Level

In the 2002 *World Development Indicators* published by the World Bank, countries are divided into three groups: high-income economies, in which the gross national income (GNI) per capita is US$9,266 or more; middle-income economies, with a GNI per capita of between US$755 and US$9,265; and low-income economies, with a GNI per capita below US$755. This information can be transformed into a quantitative variable by assigning the value 1 to countries in the low-income group, value 2 to countries in the middle-income group, and value 3 to countries that belong to the high-income group.

Having created this variable, the analysis was able to investigate whether there is a relationship (and if so, what type of relationship) between income levels of a country and the oversight potential of its legislature. By cross-tabulating the income variable with the number of oversight tools available to a given country's legislature, the analysis finds a clear relationship between income level and the number of oversight tools. The number of oversight tools in the countries that have provided information in this respect varies from a

Table 1.4. Tools of Legislative Oversight, by Form of Government
(percent; N = 82)

Form of government	Committee hearings	Hearings in plenary sittings	Committee of inquiry	Questions	Question time	Interpellations	Ombudsman
Parliamentary	100	97	97	100	89	77	78
Presidential	88	83	100	86	79	72	78
Semipresidential	93	81	87	100	87	75	53

Source: Authors' compilation from the IPU-WBI survey (Pelizzo and Stapenhurst, 2004a).

Table 1.5a. Number of Legislative Oversight Tools, by Form of Government and Country

Form of government	Number of tools			
	Four	Five	Six	Seven
Presidential	Côte d'Ivoire	Nicaragua	Benin	Costa Rica
	Kazakhstan	Palau	Brazil	Indonesia
			Chad	
			Cyprus	
			Guinea	
			Korea, Rep. of	
			Tunisia	
Parliamentary	Liechtenstein	Australia	Canada	Austria
		Turkey	Germany	Belgium
			Guinea-Bissau	Croatia
			Jamaica	Czech Republic
			Luxembourg	Estonia
			United Kingdom	Greece
				Hungary
				Japan
				Lithuania
				Spain
				Sweden
Semipresidential	Angola	Cameroon	Niger	France
	Armenia	Senegal	Togo	Gabon
	Rwanda	Yemen, Rep. of	Yugoslavia	Madagascar
				Mali
				Romania
Other			Switzerland	

Source: Authors' compilation from the IPU-WBI survey (Pelizzo and Stapenhurst, 2004a).
Note: Zambia was not included in this table as it did not provide an answer as to its form of government.

Table 1.5b. Number of Oversight Tools, by Form of Government

Form of government	Number of oversight tools					
	Four	Five	Six	Seven	Total	Mean
Presidential	2	2	7	2	13	5.69
Semipresidential	3	3	3	5	14	5.71
Parliamentary	1	2	6	11	20	6.35
Total	6	7	16	18	47	

Source: Authors' compilation from the IPU-WBI survey (Pelizzo and Stapenhurst, 2004a).

minimum of four tools to a maximum of seven. Legislatures in low-income countries have an average of five and a half oversight tools at their disposal, while legislatures in middle-income and high-income countries have an average of six and a quarter (see table 1.6).

Regarding the distribution of each of the oversight tools by income level, the data presented in table 1.7 suggest that committee hearings become an increasingly popular oversight tool as countries move from low income to middle and high income. Such hearings are used in less than 91 percent of the low-income countries, in almost 97 percent of the middle-income countries, and in all of the high-income countries for which survey data are available.

Hearings in plenary sittings are not as common as committee hearings (see table 1.8), but even these oversight tools become increasingly common with the move from low-income to middle- and high-income countries. Hearings in plenary sittings are used in about 82 percent of the low-income countries, about 94 percent of the middle-income countries, and more than 95 percent of the high-income countries.

The use of questions and question time as oversight tools follows the same pattern observed with regard to both committee hearings and hearings in plenary sittings, becoming more common in higher income countries. Questions

Table 1.6. Number of Oversight Tools, by Income Level

Income level	Number of oversight tools					
	Four	Five	Six	Seven	Total	Mean
Low	4	4	7	3	18	5.50
Middle	1	2	5	8	16	6.25
High	1	1	6	7	15	6.27
Total					49	

Source: Data on income level are taken from the 2002 World Development Indicators, while data on oversight tools are taken from the IPU-WBI survey as indicated above.

Table 1.7. Use of Committee Hearings, by Income Level

Income level	Countries' use of tool			
	No	Yes	Total	% Yes
Low	2	19	21	90.5
Middle	1	29	30	96.7
High	0	21	21	100.0
Total	3	69	72	

Source: Authors' compilation from the IPU-WBI survey (Pelizzo and Stapenhurst, 2004a).

Table 1.8. Use of Hearings in Plenary Sittings, by Income Level

Income level	Countries' use of tool			
	No	Yes	Total	% Yes
Low	4	18	22	81.8
Middle	2	30	32	93.8
High	1	20	21	95.2
Total	7	68	75	

Source: Authors' compilation from the IPU-WBI survey (Pelizzo and Stapenhurst, 2004a).

are used in over 92 percent of the low-income countries surveyed, 97 percent of the middle-income countries, and all of the high-income countries. Question time is used in about 79 percent of the low-income countries, 83 percent of the middle-income countries, and slightly more than 90 percent of the high-income countries (see tables 1.9 and 1.10).

By contrast, use of committees of inquiry, of interpellations, and of an ombudsman's office follows a different pattern (see table 1.11). The survey data suggest that the use of interpellations as an oversight tool is more common in high-income countries (81 percent), less common in low-income countries (about 77 percent), and least common in middle-income countries (less than 70 percent).

Finally, the use of committees of inquiry and an ombudsman as oversight tools are most common in middle-income countries, less common in high-income countries, and least common in low-income countries (see tables 1.12 and 1.13).

Table 1.9. Use of Questions, by Income Level

| Income level | Countries' use of tool | | | |
	No	Yes	Total	% Yes
Low	2	24	26	92.3
Middle	1	33	34	97.1
High	0	21	21	100.0
Total	3	78	81	

Source: Authors' compilation from the IPU-WBI survey (Pelizzo and Stapenhurst, 2004a).

Table 1.10. Use of Question Time, by Income Level

| Income level | Countries' use of tool | | | |
	No	Yes	Total	% Yes
Low	5	19	21	79.2
Middle	5	25	30	83.3
High	2	19	21	90.5
Total	12	63	75	

Source: Authors' compilation from the IPU-WBI survey (Pelizzo and Stapenhurst, 2004a).

Table 1.11. Use of Interpellation, by Income Level

| Income level | Countries' use of tool | | | |
	No	Yes	Total	% Yes
Low	5	17	22	77.3
Middle	8	18	26	69.2
High	3	13	16	81.3
Total	16	48	64	

Source: Authors' compilation from the IPU-WBI survey (Pelizzo and Stapenhurst, 2004a).

Table 1.12. Use of Committees of Inquiry, by Income Level

Income level	Countries' use of tool			
	No	Yes	Total	% Yes
Low	2	20	22	90.9
Middle		30	30	100.0
High	1	19	20	95.0
Total	3	69	72	

Source: Authors' compilation from the IPU-WBI survey (Pelizzo and Stapenhurst, 2004a).

Table 1.13. Presence of Ombudsman as Oversight Tool, by Income Level

Income level	Countries' use of tool			
	No	Yes	Total	% Yes
Low	11	14	25	56.0
Middle	5	25	30	83.3
High	5	16	21	76.2
Total	21	55	76	

Source: Authors' compilation from the IPU-WBI survey (Pelizzo and Stapenhurst, 2004a).

Oversight Tools and Level of Democracy

Freedom House computes an annual index of freedom that is regarded by many social scientists as a proxy index of democracy for all countries. Known as the Gastil Index of Freedom, it is computed in the following way. Freedom House assigns each country a political rights score and a civil liberties score. Both scores are on 7-point scales. The index of freedom is estimated by adding a country's political rights score to its civil liberties score and dividing their sum by 2. This means that the Gastil index is also on a 7-point scale. So, for example, if the fictional country of Abbaba has a score of 3 for its political rights and of 4 for its civil liberties, then Abbaba's democratic score is (3 + 4)/2, or 3.5. Countries that score from 1.0 to 2.5 points on this scale are considered democratic; countries scoring from 3.0 to 5.5 are quasi-democratic, while countries with a score of 5.5 or higher belong to the group of nondemocratic countries. The lower the score a country is given, the more democratic it is.

The democracy variable in this chapter was constructed by recoding the Gastil index by assigning a value of 1 to democratic countries, 2 to quasi-democratic countries, and 3 to nondemocratic countries. Having created this variable, the analysis was able to investigate whether there is a relationship (and if so, what type of relationship) between the level of democracy in a given country and the number of oversight tools available to that country's legislature. By cross-tabulating the level-of-democracy variable with the number of oversight tools available to a country's legislature, the analysis shows a clear relationship between the level of democracy and the number of oversight tools. Nondemocratic countries have an average of

Table 1.14. Number of Oversight Tools, by Level of Democracy

Level of democracy	Number of oversight tools					
	Four	Five	Six	Seven	Total	Mean
Democratic	1	2	9	15	27	6.41
Quasi-democratic	2	3	6	3	14	5.71
Nondemocratic	3	2	3		8	5.00
Total	6	7	18	18	49	

Source: Data on oversight are taken from the IPU-WBI survey, while the Gastil index scores for 2001 were taken from the historical data set prepared by Freedom House. These data are available online at http://www.freedomhouse. org/template.cfm?page=15.

five oversight tools, quasi-democratic countries have an average of five and three-quarters, and democratic countries have an average of almost six and a half (see table 1.14).

The composition of the sample allows the analyst to assess whether a country is a formal democracy or a liberal democracy and to what extent the probability that it is one or the other is affected by the number of oversight tools available to the parliament (controlling for other variables of interest such as the form of government and income level). The results of such analyses, presented in the annex, reveal that once the analysis controls for the effects of income level and number of oversight tools, the form of government does not have a significant impact on whether a country is formally democratic. By contrast, the number of oversight tools is a very strong determinant of whether a country is at least a formal democracy, regardless of whether the analysis controls for income level or for both income level and form of government. The data analysis also reveals that the number of oversight tools is also a major predictor of whether a country is a liberal democracy, although the relationship between oversight potential and liberal democracy is not as strong as the relationship between oversight potential and formal democracy.

Conclusions

The major question addressed in this chapter is whether the potential for legislative oversight, as reflected in the number of oversight tools available in a given country, is related to or affected by other variables, specifically the country's form of government, per capita gross national income level, and level of democracy.

The data show that oversight potential is indeed affected by these variables. Legislatures in parliamentary systems are better equipped—in terms of oversight tools—than legislatures in either presidential or semipresidential systems, although there is little difference in oversight potential between presidential and semipresidential systems. Legislatures in parliamentary systems have an average of six and one-third oversight tools, in contrast to the average of five and two-thirds recorded in presidential systems and almost five and three-quarters recorded in semipresidential systems.

Oversight potential is also greatly affected by the income level of the country. Legislatures in low-income countries have, on average, a much smaller number of oversight tools at their disposal than their counterparts in both middle- and high-income countries. An interesting finding is that the difference in oversight potential between middle- and high-income countries is negligible.

The third set of findings concerns the relationship between oversight potential and level of democracy. The average number of oversight tools is almost linearly related to the level of democracy: the more democratic a country, the more oversight tools are at the disposal of that country's legislature. Nondemocratic countries have an average of just five oversight tools, quasi-democratic countries have an average of five and three-quarters, and democratic countries have an average of less than six and a half.

What do these findings mean? Does the adoption of additional oversight tools make countries more democratic, or is the answer that, because countries are already democratic, they adopt more oversight tools? In other words, is it possible to detect a clear arrow of causality? Based on the data and the analyses that can be performed with these data, the answer is that a unidirectional, causal influence cannot be detected. However, there are also some theoretical reasons why it may not be possible to answer the question above. The relationship between variables, instead of being unidirectional, is often bidirectional. This means that one variable (Y) is determined by another variable (X), which in turn is determined by Y. This could very well be the case in the relationship between levels of democracy and oversight potential. If what distinguishes democratic regimes from nondemocratic ones is that they entail representation, accountability, and responsiveness, and if oversight tools are the institutional instruments that contribute to keeping governments accountable, then it is not surprising that democratic countries adopt more oversight tools. Yet as a country's oversight potential increases, the level of democracy also can increase, thus creating a virtuous circle.

If as oversight potential increases, the level of democracy also increases, then this finding has important practical consequences for the international community and for international organizations seeking to reduce global poverty and to promote good governance. If democracy is "a condition without which development and poverty reduction strategies could not be properly implemented,"[7] and if oversight tools are the institutional devices that are associated with the transition of countries to full democracy, then it is important that the international community better understand the dynamics of legislative oversight. It is equally important that the international community understand the role that oversight tools can play in the promotion of government accountability, democratic development, and good governance. By identifying and disseminating examples of good practice, the international community contributes to creating the conditions for sustainable long-term development.

This chapter contributes to such an understanding, by explaining the *incidence* of parliamentary oversight tools and relating it to important economic and political variables. Further research on the *effectiveness* of such tools will further understanding; however, given the difficulties of measuring parliamentary performance across countries,[8] such research could first be undertaken through country case studies that attempt to measure changes in effectiveness over time.

Annex: Oversight and Democracy

Riccardo Pelizzo

The probability that a country is at least formally democratic is affected by the number of oversight tools available. To test that influence, one can run the following model:

$$\text{Logit (democracy)} = a + b1\ \text{tools} + b2\ \text{gofor} + b3\ \text{incomelevel} \quad (1)$$

The democracy variable takes value 1 for countries that are at least formally democratic. The number of oversight tools variables ranges from 2 to 7. The *gofor* variable refers to the form of government. This variable takes value 1 for presidential systems, value 2 for semipresidential systems, and value 3 for parliamentary systems. The *income level* variable takes values 1, 2, and 3, respectively, for low-income, middle–income, and high-income countries.

By performing this analysis one finds that the model takes the following values:

$$\text{Logit (democracy)} = -4.915 + .713\ \text{Tools} + .053\ \text{gofor}$$
$$+ 1.487\ \text{incomelevel} \quad (2)$$
$$(.008)\ (.010)\ (.913)\ (.018)$$

The form of government (gofor) variable, as seen from the p-values reported in parentheses, is entirely insignificant; thus, it is legitimate to exclude it from the model. By dropping the gofor variable, the model takes the following values:

$$\text{Logit (democracy)} = -4.958 + .775\ \text{tools} + 1.262\ \text{incomelevel} \quad (3)$$
$$(.002)\ (.005)\ (.023)$$

The meaning of these findings is quite clear. Even when controlling for the effects of the income level, the coefficient for the number of oversight tools is strong and statistically significant. In a middle-income country with seven oversight tools, the equation gives the following result:

$$\text{Logit (democracy)} = -4.958 + .775\ (7) + 1.262\ (2) =$$
$$\text{Logit (democracy)} = -4.958 + 5.425 + 2.524 = 2.991$$

Therefore, in the case of a middle-income country where the legislature has all seven oversight tools, the probability that the political system of that country is democratic is

$$e^{2.99}/(1 + e^{2.99}) = .952,\ \text{or}\ 95.2\ \text{percent}.$$

This means that a middle-income country has a phenomenally high chance of being at least formally democratic when all seven oversight tools are available to the parliament. The data presented in annex table 1 provide a clear indication of how (and how much) the probability that a country is at least formally democratic increases as the number of oversight tools available to the parliament increases.

Diamond (1999) noted that formal democracies are effectively quasi-democracies. They have the forms, the mechanisms, and the institutions that can be found in properly democratic regimes, but they do not really function like real democracies. Therefore, one might want to shift the focus of the analysis to investigate whether the probability that a country is a liberal democracy changes as the number of oversight tools available to that country's legislature increases. The following logistic regression model was run to test whether the probability that a country is a liberal democracy is affected by the number of oversight tools:

$$\text{Logit (liberaldemocracy)} = a + b1 \text{ Tools} + b2 \text{ incomelevel} \qquad (4)$$

The *liberal democracy* variable takes value 1 for countries that are ranked as free by the Gastil Index of Freedom, but it takes a value of 0 (zero) otherwise. Both the tools variable and the income level variable take the values specified above. With these considerations in mind, when one runs the model one finds that it takes the following values:

$$\text{Logit (liberaldemocracy)} = -7.193 + .576 \text{ tools} + 2.162 \text{ incomelevel} \qquad (5)$$
(.000) (.036) (.000)

The coefficient for the tools variable is still positive, and still fairly strong, but it is not as statistically significant as the income level variable. It should also be noted that the tools variable in the equation (5) is weaker and much less significant than in the equation model (3). Be that as it may, the greater the number of oversight tools in a middle-income country, the greater the probability that the country is a liberal democracy. One can compare the probability that a middle-income country is a liberal democracy when it has only two

Annex Table 1. Number of Oversight Tools and the Probability That a Country Is Formally Democratic

If in a middle-income country the number of oversight tools is:	The probability that the country is formally democratic is:
0	.08
1	.16
2	.29
3	.47
4	.66
5	.81
6	.90
7	.95

oversight tools with the probability that a middle-income country is a liberal democracy when it has seven oversight tools. When a middle-income country has only two oversight tools, the equation (5) takes the following values:

$$\text{Logit (liberaldemocracy)} = -7.193 + .576\,(2) + 2.162\,(2) = -1.72 \qquad (6)$$

This means that the probability that such a country is liberal democratic is:

$$e^{-1.72}/(1 + e^{-1.72}) = .152, \text{ or } 15.2 \text{ percent.}$$

When a middle-income country has instead seven oversight tools, the equation (5) takes the following values:

$$\text{Logit (liberaldemocracy)} = -7.193 + .576\,(7) + 2.162\,(2) = 1.16 \qquad (7)$$

This means that the probability that such a country is liberal democratic is:

$$e^{1.16}/(1 + e^{1.16}) = .762, \text{ or } 76.2 \text{ percent.}$$

As one can see from the data presented in annex table 2, as the number of oversight tools increases, the probability that a country is liberal democratic also increases, but this increase is not as marked as the probability that a country is only formally democratic. In fact, while there is about a 95 percent probability that a middle income country with seven oversight tools is formally democratic, the probability that this same country is liberal democratic is just 76.2 percent.

These findings clearly indicate that a parliament's oversight potential, as measured by the number of oversight tools, makes a difference as to whether that country is liberal democratic. The data also reveal that the oversight potential exercises greater influence on the probability that a country is formally democratic than on the probability that a country is liberal democratic. Why? The data available do not allow this question to be answered conclusively, but one can nonetheless formulate some educated guesses as to why the relationship between oversight potential and the probability that a country is liberal democratic is so tenuous.

Annex Table 2. Number of Oversight Tools and the Probability That a Country Is Liberal Democratic

If in a middle-income country the number of oversight tools is:	The probability that the country is liberal democratic is:
0	.05
1	.09
2	.15
3	.24
4	.36
5	.50
6	.64
7	.76

Liberal democracy needs to have not just potential oversight or oversight potential, but real and effective oversight. This is the major difference between formally democratic and liberal democratic regimes. In formally democratic regimes, democratic institutions have only a cosmetic function. They are present but they are either not used or they are not used effectively. This may be the case for other types of democratic institutions, including oversight tools. Legislatures in formally democratic regimes do adopt oversight tools, as if they were to effectively oversee government actions, but these tools are not used or, at least, are not used effectively. Hence, in the case of formal democracies, the form of democratic government is respected, but its substance is not.

By contrast, liberal democracies are concerned with the substance of democracy and not just its form. The presence of oversight tools, or of oversight potential, is not enough. What is peculiar to liberal-democratic regimes is the fact not only that governments are empowered to perform their duties and tasks but also that they are subject to control. Governments have the power to govern, but their power is constrained, because they are required, or at the very least may be asked, to provide justifications for their actions or inactions. In parliamentary systems, if a government fails to justify its course of action to the legislature, it may be voted out of office.

Though the presence of oversight tools is a necessary condition for effective oversight, it is not, by itself, sufficient. In addition to legislatures' oversight potential, the political will must exist to oversee government activities. In his study of public accounts committees (PACs), McGee (2002) showed that one of the major obstacles that PACs face in their attempt to oversee governments' accounts is that legislators are often unwilling to engage in serious oversight of the government's accounts.[9] Scrutinizing the government accounts may be considered a job that gives little visibility to legislators, which might act as a disincentive to members seeking to be reelected. Worse, legislators belonging to the government party (or coalition) fear that, by scrutinizing government's accounts, they may be forced to choose between performing their oversight functions effectively (possibly straining their relationship with their party) and preserving a strong tie to their party.[10] Therefore, in parliaments with PACs, the presence of these committees is a necessary but not sufficient condition for effective scrutiny of government accounts. If this conclusion could be extended from the particular case of PACs to oversight tools in general, it could equally explain why the presence of oversight tools does not necessarily amount to effective oversight—which is what is actually needed for a country to be a liberal democracy.

This annex investigated the relationship between the number of oversight tools available to a legislature, on the one hand, and the probability that a country is a formal democracy or a liberal democracy on the other hand. An analysis of the IPU-WBI survey data showed that the number of oversight tools available to a country's parliament is a strong predictor of whether a country is at least formally democratic. The findings indicate that the probability that a country is formally democratic increases as the number of oversight tools increases. Similarly, when a middle-income country has all of the seven oversight tools for which the IPU-WBI survey sought information, there is a 95 percent probability that the country is formally democratic. However, although the probability that a country is a liberal democracy increases as the number of oversight tools available to the parliament increases, the relationship between oversight potential and liberal democracy is neither as strong nor as significant as the relationship between oversight potential and formal democracy. This difference may be explained by the fact that liberal-democratic regimes are concerned not only with the formal aspects of democracy, such as the presence of democratic mechanisms and institutions, but also with the substance of democracy. Liberal democracies are not satisfied with oversight potential; rather, they seek effective oversight implementation. Furthermore, legislatures need the political will to exercise oversight effectively.

These findings suggest two additional considerations. First, the analysis, by showing that legislative oversight is good for democracy, confirms what several international organizations have often assumed, namely, that strengthening legislatures (and legislatures' oversight potential) is good for democracy building. Legislatures (and strong legislatures) are good for democracy, as recent studies have underlined (Fish 2006), and legislatures make such a significant contribution to democratic governance. By performing their oversight function, legislatures play a major role in keeping governments responsive and accountable for their actions, and thus are instrumental in preventing possible abuses of power. Second, the analysis suggests that, although international organizations are correct in arguing that strengthening legislatures is critical for the promotion and consolidation of democracy, they need to reconsider their legislature-strengthening strategies (NDI 2000; Pelizzo and Stapenhurst 2004b). In the past, programs focused mainly on strengthening legislatures' oversight potential. Yet legislatures must have not only the tools but also the political will to oversee the government. Only then can they move from formal to liberal democracy, because liberal democracy requires effective oversight and not just oversight potential. The major challenge for international organizations concerned with the promotion and consolidation of democracy is to identify and promote the conditions under which legislatures and legislators are more likely to engage in effective oversight of government activities.

Notes

1. The 2001 IPU-WBI survey on executive-legislative relations surveyed some 180 parliaments. Of those, 83 responded (82 national parliaments and the European Parliament).

2. A description of some of these tools can be found in the National Democratic Institute for International Affairs (NDI 2000), "Strengthening Legislative Capacity in Legislative-Executive Relations," particularly pages 19–32.

3. For example, questions were asked concerning the accountability of the executive to the legislature; procedures for impeachment and for dissolution of

parliament; oversight of government, the budget, budget implementation, foreign policy, and defense policy; parliament and state of emergency; verification of the constitutionality of laws; and oversight over the application or evaluation of laws.

4. A discussion on why questions, question time, and interpellations should be considered instruments of parliamentary control can be found in Maffio (2002). Also see David McGee (2002).

5. A more detailed discussion of the Gastil Index of Freedom will be provided in the course of the chapter.

6. Respondents were asked to indicate their country's form of government. Responses were coded: presidential form of government was given a value of 1, parliamentary form of government was 2, semipresidential form of government was 3, parliamentary form of government in countries with a constitutional monarchy was 4, parliamentary form of government in countries with a hereditary monarchy was 5, and other forms of government were all 6. For the purposes of this chapter, a slightly different coding scheme was adopted. Countries that were given the value 2, 4, or 5 by the IPU data set were all considered to have a parliamentrary system and were hence collapsed into a single category.

7. The quote is taken from Pelizzo and Stapenhurst (2004a, 177). See also Pelizzo and Stapenhurst (2004b) and Stapenhurst and Pelizzo (2002).

8. Laurentian Seminar Proceedings (Parliamentary Centre 1997).

9. In spite of the fact that public accounts committees are proper oversight committees, that is, committees established to oversee government accounts, the list of oversight tools considered by the IPU-WBI survey did not include PACs. Also see Wehner (2003; 2005).

10. The reasons partisanship may represent a major obstacle to the proper functioning of PACs are discussed by Stapenhurst et al. (2005).

Bibliography

Diamond, L. 1999. *Developing Democracy.* Baltimore: Johns Hopkins University Press.

Fish, M. Steven. 2006. "Stronger Legislatures, Stronger Democracies." *Journal of Democracy* 17 (1). Baltimore: Johns Hopkins University Press. http://sdnhq.undp.org/governance/parls/docs/Fish-17-1.pdf.

Lees, J. D. 1977. "Legislatures and Oversight: A Review Article on a Neglected Area of Research." *Legislative Studies Quarterly* 2 (2): 193–208.

Maffio, R. 2002. "*Quis custodiet ipsos custodes?* Il controllo parlamentare dell' attivitá di governo in prospettiva comparata." *Quaderni di Scienza Politica* 9 (2): 333–83.

McGee, D. G. 2002. *The Overseers. Public Accounts Committees and Public Spending.* London: Commonwealth Parliamentary Association, with Pluto Press.

NDI (National Democratic Institute for International Affairs). 2000. "Strengthening Legislative Capacity in Legislative-Executive Relations." Legislative Research Series, Paper No. 6, NDI, Washington, DC.

Parliamentary Centre. 1997. *Laurentian Seminar Proceedings.*

Pelizzo, R., and R. Stapenhurst. 2004a. "Legislatures and Oversight: A Note." Paper prepared for the Annual Meeting of the Southern Political Science Association, New Orleans, Louisiana, January 7–10, 2004. In *Trends in Parliamentary Oversight: Proceedings from a Panel at the 2004 Southern Political Science Association Conference*, ed. R. Pelizzo, R. Stapenhurst, and D. Olsons, 1–8. Washington, DC: World Bank Institute. Also published in *Quaderni di Scienza Politica* 11 (1): 175–88.

————. 2004b. "Legislative Ethics and Codes of Conduct." Working Paper. World Bank Institute, Washington, DC.

Stapenhurst, R., and R. Pelizzo. 2002. "A Bigger Role for Legislatures." *Finance and Development* 39 (4): 46–48.

Stapenhurst, R., V. Sahgal, W. Woodley, and R. Pelizzo. 2005. "Scrutinizing Public Expenditures: Assessing the Performance of Public Accounts Committees." Policy Research Working Paper 3613, World Bank, Washington, DC.

Wehner, J. 2003. "Principles and Patterns of Financial Scrutiny: Public Account Committees in the Commonwealth." *Commonwealth and Comparative Politics* 41 (3): 21–36.

————. 2005. "Legislative Arrangements for Financial Scrutiny: Explaining Cross-National Variation." In *The Role of Parliament in the Budget Process*, eds. R. Pelizzo, R. Stapenhurst, and D. Olson. Washington, DC: World Bank Institute.

World Bank. *World Development Indicators*. Washington, DC: World Bank.

CHAPTER 2

Oversight and Democracy Reconsidered

Riccardo Pelizzo

The purpose of this chapter is twofold. First, it investigates whether and to what extent oversight potential—measured on the basis of the number of oversight tools available to a legislature in a given country—affects the probability that a country is a formal democracy or a liberal democracy. Such an inquiry is worth conducting, as previous analyses have failed to produce conclusive evidence in this respect. Second, it challenges the idea that all oversight tools are equally effective to scrutinize the government activities, by showing that, although the presence of certain oversight tools has very little impact on whether a country is a liberal democracy, the presence of other tools, such as the ombudsman, has a major impact. Hence, the main conclusion of the chapter is that, although oversight matters, some oversight tools are more important than others in making countries democratic.[1]

The chapter is divided into four parts. The first part discusses the legislative oversight literature and how this literature has investigated the determinants, the tools, the possible consequences of legislative oversight of government activities, as well as the relationship between democracy and oversight.

In the second part of the chapter, three questions are addressed, namely, whether democracy is related to oversight potential, whether this relationship is trivial or spurious or both, and whether one should investigate the relationship between democracy and actual oversight rather than the relationship between democracy and oversight potential. In this second part, it is shown that regardless of the size of the sample and statistical technique employed, democracy is always strongly related to oversight potential. Moreover, it is argued that the measure of democracy used in this analysis captures what in the literature is known as the vertical dimension of accountability, whereas the measure of oversight potential captures what is known as the horizontal dimension of accountability, and that therefore the findings presented are neither trivial nor spurious. Finally, the second part presents evidence—based on the use of oversight tools in the Italian Parliament—that illustrates why focusing on the relationship between democracy and oversight potential is actually better than focusing on the relationship between democracy and actual oversight.

In the third part of the chapter, some empirical analyses are performed to test whether all oversight tools are equally effective to scrutinize the government activities and to affect the functioning of a political system. This is done by investigating the relationship between each of the oversight tools for which data were collected in the Inter-Parliamentary Union and World Bank Institute (IPU-WBI) survey and the probability that a country is liberally democratic. This analysis reveals that oversight tools that cannot be used in a partisan manner or to further partisan interests have a much stronger and more significant impact on whether a country is liberally democratic than do those tools that can be used in a partisan fashion.

In the fourth and concluding part, the implications of the main findings are discussed. Because the results of these analyses are not conclusive, future studies will want to use better data, methods, and techniques to investigate the relationship between (liberal) democracy and oversight—a relationship that in spite of its importance has been somewhat neglected by comparative constitutional engineers.

Legislative Oversight: Causes and Consequences

The study of legislative oversight is focused on five basic questions: What is oversight? Why is it good for a political system? How can oversight be exercised? What is the impact of oversight? And, last but not least: Is democracy affected by oversight?

The answer to the first question provided by experts in legislative studies is that oversight refers to the set of activities that a legislature performs to evaluate the implementation of policies (McCubbins and Schwartz 1984; Olson and Mezey 1991).[2] Oversight may lead to revisions of policies, and it can affect the reform of legislation, but that does not mean it is legitimate to regard a parliament's legislative function as a subset of oversight activities or to equate the legislative function to the oversight function.

Scholars have noted that oversight can be performed by employing a variety of oversight tools. Damgaard (2000, 8) notes, for example, that the list of oversight tools includes "ombudsmen, committees of inquiry, auditing institutions, specialised parliamentary committees, public hearings, interpellations that may end with a vote in the chamber," and so on. Some scholars have underlined that not all oversight tools are alike. Maffio (2002) and Maor (1999), for example, have offered two alternative groupings of oversight tools. For Maffio, oversight tools can be grouped on the basis of whether they are applied before or after a specific policy is implemented. She further argues that some tools have more bite than others. Maor argues instead that oversight tools take either the form of specific bodies (ombudsman, committees, and so on) or the form of a procedure (interpellation, questions, and so on).

Some studies have investigated the relationship between oversight tools and various political and socioeconomic conditions (Maffio 2002; Pelizzo and Stapenhurst 2004b; Pennings 2000). According to Pennings, the most important conclusion reached by these studies is that oversight "has a dynamics of its own and is not solely the derivative of other variables." Pennings in fact found that patterns of oversight could not be reduced to what he calls "families of nations," to the distinction between consensus and majoritarian democracies (Lijphart 1999), or to the distinction between presidential and parliamentary systems (Linz 1994). A similar conclusion is suggested by Pelizzo and Stapenhurst (2006).

Scholars have noted, however, that the presence of the oversight tools is a necessary but insufficient condition for effective oversight. Effective oversight depends not only on the availability of oversight tools, but also on additional conditions. Effective oversight may depend on the specific oversight powers given to the parliament, on whether the parliament has the ability to modify legislation (Loewenberg and Patterson 1979), on whether parliaments and parliamentarians are given proper information to adequately perform their oversight tasks (Frantzich 1979; Jewell 1978), on the role of individual members of parliament (Jewell 1978), on the role of committee chairs, on swings in the political mood of the country (Ogul and Rockman 1990), on tensions between the executive and the legislative branches, and on the saliency of issues and how aggressively the opposition performs its role (Maor 1999, 374; Rockman 1984; Weller 2006, 14–15).[3]

Does oversight actually affect the functioning and possibly the nature of a political system? In the course of the past decade, international organizations have conducted some studies to assess whether strengthening legislatures' oversight capacity is good for democracy or not (Pelizzo and Stapenhurst 2004a, 2004b).[4] The evidence presented in these publications was at best suggestive. It showed that, on average, liberal-democratic regimes had more oversight tools and oversight potential than formally democratic or quasi-democratic regimes, and that these, in turn, had greater oversight potential than nondemocratic regimes. But the fact that more democratic regimes tend to have, on average, more oversight tools than less democratic regimes does not say much as to whether the adoption of a larger number of oversight tools is a consequence or a cause of the higher democratic quality in a given country. More recently, Pelizzo and Stapenhurst (2006) investigated the relationship between the number of oversight tools and the probability that a country is a formal or a liberal democracy. By performing this analysis, they found that the probability that a country is a formal democracy or a liberal democracy is strongly and significantly related to the number of oversight tools.

Building on the work by Pelizzo and Stapenhurst (2006), it is worth testing whether the various oversight tools have the same impact on the probability that a country is democratic or not. This analysis is relevant for two reasons. First, it can provide constitutional engineers and practitioners alike with a better understanding of which institutional elements should be adopted to help consolidate a newly established democracy. Second, this analysis may shed some light on what makes oversight work or on what makes oversight tools affect the functioning of a political system.

Democracy and Oversight: A Disputed Relationship

Before addressing the main question of this chapter, namely, whether oversight tools are equally effective or not, two preliminary questions need to be addressed: first, whether democracy is affected by what Pelizzo and Stapenhurst (2006) call oversight potential, which is the number of oversight tools available to a legislature in a given country, and second, whether it is appropriate to investigate the impact of oversight potential on democracy.

To answer the first question (whether democracy is affected by oversight potential), three sets of analyses were performed for this chapter. In the first set, the number of oversight tools is correlated with the level of democracy (measured by the Gastil Index of Freedom) for all 82 countries included in the IPU-WBI survey (excluding the European Union), for the 47 countries originally included in the analysis performed by Pelizzo and Stapenhurst (2006), and for the subset of 16 African countries that are part of the 47-country sample used by Pelizzo and Stapenhurst (2006).[5] Results are presented in table 2.1.

The Gastil Index of Freedom is a seven-point scale in which lower values are associated with a higher level of democracy and higher values are associated with lower levels or even absence of democracy. Oversight potential is measured on the basis of the number of oversight tools, so that the larger the number of oversight tools available to a parliament, the greater the parliament's oversight potential.[6] Hence, if oversight potential were good for democracy and/or democratic quality, the correlation analysis should yield a negative coefficient. The results of the correlation analysis reveal that countries with a greater number of oversight tools have a lower score on the Gastil index and are therefore more democratic. This is true in the 82-country sample, in the 47-country sample used by Pelizzo and Stapenhurst (2006), and in the African subsample.

The analysis next performs some logistic regressions to see how the number of oversight tools a country has can affect the probability that that country is either a liberal or a formal democracy by.[7] The first step is to regress dependent variables against the number of oversight tools; then the same analyses is

Table 2.1. Correlation Analysis of Level of Democracy and Oversight Tools

	Level of democracy		
Oversight tools	−.482	−.503	−.481
Significance	(.000)	(.000)	(.059)
Sample size	82	47	16

Source: Data compiled by authors from Freedom House (for level of democracy) and IPU-WBI survey (for use of oversight tools).

replicated by regressing the dependent variables against the number of over-sight tools by controlling for the country income level.

By regressing the probability that a country is formally democratic against the number of oversight tools, it is found that the number of oversight tools is a key determinant of whether a country is at least formally democratic in the 82-country sample, in the 47-country sample used by Pelizzo and Stapenhurst (2006), and in the 16-country African subsample. Estimates of the logistic regression analyses are reported in table 2.2.

The results of the logistic regression analyses make it clear that the tools of legislative oversight are a strong predictor of whether a country is formally democratic. Similar results are achieved when the same model is used to assess how the number of oversight tools affects the probability that a country is liberally democratic (see table 2.3).

To assess the relationship between democracy and oversight, Pelizzo and Stapenhurst (2006) used the following models:

$$\text{Logit (formal democracy)} = a + b1 \text{ tools} + b2 \text{ incomelevel}$$

$$\text{Logit (liberal democracy)} = a + b1 \text{ tools} + b2 \text{ incomelevel}$$

When these models are used in the 82-country sample and the effects of income level are being controlled for, the result shows that the number of over-sight tools exercises a strong and statistically significant influence on whether a country is formally democratic or liberally democratic or both. These results are interesting in a particular respect. When Pelizzo and Stapenhurst (2006)

Table 2.2. Logistic Regression, with Formal Democratic Status as a Dependent Variable

Logit (formal democracy) =	Model 1	Model 2	Model 3
Constant	−1.433	−5.49	−10.005
	(.000)	(.017)	(.078)
Tools of legislative oversight	.532	1.223	1.733
	(.000)	(.003)	(.071)
N	82	47	16

Source: Data compiled by authors from Freedom House (for level of democracy) and IPU-WBI survey (for use of oversight tools).

Table 2.3. Logistic Regression, with Liberal Democracy as a Dependent Variable

Logit (liberal democracy) =	Model 1	Model 2	Model 3
Constant	−5.575	−5.026	−4.033
	(.000)	(.017)	(.360)
Tools of legislative oversight	1.077	.870	.441
	(.000)	(.012)	(.548)
N	82	47	16

Source: Data compiled by authors from Freedom House (for level of democracy) and IPU-WBI survey (for use of oversight tools).

performed their analyses with the 47-country sample, they found that the number of oversight tools was a stronger and more significant determinant of whether a country was formally democratic than of whether a country was liberally democratic. The results of the current analysis are slightly different, because the impact of the number of oversight tools on the logit of liberal democracy is stronger and more significant than the impact of the number of oversight tools on the logit of formal democracy (see table 2.4).

When these models are used in the small African subsample, it is found that even when controlling for the effect of income level, the number of oversight tools is a major determinant of whether a country is a formal or liberal democracy (see table 2.5).

The evidence presented thus far sustains the claim that the oversight potential, measured on the basis of number of oversight tools, is a strong determinant of a country's democratic status. Regardless of the size of the sample and regardless of which statistical technique is used to analyze the relationship between democracy and oversight, the result is always that democracy is affected by the oversight potential.

Table 2.4. Oversight Tools, Income Level, and Democracy

	Logit (formal democracy)	Logit (liberal democracy)
Constant	−3.689	−8.271
	(.007)	(.000)
Tools of legislative oversight	.398	.940
	(.060)	(.002)
Income	1.728	1.816
	(.002)	(.002)
N	82	82

Source: Data on oversight tools are taken from the IPU-WBI survey; data on income level are taken from the *World Development Indicators* (2002).

Table 2.5. Oversight Tools, Income Level, and Democracy in Africa

	Country status	
Logit	(formal democracy)	(liberal democracy)
Constant	−9.763	15.516
	(.101)	(1.00)
Tools of legislative oversight	1.947	.672
	(.071)	(.385)
Income	−1.446	−20.564
	(.442)	(.999)
N	16	16

Source: Data on oversight tools are taken from the IPU-WBI survey; data on income level are taken from the *World Development Indicators* (2002).

Actual and Potential Oversight: Evidence from the Italian Case

The results presented in the previous section are not as interesting as they first appear. After all, it can be argued that what matters is not whether legislatures have oversight tools or oversight, but whether they actually oversee government activities; that is, actual oversight matters, not potential oversight or oversight potential. This objection assumes that effective oversight is a function of actual oversight, or rather, a function of the amount of oversight performed. This means that the more the legislature oversees the executive government, the more effective legislative oversight is.

The idea of equating actual oversight to effective oversight has already been challenged in the literature. Sartori (1987), for example, noted that effective oversight depends on the parliament's ability or potential to oversee the government's activities. If the government knows that the parliament may scrutinize its actions, that the parliament has the freedom to choose the topics on which to conduct its investigations, the government may be induced to act more properly in order to avoid criticism from the legislature. A similar point was raised by Pelizzo and Stapenhurst (2006) in their discussion of public accounts committees (PACs). In their analysis of what makes PACs effective in scrutinizing government expenditures, Pelizzo and Stapenhurst argued that a PAC's ability to perform its job is significantly related to the committee's freedom to choose what to investigate rather than to investigate everything. Sartori pushed the argument even further by saying that when legislatures attempt to oversee everything, they are not very focused and perform their oversight activities in a less effective manner.

To test whether Sartori's point is actually corroborated by empirical evidence, the analysis collected some information on the use of oversight tools in both houses of the Italian Parliament. As previous studies (Pasquino and Pelizzo 2006) have already indicated, the Italian Parliament can employ various tools to oversee government activity: motions, interpellations, oral questions, oral questions that must be answered immediately on the floor, written questions, questions to be answered in committees, questions to be answered immediately in the committees, various types of resolutions (in the assembly, in the committee, and conclusive resolutions), and the final draft agenda (*Ordini del Giorno*) both in assembly and in committee. According to Wiberg (1995) the Italian Parliament can formulate three types of questions: written, oral, and interpellations that, according to Wiberg, correspond to what in Italian are known respectively as *interrogazioni parlamentari*, *interrogazioni urgenti*, and *interpellanze*. Wiberg's discussion of parliamentary questions in the Italian parliament is wrong in one respect. The standing orders of the Chamber of Deputies establish that both parliamentary questions (interrogazioni) and interpellations (interpellanze) can be "urgent."[8]

The Chamber of Deputies provides information concerning the use of these oversight tools from 1976 to 2006. Indications as to whether questions and interpellations were urgent or not are provided only for the 2001–06 period. Tables 2.6 through 2.9 show the number of interpellations, oral questions, and written questions that were produced in the seven legislatures that took office in the 1976–2006 period and that were addressed to the ministries of budget, defense, finance, foreign affairs, interior, and justice. Specifically, tables 2.6a and 2.6b show the number of oversight acts (interpellations, oral questions, and written questions) asked in each legislature. Because Italian legislatures in the period under study have lasted between two and five years, tables 2.7a and 2.7b show how the production of oversight acts per year has changed. The data make clear that there has been a remarkable increase in the number of oversight acts performed both in the Chamber of Deputies and in the Senate. These data sustain the claim that over the years, the Italian

Table 2.6a. Number of Oversight Acts in Italy's Legislature—Chamber of Deputies, 1976 to 2001

| | | Ministry to which questions are directed | | | | | |
| | | | | | Foreign | | |
Legislature	Activity	Budget	Defense	Finance	affairs	Interior	Justice
7th	Interpellations	11	24	23	41	101	65
(1976–79)	Oral questions	86	233	198	321	1,077	610
	Written questions	84	536	484	401	845	584
	Total oversight acts	181	793	705	763	2,023	1,259
8th	Interpellations	58	236	100	487	449	394
(1979–83)	Oral questions	116	581	334	1,044	1,710	1,403
	Written questions	160	1,600	1,136	571	1943	1,522
	Total oversight acts	334	2,417	1,570	2,102	4,102	3,319
9th	Interpellations	16	103	19	182	166	90
(1983–87)	Oral questions	28	215	90	324	654	411
	Written questions	183	1,611	1,328	809	3,183	2,433
	Total oversight acts	227	1,929	1,437	1,315	4,003	2,934
10th	Interpellations	27	124	55	283	352	242
(1987–92)	Oral questions	26	316	96	334	863	639
	Written questions	312	1,937	2,150	1,311	7,125	4,788
	Total oversight acts	365	2,377	2,301	1,928	8,340	5,669
11th	Interpellations	35	62	82	105	183	180
(1992–94)	Oral questions	36	162	119	116	518	391
	Written questions	834	1,038	2,043	703	6,588	4,732
	Total oversight acts	905	1,262	2,244	924	7,289	5,303
12th	Interpellations	26	43	38	68	173	120
(1994–96)	Oral questions	16	35	35	54	237	166
	Written questions	496	724	1,352	709	4,186	2,451
	Oversight acts per year	538	802	1,425	831	4,596	2,737
13th	Interpellations	34	194	186	228	648	422
(1996–2001)	Oral questions	42	406	400	449	1,645	1,076
	Written questions	406	1,766	2,878	1,121	6,795	3,861
	Total oversight acts	482	2,366	3,464	1,798	9,088	5,359

Source: Chamber of Deputies, Italy.

Table 2.6b. Number of Oversight Acts from the 7th to the 13th Italian Senate

| Legislature | Activity | Ministry to which questions are directed | | | | | |
		Budget	Defense	Foreign affairs	Finance	Justice	Interior
7th	Interpellations	11	8	6	20	18	25
(1976–79)	Oral questions	26	84	94	61	131	293
	Written questions	26	112	145	180	168	255
	Total oversight acts	63	204	245	261	317	573
8th	Interpellations	16	39	132	34	62	76
(1979–83)	Oral questions	30	233	357	104	288	421
	Written questions	43	188	154	250	245	387
	Total oversight acts	89	460	643	388	595	884
9th	Interpellations	5	84	132	19	49	57
(1983–87)	Oral questions	16	180	198	90	187	245
	Written questions	29	285	174	272	398	427
	Total oversight acts	50	549	504	381	634	729
10th	Interpellations	12	41	86	15	86	127
(1987–92)	Oral questions	21	116	216	68	217	317
	Written questions	66	567	295	429	1,044	1,279
	Total oversight acts	99	724	597	512	1,347	1,723
11th	Interpellations	20	20	38	23	46	72
(1992–94)	Oral questions	16	134	136	50	116	139
	Written questions	111	272	228	443	673	991
	Total oversight acts	147	426	402	516	835	1,202
12th	Interpellations	9	19	37	16	52	54
(1994–96)	Oral questions	26	97	88	71	105	169
	Written questions	169	429	352	656	1,041	1,610
	Total oversight acts	204	545	477	743	1,198	1,833
13th	Interpellations	44	66	100	63	266	340
(1996–2001)	Oral questions	94	418	403	265	642	962
	Written questions	786	1359	1,047	1,999	3,301	4,608
	Total oversight acts	924	1843	1,550	2,327	4,209	5,910

Source: Chamber of Deputies, Italy.

Parliament has performed more actual oversight. But was actual oversight in any way related to effective oversight? To answer this question, the focus of the analysis narrowed to investigate only the success rate of interpellations addressed by the Chamber of Deputies and the Senate to the Ministries of Budget and Foreign Affairs. Whether the *iter* (legislative procedure) initiated by an interpellation was completed is used as a measure for the effectiveness of an interpellation. The procedure initiated by interpellations could be completed in three ways: interpellations could be answered, withdrawn, or transformed.[9] The data presented in tables 2.8 and 2.9 make it clear that

Table 2.7a. The Upward Trend in Oversight Acts—Chamber of Deputies

Legislature	Years	Number of oversight acts	Number of oversight acts per year
7th	1976–79	5,724	1,908
8th	1979–83	1,3844	3,461
9th	1983–87	11,845	2,961
10th	1987–92	20,980	4,196
11th	1992–94	17,927	8,964
12th	1994–96	10,929	5,465
13th	1996–2001	22,557	4,511

Source: Chamber of Deputies, Italy.

Table 2.7b. The Upward Trend in Oversight Acts—Senate

Legislature	Years	Number of oversight acts	Number of oversight acts per year
7th	1976–79	1,663	554
8th	1979–83	3,059	765
9th	1983–87	2,847	712
10th	1987–92	5,002	1,000
11th	1992–94	3,528	1,764
12th	1994–96	5,000	2,500
13th	1996–2001	16,763	3,353

Source: Chamber of Deputies, Italy.

Table 2.8a. Interpellations Directed to the Ministry of Budget from the Chamber

(percentage of N)

Result of action	7th	8th	9th	10th	11th	12th	13th
Procedures initiated by the interpellations that were completed	63.6	32.7	25.0	18.5	2.8	21.4	64.7
Interpellations answered	45.4	27.6	25.0	14.8	0	19.2	64.7
Interpellations withdrawn	18.2	0	0	3.7	2.8	3.8	0
Interpellations transformed	0	5.2	0	0	0	0	0
	of	of	of	of	of	of	of
N	11	58	16	27	35	26	34

Source: Chamber of Deputies, Italy.

Table 2.8b. Interpellations Directed to the Ministry of Budget from the Senate

(percentage of N)

Result of action	7th	8th	9th	10th	11th	12th	13th
Procedures initiated by the interpellations that were completed	36.3	56.3	0	16.7	15.0	11.1	40.9
Interpellations answered	36.3	43.8	0	16.7	10.0	11.1	15.9
Interpellations withdrawn	0	0	0	0	0	0	4.5
Interpellations transformed	0	12.5	0	0	5.0	0	20.5
	of	of	of	of	of	of	of
N	11	16	5	12	20	9	44

Source: Chamber of Deputies, Italy.

Table 2.9a. Interpellations Addressed to the Foreign Affairs Ministry from the Chamber of Deputies

(percentage of N; N = interpellations introduced)

Result	7th (1976–79)	11th (1992–94)	12th (1994–96)	13th (1996–2001)	14th (2001–06)
Completed	73.1	42.8	32.4	46.9 47.5[a]	63.1
Answered	43.9	41.9	29.4	44.5[a]	
Withdrawn	24.4	0	1.5	0.5[a]	
Transformed	4.5	0.9	11.5	2.5[a]	
	of	of	of	of	of
N	41	105	68	228; 200[a]	171

Source: Chamber of Deputies, Italy.
a. Though the Chamber of Deputies makes it clear that 107 of the 228 interpellations were completed, it provides more detailed information concerning only the first 200 interpellations introduced in this legislature. The procedures for 95 of these 200 interpellations were completed: 89 interpellations were answered (44.5 percent), one was withdrawn (0.5%), and five (2.5%) were transformed.

increases in the numbers of oversight acts, the analysis's proxy for actual oversight, were in no way related to the effectiveness of oversight, that is, to the ability to complete oversight procedures initiated by the various acts.

The evidence based on the data from the Italian Parliament thus far sustains the claim that democracy is affected by oversight potential, that the relationship between these two variables is not spurious or trivial, that the effectiveness of the oversight process is not necessarily tied to the number of oversight activities performed, and that focusing on the relationship between actual oversight and democracy is not necessarily more instructive than investigating the relationship between democracy and oversight

Table 2.9b. Interpellations to the Ministry of Foreign Affairs, from the Senate

(percentage of N; N = interpellations introduced)

Result	7th (1976–79)	11th (1992–94)	12th (1994–96)	13th (1996–2001)	14th (2001–06)	15th (2006–pres.)
Completed	33.3	18.4	40.5	35.0	34.9	40.6
Answered	33.3	15.8	37.8	23.0		
Withdrawn	0	0	0	1.0		
Transformed		2.6	2.7	11.0		
	of	of	of	of	of	of
N	6	38	37	100	86	32*

Source: Chamber of Deputies, Italy.

*As of March 12, 2007.

potential. Although based solely on data from the Italian case study, these conclusions offer legitimate reasons to investigate the relationship between democracy and oversight potential.

Having established that oversight potential, measured by the number of oversight tools, is good for democracy, the main question of this chapter can be addressed, namely, whether all oversight tools are equally effective.

Tools of Oversight and Democracy: Evidence of Efficacy

Maffio (2002) suggested that not all oversight tools are equally powerful. She noted that oversight tools that force the government to respond quickly—such as questions with immediate answers in the assembly, questions to be answered immediately in the commissions, and interpellations to be answered immediately—are more powerful oversight tools than normal questions or interpellations and weighted them accordingly. Maffio did not provide much evidence to support her claim. The Chamber of Deputies in Italy provides some evidence that can be used to test whether Maffio was correct in claiming that urgent dispositions have a greater impact than normal ones. To test whether that is indeed the case, this chapter measures the percentage of oversight procedures that were initiated by questions and urgent questions that were also completed. Data are presented in table 2.10.

The results presented in table 2.11 highlight that whenever questions are to be answered immediately, either in the committees or in the assembly, their success rate is much higher than the success rate of normal questions. All the questions that were addressed to the Ministries of Foreign Affairs, Defense, and Justice and that were to be answered immediately in the assembly were completed. When the questions were to be given an immediate oral answer in the committees, their success rate ranged from 91.8 percent to 99 percent. Normal questions that were to be answered orally in the assembly had

Table 2.10. Effectiveness of Oversight Tools in the 14th Legislature

Ministry to which the question was addressed	Tool	Timing of the response	Number completed	Number initiated	Success rate (%) = number completed/number initiated
Foreign affairs	Questions to be answered orally in the assembly	Normal	75	486	15.4
		Immediately	48	48	100.0
	Questions to be answered orally in the committees	Normal	146	274	53.3
		Immediately	162	166	97.6
Defense	Questions to be answered orally in the assembly	Normal	55	246	22.3
		Immediately	43	43	100.0
	Questions to be answered orally in the committees	Normal	108	240	45.0
		Immediately	104	105	99.0
Justice	Questions to be answered orally in the assembly	Normal	91	382	23.8
		Immediately	55	55	100.0
	Questions to be answered orally in the committees	Normal	29	230	12.6
		Immediately	56	61	91.8

Source: Chamber of Deputies, Italy.

Table 2.11. Logit Models, with Oversight Tools and Democracy

	Logit (liberal democracy)		
	Model 1	Model 2	Model 3
Constant	−4.704	−1.004	−.288
	(1.0)	(.148)	(.514)
Committee hearings	22.6		
	(.999)		
Hearing in the assembly	.775		
	(.542)		
Creation of inquiry committees	−1.36		
	(.417)		
Question time	1.02		
	(.335)		
Interpellations	1.60	.891	
	(.061)	(.162)	
Ombudsman	2.25	1.27	1.179
	(.008)	(.038)	(.027)
Questions	20.00		
	(1.0)		

Source: Chamber of Deputies, Italy.

success rates between 15.4 percent and 23.8 percent, the success rate for normal questions in the committees ranged from 12.6 percent to 53.3 percent. This evidence indicates that Maffio (2002) was correct in suggesting that the effectiveness of legislative oversight varies depending on which tools are employed. The evidence also indicates that there is some variation in how effective oversight tools may be. Hence, it is worth investigating which tools are best for democracy or investigating how the various oversight tools affect the probability that a country is democratic.

Is it possible to formulate some educated guesses as to which oversight tools have the most significant influence on democracy and which oversight tools are most effective? Maffio (2002) related the effectiveness of oversight tools to their ability to solicit a quick government response. This chapter takes a slightly different approach. Various studies on oversight (Weller 2006) and financial scrutiny (McGee 2002; Pelizzo, Stapenhurst, Sahgal and Woodley 2006) have demonstrated that the success of these two methods depends on the extent to which they can be used in a nonpartisan fashion.

If the nonpartisanship of an oversight tool is assumed to be the key determinant of its success, then the hypothesis follows that the ombudsman is the oversight tool that exercises the strongest influence on democracy. The ombudsman is in fact a parliamentary commissioner and should, as such, be regarded as a tool of legislative oversight in the same way the auditor general or an audit office are tools of legislative oversight. However, the ombudsman, exactly like the auditor general, is an independent official. He or she receives complaints on government activity from the public, assesses whether these complaints can be substantiated, and, if they can be, makes a report.

Given the way in which the ombudsman is selected and operates, the role is not one of those oversight tools that can actually be used for partisan purposes. This is very important, because partisan use undermines the effectiveness of oversight tools. If an oversight tool, such as a parliamentary question, is used in a partisan manner, both the credibility and the effectiveness of that tool are undermined. If the public knows that a tool is used to promote personal and/or partisan interests, it would regard those oversight activities simply as politics by other means. The media would not pay much attention to those oversight activities, and the government would not feel compelled to answer to (and therefore be accountable to) the parliament. In light of this argument, a hypothesis can be suggested that, although oversight tools that cannot be used in a partisan fashion are the most effective (such as the ombudsman), oversight tools that can be used in a highly partisan manner, such as the parliamentary questions, are the least effective. But is this really the case?

In order to answer this question, this chapter estimated the effects of oversight tools on the probability that a country is liberal democratic. Each of the seven oversight tools included in the IPU-WBI survey was run in the following model:

$$\text{Logit (liberal democracy)} = a + b1 \text{ comhear} + b2 \text{ assemhear} + b3 \text{ inquiry} \\ + b4 \text{ time} + b5 \text{ interpellations} + b6 \text{ ombudsman} + b7 \text{ questions}$$

The variable comhear refers to the presence of committee hearings, assemhear refers to the presence of hearings in the plenary, inquiry refers to the parliament's ability to form inquiry committees, and time refers to legislative question time, and the remaining three variables refer to interpellations, the presence of the ombudsman, and parliamentarians' ability to ask questions. The results are presented as model 1 in table 2.11. All the coefficients are statistically insignificant, with the exception of the coefficient for the ombudsman, which is also strong and positive. The table also shows a second model, in which all the variables were removed, with the exception of ombudsman, which was statistically significant, and interpellations, which was almost statistically significant. The results of model 2 make clear that ombudsman is the only significant predictor of liberal democracy. To check whether that is indeed the case, a third model was used, in which the logit (liberal democracy) is a function of the presence of the ombudsman.

The results of this third model indicate that the presence of the ombudsman strongly and significantly affects the logit (liberal democracy). But how does the presence of this oversight tool affect the probability that a country is a liberal democracy? To answer this question, the following equation has to be solved:

$$\text{Logit (liberal democracy)} = -.288 + 1.179 \text{ ombudsman}$$

When there is no ombudsman the logit is:

$$\text{Logit (liberal democracy)} = -.288 + 1.179(0) = -.288 + 0 = -.288$$

In this case, the probability that a country is a liberal democracy corresponds to:

$$\frac{e^{-.288}}{1+e^{-.288}} = 44.3 \text{ percent}$$

When there is an ombudsman, the logit is:

$$\text{Logit (liberal democracy)} = -.288 + 1.179(1) = -.288 + 1.179 = .891$$

In this case, the probability that a country is liberal democratic corresponds to:

$$\frac{e^{-.891}}{1+e^{-.891}} = 70.9$$

This means that the probability that a country is liberal democratic increases by 26.6 percent when the ombudsman is one of the oversight tools available to the parliament.

Conclusion

The purpose of this chapter was to increase understanding of the relationship between democracy and oversight. The chapter shows that regardless of which data and statistical analyses are used to assess the relationship between democracy and oversight, the result is that democracy is always related to oversight potential. On the basis of this evidence, it can be concluded that democracy and oversight potential are related.

Furthermore, the chapter argues that what affects democracy is a legislature's oversight potential, and not actual oversight. Using case-study data on the Italian Parliament, the chapter shows that the effectiveness of oversight activities is inversely related to the quantity of oversight activities performed. The larger the number of oversight acts generated by a legislature, the lower the effectiveness of oversight. The problem is twofold. First, when a legislature devotes its attention to too many issues, it cannot be as focused at it would be if it were concentrating on a smaller number of issues, and this lack of focus negatively affects the effectiveness of oversight acts. Second, when legislators ask too many questions of the government, they paradoxically make it easier for the government to dismiss these legislative queries on the grounds that many such questions are of dubious relevance. To avoid both problems, legislators would do well to focus their attention on specific issues, and to choose when and how the government can best be overseen. To do that, legislators need oversight tools or, as Pelizzo and Stapenhurst (2006) put it, oversight potential. Given the importance of oversight potential in keeping governments accountable, it is worthwhile to investigate the relationship between oversight tools or potential on the one hand and democracy on the other hand.

Building on the discussion by Pelizzo and Stapenhurst (2006), the chapter tested which oversight tools are most important for democracy. The finding is that a country's liberal-democratic status is little affected by whether the legislature can hold committee hearings or whether parliamentarians can ask questions of the government. This result is not surprising if one considers that, as the Italian data illustrated, with the exception of the urgent questions, questions are left unanswered. Hence, whether parliamentarians have this tool or not has very little to do with keeping the government accountable and keeping a country liberal and democratic. However, the data analysis showed that although interpellations have some impact on the liberal-democratic status of a country, the only oversight tool that is strongly and significantly related to a country's liberal-democratic status is the ombudsman. In fact, countries in which the ombudsman is institutionalized have a 26.6 percent greater chance to be liberal democratic than countries without an ombudsman.

The chapter argues that the reason the ombudsman is so important for democracy, or rather liberal democracy, is that the ombudsman provides the horizontal accountability that liberal-democratic regimes need to be both liberal and democratic. The ombudsman's office is a more effective oversight tool because, unlike other oversight tools (parliamentary questions, for example), it cannot be used in a partisan manner, it does not suffer any issues of credibility and legitimacy, and it can use its legitimacy to conduct its activities in an effective manner—which is why the probability that a country is liberal democratic is more strongly affected by the presence of the ombudsman than by the presence of any other oversight tool.

Given the nature of data employed in this analysis, these findings are not the final word on the relationship between democracy and oversight. Although the Italian case-study data are a good start, better data from more countries can be collected, and more sophisticated analyses can be conducted. That being said, the findings do shed some light on a relationship that, in spite of its great importance, has been neglected and deserves more attention from both comparative constitutional engineers and practitioners (Sartori 1994a, 1994b). The findings might remind both scholars and drafters of constitutions of the old Madisonian lesson, which states: "In framing a government which is to be administered by men over men, the great difficulty lies in this: you must first enable the government to control the governed; and in the next place oblige it to control itself"—this is why oversight potential is so important for democratic government.

Notes

1. Countries are said to be formal democracies when they have formally democratic institutions on paper. Properly democratic countries are countries in which there are regular free and fair elections, universal suffrage, horizontal and vertical accountability, and protection of individual rights and freedoms. Regimes that share these characteristics are defined as liberal democracies (Diamond 1999).

2. Rockman (1984) and Ogul and Rockman (1990) noted, however, that there is much greater variety as to how oversight can be defined, and definitions of oversight range from minimalist to all-encompassing.

3. Though high partisanship and fierce opposition may be conducive to more effective oversight in general, studies on Public Accounts Committees have argued instead that cooperation between the committee members across party lines is critical in promoting effective oversight of the public accounts (McGee 2002). A similar point is made by Weller (2005, 316) who noted that "committees will be effective primarily, if at all, in areas that are not of partisan interest, such as the system of military discipline."

4. See the annex to chapter 1 in this book.

5. Pelizzo and Stapenhurst (2006) used the data collected by the Inter-Parliamentary Union (IPU) in collaboration with the World Bank Institute (WBI) in its survey on executive-legislative relations. Questionnaires were sent to 180 parliaments around the world, and 83 responded (82 national parliaments plus the European Parliament, which, given its supranational nature, is excluded from further analysis), a response rate of 46 percent. In their analyses of the relationship between democracy and oversight, the IPU-WBI used the data on the 47 parliaments that had provided complete information. This chapter later shows how this methodological choice did not affect the nature of the findings. In fact, regardless of which sample is used—the 47-country sample used by Pelizzo and Stapenhurst (2006) or the complete 82-country sample—the findings show that oversight potential, measured on the basis of the number of oversight tools, is a strong predictor of whether a country is democratic.

6. That the Gastil index scores can be used as proxies for quality of democracy was suggested by Lijphart (1999).

7. Liberal democracies are a subsample of formal democracies. Hence, the sample of formal democracies includes all the countries that are liberal and all the countries that are formal democracies without being liberal democracies.

8. Art. 135 of the standing orders of the Chamber of Deputies establishes that parliamentary questions can have "character of urgency." Art. 138-bis of the standing orders of the Chamber of Deputies establishes that "the presidents of the various parliamentary groups, on behalf of their respective groups, or a group of at least thirty MPs can ask urgent interpellations."

9. Answers could be given right away, after the members of parliament who filed the interpellation had renounced further action, after an interpellation had be joined with other interpellations on a specific topic, or after the answering of the interpellation had been postponed.

Bibliography

Damgaard, Erik. 2000. "Representation, Delegation and Parliamentary Control." Paper prepared for the workshop on "Parliamentary Control of the Executive," European Consortium on Political Research Joint Sessions of Workshops, Copenhagen, April 14–19.

Diamond, Larry. 1999. *Developing Democracy*. Baltimore: Johns Hopkins University Press.

Diamond, Larry, and Leonardo Morlino. 2004. "An Overview." *Journal of Democracy* 15 (4): 20–31.

Frantzich, Steven E. 1979. "Computerized Information Technology in the U.S. House of Representatives." *Legislative Studies Quarterly* 4 (2): 255–80.

Huntington, Samuel. 1991. *The Third Wave*: London: University of Oklahoma Press.

Jewell, Malcolm E.1978. "Legislative Studies in Western Democracies: A Comparative Analysis." *Legislative Studies Quarterly* 3 (4): 537–54.

Lijphart, Arend. 1999. *Patterns of Democracy*. New Haven, CT: Yale University Press.

Linz, Juan J. 1994. "Presidential or Parliamentary: Does It Make a Difference?" In *The Failure of Presidential Democracy*, eds. J. J. Linz and A. Valenzuela, 3–91. Baltimore: Johns Hopkins University Press.

Loewenberg, Gerard, and Samuel C. Patterson. 1979. *Comparing Legislatures*. Boston: Little, Brown & Co.

Maffio, Roberta. 2002. "*Quis custodiet ipsos custodes?* Il controllo parlamentare dell' attivitá di governo in prospettiva comparata." *Quaderni di Scienza Politica* 9 (2): 333–83.

Maor, Moshe. 1999. "Electoral Competition and the Oversight Game: A Transaction Cost Approach and the Norwegian Experience." *European Journal of Political Research* 35: 371–88.

McCubbins, Matthew, and Thomas Schwartz. 1984. "Congressional Oversight Overlooked: Police Patrols versus Fire Alarms." *American Journal of Political Science* 28 (1): 165–79.

McGee, David G. 2002. *The Overseers. Public Accounts Committees and Public Spending*, London: Commonwealth Parliamentary Association, with Pluto Press.

O'Donnell, Guillermo. 1998. "Horizontal Accountability in New Democracies." *Journal of Democracy* 9 (3): 112–26.

Ogul, Morris S., and Bert Rockman. 1990. "Overseeing Oversight: New Departures and Old Problems." *Legislative Studies Quarterly* 15 (1): 5–24.

Olson, David M., and Michael L. Mezey, eds. 1991. *Legislatures in the Policy Process: The Dilemmas of Economic Policy.* Cambridge, UK: Cambridge University Press.

Pasquino, Gianfranco, and Riccardo Pelizzo. 2006. *Parlamenti Democratici.* Bologna: Il Mulino.

Pelizzo, Riccardo, and Rick Stapenhurst. 2004a. "Legislatures and Oversight: A Note." *Quaderni di Scienza Politica* 11 (1): 175–88.

———. 2004b. "Tools for Legislative Oversight. An Empirical Investigation." Policy Research Working Paper No. 3388, World Bank, Washington, DC.

———. 2006. "Democracy and Oversight." Paper presented at the 102nd Annual Meeting of the American Political Science Association, Philadelphia, August 31–September 3.

Pelizzo, Riccardo, Stapenhurst, Rick, Sahgal, Vinod and William Woodley. 2006. "What makes public accounts committees work?" *Politics and Policy*, vol. 34, n. 4, pp. 774–793.

Pennings, Paul. 2000. "Parliamentary Control of the Executive in 47 Democracies." Paper prepared for the workshop on "Parliamentary Control of the Executive." ECPR Joint Sessions of Workshops, Copenhagen, April 14–19.

Rockman, Bert A. 1984. "Legislative-Executive Relations and Legislative Oversight." *Legislative Studies Quarterly* 9 (3): 387–440.

Sartori, Giovanni. 1987. *Elementi di teoria politica.* Bologna: Il Mulino.

———. 1994a. "Neither Presidentialism nor Parliamentarism." *The Failure of Presidential Democracy*, eds. J. J. Linz, and A. Valenzuela, 106–18. Baltimore: Johns Hopkins University Press.

———. 1994b. *Comparative Constitutional Engineering.* New York: New York University.

Schmitter, Philippe. 2004. "The Ambiguous Virtues of Accountability." *Journal of Democracy* 15 (4): 47–60.

Smulovitz, Carolina, and Enrique Peruzzotti. 2000. "Societal Accountability in Latin America." *Journal of Democracy* 11 (4): 147–58.

Weller, Patrick. 2005. "Parliamentary Accountability for Non-Statutory Executive Power: Impossible Dream or Realistic Aspiration?" *Public Law Review* 16 (4): 316–24.

———. 2006. "The Australian Senate: House of Review. Obstruction or Rubber Stamp?" *Social Alternatives* 25 (3): 13–18.

Wiberg, Matti. 1995. "Parliamentary questioning: control by communication" in Herbert Doering, *Parliaments and Majority Rule in Western Europe*, Frankfurt, Campus Verlag, 1995, pp. 179–222.

World Bank. 2002. World Development Indicators. Washington, DC: World Bank.

II. OVERSIGHT AND THE BUDGET PROCESS

CHAPTER 3

The Legislature and the Budget

Rick Stapenhurst

In most countries, the legislature is constitutionally mandated as the institution through which governments are held accountable to the electorate. In that role, the legislature can use several means: the questioning of senior government officials, including ministers; the review and confirmation of executive appointments; impeachment and the power to dismiss the government; question period; the establishment of legislative committees; and the formation of commissions of inquiry.

The accountability mechanisms available to any one legislature depend on the constitutional provisions regarding the specific powers of the legislature; the institutional arrangements between the different branches of government; and the division of authority between national, regional, and local government (Dubrow 1999). Committee hearings, hearings in plenary sittings, and commissions of inquiry are more common in the legislatures of parliamentary systems (parliaments), whereas commissions of inquiry are used more in presidential systems (Pelizzo and Stapenhurst 2004a).

Legislative oversight is nowhere more important than in the budget process. The role of the legislature in most countries is to scrutinize and authorize revenues and expenditures and to ensure that the national budget is properly implemented. How governance affects the well-being of the populace depends on tax levels, spending patterns, the impact of policies on investment and on interest rates, and the ways that domestic priorities and choices interact with international economic and financial trends.

The evolution of legislative "power of the purse" dates back to medieval times, when knights and burgesses in England were summoned to confirm the assent of local communities to the raising of additional taxes.[1] By the early 14th century, the English Parliament had begun to use its power to condition the voting of supply of funds on the acceptance and redress by the monarch to public petitions presented by Parliament.[2] This process was confirmed in

1341, when King Edward III agreed that citizens should not be "charged nor grieved to make common aid or to sustain charge" without the assent of Parliament (White 1908).

In parallel, the English Parliament began to take an interest in how money was collected, as well as how it was spent. As early as 1340, commissioners were appointed by Parliament to audit the accounts of tax collectors, and where public officials were found to have been deficient, the House of Commons would impeach the officials and the House of Lords would try the case (Norton 1993).

The English Parliament's power of the purse evolved gradually and was particularly strengthened during the 16th century, when Tudor monarchs needed parliamentary support and voting of funds for their various political and religious battles. King Henry VIII, for example, gave Parliament enhanced status in policy making, in return for support during his battles with Rome (Norton 1993).

Since that time, the power-of-the-purse function has been performed by legislatures around the world as a means to expand their democratic leverage on behalf of citizens. There is great variation, however, in the nature and effect of legislative engagement. Some legislatures effectively write the budget; others tend to approve executive budget proposals without changes. In some legislatures, most of the debate takes place in plenary, on the floor of the house; elsewhere, the emphasis is on review in committee. Some legislatures fragment scrutiny of the budget across several committees, whereas others have established a preeminent budget (or finance) committee that oversees the process. Ultimately, however, the final vote of approval of "the budget act" takes place in the chamber (Wehner and Byanyima 2004). It is this process of legislative approval of the budget that brings the rule of law to the budget process.

It is useful to conceptualize the overall budget system as a continuing and integrated *budget cycle process*, with legislatures playing a key role at different stages of the cycle. This cycle includes many institutions that, among others, form a country's governance system, namely, the executive, the public service, civil society, and the legislature. Certain facets of the budget process—for example, government accounting, managerial reporting, and internal audit—are primarily the responsibility of the executive and the public service (shown inside the circle in figure 3.1). But for the overall budget cycle to work in a transparent, open, and accountable way within the national economy, the various functions *outside* the circle—budget planning, revenue and expenditure allocation, financial reporting, external audit and evaluation, and public accountability—should involve significant interaction with civil society groups, businesses, and the public at large. It is in those functions outside the circle that legislatures have a key role to play (Langdon 1999). It is useful to consider the role of the legislature in both budget planning and expenditure allocations (ex ante) and in the financial reporting, external audit, and evaluation (ex post) phases of the budget process.

Figure 3.1. Heart of Executive-Legislative Relations: The Budget Process

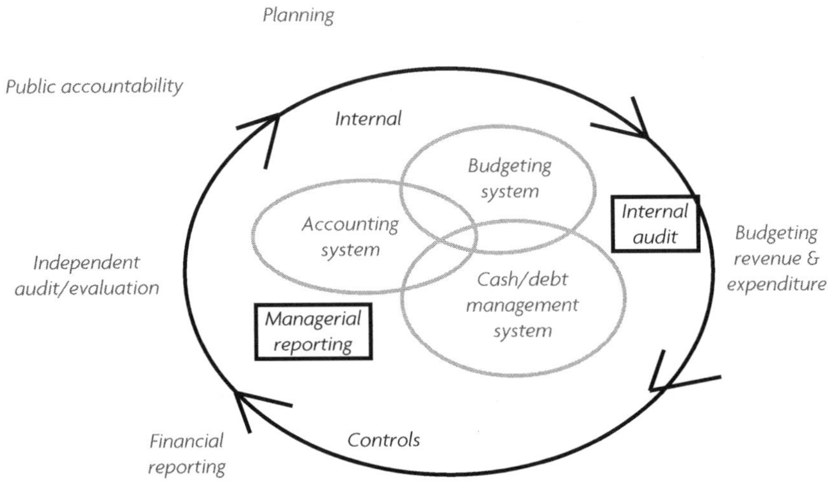

Source: WBI and Parliamentary Centre, 1999.

The Legislature and the Budget Ex Ante

Although legislatures around the world have the constitutional power to consider national budgets and authorize governments to raise revenues and carry out expenditures, the actual exercise of this power varies widely. Schick (2002), for example, noted the long-term decline in the influence of national legislatures on budget policy in industrialized countries, which results from a combination of the devolution of spending (and, to a lesser extent, revenues) to state and local governments and the expansion of both entitlement spending and national debt service. This budgetary decline is perhaps most evident in Great Britain, where Parliament has long since ceased to influence budget measures proposed by the executive (Davey 2000).

Elsewhere, there is a mixed trend, with some OECD-country legislatures launching efforts to regain a more active role in the budget process. In France, for example, the National Assembly recently initiated a wide-ranging budget reform that includes a reclassification of the budget to support parliamentary oversight and an expansion of powers to amend expenditures (Chabert 2001).

In developing and transition countries, too, there is a trend toward legislative budget activism, reflecting the process of democratization and the opening up of possibilities for legislative involvement in what were previously closed budgetary systems. In Brazil, for example, the Congress had historically played no significant role in the budget process; now, constitutional changes have given the Congress powers to modify the budget (see box 3.1). In Africa, too, changes are occurring: South Africa and Uganda have passed financial administration acts or budget acts that give more influence to the legislature during the budget formulation and approval processes.

Box 3.1. Brazilian Congress and the Budget Process

Historically, the Brazilian Congress did not play a significant role in the budget process, but democratization in the 1980s led to constitutional changes that gave Congress new powers to modify the budget. As a result, many amendments are now proposed each year. Constitutionally, the Brazilian Congress may increase one appropriation only by decreasing another. But a loophole also allows Congress to alter revenue figures if it concludes that the executive has made "errors or omissions." To exercise effective control, the Joint Committee on Plans, Public Budgets, and Auditing has moved to a practice of imposing limits on congressional amendment activity. In a recent budget approval process, the following limits applied: (1) up to 20 individual amendments for each representative, each one not reallocating more than a certain amount (of about $750,000); (2) up to five amendments for each sectoral committee in each chamber of Congress, without a monetary limit; and (3) between 15 and 20 amendments proposed by two-thirds of the representatives elected from each state, with no monetary limit.

Source: Blöndal, Goretti, and Kristensen (2003).

Even if the formal role of the legislature in amending the budget may be weak or nonexistent, this does not necessarily mean that it cannot *influence* the budget. In Ghana, for instance, the Finance Committee has had some success in influencing the budget process, in particular by requiring prebudget consultations with the minister of finance and quarterly statements from the finance minister to the Public Accounts Committee (PAC) on budget execution. One particular success was Parliament's influence in the introduction of a value added tax (see box 3.2).

Legislative activism in the ex ante budget process can cause problems for organizations such as the International Monetary Fund (IMF) and the World Bank. Von Hagen (1992), reflecting the views of many economists and an influential body of research, noted that legislative activism may weaken fiscal discipline. Wehner (2004) countered this by noting that legislatures are not the only source of overspending and that, in some instances, legislatures can rein in irresponsible government spending.[3] Wehner also argued that, even if greater legislative activism in budget formulation does lead to some fiscal deterioration, this may well be a price worth paying for greater public input into, and national consensus around, the budget.

Often, legislatures may seek public input into their deliberations on the national budget, thereby helping to develop a balance of views and inputs and providing a platform for a more broadly based consensus than would otherwise be the case. Legislatures can be the entry point into the budget process for business groups, academics, civil society organizations, and policy groups, and many actively solicit submissions from civil society (Wehner 2004).

Box 3.2. Ghana's Parliament and Introducing Value Added Tax

In 1995, Ghana's government introduced a value added tax (VAT) in an effort to remedy the deficiencies of existing consumption taxes and to boost the revenue capacity of government. Following widespread civil unrest, which resulted in several deaths and strengthened political opposition to the tax, Parliament repealed the VAT.

Subsequently, a National Economic Forum indicated that there was broad agreement on the VAT initiative but showed also that such a tax would likely have implementation problems. Perhaps more significantly, the opposition party in Parliament increasingly believed that the solution to Ghana's chronic budget deficits was not new revenue measures but rather expenditure controls and reductions.

Despite government objections, Parliament required national public hearings on the new proposals for a VAT, with the result that public support was garnered for a VAT with a lower, but broader, base (10 percent compared with the previous 17.5 percent) that excluded certain basic goods, such as unprocessed foods, drugs, and health services. The revised tax was approved by Parliament in December 1998.

In 2000, Parliament voted to increase the VAT rate to 12.5 percent, with the additional funds to be directed to a new General Education Trust Fund, operated autonomously from the Ministry of Education, that guaranteed that the new revenues would be spent on education.

Sources: Barkan, Adamolekun, and Zhou (2003); Chapman (2001); Langdon (1999).

In South Africa, the Women's Budget Initiative was established by the Parliament's Finance Committee and two nongovernmental organizations (NGOs); this partnership enabled parliamentarians to draw on the research skills of civil society and gave NGOs direct access to policy makers. The outcome is more gender-sensitive budgeting (Budlender 1996).

But if, on balance, legislative involvement in the budget process ex ante is desirable, why do so many legislatures still only play a minor role? Wehner (2004) described five explanatory variables. First, the constitutional nature of the state itself has a bearing, with legislatures in presidential systems tending to play a more significant role in budget formulation and examination than those in parliamentary or semipresidential systems. Parliamentary systems encourage a collegial approach to relations between the executive and the legislature, since the former is directly dependent on majority support in the legislature for its existence. A parliament's vote not to approve the budget would be equivalent to a vote of no confidence in the government and, in Westminster-type parliaments, could lead to the resignation of the executive. In presidential systems, by contrast, the separation of powers may lead to conflict between the executive and the legislature. Nowhere is this threat more acute than in matters relating to the budget—as, for example, in Nigeria.

The second, and related, reason that legislatures play only a minor role in the budget process is that legislatures in many of the semipresidential and non-Commonwealth parliamentary systems have the power to amend the budget. Table 3.1 indicates that more than a third of the 83 legislatures surveyed by the IPU have the power to amend the budget.

Third, some researchers (Leston-Bandeira 1999; Young 1999) have stressed that budgeting takes place in a broader political context that is ultimately subject to the power relationships of political participants. Thus, how much de facto rather than de jure influence the legislature has is largely determined by party political majorities. If the legislature comprises several parties, none of which has an overall majority, or if party discipline is weak, the executive will have to assemble a broad coalition of support for the budget, with a concomitant increase in the potential influence of the legislature in the budget (Ghana is, perhaps, a good case in point, where the government currently has a majority of 25 in Parliament). By contrast, where there is a strong or dominant political majority and where political party discipline is strong, the legislature's ability to influence the budget will be weaker. In addition, informal caucuses in some legislatures, such as women's or environmental groups, can exert influence on legislation, including budget legislation (Leston-Bandeira 1999; von Hagen 1992, quoted in Wehner and Byanyima 2004; Young 1999).

The fourth variable is that legislative budget research capacity can enable the legislature to make more informed contributions to budget formulation. Examples of such capacity include the Congressional Planning and Budget Office of the Philippines, which has a staff of 50, and the newly formed Parliamentary Budget Office in Uganda, staffed with about 27 economists, compared with the parliaments of Zambia, Namibia, and Sri Lanka, which have no specialized budget researchers. A similar case in Poland, is presented in box 3.3. Also, Pelizzo and Stapenhurst (2004b) noted a related factor: access to information. Legislators need accurate and timely information if they are to make meaningful contributions to budget formulation.

Fifth, Wehner (2004) noted that the existence of specialized budget committees, in which in-depth and technical debate can take place, supported by adequate staff and related resources, and given sufficient time for deliberation,

Table 3.1. Legislatures' Powers to Amend the Budget

Rights	No. of Countries
Have unlimited powers to amend the budget	32
May reduce existing items only	17
May reduce expenditures, but may increase them only with permission of the government	4
May increase expenditures, but increases must be balanced with commensurate cuts elsewhere	13
Rights not specified	15
Total	81

Source: Adapted from IPU (1986, table 38A), as quoted in Wehner (2004).

Box 3.3. The Polish Parliament's Budget Research Office

After years of lacking any real power, democratic changes in Poland during the late 1980s and early 1990s led to the belief that Parliament should exert greater influence over the budget. In 1991, a small budget research office was established, with a staff of six employees. Despite numerous start-up difficulties (none of the researchers had previously worked in parliamentary administration, there were early rivalries between parliamentary committee staff and the research office, and a large majority of parliamentarians were newcomers and unfamiliar with the budget process), the budget research office's stature grew. By 1995, the staff had increased from six to 12, cooperation was formalized with a university (with contracted analytical services provided by four academics), and the research office became responsible for coordination of the work undertaken by parliamentary committee staff.

As a result, the budget research office has the ability to undertake in-depth analysis of the government's proposed budget—with the office now completing more than 300 pieces of analysis each year and Parliament introducing some 700 amendments to the budget in 2000 and 350 in 2001.

Source: Staskiewicz (2002).

has an important influence on the role that the legislature can play in budget formulation. In recent years, India, Uganda, and Zambia, to name just three countries, have created specific committees to consider budget issues.

The Legislature and the Budget Ex Post

If there is controversy around the desirability of legislative activism in the ex ante phases of the budget cycle, there is much less in the ex post phases. Following implementation of the budget, government accounts and financial statements are audited by a "supreme audit institution," such as the auditor general (in Commonwealth countries) or *cours des comptes* (in francophone countries). In most countries, this audit is followed by the consideration of the audit findings—which may include value for money and performance auditing as well as financial or compliance auditing—by the legislature. If the legislature's role in the budget cycle is effective, legislative recommendations based on audit findings are reflected in future budgets, thus allowing for continuous improvements in public financial accountability.

Recent research (Pelizzo and Stapenhurst, 2004a) suggests that government reporting and legislative scrutiny of public accounts is more common in parliamentary and semipresidential systems than in presidential systems; even so, 84 percent of legislatures in presidential systems analyze financial reports from government.

The exact nature of the interaction between the legislature and the auditors partly depends on the model of the supreme audit institution and its reporting structure. In most Commonwealth countries, the auditor general is a core element of parliamentary oversight, and he or she reports directly to parliament and a specialized committee—the Public Accounts Committee. This committee reviews audit findings, considers testimony by witnesses from government departments, and sends its report to the full parliament for action. In some instances, the auditor general is an officer of parliament. In the board system, the audit board prepares and sends an annual report to the executive, which in turn submits it to the legislature, while in *cours des comptes* systems, the court can pass findings on to the legislature's finance committee. The committee can also request that a specific audit be undertaken (Stapenhurst and Titsworth 2001).

The structure and function of PACs dates back to the reforms initiated by William Gladstone, when he was chancellor of the exchequer in the mid-19th century. Replicated in virtually all Commonwealth and many non-Commonwealth countries, PACs are seen as the legislative apex for financial scrutiny in many parliamentary forms of government and have been promoted as a crucial mechanism to facilitate transparency in government financial operations (see figure 3.2).

Rules and practices affecting the operation of PACs in different countries vary greatly. A large majority of PAC work focuses on the reports from the auditor general—indeed, the PAC is the principal client of the auditor general. Financial oversight is greater when a cordial relationship is maintained between the PAC and the auditor general: the PAC requires timely, high-quality auditing, and the auditor general needs an effective PAC to ensure that the government takes audit outcomes seriously.

A recent survey by the PCA (Commonwealth Parliamentary Association) (McGee 2002) shows that several practices can enhance financial transparency by broadening access to information (see box 3.4). More than four-fifths of Commonwealth PACs make their reports freely available to the public, and more than half have their reports debated in the parliamentary chamber. In

Figure 3.2. Fiduciary Obligation

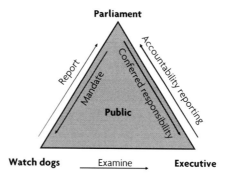

Source: Stapenhurst, Woodley, and Pelizzo, 2005.

Box 3.4. Enhancing Financial Transparency by Broadening Access to Information

In a Commonwealth-wide survey conducted in 2000 by the Commonwealth Parliamentary Association (CPA) and the World Bank Institute (WBI), it was found that 87 percent of PACs release their reports to the general public, and 57 percent of PACs stated that their reports are debated in parliament (typically with public access and media coverage). A further commitment to transparency is reflected in the fact that 55 percent of PACs open their hearings to the general public and the media.

Though some argue that the need for political consensus within the PAC requires that hearings be held in camera, there seems to be a general trend toward opening up hearings to the public and media. Indeed, some parliaments reported significant improvements in the responses from government when the PAC started holding its hearings in public. It may be instructive that, despite the advantages and disadvantages of holding public meetings, no PAC has reversed its decision to hold its meetings in public. As McGee noted, "The PAC's work is performed through the Parliament for the public benefit; it is therefore fitting that the public should know as much about [its work] as possible, without interfering with its effective performance" (73).

Source: McGee (2002).

many countries government is required to make a formal response to PAC reports, typically in the form of a Treasury (or executive) minute. Moreover, in more than half of the Commonwealth countries, PAC meetings are open to the public and the media.

Building on the CPA-WBI survey, Stapenhurst et al. (2005) have sought to identify potential success factors that influence the effectiveness of PACs. These factors include having a broad scope and mandate, thereby giving the PAC a greater potential to deter waste and wrongdoing; having the power to choose subjects for examination without government direction or advice; having the power to undertake effective analysis, publish conclusions, and use effective follow-up procedures; and having solid support, both from the auditor general and from dedicated parliamentary research staff.

At the same time, constraints to effective PAC performance have been identified (Stapenhurst et al. 2005). These constraints include a highly partisan climate where, at an extreme, the executive may be unwilling to accept any criticism or act on valid complaints; government's dislike of legislative oversight and, in some cases, its lack of interest in addressing the inherent weaknesses of the legislature; a lack of media and public involvement; and a weak ethical culture within both the executive and the legislature, which leads to public distrust of politicians in general.

The examples of effective PACs are numerous. In Uganda, the PAC increased its activism by taking many more suspects to the courts for cases of financial irregularity; in South Africa the PAC and the media have kept the "defense budget scandal" in the public eye, demanding remedial action by the executive; and in Ghana the PAC was able to enact initiatives to tighten financial administration of local school authorities (Langdon 1999). Many non-Commonwealth countries have established committees similar to PACs, and in some legislatures the committee that is responsible for scrutinizing the budget is also charged with considering audit reports.[4]

With the increasing complexity of public audits, many PACs (or their equivalent committees in non-Commonwealth countries) have created subcommittees that examine particular subject areas, such as education or health. In addition, a close relationship is often forged between the PAC and the departmental or sectoral committees that are charged with the oversight and scrutiny of specific government policies.

One weakness in many countries is that, despite debates in the chamber of the legislature and reports to the executive, the government fails to address the issues raised or to implement the PAC's recommendations. To overcome this problem, countries have adopted different follow-up procedures. In Canada, for example, government departments have the opportunity to include a chapter in the auditor general's report on their intentions for follow-up on implementation, and reports in subsequent years will review the departments' actions on these announced intentions. In Germany, by contrast, the audit institution produces a regular tracking report, which tracks the implementation of each recommendation made in earlier reports. In other countries, the legislature may require interim reporting (which can take the form of regular committee briefings by relevant officials) to ensure that the government takes timely remedial action (Wehner and Byanyima 2004).

As with legislative involvement in the budget ex ante, public input may be sought by the legislature in its ex post review of government spending; many PACs call witnesses in addition to relying on input from the auditor general. Moreover, civil society can play a supporting role. Wehner and Byanyima (2004) note a particularly innovative example from South Africa, where the Public Sector Accountability Monitor (PSAM)—a civil society initiative—follows up on reported cases of corruption and misconduct with the government departments concerned. After obtaining all relevant details, PSAM sends a fax to the relevant departmental head; a follow-up contact is made a month later by telephone, and the response, which is recorded, is made available in text and audio format on the Internet. An alternative approach is for civil society groups to seek input at the external audit stage, before the submission of the auditor general's report to parliament and the PAC. In Colombia, for example, the auditor general's program includes public forums and hearings in which complaints from citizens are heard and public feedback is generated regarding the work of the auditor general. A particularly innovative program is the establishment of "citizen watchdog committees," which monitor high-impact projects and report back to the auditor general (Krafchik 2003).

Conclusions

Legislatures have, and are using, constitutional powers to oversee budget formulation and implementation. The challenge for legislatures, in performing these functions, is to ensure both that their influence and impact reflect national, as opposed to partisan, priorities (and allow for input from broader civil society) and that fiscal discipline is maintained. Indeed, Schick (2002) noted that, rather than act as controllers of public finance, legislatures should perhaps aim to promote fiscal discipline, improve the allocation of public money, and stimulate public bodies to manage their financial operations more efficiently. To do that, it is necessary for governments to enhance, among other efforts, their legislative capacity to deal with budget issues.

Providing legislatures with adequate resources involves, among other things, strengthening the "money committees" (for example, the finance, budget, and public accounts committees), establishing dedicated research staff, enhancing the capacity of national audit offices, and encouraging public input at the various stages of the budget cycle. Over the past decade or so, numerous organizations, including bilateral donors, multinational organizations, and international financial institutions, have assisted legislatures in carrying out financial oversight. Such assistance has ranged from supplying office and other equipment, information, and training, to helping establish legislative budget offices and strengthening committees. However, results have been mixed; Carothers (1999) noted that in the area of democracy assistance, it is support to the legislatures that most often falls short of its goals. Why is this? And what lessons can be learned from the 1990s to help legislatures and multilateral institutions alike design such projects in the future?

Carothers noted that "...aid providers' lack of knowledge about the political and personal dynamics of the institutions they are trying to reshape" was a common deficiency, as was "the lack of interest in reform among the power-holders in the legislatures of [certain] countries" (1999, 183), a fact reiterated by Messick (2002), who highlighted the need to undertake a thorough analysis of the political environment in which the legislature operates.

Clearly, political will is a prerequisite for legislative strengthening. In Bolivia, the multiparty Committee for Legislative Modernization, which was established in 1995, took ownership of the reform process and functioned as the internal locus for identifying problems, setting priorities, and proposing future directions. Despite partisan bickering, by 1999 the committee had survived three national elections and three changes of parties in power, and it had spearheaded constitutional and rules reforms that established direct elections for half of the lower house and required congressional committees to conduct public hearings. Similar mechanisms were established, with varying success, in Colombia and Nicaragua. In Uganda, a private-member's bill established an independent parliamentary commission, that is, a joint parliamentary-executive board that oversees the management and modernization of the National Assembly. The commission's functions include, among other things, creating a permanent, independent nonpartisan staff for Parliament and coordinating donor support to Parliament (USAID 2000). By contrast, in Nepal the first speaker was instrumental in legislative reform, but his successor showed less interest in the program (Lippman and Emmert 1997). In the case of support to the budget oversight function, the example of Nepal means that the chairs of the money committees, as well as the parliamentary leadership, need to be fully supportive of the capacity-building efforts.

Furthermore, legislative strengthening efforts should be seen as complements to related governance improvements. To quote Carothers (1999):

> Treating legislatures as self-contained entities that can be fixed by repairing internal mechanisms is unlikely to get very far. Rather, … it is more useful to think in terms of helping a society develop the capacity to enact laws that incorporate citizens' interests. [This means] working with many people and groups outside the legislature, including political parties, citizens groups, the media, officials from the executive branch, jurists and others. (188)

In the case of money committees, use of the complementary approach means dovetailing reform activities with broader efforts to enhance government accountability and to strengthen public financial oversight. It also means ensuring that training activities include participants from other stakeholder

Box 3.5. Analyzing the Political Context

Lippman and Emmert (1997) recommend using a typology to analyze the political context within which the legislature operates.

Type 1: No democratic legislature (pre-democratic country, failed state, or "rubber stamp" legislature)—here, only limited success can be anticipated (at best).

Type 2: Just after a defining democratic event—such as the establishment of democratic institutions or the redrafting of the constitution in the East European and Commonwealth of Independent States (CIS) countries in the early 1990s—often, timing is of the essence, and the nature and extent of the event may determine the type of assistance.

Type 3: Fledgling democratic legislature—here, helping the legislature define its basic role and function may be helpful.

Type 4: Established democratic legislature—here, focus could most usefully be on helping the legislature become more accountable, transparent, and responsive.

It is also important to analyze the legislature's relationship with other branches of government, political parties, and civil society. In particular, it is important to determine if the legislature has real power, to what extent political parties respect and cooperate with each other, and how civil society organizations and interest groups interact with the legislature.

Source: Lippman and Emmert (1997).

organizations, such as the Ministry of Finance, the Auditor General's Office, and representatives from civil society.

Finally, legislative strengthening is a long-term process that requires long-term commitment—but short-term visible results are both possible and important. Sometimes time constraints result from training new legislators at the beginning of their term, but the requirements of sustainability and institutionalization typically require a more long-term process, and even then the results may not always be tangible. The United Nations Development Programme (UNDP) faced this lack of visible progress in Ethiopia by having the legislature hold regular public hearings to mark the impact of the project (UNDP 2001).

Legislative assistance will inevitably continue to evolve, with growing emphasis on, among other things, training legislators on budget processes and improving research and information capabilities (Manning and Stapenhurst 2002). Indeed, though it is necessary to examine holistically the legislature's needs, including looking at the roles of legislators and staff, and the legislature's relationships with other branches of government and the public, enhancing the legislature's role in the budget process can be a powerful tool in developing checks and balances within governance systems. In Bolivia, for example, support to the staff of Congress facilitated more capable analyses of the budget, which in turn improved the ability of legislators to become more meaningfully engaged in a policy area that previously had been the sole preserve of the executive (Lippman and Emmert 1997).

Notes

1. There was, however, no suggestion that they had the power to *refuse* such assent (Norton 1993).

2. From such petitions evolved *statutes*, which required the assent of Parliament and the King. Statutes were distinguishable from *ordinances*, which were the product solely of the King, thus marking the beginning of the transfer of power from the King to Parliament for the development of statute law (Norton 1993).

3. Wehner cited the United States, Germany, and the South African province of Mpumalanga, where executive initiative, rather than the legislature, caused deterioration in fiscal discipline.

4. This is the case in France, Germany, and several East European, Latin American, and francophone African countries. In addition, New Zealand, a Commonwealth country, does not have a PAC; its functions are incorporated into the Finance and Estimates Committee.

Bibliography

Barkan, J., L. Adamolekun, and Y. Zhou (with M. Laleye and N. Ng'e). 2003. "The Emerging Legislatures in Emerging African Democracies." Unpublished report, World Bank, Washington, DC.

Blöndal, J. R., C. C. Goretti, and J. K. Kristensen. 2003. "Budgeting in Brazil." Paper presented at the 24th Annual Meeting of OECD Senior Budget Officials, Rome, June 3–4.

Budlender, D., ed. 1996. *The Women's Budget.* Cape Town: Institute for Democracy in South Africa.

Carothers, T. 1999. *Aiding Democracy Abroad: The Learning Curve.* Washington, DC: Carnegie Endowment for Peace.

Chabert, G. 2001. "La Reforme de l'Ordonnance de 1959 sur la Procedure Budgetaire: Simple Amenagement Technique ou Prelude a des Veritables Bouleversements?" Regards sur l'Actualité, No. 275.

Chapman, E. 2001. "Introducing a Value Added Tax: Lessons from Ghana." PREM Note No. 61, World Bank, Washington, DC.

Davey, E. 2000. "Making MPs Work for Our Money: Reforming Parliament's Role in Budget Scrutiny." Paper No. 19, Centre for Reform, London.

Dubrow, Geoff. 1999. "Systems of Governance and Parliamentary Accountability." In *Parliamentary Accountability and Good Governance.* Washington, DC: World Bank Institute and the Parliamentary Centre.

Krafchik, Warren. 2003. "What Role Can Civil Society and Parliament Play in Strengthening the External Auditing Function?" Paper presented at the workshop "Towards Auditing Effectiveness," Addis Ababa, Ethiopia, May 12–15.

Langdon, Steven. 1999. "Parliament and the Budget Cycle." In *Parliamentary Accountability and Good Governance.* Washington, DC: World Bank Institute and the Parliamentary Centre.

Leston-Bandeira, C. 1999. "The Role of the Portuguese Parliament Based on a Case Study: The Discussion of the Budget, 1983–95." *Journal of Legislative Studies* 5 (2): 46–73.

Lippman, H., and J. Emmert. 1997. "Assisting Legislatures in Developing Countries." Programs and Operations Assessment Report No. 20, USAID, Washington, DC.

Manning, Nick, and Rick Stapenhurst. 2002. "Strengthening Oversight by Legislatures." PREM Note No. 74, World Bank, Washington, DC.

McGee, David. 2002. *The Overseers: Public Accounts Committees and Public Spending.* London: Commonwealth Parliamentary Association.

Messick, Rick. 2002 (March). "Strengthening Legislatures: Implications from Industrial Countries." PREM Note No. 63, World Bank, Washington, DC.

Miller, Robert, Riccardo Pelizzo, and Rick Stapenhurst. 2004. "Parliamentary Libraries, Institutes and Offices. Sources of Parliamentary Information." Working Paper, World Bank Institute, Washington, DC.

Norton, Philip. 1993. *Does Parliament Matter?* Hemel Hempstead, UK: Harvester Wheatsheaf.

Pelizzo, Riccardo, and Rick Stapenhurst. 2004a. "Legislatures and Oversight: A Note." Paper presented at the Southern Political Science Association Conference, New Orleans, January 8–10.

Pelizzo, Riccardo, and Rick Stapenhurst. 2004b. "Legislative Ethics and Codes of Conduct." Working Paper, World Bank Institute, Washington, DC.

Schick, Allen. 2002. "Can National Legislatures Regain an Effective Voice in Budget Policy?" *OECD Journal on Budgeting* 1 (3): 15–42.

Stapenhurst, Rick, Vinod Sahgal, William Woodley, and Riccardo Pelizzo. 2005. "Scrutinizing Public Expenditures: Assessing the Performance of Public Accounts Committees." Policy Research Working Paper No. 3613, World Bank, Washington, DC.

Stapenhurst, Rick, and Jack Titsworth. 2001. "Features and Functions of Supreme Audit Institutions." PREM Note No. 59, World Bank, Washington, DC.

Staskiewicz, W. 2002. "Budget Analysis for Parliaments: The Case of Poland." Paper prepared for the 68th IFLA Council and General Conference, Glasgow, August 18–24.

UNDP (United Nations Development Programme). 2001. Legislative Assistance Retrospective. Background paper, UNDP Bureau for Development Policy, New York.

USAID (U.S. Agency for International Development). 2000. *Handbook on Legislative Strengthening.* New York: USAID.

von Hagen, J., 1992. "Budgeting Procedures and Fiscal Performance in the European Communities," European Economy - Economic Papers 96, Commission of the EC, Directorate-General for Economic and Financial Affairs (DG ECFIN), Brussels.

Wehner, Joachim. 2004. *Back from the Sidelines? Redefining the Contribution of Legislatures to the Budget Cycle.* Washington, DC: World Bank Institute.

Wehner, Joachim, and Winnie Byanyima. 2004. "Budget Handbook for Parliamentarians, including from a Gender Perspective." Geneva: Inter-Parliamentary Union; Washington, DC: World Bank Institute.

White, Albert. 1908. *The Making of the English Constitution 449–1485.* London: G. P. Putnam's Sons.

Young, L. 1999. "Minor Parties and the Legislative Process in the Australian Senate: A Study of the 1993 Budget." *Australian Journal of Political Science* 34 (1): 7–27

CHAPTER 4

Budgets—An Accountant's Perspective

Kerry Jacobs

Anyone who has visited London will have heard the warning in the underground to "please mind the gap" between the train door and the platform. In so many areas of thought, a gap represents something to be avoided. However, for accountants, the term GAAP is an abbreviation for generally accepted accounting practice, that is, the rules and traditions that guide accounting practice within the private sector. Some of these have been formalized as laws and regulations; others exist merely as guidelines and traditions. Unfortunately these rules and regulations render the relatively simple nature of good accounting complex and virtually impenetrable to the uninitiated. The danger in the public sector is that financial oversight becomes too technically complex for politicians charged with oversight and too political for accountants with the technical skills. This chapter represents an attempt to construct a bridge between these two worlds and to present key accounting concepts in such a way that they are clear and simple.

Control over financial resources is a form of power. Reformers have realized that significant social and structural changes can be achieved through the reduction and redirection of financial resources (Newberry and Jacobs 2007), to the extent that the distinction between fiscal and social policy has blurred. Jürgen Habermas (1984, 1997) suggested that money is one of the great social steering media that influence the nature of social systems and behavior. Yet the institutions and practices of accounting within the context of the public sector have received little attention from political science. Although the use and distribution of money within a political system provide a powerful way to explore the nature of power and influence, these are seen as technical accounting issues by both researchers and politicians. This perspective has been encouraged by the accountants involved, and further reinforced by the introduction of private sector accounting practices—GAAP—within the public sector. The danger is that issues that should be debated openly by politicians will be relegated to the area of professional expertise, leading to reduced legislative oversight.

Central to all discussions of legislative oversight, and indeed any form of oversight, are the broader but associated issues of accountability, control, and governance. Day and Klein (1987, 6) argued that the concept of accountability today represents the merging of two different ideas. Political accountability goes back to the development of society and social structures, when individuals were given the responsibility to carry out tasks on behalf of their fellow citizens. To have responsible officials is what differentiated the emergence of democracy in cities such as Athens from those under tyrants and despots. The second tradition was the idea of stewardship associated with estate management. In contrast to the political accountability of classical Greek society, stewardship and estate management introduced concepts of financial accountability, managerial accountability, and audit. Much of the confusion over accountability arises from the simple fact that different people are talking about different things when they use the word *accountability*.

It is the second type of accountability that has expanded, potentially to the detriment of the first. Michael Power (1994, 1997) argued that this tradition of stewardship has been transformed into the practice of audit, which has come to have an increasingly dominant social and political role, particularly within the public sector. Power (2003) suggested that the power of auditing was not as a neutral or objective technology but as a process of building credibility and constructing legitimacy. Given the growth of these regimes of audit and inspection within the public sector, many aspects that may have previously been the jurisdiction of the elected politician have become the jurisdiction of the professional accountant, and therefore are no longer subjected to the public debate (Power and Laughlin 1992). One example of this process is the way that particular forms of asset valuation can make the public provision of services appear uneconomical when compared with alternative private providers. A second example is where national archives or art collections are downsized because of depreciation costs.

Although issues such as asset values and depreciation costs may appear to be technical accounting judgments, they are really matters of public policy that need to be subject to political debate. Some politicians have attempted to use these accounting tools for their own political ends (Newberry and Jacobs 2007). However, while attempting to exclude others from the debate, these politicians risk losing control themselves. One example of this problem has been the introduction of accrual accounting within the public sector, with the associated private sector accounting rules and standards. From an accounting perspective, this is an elegant technical solution that provides sector-neutral consistency and comparability, which are needed because many aspects of the public sector experience the same commercial dictates as the private sector. However, few politicians (aside from those who have professional accounting or commercial experience) actually understand the nature of an accrual-based budgetary system or the resulting financial statements. If these innovations are not, or cannot be, used for decision making, it poses a serious question as to why they were implemented and why they are being promoted as the solution to the problems of the public sector.

The next section of this chapter attempts to lift the veil on the secret art of budgeting, illustrating that many of the complex and confusing aspects of accounting are actually just an application of common sense. In particular, it emphasizes the central role of ideas of control and control theory in accountants' understanding of budgets and oversight systems.

The Secret Art of Budgeting

From an accounting perspective a budget is no more than a plan for revenue and spending, normally for a year. However, as most accountants do not come equipped with perfect foresight, the actual spending and revenue for most organizations will deviate from the budget. It is the variances or deviations from the budget that are the most interesting, as they direct attention to some aspect of activity that has deviated from the plan. In the case of expenditures, this deviation could be because an organization is using more of a particular resource than expected, resulting in a quantity variance, or the resource could have cost more than expected, resulting in a price variance. All variances need to be explored and explained and are not necessarily bad. The concept of variance calculation and the associated practice of "management by exception" illustrate that budgets can serve a number of different purposes. As a plan or target for the year, the budget represents a key tool of planning for the financial and resource needs of any organization. However, the calculation and reporting of variances illustrate the role of budgets in facilitating top management oversight (good governance) and in motivating staff. One difficulty is that although a realistic target or budget may represent the most effective tool for planning, a challenging and therefore optimistic budget may be the most effective tool for staff motivation. Accountants remain divided about these two alternatives, although in practice most budgets are realistic rather than motivational.

Budgets and Control

The nature and role of budgets tend to be presented within a general model of control that represents all systems and processes within an "inputs-process-outputs" model (see figure 4.1). Any process or system, be it biological, social, or mechanical, can be presented in this way. The central process or real activity is represented by the shaded boxes, with the movement going from inputs, through the processes, and resulting in outputs. Within the public sector the appropriated funds or taxes represent the input, which is converted through the processes of public administrative and public agency activities into the output of given services, products, and social impacts. Often both public sector reform and public sector performance measurement are described in this way; for example, Hood (1991, 1995) suggested that a

Figure 4.1. Model of a Controlled Process

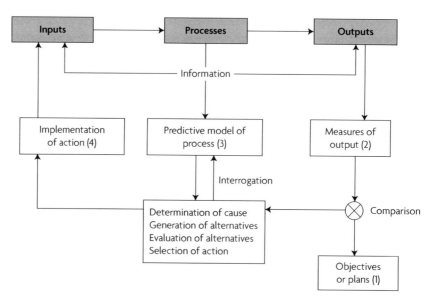

Source: Parker, Ferris, and Otley (1989, 48).

defining characteristic of public sector reform in many countries is a shift of focus away from managing inputs and bureaucratic processes and toward a greater focus on outputs. From an accounting perspective it is this control model that forms the basis of a process of oversight and governance.

The unshaded boxes and lines in figure 4.1 represent the information and actions required for control. Otley and Berry (1980) argued that there are four requirements or conditions for control. These requirements are represented as the numbered boxes in figure 4.1. In order to control outputs it is necessary that (1) clear objectives exist and (2) the outputs of the process are measurable in the same terms as the objectives being pursued. Budgets often play this role by providing a clear objective that can be compared to actual spending. However, Otley and Berry also suggested that control requires (3) a predictive model of the process, which makes it possible to identify and correct any deviation from the desired targets and goals, and (4) the ability to implement corrective action to address any deviation of actual performance from the desired outcomes.

In practice, Otley and Berry's (1980) four requirements can be difficult to achieve. A clear objective can be harder than it sounds, as public sector entities often face multiple and conflicting requirements. It is naive to suggest that goal ambiguity can be legislated away, as political processes and decisions are also subject to multiple and conflicting demands. Budgets are often part of the broader planning and strategy processes involved in the establishment of goals and objectives and therefore can play an important role in facilities' negotiation and compromise between different objectives and agendas.

Where clear objectives, budgets, or targets exist, it is the variance between actual output and planned output rather than the budget itself that is the most interesting. This process is called *feedback control*, because once the cause of the variance is determined, the information is fed back to implement a change in the available inputs to restore the desired outcome. The process of feedback implies a predictive model of how a given change in inputs will result in the desired outcomes and the ability to implement the desired change. An example of this would be the comparison of actual spending and desired spending, leading to the discovery of gross overspending, after which real action would be taken to alter some aspect of the inputs to ensure that the overspending does not continue. Clearly the difficult question is, what actions would reduce overspending, and is it possible to take those actions?

The nature and role of a predictive model is the most difficult element of control. A predictive model can be a highly structured and formal organizational learning system or it can be informal and intuitive, existing only in the minds of the staff. However, the inability to predict how a change in actions or in input resources will affect the organizational outputs, and therefore goal achievement, will limit the possibility of control and therefore the practical (as opposed to rhetorical) contribution of budget systems.

The second approach to control is known as *feed-forward* control, or *process* or *bureaucratic* control, and it requires an effective predictive model. Under this approach the ongoing process is compared with a standard or regulation, and this provides a prediction of how to alter actions or processes so that the targeted goals can be achieved. Many of the traditional regulation and compliance-based governance systems within the public sector represent this kind of approach. The danger is that the predictive model gains a life of its own and no longer exists in relation to the central goals and objectives of an organization, a government, or the population as a whole. In such a context the central question becomes whether the rules have been followed, rather than whether the objectives of the organization have been achieved. Often budgets become perceived in this way as an end in themselves rather than as a means to an end.

Within the public sector, budgets historically have not been a form of feedback control in which actual performance is compared with desired or planned performance but rather have been a form of due process compliance that aims to show that the funds and resources have been spent in line with the objectives they were appropriated for. This focus on due process of the appropriation system and of the budget can be traced back to the evolution of the Westminster Parliament and the negotiated compromise between the Parliament and the Crown, where the appropriation of taxation must have the approval of Parliament. This historical development is more fully described in chapter 3, "The Legislature and the Budget." Therefore historical budgetary control has been focused on identifying any variance between parliamentary budgetary appropriations and actual spending. The implication is that if the money has been spent in line with the appropriated objectives, then the goals and policies of government, as approved by Parliament, will have been achieved. Therefore budgets embody the dual nature of accountability identified by Day and Klein (1987), which is reflected in the question of whether the role of budgets is to ensure the achievement of policy goals or whether it is to ensure compliance with regulatory systems.

To summarize, budgets can be understood as a form of control within the public sector. They have a historical role in establishing the legitimacy of government spending but also play an important role in comparing actions against organizational targets and developing best practice guidelines for regulation and good governance. However, the growth of budgets and associated control practices within the public sector has also been subject to criticism. Gregory (1995) argued that within the New Zealand public sector this model of control has resulted in a bureaucratic paradox, where a gap exists between the need to let managers manage and the need for accountability and control, and between systems based on clear objectives and clear rules and the reality of public sector requirements and pressures that are often far from clear or explicit. The restructuring of the public sector to satisfy the conditions for control, as described by Otley and Berry (1980), has, according to Gregory, provided a system that fails to recognize the complexity and ambiguity experienced by those working within the public sector.

One area in which this model of control does fall down is the issue of outcomes. In practice, outcomes give accountants a great deal of difficulty because they are hard to measure and quantify. Outcomes are probably better addressed by program evaluation and performance audit; however, outcomes also represent the outputs of a larger (macro) system that maps how the overall objectives or goals of the government are implemented across a number of agencies and activities. This has been recognized in jurisdictions that have developed broader performance planning approaches, such as the medium-term expenditure framework. The central problem in these performance frameworks is that the predictive model is usually poor, and the cause-effect relationships are uncertain. For example, it is never clear exactly how additional spending on police will reduce crime or how additional teachers will improve literacy. Therefore, what is required is not a strict reporting or control system but rather a learning system in which policy makers and members of parliament can experiment with different activities and programs and monitor the resulting impact on the relevant outcomes. Though this sounds reasonable and sensible, clearly it is very difficult in a political environment where any perceived evidence of failure represents an opposition sound bite rather than an opportunity to learn.

Beyond Budgets

Although the establishment of a budget is presented as a technical process, it is always a judgmental process, because no one is able to accurately predict the future. On the whole, budgets are based on the previous year's cost and revenue figures adjusted for expected activity and predicted cost changes. However, in organizations this method tends to lead to an incremental approach in which existing activity is rarely questioned or challenged. One solution to this problem is the use of zero-based budgeting. This solution involves the abandonment of the incremental approach and the requirement that existing activities and spending be justified in order to be included in the budget. However, the administrative costs associated with this kind of review are particularly high, and established organizations normally maintain their current practices, assets, and structures. Therefore, although zero-based budgeting is powerful as an occasional organizational review process, it is usually unrealistic and expensive on an ongoing basis.

Some companies have even started to question and challenge the value and contribution of budgets altogether. This "beyond budgets" movement has come from European companies such as the Swedish bank Svenska Handelsbanken and the information technology (IT) company SAP AG. They argue that budgets lead to backward and incremental thinking, centralize power, reduce innovation, and focus on expense reduction rather than revenue growth. Instead of advocating budgets, these companies argue for more adaptive and devolution-focused approaches to management, which place a greater emphasis on ratios, efficiency measures, and performance targets.

Budget and Performance Centers

Even within companies, performance measurement poses problems. Most companies have only one real investment center and just a few profit centers. A profit center is where a manager can control both costs and revenue, and an investment center is where a manager can control capital investment (the purchase and sale of assets), in addition to controlling cost and revenue. For most organizations this would only exist at the total-company level. Because of this, measuring the financial and budgetary performance of smaller units, departments, divisions, or particular managers within an organization is particularly difficult. Most managers can only control their costs or spending (cost center) or occasionally revenue received (revenue center). Because of this performance measurement problem, accountants have invented a form of creative bookkeeping called *transfer pricing*.

Transfer pricing is a form of performance measurement that places a financial value on the transfer of goods or services within an organization, enabling the creation of an internal-market selling price. In effect, the "products" of one unit are "sold" to another unit at a given "price." As a consequence, both costs and revenues can be calculated, and the performance of many more parts of the organization can be evaluated as profit centers, making it possible to measure performance using measures of efficiency and effectiveness.

It is in the business of determining the nature of the products sold and establishing the price to be charged that the real difficulties exist, because the products sold are not normally real products but are something that is partially completed or some internal service. The price is also not a real price but an estimate or judgment, as a real price will only exist when the product is finally sold to an external customer. However, economists have implemented transfer pricing within the public sector under the title of *internal markets*. Therefore internal markets reflect the fundamental difficulties associated with an arbitrary determination of the sale price as opposed to a market determination. The danger of the internal market approach is that it ignores the fact that many public sector organizations exist because certain activities are easier to manage through bureaucratic structures rather than through the market (Williamson 1975).

Although additional (well-directed) activity will often result in additional income for a corporation (be it private or state owned), additional activity by organizations funded through taxes, however merited or praiseworthy the activity, will rarely result in additional income. Because most publicly funded entities have no control over income (beyond creative lobbying and political persuasion), they are cost centers, and their primary focus is to manage their expenses and to eke out their voted allowance to the end of the period. It is this cost center focus, combined with the annual funding arrangements (possibly biannual, if supplementary votes are available), that leads to much of the destructive budgetary activity so often seen in public sector organizations. One example of this is that toward the end of the budgetary year the organization or agency will have either too much or too little money left. Too much money most often leads to a spending spree, where the money is quickly spent on whatever presents itself, with the sure understanding that an underspent budget is perhaps the most dangerous condition the public sector can confront. Not only will the unspent funds be lost (as they are rarely rolled over into next year's budget), but the agency risks being viewed as overfunded (rather than economical) and thus receiving reduced funding in the next round. However, overspending is also a danger, resulting in the forced reduction of necessary and important activities, with potentially negative long-term results in costs and policy outcomes.

The introduction of accrual-based appropriation is one solution to the problems of both over- and underspending. However, this accounting-based approach may be more complex than is required. A simpler solution would be to allow a measure of transfer between one spending area and another. In addition, the accrual-based approach may create additional problems, such as the requirement in New Zealand that if an agency makes a surplus in any area or unit it must pay that surplus back to the Treasury, but when it has a deficit in any area, it must cover this deficit from its own resource base. The result is that, over time, the resource capacity of the agency is reduced (Newberry 2002).

Implications for Parliamentary Oversight

This general discussion of the nature and role of budgets has a number of practical implications for those charged with exercising budgetary oversight within public sector jurisdictions. The first point is that, because public entities are cost centers rather than profit centers, the most important control activity is monitoring actual spending levels against the budget using a cash focus. The most interesting aspect of the budget process is not the budget itself but the deviations from the budget (known as the variances). In that sense, a budget by itself is fairly useless, and in reviewing budgetary performance, the first action is always to look at the variances between the budget and actual spending. Most accountants will immediately focus on these variances, particularly the large ones. This review can always be extended to the previous year's actual activity and budget. In exploring a budgetary variance, both over- and underspending are interesting but should be closely followed by the question "Why?" Unfortunately, the answer is not always clear. Overspending can be a result of inefficiency and waste on the part of a department. However, it can also be a result of an initially unrealistic budget or a fundamental change in costs (such as an increase in the price of fuel or a higher-than-expected increase in civil servants' salaries) or a change in the work processes (such as new security requirements).

From the perspective of parliamentary oversight, the government or the appropriate civil servant must be called to account for why expenditures are different from the budgetary appropriation. Although many oversight processes stop at the identification of any over- or underspending, it is important to consider how over- or underspending has affected the program outcomes. It is this link between spending and the desired outcomes that should provide a central focus to both government and opposition party members in the exercise of parliamentary oversight and debate. It is only when the link between spending and performance is addressed that learning can occur and performance measurement has any real value, because action can be taken to change future behavior.

Unless there is clarity on what the actual objectives were, budgets and performance measurement will be at best symbolic. Therefore an important oversight role is to ensure that project goals and targets are clearly stated before funding is allocated and that the link between policy goals and budgetary allocations is clear. Broad multiperiod frameworks such as medium-term expenditure frameworks can be used to link policies, programs, and budget allocations. As most policies will involve expenditures over more than one year, the provision of forward estimates makes it possible to track how actual expenditure compares with the forward estimate and, if the forward estimate is published separately from the budget, whether the budget allocations are consistent with the forward estimate. From an accounting perspective, the annual budget is normally accompanied by a three-year rolling budget that shows the expected costs and revenues over that three-year period and for any proposed project that will involve a multiperiod evaluation of costs and benefits. Policy initiatives represent a form of multiperiod project, so it is critical that a similar evaluation be done and that costs (and revenues, when present) be monitored over multiple periods.

Protecting against the underfunding of projects is an important part of the oversight role and an issue for both new and ongoing programs. For a new or single-year program, this would involve a proposed budgetary allocation that is clearly insufficient for the task required. The danger is that this underfunding would result in waste if it undermined the goals of the policy. The appropriations for a multiyear ongoing initiative can also be cut to the point that the policy is no longer viable and therefore likely to be ineffective.

Conclusion

Within the context of the public sector there is a strong link between the idea of accountability and the management of the budget. From an accounting perspective, budgets are understood as being part of a process of control, learning, and feedback. However, effective control requires clear objectives and a predictive model of the process being controlled. Even within private sector organizations these requirements can pose problems. Public sector organizations and entities are in an even more difficult proposition because of the complex nature of their objectives and processes. Once steps are taken to clarify objectives it is easier to exercise control.

This chapter warns against the introduction of accounting technologies and practices within the public sector as ends in themselves rather than as means to an end. Although such practices provide excellent employment opportunities for accountants and consulting firms, serious questions exist as to whether these new accounting tools and measurements are actually understood by those charged with exercising oversight and accountability. If politicians do not understand accounting and budgetary processes then the tools may undermine rather than enhance accountability. Power and Laughlin (1992) warned that the commonsense view—that accounting is just an unbiased reflection of economic realities—has been questioned from a number of directions, and they pointed out the danger that accounting and associated regulatory systems become disconnected from the rest of the world. The implication is that the systems and practices of accounting can damage public debate and democracy, rendering the domains of parliamentary oversight beyond the reach of the members of parliament (MPs) charged with the responsibility. There are three alternative but not mutually exclusive solutions. One is to find forms of reporting that are more comprehensible to MPs, the second is to provide training to the MPs to better equip them to understand and interpret these reports, and the third is to establish an independent agency in the style of the U.S. Congressional Budget Office to advise and support MPs in their oversight role.

When importing managerial techniques and tools from the private sector into the public sector, it is important to remember the key differences between the two. First, whereas additional activity can lead to additional income within private sector entities, this is not the case in public sector organizations, whose primary source of income is tax-funded appropriation. Therefore, a number of the private sector budgeting techniques are inappropriate in the public sector. Second, measuring performance is also easier in the private sector than in the public sector. Within the private sector, profit is used as a basic proxy for both efficiency and effectiveness, although measures of efficiency that also consider the use of capital are superior. For public sector organizations, the measurement of effectiveness against output objectives is more complex than for the private sector, as it may involve a trade-off between different and incompatible measurement bases (as shown in the control model in figure 3.1). The complex output objectives also make it harder to measure efficiency.

Despite the issues of performance measurement within the private sector being simpler than in the public sector, private sector best practice is now moving away from the bottom-line focus on profit to consider a broader range of measures, sometimes described as a balanced scorecard (Kaplan and Norton 1996). The key characteristics of the scorecard approach are that they use multiple measures of performance, link the strategy and the measurement of performance, and require the development of explicit cause-and-effect relationships between organizational inputs, activity, and the desired output goals. Best practice within both the public and the private sector in budgetary and performance management requires this more complex and systems-focused approach. It is this kind of approach, with a greater emphasis on process accountability, that makes better efficiency, governance, and accountability possible (Model, Jacobs, and Wiesle 2007).

Note

The author is Professor of Accounting, College of Business and Economics, Australian National University, Canberra.

Bibliography

Day, Patricia, and Rudolf Klein. 1987. *Accountabilities: Five Public Services*. London: Tavistock.

Gregory, Robert. 1995. "Accountability, Responsibility, and Corruption: Managing the '"Public Production Process."'" In *The State under Contract*, ed. J. Boston, 97–114. Wellington, NZ: Bridget Williams Books.

Habermas, Jürgen. 1984. *The Theory of Communicative Action*, vol. 1. Trans. Thomas McCarthy. Boston: Beacon Press.

———. 1987. *The Theory of Communicative Action*, vol. 2. Trans. Thomas McCarthy. Boston: Beacon Press.

Hood, Christopher. 1991. "A Public Management for All Seasons?" *Public Administration* 69: 3–19.

———. 1995. "The 'New Public Management' in the 1980s: Variations on a Theme." *Accounting, Organizations and Society* 20 (2/3): 93–109.

Hood, Christopher, Henry Rothstein, and Robert Baldwin. 2001. *The Government of Risk*. Oxford, U.K.: Oxford University Press.

Kaplan, Robert, and David Norton. 1996. *The Balanced Scorecard: Translating Strategy into Action*. Boston: Harvard Business School Press.

Model, Sven, Kerry Jacobs, and Fredrika Wiesle. 2007. "A Process (Re)turn? Path Dependencies, Institutions and Performance Management in Swedish Central Government." *Management Accounting Research* 18 (4): 453–75.

Newberry, Sue, and Kerry Jacobs. 2007. "Obtaining the Levers of Power: The Treasury and the Introduction of New Zealand's Public Sector Financial Reforms." *Advances in Public Interest Accounting* 13: 115–50.

Newberry, Sue. 2002. "Intended or Unintended Consequences? Resource Erosion in New Zealand's Government Departments." *Financial Accountability and Management* 18 (4): 309–30.

Otley, David, and Anthony J. Berry. 1980. "Control, Organisation and Accounting." *Accounting, Organizations and Society* 5 (2): 231–46.

Parker, Lee, Kenneth Ferris, and David Otley. 1989. *Accounting for the Human Factor*. Sydney: Prentice Hall.

Power, Michael. 1994. *The Audit Explosion*. London: Demos.

———. 1997. *The Audit Society: Rituals of Verification*. Oxford, U.K.: Oxford University Press.

———. 2003. "Auditing and the Production of Legitimacy." *Accounting Organizations and Society* 28 (4): 379–94.

———. 2004. *The Risk Management of Everything*, London, Demos.

Power, Michael, and Richard Laughlin. 1992. "Critical Theory and Accounting." In *Critical Management Studies*, eds. Mats Alveson and Hugh Willmott, 113–35. London: Sage.

Williamson, Oliver, E. 1975. *Markets and Hierarchies Analysis and Antitrust Implications*. New York/London: Free Press.

CHAPTER 5

Assessing the Power of the Purse: An Index of Legislative Budget Institutions

Joachim Wehner

This power over the purse may, in fact, be regarded as the most complete and effectual weapon with which any constitution can arm the immediate representatives of the people, for obtaining a redress of every grievance, and for carrying into effect every just and salutary measure.

(James Madison, *Federalist No. 58*)

The requirement for legislative approval of financial measures is a democratic foundation that is enshrined in constitutions around the world.[1] Despite this widespread formal recognition, the actual budgetary role of national legislatures apparently differs sharply across countries. Members of the U.S. Congress "have long seen themselves as the bulwark against [executive] oppression," and their "major weapon" is the constitutional requirement for congressional approval of appropriations (Wildavsky and Caiden 2001, 10). Scholars and practitioners agree that the U.S. Congress is a powerful actor that can have decisive influence on budget policy (Meyers 2001; Schick with LoStracco 2000; Wildavsky 1964).[2] On the other hand, the budgetary influence of legislatures is said to be marginal in several other industrialized countries, including France and the United Kingdom (Chinaud 1993; Schick 2002). Existing comparative work on legislative budgeting contributes selected case studies (Coombes 1976; LeLoup 2004) but lacks systematic analysis on the basis of a common framework. Moreover, though the literature on the U.S. Congress is extensive, legislative budgeting in parliamentary systems, and in developing countries in particular, remains understudied (Oppenheimer 1983). As a basis for more systematic comparative work, this chapter proposes and applies an index of legislative budget institutions that can be used to assess and compare the budgetary power of national legislatures.

A number of authors refer to the cross-national distribution of legislative power over the purse (Coombes 1976; Meyers 2001; Schick 2002), but few have constructed quantitative measures. Although some previous studies present indexes of budget institutions, these pay only limited attention to legislative variables. Fiscal institutionalists are concerned with explaining fiscal performance, typically public debt and deficits, with the design of the budget process (Kirchgässner 2001). Most of this literature does not focus exclusively on the role of the legislature but on a broader selection of variables that are said to promote fiscal discipline in budgetary decision making. Von Hagen's (1992, 70) pioneering index includes one composite item on the structure of the parliamentary process that mainly considers the amendment powers of a legislature. Alesina et al. (1999) constructed an index of budgetary procedures with two out of 10 variables as indicators of the position of the government in relation to the legislature, namely, amendment powers and the nature of the reversionary budget (see also Hallerberg and Marier 2004). Other studies focus exclusively on the fiscal effect of specific legislative institutions (for example, Crain and Muris 1995; Heller 1997).

Lienert (2005) offers a broader consideration of legislative budget institutions. His index of legislative budget powers covers five variables, namely parliament's role in approving medium-term expenditure parameters, amendment powers, time available for the approval of the budget, technical support to the legislature, and restrictions on executive flexibility during budget execution. The index provides a basis for more systematic comparative analysis of legislative budgeting but also raises some methodological issues. For example, there is hardly any variation on the first variable, the legislature's role in approving medium-term spending plans. Only one out of 28 legislatures in the sample formally passes a law on the medium-term strategy (Lienert 2005, 22). The lack of variation calls into question the usefulness of this variable as a comparative indicator. In addition, the differential weighting of variables is not explicitly motivated. In short, what is missing so far is a broader measure of legislative budget institutions that is based on a thorough discussion of relevant indicators and methodological issues.

The aim of this chapter is to present a comparative framework to assess legislative budget capacity that can be applied, potentially, to any national legislature in a modern democracy. The framework consists of a series of variables that are combined into an index to measure cross-country variation in legislative budgeting. The operationalization is based on survey data from the Organisation for Economic Co-operation and Development (OECD) and the World Bank. More specifically, the chapter asks which institutional arrangements facilitate legislative control over budgets. Thus, a crucial assumption is that institutional arrangements reflect the budgetary power of a legislature; *control* is defined as the power to scrutinize and influence budget policy and to ensure its implementation. As Wildavsky and Caiden (2001, 18) observed: "Who has power over the budget does not tell us whether or not the budget is under control." The question of whether legislative power over the budget is fiscally desirable is explicitly excluded from this chapter. Although some studies argue that limiting parliamentary involvement is conducive to fiscal discipline (Poterba and von Hagen 1999; Strauch and von Hagen 1999), other studies highlight the risks of weak legislative scrutiny (Burnell 2001; Santiso

2004). The debate will not be settled in this chapter, which primarily aims at providing a fresh conceptual and empirical basis for engaging with this issue in follow-up research.

The chapter proceeds by first outlining and explaining the selection of the variables included in the index, followed by an overview of the data used. The third section discusses issues related to index construction and selects a method for use in this chapter. A number of experiments are conducted to check the robustness of the index. Next is an overview of the results, presented as a ranking of legislatures. Two approaches are used to validate the index. The first is to compare the resulting ranking with findings from case study literature, and the second is to test the association of the index with an indicator of legislative amendment activity. The conclusion summarizes the main results and highlights implications.

Variables

The construction of an index for the purpose of cross-national comparison requires the identification of essential differences. Invariably, some of the richness of qualitative analysis has to be forfeited to gain a tractable tool for comparative research, which is necessary to venture beyond particular cases in order to discover broader patterns. No single variable can be considered sufficient on its own, nor is every potentially relevant variable covered. Rather, the chapter adopts an approach that is based on assessing the *institutional capacity* for legislative control (Meyers 2001, 7). To that end, this analysis assumes that the presence of a minimum number of institutional prerequisites, including formal authority and organizational characteristics, is necessary to facilitate budgetary control. The six prerequisites used for the index relate to amendment powers, reversionary budgets, executive flexibility during implementation, time for scrutiny, committee capacity, and access to budgetary information.

First, *amendment powers*—the formal powers granted to amend the budget—determine the potential for legislative changes to the budget policy proposed by the executive (Inter-Parliamentary Union 1986, table 38A).[3] Most constraining are arrangements that disallow any amendments to the executive's proposal and merely give a legislature the choice between approval and rejection of the budget in its entirety. Also severely restrictive are "cuts only" arrangements that allow only amendments that reduce existing items but not those that shift funds around, increase items, or introduce new ones. This arrangement precludes a creative budgetary role for the legislature. More permissive are powers that allow some amendments to the budget as long as the aggregate totals or the deficit in the draft budget are maintained. This enables engagement with budget priorities while protecting executive fiscal policy. Finally, most permissive are unfettered powers of amendment. Here, a legislature has full authority to cut, increase, and reallocate.

The second variable, *reversionary budgets*, defines the cost of nonapproval by spelling out what happens should legislative authorization be delayed beyond the commencement of the fiscal year. Alesina et al. (1999, 258) used the reversionary budget variable in conjunction with legislative amendment powers to assess the position of the government in relation to the legislature. If the reversionary outcome is far from the executive's preferred budget, then there is potential for the legislature to extract concessions in return for approval. In the extreme case of reversion to zero spending, the executive is likely to prefer a compromise to the possibility of no supply and hence government shutdown. Conversely, when the executive budget proposal takes effect, the executive has no incentive to avert nonapproval. Reversion to last year's budget typically constitutes an intermediate case.

Third, provisions that allow *executive flexibility during implementation* enable the executive to alter spending choices following the approval of the budget by the legislature. One mechanism is impoundment, which allows the withholding of particular funds that have been appropriated by the legislature. Another is *virement*, that is, the ability of the executive to reallocate or transfer funds between budget items during the execution of the budget. Finally, some executives can introduce new spending without legislative approval (Carey and Shugart 1998). If the executive can withhold funds, transfer between items, and initiate fresh funding without the consent of the legislature, it has significant leeway to unilaterally alter the approved budget, which diminishes legislative control over implementation. In effect, such powers constitute amendment authority in reverse, and in extreme cases allow the executive to undo legislative choices during implementation (Santiso 2004).

The fourth variable is *time for scrutiny*. Time is a precious resource, given a typically tight and crowded legislative calendar (Döring 1995). Budgets take many months to put together, and a couple of weeks are insufficient to make sense of such complex sets of information. International experience suggests that the budget should be tabled at least three months in advance of the fiscal year to enable meaningful legislative scrutiny (OECD 2002a). The timing of scrutiny partly depends on how effectively a legislature can control its own timetable and the legislative agenda, but it may also reflect constitutional prescriptions.

Committee capacity, or a well-developed committee system, appears to be "at least a necessary condition for effective parliamentary influence in the policy-making process" (Mattson and Strøm 1995, 250). This fifth variable is selected because the importance of legislative committees is widely recognized, although their primary function is disputed between proponents of distributive, informational, and partisan explanations (Cox and McCubbins 1993; Krehbiel 1991; Shepsle 1979). The use of committees can present several benefits. First, committees establish a division of labor that facilitates specialization and the development of "legislative expertise" (Mezey 1979, 64). Second, committees allow parliaments to deal with various matters simultaneously and, hence, to increase productivity. These benefits are crucial for the budget process, which requires the processing of substantial volumes of information. Moreover, committees can play an important role in monitoring implementation (McCubbins and Schwartz 1984). Legislative approval matters only when budgets are meaningful. Otherwise, budgetary drift allows the government to get what it wants irrespective of what the legislature approved. Committees with a specialized monitoring function, in particular audit committees, help to detect implementation failures and improve compliance (McGee 2002). In short, a well-designed committee system enables budget scrutiny and oversight of implementation.

The sixth and final variable used for the index is *access to budgetary information*. Budgetary decision making requires access to comprehensive, accurate, and timely information. Crucial for this is the breadth and depth of supporting documentation that accompanies the budget figures submitted to the legislature. In addition, in-year revenue and expenditure updates as well as high-quality audit reports, including performance audits (Pollitt 2003), are crucial types of information for legislative oversight of budget implementation. Key standards for budget reporting are set out in the "OECD Best Practices for Budget Transparency" (OECD 2002a). Still, an executive monopoly on budgetary information can put the legislature at a severe disadvantage, as it is easy to manipulate budget figures and limit disclosure (Wildavsky and Caiden 2001, 78). The benefits of an independent legislative budget office include that it can help to simplify complexity and make the budget accessible for legislators, enhance accountability through its scrutiny of executive information, and promote transparency by discouraging "budgetary legerdemain" (Anderson 2005, 2).

Other variables could also be included. For instance, von Hagen (1992) considered the confidence convention. Notwithstanding a legislature's formal constitutional powers to amend the budget, in some parliamentary systems any change to the executive's draft budget is by convention considered a vote of no confidence in the government (Blöndal 2001, 53). In effect, the confidence convention reduces legislative authority to a stark choice between accepting the budget unchanged, or forcing the resignation of the government and holding fresh elections. The confidence convention is most common in Westminster-type systems that in any case restrict legislative powers to amend the budget, such as Australia, Canada, New Zealand, and the United Kingdom (OECD 2002b, 159). As amendment powers are already included in the index, this variable suffices to signal restrictions on legislative policy making.

Also, some presidential systems counterbalance legislative powers over the budget with executive veto authority that can be overridden only with a heightened legislative majority. Package vetoes allow the executive to veto entire bills passed by the legislature, and a line-item or partial veto allows the president to reject individual items in a bill. Some authors give great importance to veto authority in assessing executive power over policy (for example, Shugart and Haggard 2001, 75–77). However, the power a package veto gives to the executive depends critically on the reversionary budget, which is already part of the index. For instance, if spending is discontinued without an approved budget in place, then to veto the budget would be a very extreme measure that the executive is likely to use only in extraordinary circumstances (Williams and Jubb 1996). In addition, line-item vetoes are exceptionally rare at the national level. Shugart and Haggard (2001, 80) found that only two out of 23 countries with pure presidential systems use a version of the line-item veto with extraordinary majority override, namely Argentina and the Philippines. Executive vetoes are excluded from the index for the above reasons.

Data

During 2003 the OECD, in collaboration with the World Bank, conducted the Survey on Budget Practices and Procedures, which was administered to specially identified budget officials in each participating country. The data set for this chapter draws heavily on the results of this survey, which are available online (OECD and World Bank 2003). The survey covers 27 OECD members plus 14 other countries. Some of the non-OECD countries have limited democratic credentials and are excluded from the scope of this chapter.[4]

The data are unique in that a similarly comprehensive budget system survey had not been previously carried out for such a large number of countries. On the other hand, responses were not always rigorously checked, and in certain cases the quality of the data is questionable. The data used in this chapter were double-checked as extensively as possible against information from online sources, such as finance ministry and parliamentary Web sites, as well as against previous survey results (OECD 2002b). Where necessary, clarification was sought from country experts who are identified in the acknowledgments. The following paragraphs introduce the specific data used for the construction of the index of legislative budget institutions. The full data set is reproduced in annex table 1, and annex table 2 details the construction of two composite variables. Any adjustments made to the original OECD data are documented.

Following Alesina et al. (1999, 257–58), the index codes all variables on a range between zero (the least favorable from a legislative perspective) and 10 (the most favorable). The maximum figure is divided equally between the categories. The subsequent section documents the conduct of robustness checks to see whether this coding procedure significantly affects the ranking of legislatures compared with alternative methods. The score given for each response option is in parentheses following the category.

The OECD survey (questions 2.7.d and 2.7.e) asked respondents to indicate whether legislative powers of amendment are restricted, and if so, which form the restrictions take. The index codes these answers in four categories; that is, the legislature may only accept or reject the budget as tabled (0), it may cut existing items only (3.3), it may shift funds as long as a specified aggregate constraint is met (6.7), or it has unfettered powers (10).

Survey question 2.7.c asked about the consequences should the budget not be approved at the start of the fiscal year. The responses are grouped into four categories: the executive budget (0), vote on account (3.3), last year's budget (6.7), or no spending (10). The second category requires elaboration. Historically, the English Parliament devised the tactic of voting appropriations near the end of the session to force economies on the Crown and to extract concessions (Schick 2002, 18). This historical rationale is now obsolete, but delayed approval nonetheless remains the norm. Formally, supply would cease without an approved budget in place. In practice, the parliaments of the OECD Commonwealth countries routinely approve interim spending, which is referred to as a "vote on account" in the United Kingdom.[5] Although some might argue that this system preserves the threat of reversion to zero spending, this practice is so standardized and predictable that it would be misleading to assign a score of 10.

The index tests executive flexibility during budget execution by combining three items. The OECD survey asked whether there is scope for appropriations to be reallocated from one program to another without parliamentary approval (question 3.2.a.4), whether the executive may withhold funds that are appropriated but not available on a legal or entitlement basis without legislative consent (question 3.1.c), and whether the annual budget includes any central reserve funds to meet unforeseen expenditures (question 3.2.c.1). Each answer is assigned a score of 3.3 if it is negative, because a positive answer implies executive flexibility to vire (reallocate or transfer funds between budget items), impound, and authorize fresh funds, respectively. The sum of the scores for each case can range between zero and 10 and is interpreted as an indicator of executive flexibility during budget execution. Annex table 2 provides full details.

The OECD also asked how far in advance of the beginning of the fiscal year the executive presents its budget to the legislature and provided four response options (question 2.7.b): up to two months (0), two to four months (3.3), four to six months (6.7), and more than six months (10).

The role of parliamentary committees is measured using two items in the OECD survey, relating to committee involvement in budget approval (question 2.10.a) and whether audit results are circulated and discussed in parliament (question 4.5.m). However, the answer options for the latter question are ambiguous with regard to the nature of committee engagement with audit findings. Therefore, the index also uses data on parliamentary audit committees, gathered in a separate survey of parliamentary Web sites (January 2004). The index distinguishes the involvement of three sets of specialized committees, with equal scores given to each category (3.3), that is, a budget or finance committee, sectoral or departmental committees, and an ex post audit committee. For instance, if a parliament uses a finance committee and sectoral committees for budget approval, as well as an audit committee for ex post scrutiny of audit findings, it gets the highest possible score of 10, and without any committee involvement it gets a score of zero. Involvement of sectoral committees gets a score of 3.3 only if they have actual authority over departmental budgets, but not if they are merely consulted or submit nonbinding recommendations while a finance or budget committee retains full authority. Also, if a legislature uses an audit subcommittee of the budget committee for parliamentary audit, it receives half the available score for this item (1.7) (annex table 2 presents full details).

Legislative access to budgetary information is very difficult to assess. It was not possible to use the survey results to construct a reliable and fine-grained measure of the quality of budgetary information supplied by the executive. However, most of the countries included in this analysis are OECD members and hence subscribe to the "OECD Best Practices for Budget Transparency" (OECD 2002a). In addition, studies confirm that several non-OECD countries in the sample provide high-quality budgetary information, for instance Chile (Blöndal and Curristine 2004), Slovenia (Kraan and Wehner 2005), and South Africa (Fölscher 2002). Therefore, it is reasonable to assume adherence to a common minimum standard for budgetary documentation in most cases. However, one of the key differences between countries is the level of legislative budget research capacity (question 2.10.e). This analysis distinguishes legislatures without such research capacity (0) from those with a budget office of up to 10 professional staff (2.5), 11 to 25 (5), 26 to 50 (7.5), and more than 50 (10). The last category acknowledges the uniqueness of the U.S. Congressional Budget Office, which has about 230 staff (Anderson 2005).

Construction of the Index

The task of constructing the index raises, in particular, theoretical questions about the substitutability of components. This section discusses various possible methods for index construction and then compares the results in order to check the robustness of the index. The starting point for this discussion is the additive index. This frequently used method consists of summing up all scores for a given case to derive the index score for that case (Lienert 2005; von Hagen 1992). The simple sum index can be represented as a special case of the following formula (Alesina et al. 1999, 260):

$$I_j = \sum_{i=1}^{6} c_i^j$$

The term c_i captures the value of component i, and j is a power term that can be adjusted to reflect different assumptions about substitutability. If $j = 1$, then the result is the simple sum index. If $0 < j < 1$, this favors cases with consistently intermediate scores over those with a mixture of high and low scores; that is, this approach assumes a limited degree of substitutability. Conversely, with $j > 1$, a greater degree of substitutability is assumed, since high scores are rewarded. In addition, it would be possible to allow differential weights for each of the components. However, the theoretical discussion does not imply that some of the variables are more important than others, so the possibility of using differential weights is not pursued in this case.

To assume complete nonsubstitutability, the components can also be multiplied. This typically generates highly skewed distributions, because a single low score substantially drags down the index. Since the majority of cases included in this analysis have scores of zero on at least one of the components, this method does not yield useful results. Nor does it appear theoretically plausible to assume complete nonsubstitutability for all components. In addition, this method is highly sensitive to small mistakes in the data, which can lead to severe misrepresentation of the affected cases. These are strong reasons for rejecting the purely multiplicative approach for this analysis.

This analysis preferred a third method, which is based on subindexes:

$$I_s = \prod_{k=1}^{2} s_k, \text{ where } s_1 = \sum_{i=1}^{3} c_i \text{ and } s_2 = \sum_{i=4}^{6} c_i$$

Here, s_k represents two subindexes, each consisting of the sum of three different components, which are then multiplied. It is possible to again incorporate a power term into the formulas for the subindexes, but most essential is the underlying approach. The rationale for this index is as follows. Variables one through three (amendment powers, reversionary budgets, and executive flexibility) can be interpreted as formal legislative authority in relation to the executive. Amendment powers and reversionary budgets are frequently stipulated in constitutions, and organic budget laws typically regulate flexibility during implementation (Lienert and Jung 2004). In contrast, variables four through six (time, committees, and research capacity as a proxy for access to budgetary information) are taken to represent the organizational capacity of the legislature. If it is assumed that both formal powers and organizational capacity are necessary for effective scrutiny, multiplication of the two subindexes is called for. However, within each subindex, at least a degree of substitutability is plausible. For instance, if committees are weakly developed, then this lack in division of labor might be compensated by using a lot of time to scrutinize the budget or by delegating scrutiny to a well-resourced parliamentary budget office. Similarly, even when amendment powers are limited, the legislature may still be effective in extracting concessions from the executive if spending reverts to zero in the case of nonapproval.

The next step is to check the robustness of results. Table 5.1 contains the Spearman rank correlations between four alternative indexes, which are labelled according to their subscripts in the above formulas. To consider the impact of different substitutability assumptions, the simple sum index with $j = 1$ computed with the first formula is compared with indexes using two other arbitrary numbers for the power term—that is, $j = .5$ (half the value of the simple sum version) and $j = 2$ (double the value). The fourth index labelled s is calculated using the second formula based on the two subindexes. All of the correlations between these four versions of the index are positive and very strong. The lowest coefficient is .86 between the two indexes that use extreme

Table 5.1. Spearman Correlations between Indices

	$j=1$	$j=.5$	$j=2$
$j=.5$	.97	...	...
$j=2$	.95	.86	...
s	.99	.97	.94

Note: N = 36.

values for j, which is expected. Overall, the results are very robust. For this reason, the simple sum index is used in the remainder of the chapter.

Discussion and Analysis

This section presents the index of legislative budget institutions and discusses main results. For presentational purposes, the index is rescaled to range between 0 and 100. The resulting ranking is presented in figure 5.1. Next, two approaches are used to evaluate the index: first, to consider whether the results are broadly in line with case study literature, second, to check the validity of the index by testing its association with a simple indicator of legislative amendment activity.

The U.S. Congress emerges as an outlier by a substantial margin. Its score is more than three times as great as those for the bottom nine cases, predominantly Westminster systems. According to the index, the U.S. Congress is the only legislature with the institutional foundation to exercise very strong influence over public finances. The importance of Congress in the U.S. budget process is widely acknowledged. Aaron Wildavsky's seminal work on the politics of the budget process is, in essence, a study of congressional policy making (Wildavsky 1964; Wildavsky and Caiden 2001). Although the U.S. president submits a draft budget, it does not bind Congress in any way (Schick with LoStracco 2000, 74–104). Oppenheimer (1983, 585) concluded a wide-ranging literature review with the observation that Congress is "the most influential legislature" in policy making. The index is in line with this judgment.

On the other extreme, the case of the United Kingdom is often said to epitomize the decline of parliaments (Adonis 1993; Einzig 1959; Reid 1966). In a recent paper, Allen Schick (2002, 27) went as far as to claim: "Nowhere is the budgetary decline of parliament more noticeable than in Britain … [The] House of Commons, the cradle of budgetary democracy, [has] lost all formal influence over revenues and expenditures." In 1998–99 the Procedure Committee of the House of Commons bluntly referred to its power over expenditure as, "'if not a constitutional myth, very close to one" (quoted in Walters and Rogers 2004, 257). Although no time series data are available for testing the decline thesis, the index confirms that current capacity in the British Parliament is extremely limited. The rankings of other parliaments with a Westminster heritage are very similar, which again is supported by case study evidence. For instance, in Canada members characterize legislative scrutiny of the budget as a "cursory review," "a total waste of time," and "futile attempts to bring about change" (quoted in Blöndal 2001, 54). Another example is the paper by Krafchik and Wehner (1998), which highlights the great difficulty of the South African Parliament in transcending its Westminster heritage in the postapartheid environment.

Few national legislatures have been as extensively studied as the U.S. Congress and the British Parliament; nonetheless, some other rankings can also be

Figure 5.1. Index of Legislative Budget Institutions

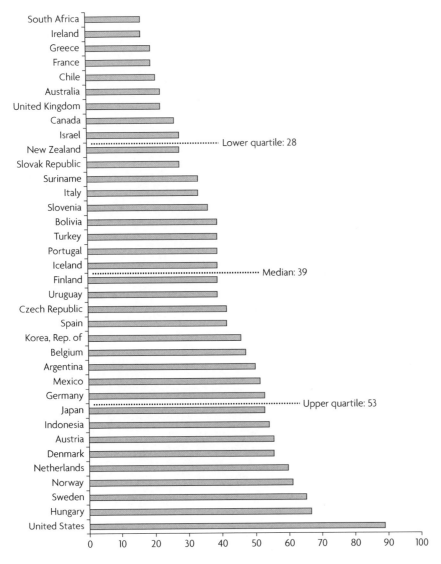

assessed against the literature. Notably, the Danish, Norwegian, and Swedish parliaments achieve relatively high scores on the index. This corresponds with literature that has pointed out the distinctiveness and relative strength of these parliaments (Arter 1984; Esaiasson and Heidar 2000; Wehner 2007). In addition, a large number of cases fall between the extremes of the U.S. Congress and Westminster-type legislatures. Notably, continental European parliaments make up much of the middle mass on the index. Case study work shows that in a number of these countries, parliaments retain a limited level of influence on budgets.[6] It is beyond the scope of this chapter to present a full literature review. Still, this brief comparison with some of the case study literature suggests that the index generates plausible scores.

The validity of the index can also be tested statistically. Given that the index captures institutional preconditions for legislative control, it should be associated with a measure of policy influence. One such indicator is amendment activity. The OECD asked (question 2.7.i) if, in practice, the legislature generally approves the budget as presented by the executive. Eleven out of 36 respondents in this sample indicated that the legislature "generally approves the budget with no changes." More finely grained measures of amendment activity would be preferable, such as the number of amendments and their magnitude, but comprehensive data are not available. Also, it is true that a legislature may not have to amend the budget to affect policy. Hidden actions, such as a short phone call from a powerful committee chair to an executive official, can be important means of legislative influence (Meyers 2001, 7). Moreover, the executive may anticipate legislative reactions and fashion the draft budget accordingly, thereby reducing the likelihood of amendments. However, it would be naive to conclude that the absence of amendments indicates that the legislature is getting its way. An executive has no reason to be responsive to legislative preferences unless the absence of such consideration has consequences. For example, in the United Kingdom the last government defeats over estimates date back more than 80 years.[7] It makes sense for legislative actors to maintain a modicum of amendment activity in order to signal to the executive their capacity for substantial revision should the draft budget not take sufficient account of their preferences.

Accepting the above premise, one would expect budget-amending legislatures to have more developed institutional capacity. This analysis uses a *t*-test to assess whether index scores are higher for budget-amending legislatures compared with those that do not amend the budget (Bohrnstedt and Knoke 1994, 139). Setting $\alpha = .05$ for 34 degrees of freedom gives a critical value of 1.7 for a one-tailed test to reject the null. Using the data in table 5.2, the analysis obtains a value of 2.3, which falls within the rejection region. This supports the prediction that budget-amending legislatures maintain higher levels of institutional capacity for financial scrutiny.

The evidence in this section is mutually reinforcing and confirms that the index is a useful summary indicator of legislative capacity to influence budget

Table 5.2. Comparison of Budget-Amending and Non-Budget-Amending Legislatures

	Amending	Nonamending
Number of cases	25	11
Mean index score	44.9	31.8
Standard deviation	15.3	16.3

Source: Annex table 1.

policy. The ranking is broadly in line with case study literature, and the index is positively associated with a simple measure of legislative impact on public finances. Not too much should be read into small score differences between national legislatures, as the index makes no qualitative statements on the margin. Nonetheless, whether a legislature ranks toward the top, middle, or bottom of the index conveys an overall perspective on the state of legislative budgeting in a particular country. Indeed, if the power of the purse is a sine qua non for legislative control in general, then the results also reflect the overall status of the legislature in the political system of a country.

Conclusions

This chapter has expanded the methodological toolkit for cross-national research on the legislative power of the purse. Previous efforts to construct quantitative measures of legislative budget power were either extremely limited in their coverage of relevant variables or neglected detailed discussion of related methodological issues. The index constructed here is robust and delivers results that can be checked against case-study evidence and with the use of statistical tests. It provides a sound basis for investigating cross-national patterns in legislative budgeting, their causes, and consequences. However, the findings do not suggest that quantitative analysis should be a substitute for the detailed study of particular cases. Rather, there is an emerging debate on comparative research methods that argues strongly in favor of a carefully designed combined use of statistical and small-N approaches (Lieberman 2005). For instance, large-N analysis can provide the basis for a more deliberate choice of case studies, which in turn may deepen understanding and add important contextual variables.

The empirical results of this analysis raise questions about the prerequisites for democratic governance. Despite widespread constitutional recognition of the importance of legislative control over the purse, this chapter reveals substantial variation in the level of financial scrutiny of government by the legislature among contemporary liberal democracies. The U.S. Congress has an index score that is more than three times as great as those for the bottom nine cases, predominantly Westminster-type systems. Even allowing for U.S. exceptionalism, the top-quartile legislatures score twice as high on this index as the bottom quartile. In between the extremes of Westminster and the U.S. Congress, continental European parliaments make up much of the middle mass of the ranking. To what extent legislative involvement or the absence of effective checks and balances imposes costs is an empirical question to be tackled in follow-up research. The findings presented here suggest that the power of the purse is a discrete and nonfundamental element of liberal democratic governance. For some countries it is a key safeguard against executive overreach, while other countries maintain a constitutional myth of legislative control.

Annex

Annex Table 1. Data for the Index and Amendment Dummy

Legislature	1 Powers	2 Reversion	3 Flexibility	4 Time	5 Committees	6 Research	$\Sigma/.6$ Index	7 Amendments
Argentina	6.7	6.7	6.7	3.3	6.7	0	50	1
Australia	3.3[a]	3.3[b]	0	0	6.7	0	22.2	0
Austria	10	6.7	6.7	3.3	6.7	0	55.6	1
Belgium	10	10	0	0	8.3	0	47.2	0
Bolivia	10	0	6.7	3.3	3.3	0	38.9	1
Canada	3.3	3.3[b]	0	0	6.7	2.5	26.4	0
Chile	3.3	0	0	3.3	3.3	2.5	20.8	1
Czech Republic	10	6.7	0	3.3	5	0	41.7	1
Denmark	10	6.7	3.3	6.7	6.7	0	55.6	1
Finland	10	0[c]	6.7	3.3	3.3	0	38.9	1
France	3.3[d]	0[e]	0	3.3	5	0	19.4	1
Germany	10	6.7[f]	3.3	6.7	5	0	52.8	1
Greece	0	6.7[g]	0	0	5	0[h]	19.4	0
Hungary	10	10	6.7	3.3	10	0	66.7	1
Iceland	10	0[i]	6.7	3.3	3.3	0	38.9	1
Indonesia	6.7	6.7	3.3	6.7	6.7	2.5	54.2	1
Ireland	0	0	3.3	0	6.7	0	16.7	0
Israel	0	6.7	0	3.3	6.7	0	27.8	1
Italy	10	0	3.3	3.3	3.3	0	33.3	1
Japan	0	10	6.7	3.3	6.7	5	52.8	0
Korea, Rep. of	3.3	6.7[j]	3.3	3.3	3.3	7.5	45.8	1
Mexico	6.7	10[k]	0	0	6.7	7.5	51.4	1
Netherlands	10	6.7	6.7	6.7	3.3	2.5	59.7	1
New Zealand	3.3[l]	3.3[b]	6.7	0	3.3	0	27.8	0
Norway	10	10[m]	6.7	3.3	6.7	0	61.1	1
Portugal	10	6.7	0	3.3	3.3	0	38.9	1
Slovak Republic	6.7	0	3.3	3.3	3.3	0	27.8	1
Slovenia	6.7	6.7	0	3.3	5	0	36.1	1
South Africa	0	0[n]	0	0	10	0	16.7	0
Spain	6.7	6.7	3.3	3.3	5	0	41.7	1
Suriname	10	0	0	3.3	6.7	0	33.3	0
Sweden	10	10	6.7	3.3	6.7	2.5	65.3	0
Turkey	6.7	10	0	3.3	3.3	0	38.9	1
United Kingdom	3.3[o]	3.3[b]	3.3	0	3.3	0[h]	22.2	0
United States	10	10	6.7	10	6.7	10[p]	88.9	1
Uruguay	6.7[q]	6.7	3.3	3.3[r]	3.3	0	38.9	1

Source: Data are from OECD and World Bank (2003) except certain committee data (see text and annex table 2).

Note: Additional comments where responses were missing or ambiguous: a. Members of the House of Representatives may reduce existing items only. The Senate can propose amendments only to parts of the budget that are other than the ordinary annual services of government. b. Vote on account or other regularized interim supply measure. c. Constitution Section 83. d. Constitution Article 40. e. Constitution Article 47(3). f. Article 111 of the Basic Law. g. Constitution Article 79. h. Based on OECD (2002b). i. The executive would resign and new elections would be held. j. Constitution Article 54(3). k. There are no provisions. l. Standing Orders 312–316 give the Crown a financial veto over amendments with more than a minor impact. m. There are no clear formal rules describing the consequences. n. The executive budget takes effect subject to restrictions related to the previous year's expenditure limits, according to Section 29 of the Public Finance Management Act. o. Standing Order 48 of the House of Commons allows cuts only to existing items. p. The Congressional Budget Office has about 230 staff. q. Constitution Article 215. r. Based on Santiso (2004).

Annex Table 2. Construction of Composite Variables

Legislature	1 Withhold	2 Virement	3 Reserve	Σ Flexibility	4 Budget	5 Sectoral	6 Audit	Σ Committees
Argentina	3.3	0	3.3	6.7	3.3	0	3.3	6.7
Australia	0	0	0	0	0	3.3[a]	3.3	6.7
Austria	3.3	3.3	0	6.7	3.3	0	3.3	6.7
Belgium	0	0	0	0	3.3	3.3	1.7[b]	8.3
Bolivia	3.3	0	3.3	6.7	3.3	0	0	3.3
Canada	0	0	0	0	0	3.3	3.3	6.7
Chile	0	0	0	0	3.3	0	0	3.3
Czech Republic	0	0	0	0	3.3	0	1.7[b]	5
Denmark	3.3	0[c]	0	3.3	3.3	0	3.3	6.7
Finland	3.3	3.3	0	6.7	3.3	0	0	3.3
France	0	0	0	0	3.3	0	1.7[d]	5
Germany	0	0	3.3	3.3	3.3	0	1.7[b]	5
Greece	0	0[e]	0	0	3.3	0	1.7[f]	5
Hungary	3.3	3.3	0	6.7	3.3	3.3	3.3	10
Iceland	3.3	3.3	0	6.7	3.3	0	0	3.3
Indonesia	0	3.3	0	3.3	3.3	3.3	0	6.7
Ireland	0[g]	0	3.3	3.3	3.3	0	3.3	6.7
Israel	0	0	0	0	3.3	0	3.3	6.7
Italy	3.3	0	0	3.3	3.3	0	0	3.3
Japan	3.3[h]	3.3	0	6.7	3.3	0	3.3	6.7
Korea, Rep. of	3.3	0[i]	0	3.3	3.3	0	0	3.3
Mexico	0	0	0	0	3.3	0	3.3	6.7
Netherlands	3.3	0	3.3	6.7	0	3.3	0	3.3
New Zealand	3.3	3.3	0	6.7	3.3	0[j]	0[k]	3.3
Norway	3.3	3.3	0	6.7	3.3	3.3	0	6.7
Portugal	0	0	0	0	3.3	0	0	3.3
Slovak Republic	0	0	3.3	3.3	3.3	0	0	3.3
Slovenia	0	0	0	0	3.3	0	1.7[l]	5
South Africa	0	0	0	0	3.3	3.3	3.3	10
Spain	3.3	0	0	3.3	3.3	0	1.7[m]	5
Suriname	0	0	0	0	3.3	3.3	0	6.7
Sweden	3.3	3.3	0	6.7	3.3	3.3	0	6.7
Turkey	0	0	0	0	3.3	0	0	3.3
United Kingdom	0	3.3	0	3.3	0	0[n]	3.3	3.3
United States	3.3	3.3[o]	0	6.7	3.3	3.3[p]	0	6.7
Uruguay	3.3	0	0	3.3	3.3	0	0	3.3

Source: Data were compiled from OECD and World Bank (2003) except data on audit committees, which were gathered through a survey of parliamentary Web sites in January 2004.
Note: Additional comments where responses were missing or ambiguous: a. Sectoral committees in the Senate examine and report on relevant areas of the budget. b. Budget committee with an audit subcommittee. c. Reallocations between operating appropriations are allowed. d. The Evaluation and Control Delegation of the Finance Commission in the National Assembly has tried to improve interaction with the Court of Audit. e. Reallocations are allowed for the Public Investment Programme and with the approval of the Ministry of Economy and Finance. f. Standing Order 31A establishes a Special Standing Committee on Financial Statement and General Balance Sheet of the State. g. Provision in an estimate passed by the Dail does not convey authority to spend without sanction of the Minister for Finance. h. Author's research. i. There can be transfers with the approval of the central budget authority or the legislature depending on budgetary classification. j. The Finance and Expenditure Committee scrutinises the Budget Policy Statement and Estimates. Other committees may debate the estimates and policy for specific departments. k. The Public Accounts Committee was abolished in 1962. l. The Commission for Budgetary and other Public Finance Control receives audit reports, but in the past it has dealt with very few of them (Kraan and Wehner 2005). m. There is a Commission for Relations with the Tribunal of Accounts, but its role is limited. n. Based on Walters and Rogers (2004). o. Most transfers require approval by the legislature, some only notification. p. The Appropriations Committees in both houses operate elaborate subcommittee structures.

Notes

The author would like to acknowledge Keith Dowding, Patrick Dunleavy, Achim Hildebrandt, Jouni Kuha, Ian Lienert, David Marshall, Michael Ruffner, Carlos Santiso, Sally Stares and Andreas Warntjen, as well as three anonymous referees and the editor of the journal Political Studies, Martin Smith, who provided valuable comments on drafts of this paper. Also thanks to Vasilios Alevizakos, Mario Arriagada, Jón Blöndal, Torun Dewan, Gabriel Farfan-Mares, Keiichi Kubo, Rajagopalan Ramanathan, Vinod Sahgal, Mike Stevens, and Francesco Stolfi for help with various issues. The author is particularly indebted to Michael Ruffner, previously with OECD, for patiently dealing with questions about the 2003 Survey of Budget Practices and Procedures. The usual caveat applies. Research for this chapter was partly funded by the German Academic Exchange Service (DAAD). A previous version was published in Political Studies Vol. 54, No. 4 (December 2006), pp. 767–85.

1. Refer to the International Constitutional Law Project Web site, which includes references to the financial provisions of various constitutions: http://www.servat. unibe.ch/icl/.

2. Definitions of the budget differ across countries. The word *budget* in the United Kingdom now refers to the Spring Financial Statement, which focuses on taxation measures. In many countries, however, the term has a broader meaning, which is captured in the first traceable legal definition of the budget in a French decree of 1862: "The budget is a document which forecasts and authorizes the annual receipts and expenditures of the State ..." (quoted in Stourm 1917, 2). This chapter uses the word in this broader sense.

3. In virtually all countries the executive prepares a draft budget that is then submitted to the legislature for approval (Schick 2002). The U.S. Congress held out longest compared with other legislatures before establishing an executive budget process, until in 1921 the Budget and Accounting Act required the president to coordinate the drafting of a budget proposal to be submitted to Congress (Webber and Wildavsky 1986, 411–16).

4. Several countries included in the survey have low scores on the 2003 Gastil index produced by Freedom House and available at http://www.freedomhouse.org. The somewhat arbitrary cutoff point of 3.5 used in this chapter excludes Cambodia, Colombia, Jordan, Kenya, and Morocco.

5. This practice is referred to as *interim supply* in Canada, *supply* in Australia, and *imprest supply* in New Zealand.

6. Chinaud 1993; Coombes 1976; Eickenboom 1989; LeLoup 2004; Leston-Bandeira 1999.

7. In 1919 the Commons, in what the chancellor criticised as a "virtuous outburst of economy," denied the lord chancellor funding for a second bathroom and other amenities, and in response Lord Birkenhead refused to move into his official residence. The last government defeat over estimates was in 1921, when members' traveling expenses were the objects of criticism (Einzig 1959, 274–75).

Bibliography

Adonis, A. 1993. *Parliament Today*. Manchester, U.K.: Manchester University Press.
Alesina, A., R. Hausmann, R. Hommes, and E. Stein. 1999. "Budget Institutions and Fiscal Performance in Latin America." *Journal of Development Economics* 59 (2): 253–73.

Anderson, B. 2005. "The Value of a Nonpartisan, Independent, Objective Analytic Unit to the Legislative Role in Budget Preparation." Paper presented at the annual meeting of the Southern Political Science Association, New Orleans, January 7.

Arter, D. 1984. *The Nordic Parliaments: A Comparative Analysis.* New York: St. Martin's Press.

Blöndal, J. R. 2001. "Budgeting in Canada." *OECD Journal on Budgeting* 1 (2): 39–84.

Blöndal, J. R., and T. Curristine. 2004. "Budgeting in Chile." *OECD Journal on Budgeting* 4 (2): 7–45.

Bohrnstedt, G. W., and D. Knoke. 1994. *Statistics for Social Data Analysis.* Itasca, IL: F. E. Peacock.

Burnell, P. 2001. "Financial Indiscipline in Zambia's Third Republic: The Role of Parliamentary Scrutiny." *Journal of Legislative Studies* 7 (3): 34–64.

Carey, J. M., and M. S. Shugart, eds. 1998. *Executive Decree Authority.* Cambridge, U.K.: Cambridge University Press.

Chinaud, R. 1993. "Loi de Finances - Quelle Marge de Manœuvre Pour le Parlement?" *Pouvoirs* 64: 99–108.

Coombes, D. L., ed. 1976. *The Power of the Purse: The Role of European Parliaments in Budgetary Decisions.* London: George Allen and Unwin.

Cox, G. W., and M. D. McCubbins. 1993. *Legislative Leviathan: Party Government in the House.* Berkeley: University of California Press.

Crain, M. W., and T. J. Muris. 1995. "Legislative Organization of Fiscal Policy." *Journal of Law and Economics* 38 (2): 311–33.

Döring, H. 1995. "Time as a Scarce Resource: Government Control of the Agenda." In *Parliaments and Majority Rule in Western Europe*, eds. H. Döring, 223–46. Frankfurt: Campus.

Eickenboom, P. 1989. "Haushaltsausschuß und Haushaltsverfahren." In *Parlamentsrecht und Parlamentspraxis in der Bundesrepublik Deutschland: Ein Handbuch*, eds. H.-P. Schneider and W. Zeh, 1183–1220. Berlin: De Gruyter.

Einzig, P. 1959. *The Control of the Purse: Progress and Decline of Parliament's Financial Control.* London: Secker and Warburg.

Esaiasson, P., and K. Heidar, eds. 2000. *Beyond Westminster and Congress: The Nordic Experience.* Columbus: Ohio State University Press.

Fölscher, A., ed. 2002. *Budget Transparency and Participation: Five African Case Studies.* Cape Town: IDASA.

Hallerberg, M., and P. Marier. 2004. "Executive Authority, the Personal Vote, and Budget Discipline in Latin American and Caribbean Countries." *American Journal of Political Science* 48 (3): 571–87.

Heller, W. B. 1997. "Bicameralism and Budget Deficits: The Effect of Parliamentary Structure on Government Spending." *Legislative Studies Quarterly* 22 (4): 485–516.

IPU (Inter-Parliamentary Union). 1986. *Parliaments of the World: A Comparative Reference Compendium.* Aldershot, U.K.: Gower.

Kirchgässner, G. 2001. "The Effects of Fiscal Institutions on Public Finance: A Survey of the Empirical Evidence." Working Paper 617, CESifo, Munich.

Kraan, D.-J., and J. Wehner. 2005. "Budgeting in Slovenia." *OECD Journal on Budgeting* 4 (4): 55–98.

Krafchik, W., and J. Wehner. 1998. "The Role of Parliament in the Budgetary Process." *South African Journal of Economics* 66 (4): 512–41.

Krehbiel, K. 1991. *Information and Legislative Organization.* Ann Arbor, MI: University of Michigan Press.

LeLoup, L. T. 2004. "Uloga parlamenata u određivanju proračuna u Mađarskoj i Sloveniji" (Parliamentary Budgeting in Hungary and Slovenia). *Financijska teorija i praksa* 28 (1): 49–72.

Leston-Bandeira, C. 1999. "The Role of the Portuguese Parliament Based on a Case Study: The Discussion of the Budget, 1983–95." *Journal of Legislative Studies* 5 (2): 46–73.

Lieberman, E. S. 2005. "Nested Analysis as a Mixed-Method Strategy for Comparative Research." *American Political Science Review* 99 (3): 435–52.

Lienert, I. 2005. "Who Controls the Budget: The Legislature or the Executive?" Working Paper WP/05/115, IMF, Washington, DC.

Lienert, I., and M.-K. Jung. 2004. "The Legal Framework for Budget Systems: An International Comparison." Special issue, *OECD Journal on Budgeting* 4 (3).

Madison, James (Publius, pseud.). 1788/1961. *The Federalist Papers.* Ed. C. L. Rossiter. New York: New American Library.

Mattson, I., and K. Strøm. 1995. "Parliamentary Committees." In *Parliaments and Majority Rule in Western Europe,* ed. H. Döring, 249-307. Frankfurt: Campus.

McCubbins, M. D., and T. Schwartz. 1984. "Congressional Oversight Overlooked: Police Patrols versus Fire Alarms." *American Journal of Political Science* 28 (1): 165–79.

McGee, D. G. 2002. *The Overseers: Public Accounts Committees and Public Spending.* London: Commonwealth Parliamentary Association and Pluto Press.

Meyers, R. T. 2001. "Will the U.S. Congress's 'Power of the Purse' Become Unexceptional?" Paper presented at the annual meeting of the American Political Science Association, San Francisco, August 30.

Mezey, M. L. 1979. *Comparative Legislatures.* Durham, NC: Duke University Press.

OECD (Organisation for Economic Co-operation and Development). 2002a. "OECD Best Practices for Budget Transparency." *OECD Journal on Budgeting* 1 (3): 7–14.

———. 2002b. "The OECD Budgeting Database." *OECD Journal on Budgeting* 1 (3): 155–71.

OECD and World Bank. 2003. "Results of the Survey on Budget Practices and Procedures." http://ocde.dyndns.info/.

Oppenheimer, B. I. 1983. "How Legislatures Shape Policy and Budgets." *Legislative Studies Quarterly* 8 (4): 551–97.

Pollitt, C. 2003. "Performance Audit in Western Europe: Trends and Choices." *Critical Perspectives on Accounting* 14: 157–70.

Poterba, J. M., and J. von Hagen, eds. 1999. *Fiscal Institutions and Fiscal Performance.* Chicago: University of Chicago Press.

Reid, G. 1966. *The Politics of Financial Control: The Role of the House of Commons.* London: Hutchinson University Library.

Santiso, C. 2004. "Legislatures and Budget Oversight in Latin America: Strengthening Public Finance Accountability in Emerging Economies." *OECD Journal on Budgeting* 4 (2): 47–76.

Schick, A. 2002. "Can National Legislatures Regain an Effective Voice in Budget Policy?" *OECD Journal on Budgeting* 1 (3): 15–42.

Schick, A., with F. LoStracco. 2000. *The Federal Budget: Politics, Policy, Process.* Washington, DC: Brookings Institution Press.

Shepsle, K. A. 1979. "Institutional Arrangements and Equilibrium in Multidimensional Voting Models." *American Journal of Political Science* 23 (1): 27–59.

Shugart, M. S., and S. Haggard. 2001. "Institutions and Public Policy in Presidential Systems." In *Presidents, Parliaments, and Policy,* eds. S. Haggard and M. D. McCubbins, 64–102. Cambridge, U.K.: Cambridge University Press.

Stourm, R. 1917. *The Budget*. New York: D. Appleton, for the Institute for Government Research.

Strauch, R. R., and J. von Hagen, eds. 1999. *Institutions, Politics and Fiscal Policy*. Boston: Kluwer Academic.

von Hagen, J. 1992. *Budgeting Procedures and Fiscal Performance in the European Communities*. Brussels: Commission of the European Communities, Directorate-General for Economic and Financial Affairs.

Walters, R. H., and R. Rogers. 2004. *How Parliament Works*, 5th edition. New York: Longman.

Webber, C., and A. B. Wildavsky. 1986. *A History of Taxation and Expenditure in the Western World*. New York: Simon and Schuster.

Wehner, J. 2007. "Budget Reform and Legislative Control in Sweden." *Journal of European Public Policy* 14 (2): 313–32.

Wildavsky, A. B. 1964. *The Politics of the Budgetary Process*. Boston: Little Brown.

Wildavsky, A. B., and N. Caiden. 2001. *The New Politics of the Budgetary Process*, 4th edition. New York: Addison Wesley/Longman.

Williams, R., and E. Jubb. 1996. "Shutting Down Government: Budget Crises in the American Political System." *Parliamentary Affairs* 49 (3): 471–84.

CHAPTER 6

The Role of the Legislature in the Budget Drafting Process: A Comparative Review

Katherine Barraclough and Bill Dorotinsky

Increasingly, legislatures are focusing on their role in public resource management. This role generally falls into two areas: steering (setting policy and direction) and accountability (monitoring implementation and ex post review of budget execution regarding the purpose, amounts, and compliance with laws). Within the steering role, one aspect of the public finance process influencing legislative effectiveness is executive-legislative interaction during the process. This chapter examines the legislature's role at the drafting stage of the budget and identifies factors that influence different degrees of legislative involvement. It also highlights some good practices for optimizing the role of the legislature in the budget process to improve fiscal discipline, strategic allocation of resources, and operational efficiency, including the availability of information to the legislature, internal legislative organization and processes for engaging in budget decisions, the capacity of the legislature to analyze information, and the role of political parties. These factors are enablers of enhanced legislative engagement in the budget process and are relevant to all countries. However, it should be noted that country-specific historical, cultural, and political factors will also influence the relationship between the executive branch and legislature, particularly around the budget process.

Information for this chapter is drawn mainly from the World Bank-OECD budget procedures database and with data from the Open Budget Survey (OBS), conducted by the Center on Budget and Policy Priorities' International Budget Project (IBP).[1]

Recommendations of International Good Practices[2]

The International Monetary Fund's *Manual on Fiscal Transparency* (2001) recommends regular fiscal reporting "in a way that facilitates policy analysis and promotes accountability." For budget preparation, execution, and reporting, the manual states that budget documentation should specify fiscal objectives and sustainability, fiscal rules, the macroeconomic framework, new policies, and fiscal risks using qualitative and quantitative information.

The "OECD Best Practices for Budget Transparency" advocates a prebudget report to "encourage debate on the budget aggregates and how they interact with the economy." The prebudget report should include the "government's long-term economic and fiscal policy objectives and the government's economic and fiscal policy intentions." It further recommends that Parliament have "the opportunity and the resources to effectively examine any fiscal report that it deems necessary" (OECD 2001, 37).

The International Budget Project (which conducts the OBS) recommends that the budget include "sufficient disaggregated information to assess the distribution of spending within departments, at least including major programs and line items, backed by clear program objectives," and that consistency be maintained over time for comparison purposes (Krafchik and Wehner 2004, 3–7). The International Budget Project (IBP) also recommends that legislatures concentrate their attention on the decisions and allocations between departments and within departments, rather than on the overall size of the budget and deficit, and that they allocate proportionately more time to scrutinizing the distribution of resources against priorities at a departmental and subdepartmental level.

Both the IBP's and OECD's recommended good practices are uniform in advocating sufficient transparency of executive budget proposals to enable meaningful engagement in the budget process by the legislature, and also in advocating that legislatures focus on accountability and on making strategic resource allocation choices.

Early Release of Budget Information

Two important factors in determining the legislature's role in the draft stage of the budget are (1) the timeliness and content of information released by the executive to the legislature, and (2) whether there are formal arrangements for legislative debate of budget ceilings in the process. Early release of information to the legislature typically comes in the form of a prebudget statement. According to the OECD's best practices guidelines for fiscal transparency, the prebudget report should be released no later than one month prior to the budget proposal. The Center on Budget and Policy Priorities' International Budget Project stipulates that a prebudget statement should disclose expenditure and revenue parameters of the budget proposal and be released in the formulation phase of the budget.

Recognizing that countries' prebudget statements vary in the content, timing, and submission procedure, this chapter broadly defines *prebudget statements* as any formal document that is released to the legislature before the start of the fiscal year and before delivery of the formal budget document to the legislature for approval, that are publicly announced, and that contain information on government policy and priorities, aggregate revenue, expenditure, surplus or deficit, and debt forecasts in greater or lesser detail. The OBS data set offers some insight into the issue of early release of information to the legislature.[3]

Of the 36 countries that responded to the OBS, 24 have presidential systems and 12 have parliamentary systems. Twelve of the 36 may be considered middle-income countries (MICs) (with purchasing power parity (PPP), or GDP per capita greater than US$7,600). The remaining countries are lower-income countries (LICs). Among the countries with a presidential system, 10 have a bicameral legislature, while 7 of the 12 countries with parliamentary systems have a bicameral legislature. Overall, the OBS found that most executive branches fail to provide sufficient information to the legislature to assist them in making informed decisions about the budget.

Timeliness

Releasing budget information before the start of the fiscal year, and before delivery of the formal budget for approval, enables the legislature to engage more meaningfully in the budget debate. Table 6.1 presents results of when the prebudget statement is released to the public, based on the IBP data set.

Most countries release a prebudget statement before the start of the fiscal year. Fifty-three percent of all countries release a prebudget statement to the public. Fifty-nine percent of countries with presidential systems of government and 67 percent of MICs release a prebudget statement to the public. Sixty percent of countries with presidential systems and bicameral legislatures release a prebudget statement, compared with 35 percent of countries with presidential systems and unicameral legislatures. By contrast, only 29 percent of parliamentary systems with bicameral legislatures release a prebudget statement. Overall, slightly more countries with presidential systems than with parliamentary systems release prebudget statements.

Table 6.1. When Does the Executive Release a Prebudget Statement to the Public?
(percent)

Answer	All countries (36)	Presidential (24)	Parliamentary (12)	MIC (12)	LIC (24)
a. The executive releases a prebudget statement at least four months in advance of the start of the budget year.	31	33	25	50	21
b. The executive releases a prebudget statement at least two months (but less than four months) in advance of the start of the budget year.	11	13	8	17	8
c. The executive releases a prebudget statement, but it is released less than two months before the start of the budget year.	11	13	8	0	17
d. The executive does not release a prebudget statement.	47	42	58	33	54
e. Not applicable/other (please comment).	0	0	0	0	0

Source: Open Budget Survey (question 71).
Note: MICs = middle-income countries (or GDP per capita greater than US$7,600); LICs = low-income countries.

Most countries that release a prebudget statement do so at least four months before the start of the fiscal year. This is true for 33 percent of countries with presidential systems of government and 50 percent of middle-income countries. By contrast, only 21 percent of low-income countries release a prebudget statement at least four months before the start of the fiscal year. Sixty-seven percent of MICs release a prebudget statement at least two months before the start of the budget year—more than countries with presidential systems of government (46 percent), and more than the 42 percent average for all countries in the sample.

Content of Prebudget Statement

In addition to early release of information, the content of the prebudget statement is important to enable meaningful debate. Table 6.2 presents information on the content of the prebudget statement, using IBP data.

Despite the relatively large proportion of countries providing a prebudget statement, the content and quality of those statements varies considerably, as follows:

• In terms of inclusion of the government's macroeconomic and fiscal framework, 50 percent of the sample provide some explanation, but only 17 percent include both narrative detail and quantitative estimates.

• For countries with presidential systems of government, 55 percent provide at least an explanation of macroeconomic and fiscal policy, but only 13 percent provide narrative detail and quantitative estimates.

Table 6.2. Does the Prebudget Statement Describe the Government's Macroeconomic and Fiscal Framework?
(percent)

Answer	All countries (36)	Presidential (24)	Parliamentary (12)	MIC (12)	LIC (24)
a. Yes, an extensive explanation of the government's fiscal and macroeconomic policy is presented, including both a narrative discussion and quantitative estimates.	17	13	25	33	8
b. Yes, an explanation is presented, highlighting key aspects of the fiscal and macroeconomic framework, but some details are excluded.	22	25	17	33	17
c. Yes, some explanation is presented, but it lacks important details.	11	17	0	0	17
d. No, an explanation is not presented, or the executive does not release a prebudget statement to the public.	50	46	58	33	58
e. Not applicable/other (please comment).	0	0	0	0	0

Source: Open Budget Survey (question 72).
Note: MICs = middle-income countries (or GDP per capita greater than US$7,600); LICs = low-income countries.

- Of countries with presidential systems and bicameral legislatures, 20 percent release a prebudget statement that includes narrative detail and quantitative estimates. Fifty-seven percent of countries with presidential systems and unicameral legislatures release prebudget statements, but only 7 percent of those include narrative discussion and quantitative estimates.

- Of middle-income countries, 66 percent provide at least an explanation, and 33 percent provide both narrative detail and quantitative estimates.

Middle-income countries, regardless of whether they have a presidential or parliamentary system, would be expected to have a prebudget statement explaining macroeconomic and fiscal policy, and many would also be expected to include both narrative detail and quantitative estimates.

In addition to macroeconomic information, prebudget statements are valuable as statements of government policy intentions. Table 6.3 presents information on the policy content of prebudget statements.

These data most directly answer the question of whether detailed policy information for guiding executive budget development is included in the prebudget statement. For all countries in the sample, 34 percent provide an explanation that at least highlights the key priorities for executive budget development; 17 percent detail narrative and quantitative estimates (for example, ceilings or spending targets). For countries with presidential systems, 30 percent provide an explanation that at least highlights the key priorities for executive budget development, while 13 percent give detailed narrative and quantitative estimates (for example, ceilings or spending targets)—both somewhat less than the average for the entire sample. Among countries with presidential systems with bicameral legislatures, 20 percent give detailed

Table 6.3. Does the Prebudget Statement Describe the Government's Policies and Priorities That Will Guide the Development of Detailed Estimates for the Upcoming Budget?
(percent)

Answer	All countries (36)	Presidential (24)	Parliamentary (12)	MIC (12)	LIC (24)
a. Yes, an extensive explanation of the government's budget policies and priorities is presented, including both a narrative discussion and quantitative estimates.	17	13	25	33	8
b. Yes, an explanation is presented, highlighting key aspects of the government's budget policies and priorities, but some details are excluded.	17	17	17	25	13
c. Yes, some explanation is presented, but it lacks important details.	17	25	0	8	21
d. No, an explanation is not presented, or the executive does not release a prebudget statement to the public.	50	46	58	33	58
e. Not applicable/other (please comment).	0	0	0	0	0

Source: Open Budget Survey (question 73).
Note: MICs = middle-income countries (or GDP per capita greater than US$7,600); LICs = low-income countries.

narrative explanations, compared with only 7 of those with unicameral legislatures. For countries with parliamentary systems, the figures are 29 percent and 20 percent for those with bicameral and unicameral legislatures, respectively.

Within the OBS, higher-income countries clearly provide more detailed information. For MICs, 58 percent provide an explanation that at least highlights the key priorities for executive budget development, and 33 percent provide both narrative detail and quantitative estimates.

Formal Legislative Debate on Ceilings

To help set policy priorities and bind both the executive branch and the legislature to those priorities during detailed development and consideration of the budget, some countries establish formal legislative consideration of the budget ceilings. Table 6.4 presents data on whether such a formal process exists.

In addition to providing information on government policies and priorities, 57 percent of countries' legislatures in the World Bank-OECD database engage in debates on the aggregates in a binding or nonbinding capacity, and 20 percent have the legislature set hard spending ceilings. Among OECD countries the figure is slightly higher, at 60 percent, and even greater among countries with presidential systems of government, where 64 percent engage in either binding or nonbinding debate. (Note that the OECD countries category includes presidential and parliamentary systems, and that presidential and parliamentary, respectively, include OECD and non-OECD countries.) Strikingly, 20 percent of countries with presidential systems and bicameral legislatures set hard ceilings while none with presidential systems and unicameral legislatures set hard or even notional spending limits. Twenty percent of parliamentary systems with bicameral legislatures and 25 percent with unicameral legislatures set hard ceilings. Of the OECD countries that are also presidential, 88 percent (five out of six countries) answered positively to having binding or nonbinding discussions. However, the table does not clarify whether this debate occurs at the prebudget stage or at the time of budget proposal is submitted.

Table 6.4. Are Any Arrangements in Place for the Legislature to Establish Aggregate Expenditure Ceilings before Beginning Debate on Individual Expenditure Items?
(percent)

Answer	All countries (41)	OECD countries (27)	Presidential (14)	Parliamentary (27)
A1. Yes, the legislature sets hard spending ceilings.	20	30	14	22
A2. Yes, the legislature sets notional spending constraints.	0	0	0	0
A3. No, but the legislature engages in a nonbinding debate on aggregate spending.	37	30	50	30
A4. No.	44	41	36	48

Source: World Bank-OECD 2003 (question 2.7.j).

Summarizing the comparative information, any MIC country and any system of government could be expected to have a prebudget statement with the following characteristics:

- Is released publicly.

- Explains government's proposed macroeconomic and fiscal policy. Many would also be expected to include both narrative detail and quantitative estimates.

- Highlights the key government policy priorities for executive budget development. Many would also be expected to include both narrative detail and quantitative estimates (for example, ceilings or spending targets).

Certainly, any OECD country and those countries with comparable GDP per capita levels might be expected to at least have a legislature that engages in a nonbinding debate on the expenditure aggregates.

The Role of the Legislature

How and why some legislatures play a greater role in the budget process can also depend on the conferred powers and on the effective role of committees within legislatures. As noted earlier, legislatures require access to timely and appropriate information from the executive. They also require the technical capacity to use this information. Certain factors can affect the ability of a given legislature to play an active and relevant role in the budgetary process. Even where a legislature has the authority to modify the budget, it might not always use that authority. Factors such as supportive institutions (legislative budget offices), internal legislative processes enabling collective decision-making (parliamentary procedures), and the number of political parties also influence outcomes.

Use of Powers

The primary example of a legislature having unrestricted powers in budget formulation is the United States Congress. Many legislatures have more restricted powers, with an ability to make some changes to the proposed budget within set limits. However, having such powers does not seem to indicate that they will always be used. As table 6.5 shows, 97 percent of respondents to the World Bank-OECD survey said the legislature made little to no change to the budget. Even the United States, whose Congress has the power to change the budget in its entirety, indicated that it generally approves the budget with minor changes only. This figure is higher still among OECD countries, with 99 percent responding that the legislature makes few, if any, changes.

Along with having the power to change the budget, legislatures with a greater involvement in the budgetary process also require the capacity to analyze budgetary information. Seventy-two percent of countries do not have specialized budget organizations (see table 6.6). However, among the OECD

Table 6.5. In Practice, Does the Legislature Generally Approve the Budget as Presented by the Executive?
(percent)

Answer	All countries (41)	OECD countries (27)	Presidential (14)	Parliamentary (27)
A1. It generally approves the budget with no changes.	34	33	21	41
A2. It generally approves the budget with minor changes only (affecting less than 3 percent of total spending).	63	67	71	59
A3. It generally approves the budget with major changes (affecting more than 3 percent but less than 20 percent of total spending).	2	0	7	0
A4. It generally approves a budget significantly different from the executive (affecting more than 20 percent of total spending).	0	0	0	0

Source: World Bank-OECD 2003 (question 2.7.i).

Table 6.6. Is There a Specialized Budget Research Organization Attached to the Legislature That Conducts Analyses of the Budget (Organization May Be Part of the Audit Office)?
(percent)

Answer	All countries (39)	OECD countries (25)	Presidential (14)	Parliamentary (25)
A1. Yes, with fewer than 10 professional staff.	18	12	14	20
A2. Yes, with 10 to 25 professional staff.	3	4	0	4
A3. Yes, with 26 or more professional staff.	8	12	21	0
A4. No.	72	72	64	76

Source: World Bank-OECD 2003 (question 2.10.e).

countries with presidential systems, 50 percent have a research organization with 26 or more professional staff. Legislatures in countries that have established research bodies with sufficient professional staff to assist the legislature should have a greater capacity to analyze budgetary documents.

Committees

Lack of, or weak, committees may compromise a legislature's ability to influence budget policy or make amendments (Krafchik and Wehner 2004, 7). Strong committees are generally characterized as having sufficient resources, skilled staff, and plenty of time to debate. Sixty-three percent of countries have a single budget committee dealing with all budget issues, with members from sectoral committees sometimes attending for specific discussion (see table 6.7). This is consistent for both OECD countries and countries with presidential systems.

In addition to committee structure, whether committees hold public hearings at which executive agencies must justify their budget requests can be an important tool enabling legislative understanding of the budget and influence over policy content. Table 6.8 presents results on legislative committee involvement in public hearings using IBP data.

Forty-two percent of countries hold public hearings either extensively or on key administrative units. Among MICs and among countries with presidential systems, 75 percent and 42 percent, respectively, hold hearings either extensively or on key administrative units.

Table 6.7. What Best Describes the Committee Structure for Dealing with the Budget?
(percent)

Answer	All countries (40)	OECD countries (26)	Presidential (14)	Parliamentary (26)
A1. A single budget committee deals with all budget-related matters with no formal input from other committees. Sectoral committees may make recommendations, but the budget committee does not have to follow them.	48	46	50	46
A2. A single budget committee deals with the budget, but members from other sectoral committees attend meetings of the budget committee when expenditures in their specific areas are being dealt with. For example, members of the education committee would attend meetings of the budget committee when expenditures for the ministry of education were being discussed.	15	15	21	12
A3. A single budget committee deals with budget aggregates (total level of revenue and spending and their allocation to each sector), and sectoral committees deal with spending at the level of each appropriation. For example, the budget committee would establish the total level of expenditure for education, but members of the education committee would allocate the total among each appropriation within the education sector.	18	15	14	19
A4. Sectoral committees deal with appropriations for each respective sector. No budget committee is in place, or it offers only technical assistance.	5	8	0	8
A5. Other, please specify.	15	15	14	15

Source: World Bank-OECD 2003 (question 2.10.a).

Table 6.8. Does a Legislative Committee (or Committees) Hold Public Hearings on the Macroeconomic and Fiscal Framework Presented in the Budget in Which Testimony from the Executive Branch and the Public Is Heard?
(percent)

Answer	All countries (36)	Presidential (24)	Parliamentary (12)	MIC (12)	LIC (24)
a. Yes, extensive public hearings are held on the budgets of administrative units in which testimony from the executive branch is heard.	11	13	8	17	8
b. Yes, hearings are held, covering key administrative units, in which testimony from the executive branch is heard.	31	29	33	58	17
c. Yes, a limited number of hearings are held in which testimony from the executive branch is heard.	17	25	0	17	17
d. No, public hearings are not held on the budgets of administrative units in which testimony from the executive branch is heard.	42	33	58	8	58
e. Not applicable/other (please comment).	0	0	0	0	0

Source: Open Budget Survey (question 76).

Political Parties

Where one party does not dominate the legislature, the executive is more likely to have to amend the budget proposal to gain sufficient support for passage of the budget. Where a single party dominates, especially if it is the same party as the executive, less compromise may be necessary (Krafchik and Wehner 2004, 7). Table 6.9 presents IBP data on executive responsiveness to legislative requests for information. Eighty-three percent of respondents indicated that the executive responds to requests, although the responses have mixed results on how timely and appropriate the information is. Sixty percent of countries with presidential systems and bicameral legislatures respond in a timely manner to legislative requests, compared with 21 percent of countries with presidential systems and unicameral legislatures. Notably, half of MICs responded positively to providing timely and appropriate information, suggesting that more developed countries' executive branches have a higher rate of providing accurate information and a more harmonious relationship with parties in the legislature.

Parliamentary versus Presidential Systems

Parliamentary systems tend to have more cooperative legislative-executive relations. Conversely, the separation of powers characteristic of presidential systems can lead to great antagonism in executive-legislative relations (Krafchik and Wehner 2004, p. 6). This difference in the two systems may influence the flow of information between these two bodies. For example, parliamentary systems tend to make fewer and less-significant changes to the budget but

Table 6.9. Does the Executive Present More Details or Provide a Better Explanation of any Budget Proposal, if Members of the Legislature (Including from Minority Parties) Request Such Information?
(percent)

Answer	All countries (36)	Presidential (24)	Parliamentary (12)	MIC (12)	LIC (24)
a. The executive responds to such legislative requests, and it generally provides an appropriate and timely response.	36	38	33	50	29
b. The executive responds to such legislative requests, but its responses are sometimes not appropriate or timely.	47	42	58	50	46
c. The executive responds to such legislative requests, but its responses are typically not appropriate or timely.	11	17	0	0	17
d. The executive responds selectively or ignores such legislative requests.	6	4	8	0	8
e. Not applicable/other (please comment).	0	0	0	0	0

Source: Open Budget Survey (question 79).

there is usually substantial presentation of information on the fiscal framework ahead of tabling the budget, and there is often more parliamentary debate, backed by greater transparency.

Conclusion

Transparency and legislative engagement varies, even among countries of comparable economic development and with similar systems of government. Most notable in many countries is the lack of public prebudget statements outlining information on macroeconomic estimates and fiscal policy, and the absence of any debate on these issues in the legislature. Countries develop their own systems and processes for budgeting; preparing a prebudget statement should take country-specific factors into consideration. Understanding the role and power conferred upon and practiced by the legislature is crucial. Transparency of budget systems depends on the legislature's analytic capacity, the strength and composition of committees, and the existence of adequate procedures within the legislature to enable coherent consideration of fiscal policy and sectoral allocations.

Legislatures are increasingly exercising their role in resource allocation and public finance—a fact of life that the executive branch must address. Some concrete steps can be taken to improve the quality of legislative engagement. Provision of more complete information is a minimum step to enable better legislative engagement. But increasingly this seems insufficient; the executive branch and legislature need to work closely together to craft common processes and constraints and to better define appropriate roles to achieve more appropriate outcomes.

Notes

1. The Center on Budget and Policy Priorities (CBPP) is a nongovernmental research organization providing policy analysis in the United States on federal and state fiscal policy and low- to moderate-income family policies (http://www.cbpp.org). The International Budget Project (IBP) was formed within the CBPP in 1997 to nurture the growth of civil society capacity to analyze and influence government budget processes, institutions, and outcomes. For more on the IBP, see http://www.internationalbudget.org/.

2. Best practices are designed to provide guidelines against which individual countries can assess their own standards and share lessons from the experiences of other countries. They should not to be taken as concrete rules.

3. The CBPP (http://www.cbpp.org), through its' International Budget Project, developed the Open Budget Survey questionnaire to evaluate public access to budget information and involvement in the budget debate. In 2004 researchers from 36 countries examined procedures for budget drafting, budget execution, and auditing. The data from the survey, which was filled out by the NGO researchers, have been questioned because they represent the judgment of these NGO researchers and have not been vetted by governments or other sources for accuracy. In some cases, the data are known to be problematic. Nonetheless, the survey poses several questions related to early release of budget information to the legislature. The countries surveyed are Argentina, Azerbaijan, Bangladesh, Bolivia, Botswana, Brazil, Bulgaria, Burkina Faso, Colombia, Costa Rica, Croatia, Czech Republic, Ecuador, El Salvador, Georgia, Ghana, Honduras, India, Indonesia, Jordan, Kazakhstan, Kenya, Malawi, Mexico, Mongolia, Namibia, Nepal, Nicaragua, Peru, Poland, Romania, Russia, Slovenia, South Africa, Uganda, and Zambia.

Bibliography

IMF. 2001. *Manual on Fiscal Transparency*. Washington, DC: International Monetary Fund. http://www.imf.org/external/np/fad/trans/manual/index.htm.

Krafchik, Warren, and Joachim Wehner 2004. "Legislatures and Budget Oversight: Best Practices." Paper presented at the Kazakhstan Revenue Watch Open Forum, Almaty, Kazakhstan, April 8. http://www.revenuewatch.org/reports/kazakhstan_parliament_budget_forum.pdf.

OECD (Organisation for Economic Co-operation and Development). 2001. "Best Practices for Budget Transparency." OECD, Paris. http://www.oecd.org/dataoecd/33/13/1905258.pdf.

CHAPTER 7

A Note on What Happens if No Budget Is Passed before the Fiscal Year Begins
A Comparison of OECD and Non-OECD Provisions

Bill Dorotinsky

In the annual budget game between the executive branch and legislature, the incentives are influenced by the rules of the game. The cost of failing to reach agreement can vary and can influence results, with implications for service delivery as well as political economy.

Generally, there are two broad approaches to structuring what happens if no budget agreement is reached before the fiscal year begins. One emphasizes the importance of positive action by the authorities to continue spending, thus empowering the relevant institutions with an effective veto over new budgets unless agreement is reached. Compromise is an essential feature. The second approach deemphasizes the importance of reaching an agreement, and stresses the importance of continuation of government services in the event no budget is enacted.

Underlying the former approach is the assumption that the cost of non-agreement is high, with the government shutting down in the new fiscal year if there is no approved budget. In this event, the general population and interest groups are likely to be dissatisfied and exert pressure on both branches to reach some agreement. The caveats, of course, involve political gamesmanship and communication, in which one branch—the legislature or the executive—might be able to persuade the citizenry that the other is at fault. In any event, one or all political parties are thought to suffer in the polls and the election if they fail to reach agreement. However, memory is short, and if such a failure occurs early in a term of office, it may not manifest itself as an issue in subsequent elections.

The second approach deemphasizes agreement, and the direct consequences of failure to reach agreement are minimized. There may be some residual reputation damage to authorities, as new spending in support of new policies may not be realized, and electoral promises may remain unfulfilled, depending on the rules. In these cases, some spending would be allowed to continue in the new fiscal year, pending resolution of the impasse between branches of government.

In the latter case, different levels of spending may be permitted to continue, and these may favor the executive branch, the legislature, or neither. For example, in Bolivia, Chile, and Suriname, the executive branch's budget proposal takes effect—either permanently, or as in Bolivia, on an interim basis—if no budget is approved by the legislature by the beginning of the fiscal year. Such rules favor the executive branch and reduce the incentive of the executive to compromise at all on the budget proposal. In other cases, the legislature must enact special measures to allow spending to occur, such as in Canada, the United Kingdom, and the United States. Alternatively, the prior year's approved budget—representing the most recent consensus budget—continues to operate, with or without special adjustments. Argentina, Colombia, Portugal, Spain, Uruguay, and República Bolivariana de Venezuela operate under this regime. Table 7.1 presents data on this question from the 2003 World Bank-OECD survey of developed and developing country budget processes.[1]

For all countries, the largest group (41 percent) is countries that have provisions for adopting the prior year's budget in the event no budget is passed prior to the start of the fiscal year, followed by 26 percent of countries requiring the legislature to take special action to continue government operations.

The most striking difference is between OECD and non-OECD countries. Roughly 40 percent of OECD countries—the largest number —require legislative action to continue spending in the event of no approved budget, whereas *none* of the non-OECD countries reporting required legislative action. The majority (62 percent) of the non-OECD countries had measures for adopting the prior year's budget to continue spending, compared with only about one-quarter of OECD countries. Furthermore, only 15 percent of OECD countries had measures adopting the executive budget in the absence of an approved budget, compared with 31 percent of non-OECD countries. Interestingly, 19 percent of OECD countries listed "other" provisions, including no provisions for continuing spending in the event no budget is passed before the beginning of the fiscal year, compared with only 8 percent of non-OECD countries.

Table 7.1. If the Budget Is Not Approved by the Legislature before the Start of the Fiscal Year, Which of the Following Describes the Consequences?
(percent)

	All countries	Non-OECD	OECD
Executive's budget takes effect	16	31	15
Previous year's budget takes effect	41	62	23
Legislature must vote in other measures	26	—	38
Executive falls, new elections held	3	—	4
Other (including no provisions)	13	8	19

Source: World Bank-OECD 2003 budget procedures database at http://ocde.dyndns.info/.
Note: — = not available.

Generally, non-OECD countries tended to have measures that increase certainty of spending (adopting either the executive budget or the prior year's budget) and reduce conflict (adopting the prior year's approved budget, which can be considered the most recent political consensus budget). OECD countries, in contrast, had a wider variety of systems, with the largest number of countries having measures emphasizing legislative leadership, greater executive accountability (weaker executive negotiating power), and greater potential for interbranch conflict and uncertain spending in the new fiscal year.

Presidential versus Parliamentary Systems

Table 7.2 presents the same data, arrayed for OECD and non-OECD countries by system of government—presidential or parliamentary. Among the 26 OECD countries reporting, 88 percent have parliamentary systems of government, compared with 38 percent of the 13 non-OECD countries reporting.

In a comparison of presidential systems of government, 50 percent of non-OECD presidential systems adopt the prior year's budget when no budget is enacted before the beginning of the fiscal year; one-third adopt the president's budget.2 Again, the tendency seems to be for more certainty in continuation of spending and lower conflict for non-OECD countries.

In marked contrast, most OECD presidential systems tend to use other provisions (including no formal provisions), followed by provisions requiring legislative action for continued spending.[3] OECD countries are generally assumed to represent higher income or more developed country status, which raises an interesting issue of whether potential spending disruptions and interbranch conflict are more affordable with higher income status, and whether similar institutional arrangements (or nonarrangements) might be inappropriate for less developed countries.

For parliamentary systems of government, most non-OECD countries (80 percent) have provisions for adopting the prior year's budget in the event no budget is passed for the new fiscal year, with the remaining 20 percent adopting the executive branch budget.

Table 7.2. Provisions for Spending in the Event No Budget Is Enacted before the Fiscal Year, by System of Government

(percent)

	Non-OECD		OECD	
	Presidential (8)	Parliamentary (5)	Presidential (3)	Parliamentary (23)
Executive's budget takes effect	38	20	—	17
Previous year's budget takes effect	50	80	—	26
Legislature must vote in other measures	—	—	33	39
Executive falls, new elections are held	—	—	—	4
Other (including no provisions)	12	—	66	13

Source: World Bank-OECD (2003). "Results of the Survey on Budget Practices and Procedures." http://ocde.dyndns.info/.
Note: — = not available.

For OECD parliamentary systems, the largest number (38 percent) require legislative action for further spending, clearly giving precedence to the legislative body in budget negotiations.[4] In a nearly direct inverse to non-OECD country tendencies, only 26 percent of OECD parliamentary systems adopt the prior year's budget as the basis for continued spending in the new fiscal year where no budget is formally enacted. A similar percentage of OECD (17 percent) and non-OECD (20 percent) parliamentary systems adopt the executive budget for continued spending.

Notes

1. Thirty-nine countries responded to this question, of which 26 were OECD countries and 13 were developing countries.

2. Budget law provisions for adopting the prior year's budget can be detailed and sound bases for continued spending. Both Argentina (Section 27 of the Financial Administration and Control Systems Act) and República Bolivariana de Venezuela (Article 39 of the Organic Budget Law 2000) have similar provisions. Below is the relevant section of the Venezuelan law for reference.

Article 39. If for any reason, the Executive has not submitted the budget bill to the National Assembly within the period established in the preceding article, or the bill is rejected or not passed by the National Assembly before December 15 each year, the budget in effect shall be prolonged, with the following adjustments introduced by the National Executive:

1. In the revenue budgets:
   a) Eliminate the sections of revenue that cannot be collected again.
   b) Estimate each type of revenue for the new period.
2. In the expenditure budgets:
   a) Eliminate the budget credits that cannot be repeated, because the objectives for which they were budgeted have been accomplished.
   b) Include in the budget of the Republic the allocation for Constitutional Appropriation (Situado) corresponding to the ordinary revenue estimated for the new financial year, and legal contributions that must be made in accordance with the provisions of the laws in effect on the date of submission of the respective budget bill.
   c) Include the budget credits indispensable for payment of interest on the Public Debt and the installments that must be paid for commitments arising from the execution of international treaties.
   d) Include indispensable budget credits to guarantee the continuity and efficiency of the State administration, especially educational, health, welfare and security services.
3. In the financing operations:
   a) Eliminate resources from authorized public credit operations for the amount utilized.
   b) Exclude the surpluses from previous periods, when the prolonged budget included its utilization.
   c) Include the resources from public credit operations, whose receipt must occur in the related year.

      d) Include financial applications indispensable for the amortization of the Public Debt.

    4. Adapt the objectives and targets to the modifications that result from the preceding adjustments.

    In any event, the National Executive shall comply with the multi-annual budget framework and the agreement referred to in Article 28 of this Law.

    3. Note that this is for formal budgets. Much OECD spending tends to be governed outside the budget process, and this spending would continue regardless of passage of the annual budget.

    4. The category of "government falls if budget is not passed by legislature" also strengthens the legislative body relative to the executive and could be added to the previous category of "legislative action required for spending," further reinforcing the OECD tendency to give precedence to the legislative body.

CHAPTER 8

Public Accounts Committees

Riccardo Pelizzo and Rick Stapenhurst

The collapse of many authoritarian regimes in the course of what Samuel Huntington called "the third wave of democratization" (Huntington 1991), along with the democratic transitions in Eastern and Central Europe, Latin America, and Asia, have increased interest among political scientists in what Giovanni Sartori calls "constitutional engineering" (Sartori 1994a).[1] Political scientists are paying new, and increasing, attention to which institutions are more likely to lead to the consolidation of the democracies that emerged in this "third wave" (Stepan and Skach 1994, 119). More specifically, political scientists have investigated whether and to what extent democratic consolidation or democratic collapse is affected by the form of government.

In the course of this debate several positions have emerged. Juan Linz (1994) posited that the parliamentary form of government better suits democracy and democracy's consolidation. He argued that the presidential form of government, because of its rigidity and the dual legitimacy of the executive and the legislative, is less likely to sustain democracy. Przeworski and others (1997, 301) have provided extensive empirical evidence supporting Linz's argument. They showed through statistical analysis that the probability of a democratic breakdown in countries with a presidential form of government is three times higher than it is in countries with a parliamentary form of government. At the same time, Scott Mainwaring (1993) underlined that the survival of democratic regimes under the presidential form of government is only in danger when coupled with a hyperfragmented party system.[2]

While political scientists investigated which forms of government are more likely to ensure the survival of democratic regimes, several international organizations began to investigate the relationship between democracies and institutions. Organizations such as the World Bank Institute (WBI) and the United Nations Development Programme (UNDP) are paying increasing attention to legislatures and the role they can play in consolidating democracy, improving governance, curbing corruption, and, ultimately, reducing poverty (NDI 2000;

Pelizzo and Stapenhurst 2004a, 2004b; Pelizzo, Stapenhurst, and Olson 2004; Stapenhurst and Pelizzo 2002).

International organizations have adopted an interesting approach to the study of legislatures. They acknowledge that modern political systems are often characterized by a sort of executive dominance, or executive preeminence, which describes governments that have the political and the legislative initiative, along with the resources, competence, information, and know-how, necessary to analyze pressing problems and formulate policies and solutions. Meanwhile, legislatures are responsible for overseeing governments and holding them to account. They evaluate the virtues (or the lack thereof) of government policies, keep governments in check, prevent governments from abusing their power, and examine and assess the merits of governments' legislative proposals and vote to amend, approve, or reject them. In addition to this ex ante oversight function (oversight that is exercised before a policy is enacted), legislatures also perform an ex post oversight function: they are in charge of overseeing policy implementation, thereby ensuring that policies are implemented as they were approved by the legislature.

The above suggests that legislatures may be less capable of initiating policies than they were in the past, but they counterbalance this loss of political initiative by intensifying their oversight activities. International organizations are thus paying increasing attention to which institutional instruments may help legislators and legislatures to oversee governments' actions and activities (NDI 2000; Pelizzo and Stapenhurst 2004a, 2004b; Pelizzo, Stapenhurst, and Olson 2004; Stapenhurst and Pelizzo 2002). The interest in Public Accounts Committees (PACs) originated within this context. This chapter first looks closely at PACs, how they are established and institutionalized, and the functions that they perform. The chapter also analyzes a selection of survey data collected by the WBI in collaboration with the World Bank's South Asia Region Financial Management Unit (SARFM) to assess the good functioning of the PACs and factors that enable such good functioning.

Public Accounts Committees (PACs)

PACs are one of the instruments that parliaments can use to check governments' activities.[3] These committees, first instituted in the United Kingdom by a resolution of the House of Commons in 1861, are now fairly common in the countries of the Commonwealth. In general, PACs are parliamentary standing committees of the lower house. However, there are some exceptions to this general trend. In Australia and India, for example, the PAC is a bicameral committee, and in Nigeria, both chambers have established PACs.

PACs may be institutionalized in different ways: by a country's constitution, by the standing orders of the assembly, or by an act of parliament. PACs were established by constitution in Antigua and Barbuda, Bangladesh, the Cook Islands, Kiribati, Saint Vincent, the Seychelles, Trinidad and Tobago, and Zambia. In a second group of countries PACs were institutionalized by the standing orders of the assembly in Canada, Guyana, Jamaica, Malta, Tanzania, and Uganda, and by the rules of procedures in India. The PAC in Trinidad and Tobago was established by both the constitution and by standing orders. In a third group of countries, which includes Australia and the United Kingdom, the PAC was instituted by an act of Parliament.[4]

The number of members in a PAC varies from country to country. There are seven members in Malta, 17 in Canada, and 22 in India.[5] Interestingly, despite the size of the membership, the distribution of seats within a PAC corresponds, as much as possible, to the distribution of seats in the whole assembly. This means that the government party (or the government coalition) controls a majority of the seats in the PAC.

To counterbalance the power of the majority in the PAC, the opposition party is generally given the chairmanship of the PAC. David McGee noted that "in two-thirds of the cases PACs are chaired by an opposition member" (2002, 66). McGee underlines that in countries such as the United Kingdom or India, this practice is the result of "a very strong convention." In other countries it is codified by the same norms and rules that establish the PAC itself (for example, Malta and Tanzania). For example, Art. 120E(4) of the standing orders of Malta's parliament establishes "one of the members nominated by the Leader of the Opposition and so designated by him in consultation with the Leader of the House shall be appointed as Chairman of the Public Accounts Committee." Similarly, Art. 87(5) of the standing orders of the Tanzanian parliament establishes that "the Chairperson for the Public Account Committee shall be elected from amongst the Members of the Committee from the Opposition."

The practice of making an opposition member the chair of the PAC performs two basic functions. First, it balances the power between the government and the opposition. Second, it performs a symbolic function: it indicates the willingness of both the majority and the minority to operate within the PAC in a bipartisan manner.

Australia represents an interesting exception to this general trend. In Australia, the chair of the PAC is generally a member of parliament (MP) from the parliamentary majority. This choice is motivated by the fact that having a government member as chair can make implementation of the PAC's recommendations easier. "It is regarded as the duty of the Chair to advocate that the PAC's recommendations be taken up and implemented by the government. This can involve behind the scenes work persuading reluctant ministers to act. A government Member can do this more effectively than an opposition Member who as political opponent will not have the confidence of the ministers" (McGee 2002, 66).

Roles and Functions of PACs

PACs are standing committees that help parliament oversee the activities performed by the government. Like any other standing committee, a PAC has the power to investigate and examine all the issues that are referred to it by the parliament.[6] A PAC can also investigate specific issues, such as government accountability to parliament regarding expenses approved by the government, effectiveness and efficiency of government-enacted policies, and the quality of the administration.

To fulfill its role, the PAC is given additional and more specific powers, such as the power to examine the public accounts, the comments on the public accounts, and all the reports drafted by the Office of the Auditor General and the National Audit Office. The PAC also has the power to conduct investigations (directly or indirectly), to receive all the documentation it considers necessary to adequately perform its functions, to invite government members to attend PAC meetings and respond to questions, to publicize the PAC's conclusions, to report to the parliament, and to present the PAC's recommendations to the government.

The Success of PACs

The WBI and SARFM surveyed 33 PAC chairs from national and subnational parliaments in the Commonwealth (Stapenhurst et al. 2005). This chapter discusses the data generated in the course of that survey. Until recently, very little was known about the effectiveness of PACs. No comparative study had systematically investigated whether, and to what extent, PACs actually contribute to effective oversight of government activities and expenses. The WBI-SARFM survey has generated fairly interesting data. The survey data can be used to perform two tasks: first, to assess results achieved by the PACs under specific conditions, and second, to assess which conditions and factors may help PACs work well.

The data on the success of the PACs show that their success rates vary significantly, depending on the nature of the results they seek to achieve. For example, although 78.8 percent of the chairs surveyed reported that the recommendations formulated by the PAC are frequently accepted by the government, only 63.6 percent of respondents stated that the recommendations formulated by the PAC are frequently implemented. Conversely, while only 15.2 percent of the respondents reported that the PAC's recommendations are rarely accepted, 27.3 percent of respondents indicated that the recommendations formulated by the PAC are rarely implemented by the government (see table 8.1).

Further analysis of the data suggests some additional considerations. For more than 60 percent of respondents, the government frequently provides better information to the parliament in light of the PAC's recommendations. However, it is rare that the actions, suggestions, and recommendations of the PAC lead to disciplinary action against public officials who have violated the existing rules and norms. Less than one-third of respondents reported that disciplinary action occurs frequently in the wake of the PAC's recommendations. It is also worth noting that the government rarely modifies its legislation and legislative proposals in light of the PAC's recommendations and suggestions.

Table 8.1. Results Achieved by the PAC: How Frequently Has the PAC Achieved the Following Result?
(percent; N = 33)

Result Achieved	Frequently	Rarely
Recommendations accepted	78.8	15.2
Recommendations implemented	63.6	27.3
Better information	60.8	18.2
Disciplinary action	27.3	15.2
Modification of legislation	15.2	54.5

Source: Stapenhurst et al. 2005.

The Determinants of a PAC's Success

The WBI-SARFM survey did not simply ask whether, to what extent, and how PACs are effective or successful. It also attempted to assess which conditions facilitate the good functioning and success of PACs.

The survey administrators provided a list of 37 factors that could be considered possible determinants of a PAC's success. Respondents were then asked to indicate how much importance they attached to each of these factors, that is, whether they considered the factors to be very important, somewhat important, or not important. These factors fell into one of the following three categories: the composition of the committee, the powers of the committee, and the practices of the committee. Respondents were also asked to identify which conditions could prevent the successful functioning of a PAC.

Composition of the committee. Two of the 37 factors presented in the survey belong to this first category of determinants of a PAC's success: Two of the factors determining a PAC's success relate to its composition, namely, having (1) balanced representation of all major political parties in the committee, and (2) exclusion of government ministers from the committee.

Regarding the second factor, the mission of a PAC is to investigate the activities of the government, especially with regard to the use of public funds and resources. To perform its oversight activity, the PAC has to be free to conduct its business without any government interference. This condition (freedom from government interference) could be difficult to achieve if government ministers were also serving as members of the PAC. If members of parliament (MPs) already serving in the cabinet were allowed to serve on the PAC, they might try to slow down or mislead the investigative action of the committee in order to protect the cabinet in which they also serve.

Even if it is assumed that MPs who serve in the cabinet do not mislead or slow down the PAC in the performance of its duties, their membership in the PAC would still pose a problem for the proper functioning of the committee. The study by McGee (2002) revealed that PACs are not the most appealing committees on which MPs can serve. Some MPs fear that serving on a PAC requires a great amount of work without providing much visibility. Membership in a PAC may also be seen as not being adequately rewarded at the ballot box; in other words there may be little or no electoral incentive to serve on a PAC.

The absence of electoral incentives is coupled with the absence of partisan incentives (or the presence of partisan disincentives). MPs fear that serving on a PAC may cause them trouble with their own respective parties. MPs belonging to the majority party (or coalition) often worry that serving in a PAC might force them to choose between loyally serving their party (at the cost of not performing their committee duties) and loyally serving the PAC (potentially alienating their own party). If MPs with appointments in the cabinet were allowed to serve in the PAC, their presence in the committee would provide a further incentive to the younger MPs to favor partisan interests over committee interests. The committee would thus end up functioning in a partisan manner. As composition of the committee is fairly proportional, it reflects the distribution of seats in the assembly as a whole, and in parliamentary systems the government party (or coalition) controls the majority of the parliamentary seats. Hence, as soon as the PAC starts operating in a partisan fashion, the government would be able to control the PAC and avoid parliamentary oversight.

There is a third reason why cabinet ministers should not be allowed to serve on a PAC. Even if it is assumed that the presence of government officials in the PAC does not negatively affect its functioning, having government members in PACs certainly affects the credibility of the PAC and its deliberations, which are the PAC's true assets. For these reasons, government members should not be allowed to serve on the PAC.

Table 8.2 shows that the majority of respondents believe that the composition of the PAC is a crucial factor in making PACs work well. Excluding MPs serving in the cabinet from the PAC is considered important or very important by, respectively, 14.8 and 85.2 percent of respondents. Similarly, the proportional representation of parliamentary parties in the PAC is considered to be important or very important by 10.3 and 86.2 percent of the respondents, respectively. Only one respondent said that proportional representation of parties in the PAC is not important, and none of the respondents considered the exclusion of government members as not important.

Powers of the committee. The survey asked the 33 PAC chairs to indicate how important certain powers or characteristics were for the success of the

Table 8.2. Success and Composition of the PAC: How Important Is This Factor?
(percent)

Factor	Very important	Important	Not important	N
Proportional representation of the various parliamentary parties	86.2	10.3	3.4	29
Exclusion of MPs with cabinet posts	85.2	14.8	0	27

Source: Stapenhurst et al. 2005.

PAC. Respondents were given a list of 17 powers or characteristics and asked to indicate whether they considered these powers to be very important, important, or not important.

Analysis of the survey data reveals that the importance of certain powers or characteristics is almost unanimously acknowledged. For example, the power to formulate suggestions and to publish them, the power to choose which topics should be investigated without having to accept orders or suggestions from the government, and the power to investigate all the current and past expenses deliberated by the executive are almost unanimously considered to be important or very important. All respondents also considered as important or very important that the PAC have a clear focus on keeping the government accountable for the use of public money.

It should be noted that although a large percentage of respondents did not consider as important whether the PAC has the power to summon the cabinet ministers before the committee, they almost unanimously considered important or very important the PAC's power to force witnesses to respond to questions. More than 93 percent of the respondents indicated that it is important or very important for PACs to have the power to force witnesses to respond to questions (see table 8.3).

Success and practices of the PAC. A third set of factors may influence the success or the effectiveness of PACs in performing their tasks. This third set of

Table 8.3. Success and Powers of PACs: How Important Are These Factors? (percent)

Power of the committee	Very important	Important	Not important	N
Formulate recommendations and publish the conclusions	97.0	3.0	0	33
Investigate all past and present expenses	93.5	6.5	0	31
Choose topics for investigation without following the suggestions of the government	90.9	9.1	0	33
Focus on keeping government accountable for spending	90.9	9.1	0	33
Force witnesses to answer questions	87.1	6.5	6.5	33
Examine the budget of the legislative auditor	58.8	35.3	23.5	17
Force cabinet ministers to appear before the committee	55.0	15.0	45.0	33
View the proposed legislation or the amendments to the Legislative Auditor's Act	47.8	30.4	21.8	23

Source: Stapenhurst et al. 2005.

factors is based on practices adopted by PACs themselves and their members. To identify which practices and dynamics could improve the performance of PACs and make them more successful, the survey asked respondents to assess the importance of 18 practices.

Two practices were considered to be particularly important for the success of PACs. Respondents reported that keeping the records or the proceedings of meetings was one the most important ways to improve the PAC's performance. Respondents also noted that the PAC's performance was greatly enhanced when members of the PAC came prepared or did their homework before attending the PAC's meetings. Both practices were considered to be important or very important by 97 percent of respondents, although keeping the transcripts of the sessions was considered to be slightly more important than doing homework. In fact, while preparation for the meeting is considered to be very important by almost 80 percent of the respondents, keeping the transcripts is considered to be very important by 88 percent of the respondents.

The existence of procedures and mechanisms to assess whether the government actually implements the recommendations formulated by the PAC is also considered to be an important condition for its success. The existence of such procedures was considered to be important or very important by more than 93 percent of respondents (see table 8.4).

Bipartisanship and the bipartisan functioning of the PAC are considered the fourth most important practice for the success of a PAC. More than 90 percent of respondents indicated that a close working relationship between committee members, regardless of their partisan affiliation, is important or very important.

This is an interesting result, particularly if considered in light of the data presented above, which reveal the unanimous acknowledgment regarding the importance of certain powers being at the disposal of PACs. Why did a small percentage of PAC chairs consider parliamentary parties' representation in a PAC as unnecessary for a PAC's success? One reason may be that a PAC is, by its very nature, a committee in which partisan divisions should be sidelined

Table 8.4. Answers to the Question: Are Practices and Procedures Important for the Success of a PAC?

Practice of the committee	Very important	Important	Not important	N
Keeping the transcripts of the meetings	87.9	9.1	3.0	33
Preparation before committee meetings	78.8	18.2	3.0	33
Procedures to determine whether the government has taken any step to implement the recommendations of the committee	75.0	18.7	6.3	32
Close working relationship between the members of the various political parties	75.0	15.6	9.4	32

Source: Stapenhurst et al. 2005.

(Rockman 1984). For a PAC to work, and work well, it needs to function in a bipartisan or nonpartisan manner.[7] If MPs serving in a PAC must behave in a nonpartisan fashion, the importance of their partisan affiliation decreases, and it may be argued that, therefore, the importance of proportional representation of the various parliamentary parties also decreases.

It is worth noting that not all practices are regarded as important for the good functioning or success of the PACs. As shown in table 8.5, almost one-third of respondents indicated that economic incentives provided to members serving on the PAC are not important for a PAC's success.

In addition, more than one-third of respondents considered the establishment of subcommittees (to help the PACs perform their tasks) as unimportant. Respondents tended to agree that the political and professional experience of the PAC's members have little impact on the functioning and success of the PAC. Experience in business or administration was considered as unimportant by more than one-third of respondents. Similarly, previous experience in other parliamentary committees was considered as unimportant by almost 42 percent of the respondents. Finally, broadcasting the PACs meetings was considered the least important practice.

Obstacles to the good functioning of the PAC. The survey data presented in this chapter provide useful indications as to which institutional factors facilitate the good functioning and success of PACs. However, oversight potential does not necessarily translate into effective oversight. Some conditions also may prevent the PACs from functioning effectively.

The first obstacle to the good functioning of a PAC is partisanship, that is, some PAC members operating with a partisan spirit and using the investigative powers of the PAC to promote their own political fortunes (along with those of their respective parties). This problem is not necessarily due to institutional factors; rather, it is a behavioral problem. However, insofar as institutions provide incentives for political behavior, it may be possible to find institutional solutions to these problems. For example, to minimize

Table 8.5. The Least Important Practices and Dynamics for the Success of the PAC

Practice of the committee	Not important	N
TV broadcasting of the meetings	52.0	19
PAC members with at least two years of experience in any parliamentary committee	41.7	24
PAC members with administrative or business experience	35.7	28
Creation of subcommittees	35.3	17
Extra money or additional incentives for members to participate in the meetings scheduled outside the normal legislative session	31.8	22

Source: Stapenhurst et al. 2005.

the risk of partisan conflicts within a PAC, many parliaments assign the PAC's chairmanship to a member of the opposition. In the Australian case, where the PAC's chair is a member of the majority party, the importance of reaching unanimous decisions on suggestions and recommendations is greatly emphasized. To minimize partisan tensions within the PAC, many parliaments stress that the PAC's mandate is not that of assessing the political value or content of the policies enacted by the government, but instead, assessing whether policies are implemented in an efficient and effective manner. However, none of these solutions by themselves are sufficient to ensure bipartisan cooperation.

Another approach could be to ask individuals who join a PAC to underwrite a (formal or informal) code of conduct in which they pledge their loyalty to the good, nonpartisan functioning of the committee. Their word would be considered binding, and the PAC's chairs could use this pledge to induce members to perform their functions and respect their institutional duties.

A second, and more serious, problem for the effectiveness of the PAC's activity is that governments may have little interest in (if not an open aversion to) parliamentary oversight of their activities. Governments may consider parliamentary oversight as an intrusion into their sphere of influence. Similarly, governments may think that PACs are not sufficiently informed or competent enough to formulate suggestions, criticisms, and observations. This is a serious problem because it indicates poor understanding of the functions that the executive and legislative branches perform in parliamentary systems.

In parliamentary systems, the government governs and the parliament ensures that the government is governing well. When governments try to avoid parliamentary controls, or when governments consider parliamentary controls merely as obstacles to effective government action, they misunderstand the principle of parliamentary oversight. This said, it is important to keep in mind that this imperfect understanding is not confined to newly established democracies, or democratizing regimes, that have a fairly limited experience in the functioning of democratic institutions. This problem also exists in well-established and consolidated democracies. The Australian case is, in this respect, rather emblematic. Between 1932 and 1951, the PAC of the Australian Parliament did not meet because the government, which could not see what benefits would come out of the meetings of this committee, decided that the committee's meetings were unnecessary. This important problem can be solved only by inducing governments to be respectful of PACs and their activities.

A final observation is in order at this point. The good functioning of PACs is seriously threatened in those countries in which corruption and other forms of improper behavior (such as conflict of interest) are tolerated. In fact, if there is no demand for good governance—efficient, effective, transparent, and honest governance—by civil society and others, the political class does not have any incentive to use the available parliamentary oversight mechanisms to check and possibly improve the quality of governance.

Conclusions

The purpose of this chapter was to discuss one of the oversight tools adopted in the countries of the Commonwealth—Public Account Committees. The chapter looked at what these committees are, how and by whom they are instituted, how they function, results they are able to achieve (and therefore how they influence the political system), and the conditions that promote the PACs good functioning and success.

The analysis was performed based on the assumption that parliamentary control of government activities can prevent governments from abusing their powers and thus contribute to the promotion of good governance. In other words, it was assumed that parliaments and parliamentarians are agents of good governance. In many countries, this is indeed the case. Parliaments and parliamentarians play an important role in the promotion of good governance.

However, while parliaments control governments (and their activities), they must be controlled in their turn. In the absence of such controls, how would one know whether parliamentary control of the executive is truly exercised for the good of the country and not for the good of a few individuals? This point should receive more attention in the future. In order to ensure the success of a PAC (as well as that of the other instruments of parliamentary oversight), the morality (or ethical standards) of a PAC and its members must be above suspicion. This is the first step toward establishing a viable system of good governance.

Notes

1. A *transition* is the period between the crisis or the collapse of a political regime and the establishment of a new one. A transition is a *democratic transition* when it ends with the establishment of a democratic regime. A democratic transition is also called democratization. A wave of democratization occurs when the number of countries in transition from a nondemocratic system to a democratic one outnumbers the countries moving in the opposite direction. See Huntington (1991, 15).

2. This evidence has led many political scientists to believe that the presidential form of government is less likely to sustain the survival of a democratic regime and that, therefore, parliamentarism is the best form of democratic government. Giovanni Sartori (1994a; 1994b, 107) noted, however, that the fact that presidentialism is not good for democracy does not make parliamentarism the "good alternative." Parliamentary governments may be unstable and inefficient, and their instability and ineffectiveness may lead to a regime breakdown. Historical examples of this include the Weimar Republic, the French Fourth Republic, and the Spanish Republic—on this see Sartori (1976) or Pelizzo and Babones (2005). A critical assessment of the criticisms of presidentialism can be found in Shugart and Carey (1992, 28–54).

3. Although they are generally called Public Accounts Committees, the PAC may sometimes take a different name. For example, in the Seychelles, they are called Committees of Finances and Public Accounts (Art. 104[1a] of the Constitution. In the Cook Islands they are called Public Expenditures Committees (Art.71[3] of the

Constitution). However, it is important to note that in spite of the fact that they may assume different names, the PACs all perform the same set of functions.

4. This is the case in Antigua and Barbuda (Art. 98 of the 1981 Constitution); Bangladesh (Art. 76 of the 1972 Constitution); the Cook Islands (Art. 71(3) of the Constitution); Kiribati (Art. 115 of the Constitution); the Seychelles (Art. 104(1a) of the Constitution); Saint Vincent (Art. 76 of the 1979 Constitution), Trinidad and Tobago (Art. 119 of the 1976 Constitution); and Zambia (Art. 103[5] of the Constitution). The PAC in Trinidad and Tobago is established by both Art. 119 of the Constitution and Art. 72 of the Standing Orders. PACs were instituted by standing orders in the following countries: by Art. 70(2) of the Standing Orders of the Parliament in Guyana; by Art. 89 of the Standing Orders in Tanzania; by Art. 122 (1) of the Standing Orders in Uganda; by art. 108(3) of the Standing Orders in Canada; by Art. 120E of the Standing Orders in Malta; by Art. 69 of the Standing Orders in Jamaica; and by Articles 308 and 309 of the Rules of Procedures in India; by act of Parliament in Australia (the Public Accounts and Audit Committee Act 1951) and the United Kingdom (the National Audit Act, 1861).

5. Of these 22 members, 15 are members of the Lok Sahba (lower house) and 7 are members of the Rajya Sahba (upper house).

6. Or by the president of the chamber, as in Tanzania.

7. To create this close working relationship between a PAC's members from the various parties, some parliaments request that all the PAC's decisions be unanimous. According to McGee (2002), 33 percent of the national and subnational parliaments in the Commonwealth request that the PAC's decisions be unanimous.

Bibliography

Huntington, S. 1991. *The Third Wave: Democratization in the Late Twentieth Century.* Norman, OK: University of Oklahoma Press.

Linz, J. J. 1994. "Presidential or Parliamentary: Does It Make a Difference?" In *The Failure of Presidential Democracy*, ed. J. J. Linz and A. Valenzuela, 3–91. Baltimore: Johns Hopkins University Press.

Mainwaring, S. 1993. "Presidentialism, Multipartism and Democracy. The Difficult Combination." *Comparative Political Studies* 26 (2): 198–228.

McGee, D. G. 2002. *The Overseers. Public Accounts Committees and Public Spending.* London: Commonwealth Parliamentary Association, with Pluto Press.

NDI (National Democratic Institute for International Affairs). 2000. "Strengthening Legislative Capacity in Legislative-Executive Relations." Legislative Research Series Paper No. 6, NDI, Washington, DC.

Pelizzo, R., and S. Babones. 2005. "The Political Economy of Polarized Pluralism." Paper presented at the Annual Meeting of the Southern Political Science Association, New Orleans, LA, January 5–9.

Pelizzo, R., and R. Stapenhurst. 2004a. "Legislatures and Oversight: A Note." *Quaderni di Scienza Politica* 11 (1): 175–88.

———. 2004b. "Tools for Legislative Oversight: An Empirical Investigation." Policy Research Working Paper No. 3388, World Bank, Washington, DC.

Pelizzo, R., R. Stapenhurst, and D. Olson, eds. 2004 (October). "Trends in Parliamentary Oversight." Working Paper Series on Contemporary Issues in Parliamentary Development, World Bank Institute, Washington, DC.

Przeworski, A., Michael Alvarez, José Antonio Cheibub, and Fernando Limongi. 1997. "What Makes Democracy Endure?" In *Consolidating the Third Wave of Democracies*, eds. L. Diamond, M. F. Plattner, Y. Chu, and H. M. Tien, 295–311. Baltimore: Johns Hopkins University Press.

Rockman, B. A. 1984. "Legislative-Executive Relations and Legislative Oversight." *Legislative Studies Quarterly* 9 (3): 387–440.

Sartori, G. 1976. *Parties and Party Systems*. New York: Cambridge University Press.

———. 1994a. *Comparative Constitutional Engineering*. New York: New York University.

———. 1994b. "Neither Presidentialism nor Parliamentarism." In *The Failure of Presidential Democracy*, eds. J. J. Linz and A. Valenzuela, 106–18. Baltimore: Johns Hopkins University Press.

Shugart, M. S., and J. M. Carey. 1992. *Presidents and Assemblies. Constitutional Design and Electoral Dynamics*. New York: Cambridge University Press.

Stapenhurst, R., and R. Pelizzo. 2002. "A Bigger Role for Legislatures in Poverty Reduction." *Finance & Development. A Quarterly Publication of the International Monetary Fund* 39 (4): 46–48.

Stapenhurst, Rick, Vinod Sahgal, William Woodley, and Riccardo Pelizzo. 2005. Scrutinizing Public Expenditures: Assessing the Performance of Public Accounts Committees." Policy Research Working Paper No. 3613, World Bank, Washington, DC.

Stepan, A., and C. Skach. 1994. "Presidentialism and Parliamentarism in Comparative Perspective." In *The Failure of Presidential Democracy*, eds. J. J. Linz and A. Valenzuela, 119–36. Baltimore: Johns Hopkins University Press.

CHAPTER 9

The Value of a Nonpartisan, Independent, Objective Analytic Unit to the Legislative Role in Budget Preparation

Barry Anderson

Legislatures in different countries play a wide variety of roles in the budget formulation process (Santiso 2005). Some are very actively involved, and some are not involved at all. Moreover, the role the legislature plays in many countries has changed over time and should continue to change in the future (Schick 2002). These changing roles call into question the sources of information that are or may be made available to help the legislature participate in the budget process. Legislatures require reliable, unbiased information to be able to participate constructively in formulating the budget. This chapter discusses the value of a nonpartisan, independent, objective analytic unit to the legislative role in the budget preparation process.

The chapter does not address whether there should be a role for the legislature in budget preparation. Some have argued that legislative activism may weaken fiscal discipline (von Hagen 1992) or increase the level of pork barrel spending, although legislatures certainly are not the only source of overspending (Wehner 2004). As fundamental as these issues are, this chapter addresses only the potential value of a nonpartisan objective unit, not the larger issue of what should be the balance of power between the executive and legislative in budget preparation.

The chapter begins by discussing the potential value to the legislature of having a nonpartisan, independent, objective analytic unit. It lists and discusses each of the core functions that such a unit can perform; describes other possible functions of the unit; and describes the characteristics required to make the unit nonpartisan, objective, and independent, including other characteristics that can enhance the effectiveness of the unit. The results of a survey that lists the number of countries with specialized legislative research organizations is followed by a detailed discussion of three legislative research organizations within the United States.

Potential Value

In its most basic terms, an independent analytic budget unit can provide information to put the legislature on a more equal footing with the executive branch. This information is critical if a legislature is to play a real role in budget formulation. However, as important as this information is, such a unit can do much more than just eliminate the executive's monopoly on budget information. The following are benefits of an independent analytic budget unit:

- *Simplifies complexity.* Budget information is frequently not made available by the executive's budget office, but even when it is, it may be so complex that the legislature has difficulty understanding it. An independent unit must have the expertise to be able to make complex budget information understandable to the legislature, as well as to the media, academia, and the public.

- *Promotes transparency.* Because of the knowledge and expertise found in an independent budget unit, budgetary legerdemain can be discouraged and transparency promoted.

- *Enhances credibility.* By encouraging simplification and transparency, an independent unit also has the effect of making all budget forecasts—even those of the partisan executive—more credible.

- *Promotes accountability.* The accountability of the estimates used in the budget process can be enhanced by an independent budget unit because of the scrutiny such a unit provides to the executive's budget office.

- *Improves the budget process.* The combination of a more simple, transparent, credible, and accountable budget can promote a budget process that is more straightforward and easier to understand and follow.

- *Serves both the majority and minority.* A legislative budget unit—if it is truly nonpartisan and independent—should provide information to both the majority and all minority parties of the legislature.

- *Provides rapid responses.* As a unit that is part of the legislature, an independent budget unit can provide much more rapid responses to budget inquiries from the legislature than an executive budget unit.

The additional values of an independent legislative budget unit mean that it is much more than just an instrument to assist the legislature in the budget process, or one to help check the executive's budget power. It also serves the society at large and actually can help improve the whole budget process. However, the value of an independent unit can change over time. At first, the information produced by the unit may be more valuable to the legislature as whole, as a means to balance the executive's budget power. But as the unit ages and as the executive adjusts to the presence of the independent unit, the information it produces may be of more value to minority parties in the legislature in their relationship to the majority party.

Core Functions

An independent analytic budget unit can perform many possible functions, but to best assist the legislature in the budget preparation process, it should perform at the very least the following four core functions.

- *Economic forecasts.* All budgetary analyses begin with an economic forecast. The first core function of the unit is to perform an independent economic forecast. Although the unit's forecasts need to be objective, they should take into account the forecasts of others, such as private forecasters, central bankers (if available), and panels of experts specifically organized to assist the unit's forecasters. The forecasts should be based on laws in place at the time; that is, they should not try to anticipate future legislation. They also should not try to take into account the economic consequences, if any, of policy proposals. The assumptions used for interest rates and commodity prices should not be targets but should be based on the best information available. It is also better for a unit's forecast to be a little conservative, because it is much easier politically to reduce deficits and debt in an economy that is better than forecasted than it is to try to find last-minute spending cuts or increase taxes to meet a revised deficit target that results from a worse-than-anticipated forecast.

- *Baseline estimates.* The forecasts of spending and revenues should be *projections*, not *predictions*. That is, they should be based on laws that are currently in place, not on policy proposals. They should not try to judge the legislative intent of laws, but they should assume, for example, that the expiration dates built into legislation will actually occur, and that the spend-out rates of slow-spending capital projects are based on the best technical information available, not on biased political opinions.

- *Analysis of the executive's budget proposals.* The third core function of an independent unit is to perform a budgetary assessment of the executive's proposed budget. Such an assessment should not be a programmatic evaluation, which is basically a time-consuming political exercise, but rather a technical review of the budgetary estimates contained in the executive's budget. Such a review can actually enhance the credibility of the executive's budget, if the difference between the two estimates is not great and, for the government's forecasts as a whole, if the difference between the assessment and the actual outcome is not great.

- *Medium-term analysis.* All of the core functions mentioned above should be performed over at least the medium term. This alerts the executive and the public to the out-year consequences of current and proposed policy actions. It is particularly important to do a medium-term analysis to take into account various fiscal risks, such as those inherent in loan guarantee programs, commitments to provide pensions, public-private partnership initiatives, and other programs that contain contingent liabilities. A medium-term analysis also provides the basis for a long-term analysis, the importance of which grows as societies age and as the impact of programs that involve intergenerational transfers expands.

Other functions that the independent unit could perform include the following:

- *Analysis of proposals.* Hundreds, perhaps even thousands, of policy proposals can be made each year by members of the legislature, and the executive often makes many policy proposals in addition to those contained in the budget. An independent unit can provide valuable assistance to the legislature by estimating the costs of these proposals. But because it can be very time consuming to estimate the budgetary impact of every proposal, it may be appropriate for the legislature and the analytic unit to agree on a rule—such as estimating the costs of only the proposals with the largest budgetary impact or only those proposals approved by a full committee or significant subcommittee—that limits the number of proposals costed by the unit.

- *Options for spending cuts.* Legislatures can often benefit from having available a list of options for spending cuts prepared by an independent unit. The options should be based on program effectiveness and efficiency, not on political concerns. The unit should only list the options; it should not make recommendations for any option, because to do so could raise questions about its independence. As valuable as such a list of options can be to empower the legislature, this function can also be time consuming, although its staffing impact can be mitigated if the listing of options is produced only at the beginning of a new legislative session.

- *Analysis of mandates.* Legislation can affect the economy in more ways than just spending and taxing decisions; through regulations, or mandates, legislation can require actions on the part of corporations, individuals, or subnational governments. An independent unit can review the mandates and provide valuable information to the legislature by estimating the economic impact of the mandates, but again, this can be a time-consuming task, depending on how many mandates the unit reviews and how complex they are.

- *Economic analyses.* The expertise found in an independent budget unit can also be used to perform more extensive economic analyses. These analyses can contribute to the legislature's understanding of the near-term and long-term budgetary consequences of related policy proposals and also assist the unit's staff in preparing the core estimates of budget proposals.

- *Tax analyses.* In addition to the types of budgetary and economic analyses mentioned above, a unit can also serve the legislature by performing various types of analyses of tax policies, such as estimating the impacts of proposed or enacted tax changes on economic growth, or measuring the distributional impacts of various types of tax proposals. Again, these analyses can be time consuming, and they can require specialized staff whose skills are not easily transferred to analyses of spending proposals.

- *Long-term analysis.* As mentioned above, the value of long-term analyses—that is, analysis of potential budgetary trends for as many as 75 years—becomes more valuable to legislatures because of the aging of the populations in many countries, and because so many countries have programs that transfer resources (and costs) from one generation to another.

- *Policy briefs.* The time demands placed on policy makers in both the executive branch and the legislature, and the complexity of budgets, have created a demand for short, straightforward descriptions of complicated budget proposals and concepts. Such descriptions, or policy briefs, can be of real value not only to busy members of the legislature, but also to the media and the public.

As valuable as each of these other functions can be to the legislature, the size of the staff required to perform them usually limits the number that can be performed. Examples of the staff required to perform various functions in three independent legislative budget agencies in the United States are presented in tables 9.1 and 9.2.

Table 9.1. Distribution of U.S. Congressional Budget Office Staff

Function	Core	Other	Total
Executive direction	5	5	10
Macroeconomic analysis	5	15	20
Tax analysis	5	15	20
Budget analysis			80
Baseline	20		
Analysis of proposals		45	
Mandates		15	
Program divisions		75	75
Technical and administrative	10	20	30
Total	45	190	235

Source: Author's estimates based on U.S. Congressional Budget Office data.

Table 9.2. Staffing by Core Function

Core Function	CBO	IBO	LAO
Executive direction	5	6	3
Macroeconomic and tax analysis	10	4	5
Budget analysis	20	12	36
Technical and administrative	10	5	9
Total	45	27	53

Source: Author's estimates based on New York City's Independent Budget Office (http://www.ibo.nyc.ny.us) and California's Legislative Analyst's Office (http://www.lao.ca.gov).

Fundamental Characteristics

Establishing and maintaining a nonpartisan analytic unit that provides independent, objective budgetary information to the legislature is not easy. Certain fundamental characteristics of the unit must be present if the unit is to be successful. Foremost of these is the nonpartisan nature of the unit. Note that *nonpartisan* is much different from *bipartisan*: the former connotes lack of a political affiliation; the latter connotes affiliation with both (or all) political parties. A unit that is bipartisan would attempt to present its analysis from the perspective of both (or all) political parties, whereas a unit that is nonpartisan would not present its analysis from a political perspective at all. Clearly a nonpartisan unit would be superior in presenting objective information. The director of such a nonpartisan unit may be a member of a political party, but this does not make the unit itself partisan as long as the director is more of a technician than a politician; he or she operates the agency in a nonpartisan manner; and the staff is composed entirely of technicians.

Operation in a nonpartisan manner would require, among other things, that the same information be provided to the majority and minority parties. Other fundamental characteristics of a nonpartisan analytic unit include the following:

- Making the outputs of the unit, and the methods by which those outputs are prepared, transparent (especially reports that are critical of proposed policies) and understandable.

- Placing the core functions of the unit in law so they can't be easily changed to suit political purposes, avoiding recommendations.

- Briefing relevant members of the legislature immediately before a report is issued, especially if the report contains negative information with regard to a proposal.

- Principally serving committees or subcommittees rather than individual members.

- Being willing to meet with lobbyists or other proponents—as well as opponents—of policy proposals, keeping in mind that a fair, balanced process—and the *appearance* of a fair, balanced process—is always important.

- Locating the unit's offices separate from the legislature, but always answering requests in a responsive and timely manner.

- Avoiding the limelight.

Examples of Independent Budget Units

In 2007, the Organisation for Economic Co-operation and Development (OECD) conducted a survey of 30 OECD and 8 non-OECD countries on budget practices and procedures (OECD 2007). One of the questions in the survey was: "Is there a specialized budget research office/unit attached to the legislature to conduct analyses of the budget?" Of the 38 countries, 16 responded that they have either a specialized unit or some other kind of capacity to conduct such analyses.

The oldest and biggest of these specialized budget research offices is the U.S. Congressional Budget Office (CBO). CBO was created primarily as a tool to check the growing power of the president.[1] In the views of many in the U.S. Congress in the early 1970s, President Nixon had abused the powers of impoundment (the withholding from obligation the funds that had been appropriated by the Congress) that all presidents before him had used. In addition, he had replaced the more technical Bureau of the Budget with a more powerful and less open Office of Management and Budget (OMB). Budgets were growing ever more complex, with off-budget financing schemes, and every year budgets contained more programs that affected the long term as much as, if not more than, the short term. Moreover, for the first time in its history, the United States had consistent peacetime deficits in a period of economic expansion.

For these and other reasons Congress, which did not have a budget process that considered the fiscal situation in aggregate, passed an extensive budget law in 1974. President Nixon signed the new budget law just before he resigned. This law took the powers of impoundment away from the president, created budget committees in the Senate and the House that have powers to consider and control aggregate tax and spending levels, and authorized a new Congressional Budget Office to provide the new budget committees with roughly the same information that OMB provides to the president. Although the director of CBO is a political appointee selected by the Speaker of the House and the president pro tempore of the Senate (for a four-year term, which may be repeated), the law authorizing CBO explicitly states that all of the employees of CBO are to be selected without respect to political affiliation.

The law that created CBO provided only general guidance as to what its functions should be. Although CBO now performs all of the functions listed above, it was not clear at its inception exactly what work it would do and what work the staff of the newly created budget committees would do. In fact, a former CBO director (Reischauer, in Kates 1989) who was present at CBO's creation said that one view was to severely limit CBO's role:

> What the House wanted [when CBO was created] was basically a manhole in which Congress would have a bill or something and it would lift up the manhole cover and put the bill down it, and 20 minutes later a piece of paper would be handed up, with the cost estimate, the answer, on it. No visibility, [just] some kind of mechanism down below the ground level doing this ... non controversial [work], the way the sewer system [does].

CBO was able to expand its functions far beyond what was stated in this quote, in large part because of the efforts it made from its inception to explicitly structure itself as a nonpartisan, independent, objective analytic agency. CBO has about 235 staff to do all these functions, but it is relevant to review the distribution of CBO staff by core and other functions (see table 9.1), as discussed above, and then compare this staffing with that of two other agencies (see table 9.2) that provide information for core functions: the State of California's the Legislative Analyst's Office (LAO) and the City of New York's Independent Budget Office (IBO).[2] Core functions at CBO and LAO require about 50 staff each. However, the size and complexity of the U.S. government and California budgets are so much greater than the budgets of most other countries' that the approximately 27 staff found in New York City's IBO may offer a more appropriate comparison.

Conclusions

If legislatures are to play a substantive role in the budget formulation process, they will be well served by an independent source of budget information. Examples in the Unites States and in a number of other countries establish that a nonpartisan, independent, objective analytic unit can provide budget information without polarizing the relations between the executive and the legislature. However, a requirement for the successful establishment of such a unit is the existence of, or the desire for, some kind of balance in the political environment—a balance between political factions or a balance between the executive and the legislature. Once created, such a unit must operate in a credible and impartial manner if its value is to be sustained.

Notes

The author is currently the director of the Budgeting and Public Expenditures Division of the Organisation for Economic Co-operation and Development (OECD) in Paris. He previously served as the acting and deputy director of the U.S. Congressional Budget Office, as the senior career civil servant of the U.S. Office of Management and Budget, and as a budgetary adviser with the International Monetary Fund (IMF). The views expressed are the author's and do not necessarily represent those of the OECD. An earlier version of the chapter was presented at the Southern Political Science Association conference, January 7, 2005.

1. Much of the history of CBO is drawn from Dwayne Day's 2003 "Gourmet Chefs and Short Order Cooks: A Policy History of the Congressional Budget Office, 1975–2001."

2. See http://www.lao.ca.gov for information on California's Legislative Analyst's Office and http://www.ibo.nyc.ny.us for information on New York City's Independent Budget Office.

Bibliography

Day, Dwayne. 2003. "Gourmet Chefs and Short Order Cooks: A Policy History of the Congressional Budget Office, 1975–2001." Unpublished manuscript.
OECD. 2007. "OECD Budget Practices and Procedures Database." http://webnet4.oecd.org/budgeting/Budgeting.aspx.

Reischauer, Robert, quoted in Kates, Nancy D. 1989. "Starting from Scratch: Alice Rivlin and the Congressional Budget Office (A)." Case Program C16-88-872.0, John F. Kennedy School of Government, Harvard University, Cambridge, MA.

Santiso, Carlos. 2005. "Budget Institutions and Fiscal Responsibility: Parliaments and the Political Economy of the Budget Process." Chapter prepared for the 17th Regional Seminar on Fiscal Policy, United Nations Economic Commission for Latin America and the Caribbean, Santiago, Chile, January 24–27.

Schick, Allen. 2002. "Can National Legislatures Regain an Effective Voice in Budget Policy?" *OECD Journal on Budgeting* 1 (3): 33. page 33.

von Hagen, J. 1992. "Budgeting Procedures and Fiscal Performance in the European Communities." Economic Paper No. 96, Commission of the European Communities Directorate-General for Economic and Financial Affairs, Brussels, Belgium.

Wehner, Joachim. 2004. *Back from the Sidelines? Redefining the Contribution of Legislatures to the Budget Cycle.* World Bank Institute, Washington, DC.

CHAPTER 10

Legislative Budget Offices: International Experience

John K. Johnson and Rick Stapenhurst

As chapter 9 noted, independent, objective, nonpartisan legislative budget offices are increasingly being established for legislatures around the world. What do these offices do, and why are their numbers increasing? This chapter seeks to address these questions by examining legislative budget offices in four regions. It suggests reasons for the growing (albeit still small) number of such units and describes their functions, their characteristics, and how they can contribute to the budget process.

The focus of the chapter is on independent, nonpartisan budget offices serving legislatures. It does not address legislative research organizations that provide budget analysis as part of their services, such as the Bureau of Research of the Polish Sejm. Nor does it describe professional budget capabilities housed within finance committees, such as the three-person unit in the Guatemalan Congress's finance committee, which reports on government income and spending. Rather, this chapter focuses on the growing number of nonpartisan offices dedicated exclusively to assisting legislatures in their work with budgets.

Several chapters in this volume consider the role that legislatures are playing in national budget processes across the globe; they note that these roles vary greatly from country to country. Several factors influence these differing roles, among them are (1) the type of political system (that is, presidential, legislative, or hybrid); (2) the type of electoral system through which representatives are elected (that is, plurality-majority, proportional, and semi-proportional); (3) the legislature's formal powers (in this case, the extent of its powers to amend the executive budget); (4) the combination of the political environment within which the legislature functions, and the political will of legislators to exert parliament's powers; and (5) the technical capacity of the parliament.[1]

Philip Norton (2003) provided a simple classification of legislative roles in the budget process, identifying three types of legislatures: budget-approving, budget-influencing, and budget-making. Budget-approving legislatures lack the authority or capacity (or both) to amend the budget proposed by the executive, and they approve whatever budget the executive presents to them. Budget-influencing legislatures have the capacity to amend or reject the executive's budget proposal but do not have sufficient capacity to formulate a budget of their own. Finally, what Norton referred to as a budget-making legislature has both the legal authority and the technical capacity to amend or reject the executive's budget proposal and to substitute a budget of its own.

Because budget-approving legislatures simply "rubber-stamp" budgets submitted by the executive, they have little need for independent offices to assist them in analyzing those budgets, challenging executive assumptions, or making changes to draft budgets. By contrast, several budget-making and budget-influencing legislatures have established independent, nonpartisan budget units in the past half century or so. The first was California's Legislative Analyst's Office, established in 1941. It was followed about three decades later, in 1974, by the better-known U.S. Congressional Budget Office (CBO). The Congress of the Philippines created its independent budget office—the Congressional Planning and Budget Department (CPBD)—in 1990. The rate at which legislative budget offices are being established has increased over the past decade. Mexico's Chamber of Deputies' Center for Public Finance Studies (*Centro de Estudios de las Finanzas Publicas*—CEFP) began operation in 1999. The Uganda Legislative Budget Office (PBO) was established through an act of Parliament in 2001. Two years later, the National Assembly of the Republic of Korea passed legislation creating its own National Assembly Budget Office (NABO). Finally, both Nigeria and Kenya appear poised to establish legislative budget offices.

Examples of Specialized Legislative Budget Offices

Legislative Analyst's Office: California

Established in 1941, the California Legislative Analyst's Office (LAO) predates the Congressional Budget Office by more than three decades. According to Elizabeth Hill, California's current legislative analyst (that is, director of the LAO), the California legislature had been concerned that the balance of budget power had been shifting to the executive since the early 1930s. Rather than rely exclusively on the executive for budget information, the legislature sought an independent source of budget information and analysis, as well as professional assistance to help it conduct oversight and ensure that programs were being implemented effectively. It also sought to reduce the growing costs of state government and make government more efficient and more economical. In 1941, the state senate and the assembly passed legislation to establish their own budget office, but Governor Culbert Olsen vetoed the bill on the recommendation of his fiscal office. Undeterred, the legislature effectively overruled the governor by establishing the office through a joint rule of the senate and the assembly that same year.[2] The legislature later established the LAO by statute.

Duties. The LAO reviews and analyzes both the finances and the operations of the California state government. Unlike the U.S. Congressional Budget Office, the LAO performs specific oversight functions on behalf of the legislature, ensuring that legislative policy is implemented effectively and cost-effectively. The specific functions of the LAO include the following:

- Analyzing and publishing a detailed review of the governor's budget bill (*Analysis of the Budget Bill*). The analysis includes department reviews as well as recommendations for legislative action.

- Publishing *Perspectives and Issues*, which gives an overview of the state's fiscal status and identifies major policy issues.

- Assisting the Budget Committee throughout the budget process.

- Reviewing administration requests to make changes to the budget after it is enacted, and presenting findings to the Budget Committees.

- Publishing special reports on the state budget and on topics of interest to the legislature.

- Conducting fiscal analyses of initiatives and ballot measures. California is one of the states that allow citizens to petition the government to place special initiatives (such as tax cuts) on statewide ballots. The LAO prepares fiscal analyses of all such measures.

- Conducting legislative oversight, including evaluations of programs or agencies, and issuing recommendations to the legislature.

- Developing policy alternatives. The LAO offers the legislature options on public policy issues and is directed by statute to make recommendations on policy matters.[3]

LAO services are available to all committees and members of the legislature.

Operations and staffing. The Joint Legislative Budget Committee consists of 16 members (eight from each house) and oversees the LAO's operation. By tradition, a senator chairs the committee and a member of the assembly serves as the vice chair. Funding comes equally from each house. The legislative analyst serves at the pleasure of the Joint Legislative Budget Committee, and analysts tend to stay in their position for many years. The current legislative analyst, for example, has served for nearly 30 years.

With a staff of 56 (about 43 professional and 13 administrative staff), the LAO is divided into subject area sections (such as health, criminal justice, and social services), which are headed by directors who train staff and edit their work for content. Professional staff members generally have master's degrees in fields such as public policy, economics, public administration, and business and have strong analytical and quantitative backgrounds. Each professional staff person is responsible for, and becomes expert in, a specific portion of the state budget. The LAO 1999 budget was $4.6 million.

Congressional Budget Office (CBO): United States

The U.S. Congressional Budget Office (CBO) was established as part of the Congressional Budget and Impoundment Control Act of 1974. The Budget and Accounting Act of 1921 had centralized the budget process under the authority of the executive branch, and over the next half century the president had acquired greater and greater influence over the budget by virtue of growing control over budgetary and economic information.[4] Congress, by contrast, had not developed a similar capacity and instead continued to work through a fragmented web of committees, relying on the executive as its principal source of budgetary and economic information. The 1974 act created a new, more coherent congressional budget process, and House and Senate budget committees to oversee this new process. The act also created the Congressional Budget Office to provide committees with independent budgetary and economic information.

Duties. Each year CBO issues three major reports designed to assist the budget committees and to aid Congress in its work on the budget. These include the following:

- An annual report on the economic and budget outlook for the United States, estimating spending and revenue over the next 10 years.

- A report analyzing the president's budget. CBO generally issues this independent reestimate of the proposed budget within a month of the release of the president's budget proposal in early February.

- A report presenting various options for the budget. These options include spending cuts and increases, tax cuts and increases, and suggested implications of broad policy choices.

In addition to these yearly reports, CBO analyzes the spending and revenue effects of legislative proposals and estimates the costs of pending legislation. As part of the Unfunded Mandates Reform Act of 1995, CBO is also responsible for identifying the costs related to legislation containing federal mandates on state, local, and tribal governments, as well as on the private sector.

Finally, CBO produces reports and studies analyzing specific policy and program issues related to the budget. These are in-depth studies designed to inform the congressional budget process and may cover longer-term issues that are not dealt with in the annual budget process. In-depth studies have included reports on the long-term budgetary pressures likely to develop with the aging of the U.S. baby-boom generation (those born between 1946 and 1964), a spending issue far beyond the budget horizon lawmakers generally consider. The statute creating CBO requires agencies of the executive branch to provide CBO with the information it needs to perform its duties and functions.

Operations and staffing. CBO carries out its responsibilities with a staff of about 230 and a 2005 appropriation of just under $35 million.[5] The director of CBO is appointed jointly by the Speaker of the House of Representatives and the Senate president based on the recommendations of the budget committees of each house. They serve a four-year term, and there is no limit to the number of times they can be reappointed.

CBO's work is carried out through seven divisions; two of those are the division of tax analysis and the division of budget analysis. About 70 percent of CBO's professional staff hold degrees in economics and public policy, and all are officially employees of the House of Representatives.[6]

Each year CBO averages about 2,000 formal or informal cost estimates of pending legislative proposals before the Congress, 70–80 major reports, and dozens of testimonies for congressional committees. CBO makes its findings, methods of analysis, and assumptions widely available through the Internet (Anderson 2006).

Congressional Planning and Budget Department (CPBD): Philippines[7]

The Philippine Congress created its independent budget office in 1990 under the secretariat of the House of Representatives and modeled it after the U.S. CBO.

Duties. The CPBD has three major functions: (1) it assists the House of Representatives in formulating its agenda; (2) it provides House leaders and members with technical information, analyses, and recommendations on important social and economic policy issues; and (3) it conducts analyses on the impact of legislation and also conducts research and in-depth studies on identified policy issues.

The CPBD issues publications designed to inform House members of the implications of government policies and legislation. Among these are policy advisories (updates on emerging policy issues), an annual macroanalysis of the budget, and an analysis of the medium-term economic development plan. The CPBD gathers information to assist the House in conducting oversight, and gives technical assistance to the Speaker and the Legislative Development Advisory Committee and other interagency committees. Finally, the CPBD publishes occasional papers and a "Facts and Figures" publication signaling trends and providing statistics on socioeconomic conditions in the Philippines. Unlike the LAO and CBO, the Philippines' CPBD serves only one house of the nation's two-house legislature.

Organization and staffing. The CPBD is headed by a director general who is assisted by an executive director. Three main divisions, each headed by a service director, report to the director general and the executive director.

The Congressional Economic Planning Service conducts policy research on macroeconomic policy, competitiveness, and reform measures in infrastructure, industrial development, trade, and investments. Congressional Budget Services conducts research and analysis on fiscal measures, including the macroeconomic implications of government taxing and spending. Special Project Services focuses on policy analysis and research regarding the labor and employment, education, agriculture, and environment committees of the House of Representatives. The CPBD also has a division for support services. In addition to their in-house staff, the CPBD makes regular use of consultants. Professional staff members generally hold advanced degrees in economics, finance, and public administration.

Center for Public Finance Studies (Centro de Estudios de las Finanzas Públicas—CEFP): Mexico[8]

After functioning as a rubber-stamp legislature during the many decades of the Institutional Revolutionary Party (PRI) rule, Mexico's Congress became a more independent, assertive institution as the PRI's power waned in the late 1990s.[9] The Center for Public Finance Studies, which the House of Deputies established in 1998, has helped the House play a more effective role in the budget process.

Duties. Similar to the other units examined, the CEFP is a technical, nonpartisan office that is staffed by specialists in public finance. Like the CPBD in the Philippines, it serves the House but not the Senate. It provides budget-related assistance to committees, groups within Congress, and individual members of the House. It has the following specific functions:

- Analyze the executive's trimester reports on the national economic situation, public finance, and public debt.

- Analyze the executive's annual report on the implementation of the National Development Plan, and provide relevant information to subject area committees.

- Analyze the budget initiatives, tax laws, fiscal laws, and finance information that the executive presents to the House.

In addition, the CEFP provides budget information to committees, legislative groups, and individual deputies as needed, and maintains a library of copies of reports on finance and public debt.

Organization and staffing. A 22-member committee comprising members of the different political parties in the House of Deputies oversees the CEFP. The committee makes its decisions by consensus and, when necessary, by majority vote. The CEFP's director is selected by the whole House through an open competitive application process. He or she serves a five-year term, which can be renewed once. Staff members are also selected through an open, competitive process, and not according to political affiliation. The CEFP has four divisions: Macroeconomic and Sectoral Studies, Treasury (or budgetary) Studies, Public Budget and Expenditure Studies, and Technology and Information Systems. The center's Web site lists a total professional staff of 27.

Mexico's more independent Congress has made additional changes to strengthen its role in the budget process since establishing the CEFP in the late 1990s. Amendments to the Mexican constitution, which became effective in 2005, require the executive to present its budget to Congress more than two months earlier than before, giving Congress more time to consider and make amendments to the draft budget. Amendments also require that the national budget be approved a month earlier (November 15 rather than December 15; Art. 74), giving state and local governments more time to plan for the upcoming January 1 fiscal year.

Legislative Budget Office (PBO): Uganda

Of all the cases under consideration, Uganda's political system was perhaps the most unique at the time its legislative budget office was established (Kiraso 2006). In an effort to cool Uganda's heated politics, President Yoweri Museveni instituted a no-party political system in 1986, prohibiting political parties from fielding candidates for office. A constitutional referendum ended this practice in 2005. Hon. Beatrice Kiraso, primary author of the private member's bill establishing Uganda's PBO, believes that Uganda's no-party system actually helped the National Assembly in establishing its budget office. "There was no government or opposition side in Parliament, there was not majority or minority. It was easier for Members of Parliament to support a position favorable to Parliament against the Executive if it benefited or strengthened Parliament as an institution. Government was in a weaker position to whip members to its side" (Kiraso 2006, 4).

Uganda's Legislative Budget Office was established by an act of Parliament in 2001. Like the U.S. Congressional Budget and Impoundment Control Act of 1974, the act not only created a budget office but also created a centralized budget committee and made major changes in the role of Parliament in the budget process.

Duties. Uganda's PBO issues the following reports each year: local revenue analysis, foreign inflows analysis, expenditure reports, and other reports. For local revenue analysis, the PBO analyzes the monthly reports that the Uganda Revenue Authority submits to the Budget Committee and the PBO, identifying whether revenue collections were on target, reasons for shortfalls (if any), and whether revenue targets should be adjusted. Using information from these reports, the PBO has proposed to Parliament ways to widen the tax base and suggested possible methods to reduce taxes that would increase consumption.

The 2001 Budget Act requires the president to present information to the Parliament on state indebtedness. Uganda's PBO analyzes indebtedness reports, in the form of foreign inflows analysis, on behalf of the Budget Committee and identifies issues for committee attention. The Budget Act also requires ministers to submit a yearly policy statement to Parliament showing the funds appropriated for the ministry, funds released, and what they were used for. In addition to these expenditure reports, the PBO also produces quarterly budget performance reports, enabling Parliament to follow the general budget performance of different sectors during the year.

Other reports include a yearly economic indicator report, which the PBO provides to Parliament, as well as a report recording all of Parliament's recommendations to the government, whether government was expected to respond, whether or not it complied, and reasons for noncompliance.

The PBO also assists Parliament in the revised budget process. The Budget Act expanded Parliament's role in the budget process; technical expertise provided by the PBO helps the National Assembly fulfill this new role. The new budget process gives Parliament an opportunity to review, comment on, and propose amendments to a draft executive budget, and gives the executive branch time to respond by amending the draft budget and negotiating changes with the National Assembly, all before the budget is officially released.

Previously, the National Assembly's first glimpse of government's budget figures was when the budget was read on about June 15, just before the new fiscal year, which begins July 1. Under the new system, the president presents a draft revenue and expenditure framework for the next financial year to the National Assembly by April 1, a full three months before the fiscal year begins. Parliament's sessional committees, with the assistance of PBO economists, consider the indicative allocations and prepare reports to the Budget Committee, which may include recommended reallocations within sectoral budget ceilings.

The Budget Committee, on which the chairs of the 10 sessional committees sit, considers all proposals, and may propose reallocations both within and across sectors. The PBO helps the committee prepare a comprehensive budget report to present to the Speaker, who must forward it to the president by May 15. During the executive-legislative discussions over the remaining month leading up to the formal budget presentation, the executive generally makes a number of budget changes in response to Parliament.

Organization and staffing. The PBO is headed by a director. There are positions for about 27 experts, but at times vacancies have not been filled because of budget constraints. Professional staff members are economists with expertise in macroeconomics, data analysis, fiscal policy, and tax policy. Initially they were drawn primarily from the Ministry of Finance, the Uganda Revenue Authority, the central bank, and the Uganda Bureau of Statistics.

According to Hon. Beatrice Kiraso, author of the Uganda Budget Act, the act, along with the technical assistance provided through the PBO, has strengthened Parliament's role in the budget process in several ways. First, government now provides Parliament with three-year revenue and expenditure projections. The Budget Committee, with expert assistance of the PBO, reports to Parliament on any inconsistencies in these projections and on revenue and expenditure provisions for the following three years. Second,

policy statements from ministries are now reported on time—by June 30—
allowing sessional committees to adequately scrutinize them. The PBO, in
partnership with the Ministry of Finance, standardized the policy statement
format. With assistance from PBO economists, committees review the policy
statements. The statements must include value-for-money information, not
just spending data, and report on the extent to which sectoral targets were
achieved. Third, the 2001 Budget Act requires that every bill introduced in
Parliament be accompanied by a certificate of financial implications. The PBO
verifies the accuracy of these certificates and advises on the implications for
the budget for that financial year. The National Assembly has, in fact, made the
government delay several initiatives after the PBO determined that they were
not included in the current year's budget. Fourth, the Budget Act requires that
government keep supplementary expenditures to within 3 percent of what
is budgeted. The PBO works closely with the ministries to ensure that these
limits are adhered to. Finally, the PBO drafts an easy-to-understand version of
the president's report on state indebtedness.

National Assembly Budget Office (NABO): Republic of Korea[10]

The Republic of Korea's National Assembly Budget Office (NABO) was created in 2003 through an act of the National Assembly. NABO has a twofold
purpose—one, to encourage greater discipline in public spending, and two,
to allow the legislature to play a larger role in determining how the state
obtains its revenue and how that revenue is spent. Those who drafted the act
considered expanding the duties of the Budget Policy Bureau in the National
Assembly secretariat but concluded that NABO budget assistance was unique
and that it merited establishing a separate agency within the Assembly.

Duties. NABO provides nonpartisan, objective information and analysis to
committees and members of the National Assembly. It conducts research and
analysis on the budget and on the performance of the government's fiscal
operations, estimates the cost of bills proposed in the legislature, analyzes and
evaluates government programs and medium- to long-term fiscal needs (audit
function), and conducts research and analysis at the request of legislative committees or members of the National Assembly.

Organization and staffing. The Speaker, with the approval of the House
Steering Committee, appoints the chief of NABO. With a total of 92 full-time
staff positions (approximately 70 professional and 20 administrative), NABO
is the second largest budget office considered in this chapter. Professional staff
members hold advanced degrees in accounting, economics, public policy, law,
and related fields. The NABO chief appoints all NABO staff. As is true with
the other budget offices examined, staff members are selected solely on the
basis of professional competence (not political affiliation). NABO's 2006 budget was approximately US$12 million.

Budget offices are only as good as the information government provides
them, and if government ministries are unwilling to give them financial

information, their utility is hampered. In Korea's case, the legislation establishing the office requires executive agencies to provide NABO with the information it needs to carry out its functions. This has proved very useful in convincing reluctant agencies to provide necessary data. Like the U.S. CBO, NABO's analyses and work products are available to all members of the Assembly, and also to the public via the Internet. Also similar to the CBO, NABO shares its methodologies and assumptions freely. Each year NABO averages 80 to 90 formal cost estimates of pending legislative proposals before the Assembly and issues 30 to 40 major reports and other publications.

Proposed Budget Offices: Nigeria and Kenya

Two National Assembly budget offices appear to be so close to being established that it is useful to mention them here. Both are in Africa.

National Assembly Budget and Research Office (NABRO): Nigeria. The National Assembly of Nigeria is moving toward establishing an independent, nonpartisan National Assembly budget office to help ensure, among other functions, that the budget enacted is properly implemented (Nzekwu 2006). The bill establishing NABRO was passed by the Senate in May 2007, in the same version as that of the House of Representatives so that there would not be a need for harmonization by conference committee. However, in June 2007 the president refused to sign the NABRO bill into law and sent it back to the National Assembly for revisions.

The bill sought to clarify roles and responsibilities of the legislative and executive branches of government and required that government present its budget to the National Assembly at least three months prior to the end of the budget year, giving the Assembly ample time to consider and to pass the appropriations bill before the new year. The Assembly has a budget line and earmarked funds to establish the budget office.

According to the original agreement worked out in the National Assembly, the office will perform the following tasks:

- Review the budget submission of the executive to ensure that it is realistic and objectively defensible.

- Provide technical assistance and briefings to relevant committees to help them understand and appraise the proposed budget.

- Review, monitor, and evaluate the government's budget performance of the previous year.

- Forecast economic trends and draft budget impact briefs and statements.

- Support committee oversight functions.

Legislative office of fiscal analysis: Kenya.[11] A private member's bill by the Hon. Oloo Aringo, author of Kenya's "Independence of Parliament" Act (1999), was introduced in Kenya's National Assembly in March 2006. The bill, which is quite similar to Uganda's Budget Act (2001), now has the support of the government and is expected to pass (Kathuri 2006). Currently, however, it has remained in the third reading. Though the legislation has yet to be enacted, the Kenyan Parliament has nonetheless gone ahead with setting up a budget office and has hired several staff members.[12]

The bill seeks to ensure that government follows principles of prudent fiscal management, including reducing government debt, increasing transparency, and establishing predictable tax rates (Part 2 of the Fiscal Management Bill). Like Uganda's Budget Act, it would require government to set before the National Assembly a detailed budget statement well in advance of the new fiscal year (by March 31). It would establish a Fiscal Analysis and Appropriations Committee and an Office of Fiscal Analysis, requiring the finance minister to provide the National Assembly with specific economic and fiscal reports, and would grant the permanent secretary of the Finance Ministry specific authority to obtain information required under this legislation from public officers, setting severe penalties for public officers who fail to comply.

With regard to the Office of Fiscal Analysis and the Fiscal Analysis and Appropriations Committee, the bill states, "The Office will comprise qualified budgeteers and economists while the Committee will ideally be composed of members who have demonstrated competence or interest in the subject. Thus the two institutions will not only be reservoirs of expertise and continuity but also the fulcrum of the budgetary mechanism in the National Assembly."

Independent Budget Office Issues

Thus far this chapter has considered the duties, operations, staffing, and budgets of nonpartisan legislative budget units in several nations. The next section discusses a number of general aspects of legislative budget units.

Increase in the Number of Budget Offices

Why are a growing number of legislatures establishing nonpartisan, independent, objective analytic budget units? One reason may be that, using Schumpeter's procedural (electoral) concept of democracy,[13] there are simply more democracies today than at any other time in history. With the end of the Soviet Union and the resulting proliferation of new nations, the dramatic reduction in military governments in Latin America and Africa, and the sharp decline in African one-party states, more legislatures exist than ever before in history—and several of them have the potential to exercise some level of independent power. Independent financial expertise, such as that provided by professional nonpartisan budget units, aids them in exercising that power.

Another reason may be an extension of what Huntington called "demonstration effects or snowballing." According to Huntington, the demonstration effect of successful democratization in one country is a powerful incentive to other nations, especially countries geographically proximate, and culturally similar (1991, 100–06). It may be that the demonstration effect is important not only as an impetus to carry democracy from one nation to another, but as a model of the *infrastructure of democracy* as well. The Philippines CPBD is patterned after the U.S. CBO, and Kenya's private member Fiscal Management Bill (2006) has a great deal in common with Uganda's Budget Act (2001). Hon. Beatrice Kiraso, author of the Uganda Budget Act, conferred with her Kenya counterpart, Hon. Oloo Aringo, in developing his legislation. Indeed, much of the work of the international community to encourage legislative strengthening involves the sharing of best legislative practices across regions.[14]

A third reason for the growing number of legislative budget offices may be related to the increasing demand worldwide for government transparency and accountability. The proliferation of Transparency International offices, the growth of anticorruption agencies and watchdog organizations, and the increasing number of budget transparency think tanks all indicate a greater interest in and scrutiny of government finances. Legislatures need the assistance of budget experts if they are to play their role in developing and overseeing the budget, and in controlling government spending.

Potential Value

What benefits do legislative, independent, nonpartisan, objective analytic budget units provide for legislatures, committees, legislators, and citizens?[15] First, independent legislative budget units break the executive's monopoly on budget information, placing legislatures on more equal footing with the executive. In the cases of the California legislature and U.S. Congress, legislative leaders were concerned that their budget powers were being eclipsed by those of the executive, and they established budget offices to help redress that imbalance.

Budget offices simplify complexity. Executive budget agencies often fail to provide legislatures with the budget information they need, but even when they do it may be presented in a form too complex for legislators to understand. Effective legislative budget offices simplify complex budget information provided by executives so that legislators can understand and use it.

Next, these offices help promote budget transparency—not just between the executive and legislatures, but for the public as well. Many legislative budget offices publish national budget information and analyses on Internet sites (see, for example, reports by the Mexican House of Deputies' CEFP at http://www.cefp.gob.mx, or the Congressional Budget Office at http://www.cbo.gov/). Greater transparency discourages subterfuge by executives and executive agencies.

Effective budget offices can also help enhance the credibility of the budget process. Because these services encourage simplification and transparency, they help make budget forecasts easier to understand and more credible. Nonpartisan budget offices often reveal their assumptions and methods along with their findings, enabling everyone to understand the bases on which the offices make projections.

Budget offices can help increase accountability. The offices' scrutiny of executive estimates used in the budget process enhances executive accountability. The realization that their assumptions and figures will be carefully reviewed by budget experts from a separate branch of government encourages executive budgeters to be more careful and precise. In addition, the simpler, more transparent and accountable budget resulting through the work of a legislative budget unit makes the budget process more straightforward and easier to follow. Hon. Beatrice Kiraso, for example, stated that because of the work of the Uganda PBO, Ugandan ministries now produce yearly spending reports to Parliament in a standardized, easy-to-use, and more understandable format.

Having effective legislative budget offices may also lead to greater discipline in public spending. An important purpose of the U.S. Congressional Budget and Impoundment Control Act of 1974 was to control government spending, and rationales for establishing several of the budget offices examined here include this same justification.

Functions

According to Anderson (2006), the first core function of an independent analytic budget office is to make independent budget forecasts. He states that these forecasts should be objective; take into account the forecasts of private forecasters, bankers, and experts; and be a bit conservative. Conservative forecasts are preferable, because politically it is easier to use the results of a better-than-forecasted economy to reduce deficits than to find last-minute spending cuts or tax increases to deal with unanticipated deficits.

Second, independent legislative budget offices establish baseline estimates, and they do so by making *projections*, not *predictions*. That is, they should assume that laws in place will stay in place, and should not factor in policy proposals not yet enacted. The third core function of budget units is to analyze executive budget proposals, making a *technical* (not political) review of the budgetary estimates contained in the executive budget. A final core function is to conduct medium-term analyses. A medium-term analysis alerts policy makers and the public to possible future consequences of proposed policy actions. It also provides a basis on which to build long-term analyses.

Independent budget units may perform several other functions as well, among which are estimating costs of both executive and legislative policy proposals; preparing spending-cut options for legislative consideration; analyzing the costs of regulations and mandates to corporations, subnational governments, and the economy; conducting more in-depth and longer-term economic analyses; analyzing the impacts of proposed and actual tax policies; and producing policy briefs that explain complex budget proposals and concepts.

Other budget offices that were examined offer different functions. For example, California's LAO makes recommendations to the legislature on ways government can run more efficiently and economically. Also, acting as institutional watchdogs, LAO seeks to ensure that the executive has complied with the letter and spirit of legislative intent, and Uganda's PBO keeps a record of how well the executive has complied with legislative recommendations to government. Finally, the CPBD in the Philippines assists in formulating the legislative agenda of the House of Representatives.

Considerations in Establishing Effective Legislative Budget Units

The budget offices described in this chapter must be nonpartisan if they are to be effective. Anderson (2006) made a distinction between bipartisan (or multipartisan) and nonpartisan services. A bipartisan or multipartisan service would attempt to analyze matters from the perspective of both (or all) political parties, whereas a nonpartisan office would attempt to present information objectively, not from a political perspective at all.

Legislatures use several means of ensuring that their budget units become, and stay, nonpartisan. In some (for example, California and Mexico), bipartisan or multipartisan committees oversee the budget units. Directors might be selected through open competitive processes or they might have broad support in the legislature. In all cases, legislatures select unit staff for their professional expertise, not for their political affiliation.

Nonpartisan, independent budget offices should serve all parties in the legislature, potentially providing minority parties a greater voice in the budget process than they would otherwise enjoy. Anderson (2006) noted, in fact, that as independent budget units age and executives adjust to their presence, their information may become more valuable to minority than to majority powers in the legislature. Parties in power should resist the temptation to underfund, undermine, or politicize independent budget units, realizing that they may be in the opposition someday and will need access to professional budget services.

Effective legislative budget units should also have their existence and their core functions codified in law, so they cannot be easily shut down or changed to suit some political purpose. Anderson states that budget units should avoid making recommendations to their legislatures. Many do, however, as table 10.1 indicates. Anderson further recommends that legislative budget units should principally serve committees and subcommittees, rather than serve individual members; meet with representatives from all sides of an issue in order to be able to present informed and balanced analyses, and avoid the limelight.

Budget units need access to government budget information, and in many cases the statutes establishing the units also grant them authority to compel the executive to provide it (United States and Korea). The Kenya legislation has a creative approach to meeting this need. Rather than grant the National Assembly the authority to compel government to provide budget information, it grants the Finance Ministry the authority to obtain budget information requested by the National Assembly. Public officers who do not comply face heavy fines and jail terms.

In some of the cases considered (for example, the Philippines and California), the legislature established the budget office as a stand-alone reform to the budget process. In others, however, legislatures established budget offices as one component of a larger budget reform. The U.S. Congressional Budget and Impoundment Control Act of 1974 not only established the CBO, it also established a new congressional budget process and budget committees in each house to manage the process. Uganda's PBO was a part of a similar reform that, for the first time, made the National Assembly a major player in the budget process. Kenya's new budget legislation and Nigeria's proposal include legislative budget offices as part of broader budget process reforms. In many cases, and this may be a trend, budget offices are a component of larger reforms designed to strengthen the role of the legislatures in the budget process.

What is an appropriate size for a legislative budget unit? Those examined range from about 20 to 200 professional staff (see table 10.1). Their size helps determine the number and frequency of services they provide, but even nations as poor as Uganda consider a legislative budget office a good investment. Legislatures that pay their staff very low salaries may find it difficult to attract the level of expert staff needed in a budget office and may need to consider adjusting their pay levels.

Should unit responsibilities extend beyond pure budget work? California's LAO includes program evaluation among its responsibilities, as does Uganda's PBO. The PBO also keeps track of all of Parliament's recommendations to the government, whether government was expected to respond, whether or not it complied, and reasons for noncompliance. The Philippine's CPBD lists as its first responsibility assisting the House of Representatives in formulating its agenda. One can understand the importance of such services to legislatures, and it may be that budget offices are called upon to perform them, especially when legislative services are very thin. Nonetheless, architects of new legislative budget offices should generally keep them focused on their central mission, and thus avoid diluting the offices' effectiveness by asking them to do too much.

Table 10.1 compares the budget offices examined in this chapter in terms of professional staff size, whether or not the office conducts program evaluations

Table 10.1. Characteristics of Budget Offices Reviewed

Name and Year Founded	Professional Staff Size	Perform Program Evaluations?	Associated with a Larger Budget Reform Process?	Make Policy or Budget Recommendations to Legislature?
California Legislative Analyst's Office (LAO), 1941	44	Yes	No	Yes
U.S. Congressional Budget Office (CBO), 1974	205	No	Yes	No
Philippines, Congressional Planning and Budget Department (CPBD), 1990	——	Yes	No	Yes
Mexico, Center for Public Finance Studies (CEFP), 1998	27	No	No[a]	No
Uganda, Legislative Budget Office (PBO), 2001	27	Yes	Yes	No
Korea, National Assembly Budget Office (NABO), 2003	70	No	No	No

Source: Author's compilation.

a. Mexico's budget timetable was reformed a few years later.

Note: —— = not available.

of government agencies, whether its creation was part of a larger budget reform process, and whether or not it makes recommendations for legislative action.

Conclusion

Given the increasing rate at which independent legislative budget offices are being established, it is likely that several more will be appear over the next decade. In addition to Kenya and Nigeria, which appear close to establishing such units, interest has been shown by legislatures in Ghana, Guatemala, Thailand, Turkey, and Zambia, and undoubtedly many more countries.

Legislatures with long-standing traditions of nonpartisan legislative services (as exist in many Commonwealth nations with professional secretariats) may have an easier time establishing professional, nonpartisan budget offices. Similarly, legislatures in systems where divided government occurs, or where the legislative and executive branches are elected independently of each other, may have more incentive to develop independent budget offices than their counterparts in true legislative systems. In a true legislative system, the party or coalition controlling the legislature selects a government to represent it and thus has little incentive to use parliament's resources to develop professional capabilities to challenge that government. Legislatures without a tradition of nonpartisan staff, and those whose entire administrations consist of political appointees replaced after each election, may also find it difficult to establish independent budget offices—difficult, but not impossible. The U.S. Congress and state legislatures, which have a high level of partisan staff, have developed such professional services and nonpartisan services, and they are becoming increasingly common in Latin America as well. Institutions rarely change quickly, but they do change.

When budget offices are established, keeping them nonpartisan is a critical challenge because the institution they serve is partisan both by nature and design. When and where they succeed in remaining nonpartisan, they will improve the quality of government budgeting and budgets (thus generally enhancing the credibility of government) and make the budget process more transparent and easier to understand for both legislators and the public.

Notes

1. For a detailed discussion of these factors, see Johnson and Nakamura (1999) and Johnson (2005).

2. Much of the information on California's Legislative Analyst's Office is taken from Elizabeth G. Hill (2003a, 2003b) and Vanzi (1999).

3. "About the Legislative Analyst's Office." http://www.lao.ca.gov/2006/cal_facts/2006_calfacts_toc.htm.

4. Much of the information for this section comes from CBO Director Dan Crippen (2002).

5. U.S. Congress. House Report 109-139, Legislative Branch Appropriations Bill, 2006. Library of Congress, Thomas. http://thomas.loc.gov/cgi-bin/cpquery/

?&dbname=cp109&sid=cp109DGdGa&refer=&r_n=hr139.109&item=&sel=TOC_43975&.

6. Congressional Budget Office Web site: Staffing and Organization. http://www.cbo.gov/organization/.

7. Much of the information on the CPBD was collected from the Congressional Planning and Budget Department's Web page, "Budget Briefer." http://www.geocities.com/cpbo_hor/.

8. Most of this information on the CEFP can be found at http://www.cefp.gob.mx/.

9. This shift in power is illustrated by the dramatic reduction in the percentage of executive (relative to legislative) proposals enacted into law in the early years of the 21st century. In the spring 2001 term, 48 percent of legislation enacted into law was initiated by the president. Just four years later, in the spring 2004 term, that percentage had fallen to 7.1 percent. Figures are taken from Weldon (2004, 25–26).

10. Information in this section was provided by Dr. Jhungsoo Park, from "Budget Control and the Role of the National Assembly Budget Office in Korea" (Park 2006). Park is a professor of Ewha Woman's University and former director general for budget analysis of the National Assembly Budget Office, Korea.

11. Much of the information on the proposed Kenya Budget Office comes from the Fiscal Management Bill, 2006, introduced in the National Assembly March 24, 2006.

12. Interview with Hon. Oloo Aringo, February 2008.

13. Samuel Huntington, in *The Third Wave: Democratization in the Late 20th Century*, uses the Schumpeterian minimal definition of democracy when he defines a political system as democratic to the extent that its most powerful collective decision makers are selected through fair, honest, and periodic elections in which candidates freely compete for votes and in which virtually all the adult population is eligible to vote (1991, 6).

14. The World Bank Workshop on Legislative Budget Offices, held in Bangkok on May 15–17, 2006, was designed to share international practices regarding the establishment of legislative budget offices.

15. Several of these benefits were presented by Barry Anderson, former acting and deputy director of the U.S. Congressional Budget Office, in his paper "The Value of a Nonpartisan, Independent, Objective Analytic Unit to the Legislative Role in Budget Preparation," which was presented at the World Bank Workshop on Legislative Budget Offices in Bangkok, May 2006.

Bibliography

Anderson, Barry. 2006. "The Value of a Nonpartisan, Independent, Objective Analytic Unit to the Legislative Role in Budget Preparation," 1–9. Presented at the World Bank Institute Workshop on Legislative Budget Offices, Bangkok, May 15–17.

Crippen, Dan. 2002. "Informing Legislators about the Budget: The History and Role of the U.S. Congressional Budget Office." White paper (June 7), Congressional Budget Office, Washington, DC. http://www.cbo.gov/ftpdocs/35xx/doc3503/CrippenSpeech.pdf.

Hill, Elizabeth G. 2003a. "California's Legislative Analyst's Office: An Isle of Independence." *Spectrum: The Journal of State Government* 76 (4): 26. http://www.lao.ca.gov/laoapp/laomenus/lao_menu_aboutlao.aspx.

————. 2003b. "Nonpartisan Analysis in a Partisan World." *Journal of Policy Analysis and Management.* http://www.lao.ca.gov/laoapp/laomenus/lao_menu_aboutlao.aspx.

Huntington, Samuel. 1991. *The Third Wave: Democratization in the Late 20th Century.* Norman: University of Oklahoma Press.

Johnson, John K. 2005. "The Role of Parliament in Government." World Bank Institute, Washington, DC.

Johnson, John K., and Robert Nakamura. 1999. "A Concept Paper on Legislatures and Good Governance." United Nations Development Programme, Management Development and Governance Division, New York.

Kathuri, Benson. 2006. "MPs Get Green Light on the Budget Office." *The Standard.* May 16.

Kiraso, Beatrice Birungi. 2006. "Establishment of Uganda's Legislative Budget Office and Legislative Budget Committee." Paper presented at the World Bank Institute Workshop on Legislative Budget Offices, Bangkok, May 15–17.

Norton, Philip. 1993. *Does Parliament Matter?* New York: Harvester Wheatsheaf.

Nzekwu, Greg. 2006. "Nigeria: Role of National Assembly in Budget." Paper presented at the World Bank Institute Workshop on Legislative Budget Offices, Bangkok, May 15–17.

Park, Jhungsoo. 2006. "Budget Control and the Role of the National Assembly Budget Office in Korea." Paper presented at the World Bank Institute Workshop on Legislative Budget Offices, Bangkok, May 15–17.

Santiso, Carlos. 2005. "Budget Institutions and Fiscal Responsibility: Parliaments and the Political Economy of the Budget Process." Chapter prepared for the 17th Regional Seminar on Fiscal Policy, United Nations Economic Commission for Latin America, Santiago. Chile, January 24–27.

Schick, Allen. 2002. "Can National Legislatures Regain an Effective Voice in Budget Policy?" *OECD Journal on Budgeting* 1 (3): 15–42.

SUNY (State University of New York) Albany. 2006. *Quarterly Activity Report* 6 (July–September).

Vanzi, Max. 1999. "Liz Hill: Here Today, Here Tomorrow. *California Journal* (July). http://www.lao.ca.gov/staff/press_awards/lhill_cal_journal_7-99.html.

von Hagen, J. 1992. "Budgeting Procedures and Fiscal Performance in the European Communities." Economics Paper 96, Commission of the European Communities, Directorate-General for Economic and Financial Affairs, Brussels.

Wehner, Joachim. Forthcoming. "Back from the Sidelines? Redefining the Contribution of Legislatures to the Budget Cycle." World Bank Institute, Washington, DC.

Weldon, Jeffrey. 2004. "The Spring 2004 Term of the Mexican Congress." Center for Strategic and International Studies, Washington, DC.

III. COUNTRY CASE STUDIES

CHAPTER 11

Administrative Review and Oversight: The Experiences of Postcommunist Legislatures

David M. Olson

The postauthoritarian legislatures in communist regions have developed in different ways since the 1989–92 collapse of the communist system. Whereas some countries have become stable democracies, especially in Central Europe and the Baltics, others have become presidentially dominated, especially those in the former Soviet Union, and still others are hybrid states, engaged in a presidential-parliamentary struggle for power. The development of active and autonomous parliaments varies with these circumstances, as does the parliaments' ability to review the conduct of the administration.

The experience of the Polish Sejm, in its role of oversight, contrasts with most of the other postcommunist legislatures, both in their resources and in their use of those resources. This chapter examines the special case of the Polish Sejm's oversight activity, reviews the resources needed by parliaments to function, and examines the broader contexts of state, power, and time within which postcommunist parliaments interact with the executive.

Oversight in the Polish Sejm

The Polish Sejm (the larger and more powerful body in a bicameral parliament) is the only postcommunist parliament to devote much time and effort to administrative review and oversight. Its committees use a distinctive system to both examine and instruct ministers and administrative agency heads. However, this elaborate procedure is not a new invention. Both the committee system and the oversight procedure were developed during the last 30 years of communist rule. The Polish postcommunist parliament has been able to directly build upon its communist-era inheritance. This legislative innovation was part of a much broader process of distinctive Polish thought and action under communism (Karpowicz and Wesołowski 2002; Simon and Olson 1980).

Each of the 25 committees of the Sejm has the formal authority to investigate the administration of policies within the legislative jurisdiction of the committee. Committee jurisdictions tend to be defined not by ministry but by policy topic and the relevant administrative agencies. The administrative structure of the state is more stable than the changeable structure of ministries, and administrative personnel are far more stable than are the transient ministers. Though there is continuous high turnover among Sejm members, the committee structure is stable, as are the rules and procedures by which committees function. The Sejm also has a small, but stable, expert staff.

Ministers who are elected to parliament remain members; they know prior to their ministerial service the interaction patterns to expect with parliamentary committees. Committees are a recruitment source for ministers, and former ministers often return to their previous committees (van der Meer Krok-Paszkowska 2000, 146). Former ministers who continue as members of parliament are well equipped to know what questions to ask and which answers are believable.

The Sejm committees' attention to administrative matters is stimulated by a wide range of sources: the government's report on implementation of the previous year's budget, preparation of the new budget, citizen complaints, and reports from the external audit agency (Karpowicz and Wesołowski 2002, 62–67).

First, most committee reviews are prompted by the annual government report on administration of the previous year's budget. One example concerned the provision of care for single mothers and financial benefits for mothers with small children. Several joint meetings of two committees—the Social Policy and Health committees—addressed these problems. The initial committee meeting on this topic was postponed because the committee members considered that the ministry officials in attendance did not rank high enough to speak authoritatively for the ministry. This example illustrates that, though the plenum's approval of government's budget performance is usually pro forma, committees can use that exercise to achieve more detailed objectives.

Second, the annual budget itself is the subject of a large share of committee reviews. Committees usually estimate that any given administrative task needs greater funding, but they are prohibited from increasing the government's proposed amount. Their remedy is to direct a formal request—*desideratum*—to the government about next year's government budget proposal. The budgetary impact of parliament thus may be both larger in magnitude and longer in duration than is apparent in the budget of any one year.

Citizen complaints are a third source of committee action to examine and review administrative conduct. Citizens' letters are addressed to individual deputies, to parliamentary party clubs, and to the Sejm secretariat. For example, the Committee for Social Policy, in response to citizens' letters, investigated the provision of care for people with chronic diseases.

The fourth major source of committee action is the external audit and investigation agency (Chief Board of Supervision, the NIK). For example, several committees joined in a desideratum on procedures for teacher evaluation, in response to a NIK report critical of skills and procedures of education superintendents. Many other sources also suggest committee oversight activity, including the administrative agencies themselves and outside interest groups.

Though Sejm committees are active in administrative review and oversight, the legal status of committee desiderata pronouncements is both unclear and controversial. Judgments as to whether the desiderata are mere expressions of parliamentary opinion or authoritative pronouncements of requirements imposed upon the government have become controversial (Karpowicz and Wesołowski 2002, 67).

In addition to the continuous review of specific administrative activities, the Sejm investigates serious allegations of fraud and arbitrary behavior through special investigation committees. In the third and fourth terms, for example, the Sejm launched three investigations into bribery and fraud in film, insurance, and fuel companies and related privatization efforts. These scandals bridged the governments of both the Democratic Left Alliance and of the Solidarity-rooted parties (Nalewajko and Wesołowski 2007).

Resources for Parliamentary Review of Administration

The experience of the Polish Sejm in oversight contrasts with most of the other postcommunist legislatures, both in their resources and in their use of those resources (Norton and Olson 2007). Parliaments require resources to enable members to get work done. The main sets of resources for review of administration by parliaments around the world include (1) a committee system, (2) parliamentary party groups, (3) active participation of members of parliament, (4) a staff of competent personnel, (5) space and funding, (6) external support agencies, and (7) appropriate rules and procedures (Crowther and Olson 2002; Rockman 1985).

The Committee System

The Polish experience strongly suggests the critical importance of committees as the main source of continuous legislative review of the administration of public policy, as has been observed more generally elsewhere (Blondel 1973; Hazan 2001; LaPolombara 1974; Mattson and Stroem 1995; Mezey 1979; Olson 1994; Olson 1997; Shaw 1998).

The new parliaments of former communist countries have largely adopted the continental European system in which approximately 20 permanent committees consider legislation and review the conduct of the administration. They have not adopted the Westminster pattern of committees that separate oversight from legislative jurisdiction (Agh 1998; Crowther and Olson 2002; Khmelko, Pigenko, and Wise 2007; Olson and Norton 1996).

In the first years, the newly democratized parliaments resorted to the device of many temporary committees to cope with immediate specific tasks. Through rules revision, usually in the second or third term, these many and diverse committees were reorganized into a single system, with defined jurisdictions and procedures (Olson and Norton 2007, 176–77). Special investigative committees are temporary expedients to respond to immediate problems. The more urgent and volatile the problem (of which inefficiency or corruption are examples), the greater the need for a special committee. Special committees are used in most parliaments to cope with new problems. For example, to prepare for accession to the European Union and the North Atlantic Treaty Organization, countries developed new coordinating committees. Since then, with growing membership, the committees have become part of the permanent committee structure (Agh 1998, 94–98; Beetham 2006, 169–71).

The postcommunist parliaments are experimenting with subcommittees. In the Czech Chamber of Deputies, for example, the number of subcommittees has grown from 24 in the first parliamentary term to 49 in the fourth term (Linek and Mansfeldova 2007). The Polish subcommittees, developed during the communist period, are now frequently used as a means to coordinate two or more committees that share jurisdiction on any given legislative or oversight question.

Parliamentary Party Groups

In Western democracies the relationship of a parliamentary party to the party in an election is usually very clear. In new democracies, however, many different formations appeared during elections, and once elected, the members form still different groups within the legislature (Olson 1998c).

The British term *parliamentary party* is more vaguely and flexibly, and thus realistically, rendered as *parliamentary party group* in many parliaments of the new postcommunist democracies (Heidar and Koole 2000). The equivalent German term is *fraktion*, in Lithuanian it is *frakcija*, and in Polish it is *klub*. Members are assigned to committees through their parliamentary party groups; committee officers are similarly selected. In the early years, however, members on a committee frequently lacked party direction, for party groups both disappeared and were newly formed within a term. Members frequently changed party groups within a parliamentary term. The "party tourism" phenomenon, however, mostly disappeared by the third and fourth term of office, and party-committee links correspondingly became more firm (Crowther and Olson 2002, 182–86). Stability in the party system was a precondition to an effective committee system.

In the relatively routine type of oversight illustrated by the Sejm committees, members act without party direction or constraint. The politically visible investigations of special committees, by contrast, are more subject to party direction. Especially when the government is supported by a parliamentary majority, the government can avoid such investigations. In Bulgaria, for example, during a single term, 23 special investigation committees were created, of which only

13 issued reports. Another three investigative committees were authorized but never formed (Karasimeonov 2002).

The Members

A high turnover of parliamentary members from one election to the next has predominated in postcommunist democracies during the early terms, with incumbency rising to almost 60 percent in the third and fourth terms of the Czech and Hungarian parliaments. Most members of the new parliaments are new each term, however, bringing with them a wide range of experience and attitudes. Increasingly, the new members have had prior experience in democratic politics at the local level (Ilonszki and Edinger 2007).

Just as there has been high turnover of parliamentary members, there has been a high turnover in the membership of committees from one term to the next. In the mid-1990s, few committees had as many as 30 percent of their members continue from the previous term (Crowther and Olson 2002, 178–80). The trend in Western Europe, by contrast, has been toward continuity in both parliamentary membership and in committee membership (Patzelt 1999). Parliamentary incumbency in new parliaments thus is not the same as committee incumbency, for members switch committees from their earlier terms.

One paradoxical result of the defeat of each government in successive elections in the new democracies is that the members of the opposition parties are often more experienced in government and parliament than the new members of the new majority party or coalition. The new majority has become a majority through the acquisition of new members. Most members of the opposition parties, by contrast, are survivors from the previous government party or coalition. The new opposition is thus better equipped, through experience, to attack or investigate the new government than the new members are equipped to defend their government.

One basis on which to assign members to a committee is the experience and education of the individual members. If teachers concentrate in the Education Committee, physicians in the Health Committee, and economists in the Finance Committee, presumably their personal expertise is an asset to the committee. But are these committee members also possibly "inside lobbyists" on behalf of the ministries relevant to their professions (Agh 1998, 88)? Are their inclination and ability to investigate lessened or increased as a result? In presidentially dominated parliaments of the former Soviet Union, do a sizeable number of members of parliament have prior, or current, occupations in government and agricultural enterprises (Crowther 2007; Ilonszki and Edinger 2007; Remington 2007). The private occupation and government party connection would tend to limit parliamentary oversight activity.

Member ethics are a related consideration (NDI 1999). In some cases, the legislature investigates its own members. Court prosecution of a deputy is ordinarily possible only when immunity is explicitly removed by a vote of parliament, as in Armenia in 2006 (RFE/RL 2006).

Parliamentary Staff

The preparation of legislation and amendments, as well as the organization and conduct of administrative review, are time-consuming activities requiring technical skills. Each parliament, and each committee, requires its own professional, continuous, nonpartisan civil service (Beetham 2006, 116–17; Crowther and Olson 2002; Olson 1998b).

Typically the committees of new postcommunist parliaments have one secretary, an assistant, and perhaps one or two professional staff. Some parliaments also have technical and research staff as part of a central service. For example, the Parliamentary Institute for the Czech Parliament and the Bureau of Expertise and Research for the Polish Sejm. Most parliaments, however, complain of the lack of sufficient professional staff, whether in Latin America (Rundquist and Wellborn 1994) or in postcommunist states (Biscak 1998; Kanev 1998; Khmelko, Pigenko, and Wise 2007, 228; Sivakova 1998).

Space and Funding

The new postcommunist parliaments are frequently in cramped quarters, often in improvised modifications of the existing communist-period legislative buildings. There is also a constant shortage of funds for space, personnel, and operating expenses.

Within this shortage, parliamentary party groups seem to be provided more space, personnel, and funding than are the committees. A similar observation can be made for Western European parliaments.

To address the lack of technical staff support for committees, skilled personnel from existing investigative organs of the state could be assigned to work with a temporary investigation committee. Outside advisers and temporary consultants are resources to provide technical support as needed. A common complaint, however, is that such resources, however scarce, are allocated by committee chairs on a party basis. Thus, one organizational problem faced by all parliaments is the distribution of space and personnel among the parliamentary parties at both the plenary and committee levels.

External Support Agencies

Some countries have special investigative units with audit and other responsibilities for reporting to the legislature. They typically are more concerned with financial management and allegations of irregularity than with the substance of policy administration. The General Accounting Office in the United States and the Auditor-General's Office in Britain are examples. The NIK in Poland is an example in a postcommunist country. Another is the Supreme Audit Office (NKU) of the Czech Republic, which, for example, reported on financial irregularities in universities (Government of the Czech Republic 2001).

Rules and Procedures

Newly energized postcommunist parliaments began with the rules of the previous Communist legislatures, which were inadequate to channel the open expression of divergent points of view and to give scope to the reality of a competitive party system (Lukasz and Staskiewicz 1995; Olson 1998a). Systematic rules changes in the Czech Republic, Hungary, and Poland have increased the capacity of their parliaments for independent action (Crowther and Olson 2002). New sets of rules and procedures have likewise been developed in the democratized parliaments of southern Europe (Norton and Leston-Bandeira 2003, 180–81). Presidents in several post-Soviet countries, however, define parliamentary rules through the exercise of their decree power (Olson 1995).

A more particular question concerns the legal authority of committees to require ministries to provide documents and evidence: the greater the parliamentary authority, the greater the independence of parliament from the government in Western Europe and elsewhere (Beetham 2006, 129–30; Döring 1995).

Contexts of State, Power, and Time

The postcommunist parliaments have developed within the changing contexts of state definition, power distribution, and time, which in turn have shaped parliaments' capacity for administrative review and oversight activity.

State Definition

Of the 25 (and more) states of the formerly Communist region, most are remnants of federations. Czechoslovakia, the Soviet Union, and Yugoslavia no longer exist. Their many constituent republics have become independent sovereign states. Moving from provincial and subordinate status to the status of internationally recognized states has imposed a huge burden on their governments, their administrative structures, and their legislatures. They have experienced a dual transition, not only of their political systems, but also of their legal status and responsibilities. While the continuous states such as Bulgaria, Hungary, Poland, and Romania have experienced only the political system transition, the others also have taken on new burdens and opportunities as international actors.

However, state definition has also become one of state disintegration (Offe 1991). Georgia, Moldova, Russia, and Serbia illustrate the corrosive impact on civilian governance of internal ethnic armed secessionist movements, sometimes accompanied by transnational support. Although the collapse of communist federations has mainly been peaceful, the former Yugoslavia illustrates how secessionist military conflicts can interact with changes in political systems to redefine the borders and the populations of new states. Under these circumstances, civilian governance, whatever the wording of the constitution, is often authoritarian. Legislatures, if permitted to exist and to meet, are usually irrelevant except to express support for the current government.

Power: The Executive and the Legislature

Whereas a constitution in stable states defines a continuing set of constraints within which political conflict is expressed and resolved, the process of defining the state necessarily involves decisions about a new constitution. Once adopted, however, the meaning of the formal stipulations regarding the relationship of parliament to the executive must be worked out in practice (Olson and Norton 2007).

By and large, the Central European states have become stable democracies, with parliaments as the prime institution for the formation and dissolution of governments and prime ministers (Ilonszki 2007; Linek and Mansfeldova 2007; Nalewajko and Wesołowski 2007; Zajc, 2007). Stable democratic parliaments have the opportunity to become active both in the enactment of public policy and in the review of the administration of that policy.

By contrast, some parliaments, mainly in the former Soviet Union, have become presidentially dominated (Crowther 2007; Remington 2007). Presidents have become the leaders of dominant parties, with the legislatures acting mainly to accept presidential policy initiatives. In addition, such presidents usually have extensive decree powers enabling them to circumvent legislatures. Presidentially dominated parliaments lack the opportunity for independent action in either the enactment or review of public policy.

The continuing constitutional struggle leads to the designation of the so-called hybrid state (Diamond 2002). In Central Europe, Poland illustrated the constitutional struggle between the president and Parliament, which was not resolved until enactment of a new constitution in 1997 (Karpowicz and Wesołowski 2002). Similar struggles in the Russian Federation and Moldova were resolved somewhat later but very differently (Crowther 2007; Remington 2007).

The hybrid state phenomenon, with the contest for power taking place among presidents, legislatures, political parties, and reform movements, has more recently been experienced in Croatia, Georgia, Serbia, and Ukraine, among others (Bunce and Wolchik 2006; Khmelko, Pigenko, and Wise 2007). Continued efforts by opposition groups to contest incumbent authoritarians, in both executive and legislative offices, are currently seen in Armenia, Azerbaijan, and Kyrgyzstan, for example.

Time

The dismantling of communist rule occurred in the 1989–90 period in Central Europe, and the Republics of Yugoslavia and the Soviet Union become independent in the 1990–92 period. During the almost two decades since then, the development of stable structures of committees and parliamentary parties, made visible by the adoption of revised rules of procedure, has provided legislatures with not only autonomy but also methods of work by which prime ministers and cabinets, on one hand, and legislatures, on the other, interact both in the development of public policy and in the review of the administration of policy (Olson and Norton 2007).

These stability adaptations have followed a period of experimentation during the initial decade with policy, government interactions, and various ways of making parliament work. This emergent working stability, however, is not found in either the presidentially dominant parliaments or the hybrid states with their continuing struggles for power within the state.

Concluding Observations

The postcommunist and post-Soviet parliaments display very different patterns of development following communist system collapse. Their varied experiences suggest that a legislature's capacity to subject the government to examination for its conduct of public policy develops after the legislature has become an autonomous actor in a democratic political system. The oversight function develops from a long series of prior organizational and procedural developments within both parliament and government.

A legislature's oversight activity depends not only on its internal attributes but also on the broader institutional context within which it functions. Even in new stable democratic systems, the equally new attributes of the structure and procedures in public administration interact with the legislature's emerging characteristics to generate new patterns, including those of administrative review and oversight.

Bibliography

Agh, Attila. 1998. "Changing Parliamentary Committees in Changing East-Central Europe: Parliamentary Committees as Central Sites of Policy-Making." *Journal of Legislative Studies* 4 (1): 85–100.

Beetham, David. 2006. *Parliament and Democracy in the Twenty-First Century: A Guide to Good Practice.* Geneva: Inter-Parliamentary Union.

Biscak, Bogdan. 1998. "Professional Support in the Legislative Process." In Longley and Zajc 1998, 269–76.

Blondel, Jean. 1973. *Comparative Legislatures.* Englewood Cliffs, NJ: Prentice Hall.

Bunce, Valerie, and Sharon Wolchik. 2006. "International Diffusion and Postcommunist Electoral Revolutions." *Communist and Postcommunist Studies* 39 (3).

Crowther, William E. 2007. "Development of the Moldovan Parliament One Decade After Independence: Slow Going." *Journal of Legislative Studies* 13 (1): 99–120.

Crowther, William E., and David M. Olson. 2002. "Committee Systems in New Democratic Parliaments: Comparative Institutionalization." In Olson and Crowther 2002, 171–206.

Diamond, Larry. 2002. "Thinking About Hybrid Regimes." *Journal of Democracy* 13 (2): 21–35.

Döring, Herbert. 1995. "Time as a Scarce Resource: Government Control of the Agenda." In *Parliaments and Majority Rule in Western Europe*, ed. Herbert Döring, 223–46. New York: St. Martin's Press.

Government of the Czech Republic. 2001. "Mismanagement of University Funds Discovered by Audit Office." *Czech Happenings*. Press Release, November 5. http://www.ceskenoviny.cz/news/.

Hazan, Reuven. 2001. *Reforming Parliamentary Committees*. Columbus: Ohio State University Press.

Heidar, Knut, and Ruud Koole, eds. 2000. *Parliamentary Party Groups in European Democracies*. London: Routledge

Ilonszki, Gabriella. 2007. "From Minimal to Subordinate, A Final Verdict? The Hungarian Parliament 1990–2002." *Journal of Legislative Studies* 13 (1): 38–58.

Ilonszki, Gabriella, and Michael Edinger. 2007. "MPs in Post-Communist and Post-Soviet Nations: A Parliamentary Elite in the Making." *Journal of Legislative Studies* 13 (1):142–63.

Kanev, Dobrin. 1998. "The New Bulgarian Parliament: The Problem of Research Capabilities." In Longley and Zajc 1998, 277–86.

Karasimeonov, Georgi. 2002. "Bulgaria: Parliamentary Committees, Institutionalization and Effectiveness." In Olson and Crowther 2002, 93–114.

Karpowicz, Ewa, and Włodzimierz Wesołowski. 2002. "Committees in the Polish Sejm in Two Political Systems." In Olson and Crowther 2002, 44–68.

Khmelko, Irina S., Vladimir A. Pigenko, and Charles R. Wise. 2007. "Assessing Committee Roles in a Developing Legislature: The Case of the Ukrainian Parliament." *Journal of Legislative Studies* 13 (2): 210–34.

LaPolombara, Joseph. 1974. *Politics Within Nations*. Englewood Cliffs, NJ: Prentice Hall.

Linek, Lukaš, and Zdenka Mansfeldova. 2007. "The Parliament of the Czech Republic 1993–2004." *Journal of Legislative Studies* 13 (1): 12–37.

Longley, Lawrence D., and Drago Zajc. 1998. *The New Democratic Parliaments: The First Years. Working Papers on Comparative Legislative Studies III*. Lawrence, WI: Research Committee of Legislative Specialists, International Political Science Association.

Lukasz, Danuta, and Wiesław Staskiewicz, eds. 1995. *Rules of Procedure and Parliamentary Practice*. Warsaw: Sejm Bureau of Research.

Mattson, Ingvar, and Kaare Stroem. 1995. "Parliamentary Committees." In *Parliaments and Majority Rule in Western Europe*, ed. Herbert Döring, 249–307. New York: St. Martin's Press.

Mezey, Michael. 1979. *Comparative Legislatures*. Durham, NC: Duke University Press.

Nalewajko, Ewa, and Włodzimierz Wesołowski. 2007. "Five Terms of the Polish Parliament 1989–2005." *Journal of Legislative Studies* 13 (1): 59–82.

NDI (National Democratic Institute for International Affairs). 1999. "Legislative Ethics: A Comparative Analysis." Legislative Research Series, Paper 4, NDI, Washington, DC.

Norton, Philip, and Cristina Leston-Bandeira. 2003. "The Impact of Democratic Practice on the Parliaments of Southern Europe." *Journal of Legislative Studies* 9 (2): 177–85.

Norton, Philip, and David M. Olson, eds. 2007. "Post-Communist and Post-Soviet Parliaments: Beyond Transition." Special issue, *Journal of Legislative Studies* 13 (1).

Offe, Claus. 1991. "Capitalism by Democratic Design? Democratic Theory Facing the Triple Transition in East Central Europe." *Social Research* 58 (4).

Olson, David M. 1994. *Democratic Legislative Institutions: A Comparative View*. Armonk, NY: M. E. Sharpe.

———. 1995. "Organizational Dilemmas of Postcommunist Assemblies." *East European Constitutional Review* 4 (2): 56–60.

———. 1997. "Paradoxes of Institutional Development: The New Democratic Parliaments of Central Europe." *International Political Science Review* 18 (4): 401–16.

———. 1998a. "Parliaments of New Democracies: The Experience of Central Europe." In *World Encyclopedia of Parliaments and Legislatures*, ed. George Kurian, 838–48. Washington, DC: Congressional Quarterly.

———. 1998b. "Legislatures for Post-Conflict Societies." In *Democracy and Deep-Rooted Conflict: Options for Negotiators*, ed. Peter Harris and Ben Reilly, 212–23. Stockholm: International Institute for Democracy and Electoral Assistance.

———. 1998c. "Party Formation and Party System Consolidation in New Central European Democracies." *Political Studies* 43 (3): 432–64.

Olson, David M., and Philip Norton, eds. 1996. *The New Legislatures of Central and East Europe*. London: Cass.

———, eds. 2002. *Committees in Post-Communist Democratic Parliaments: Comparative Institutionalization*. Columbus: Ohio State University Press.

———. 2007. "Post-Communist and Post-Soviet Parliaments: Divergent Paths From Transition." *Journal of Legislative Studies* 13 (1): 164–96.

Patzelt, Werner. 1999. "What Can an Individual MP Do in German Parliamentary Politics?" *Journal of Legislative Studies* 5 (3/4): 23–52.

Remington, Thomas F. 2007. "The Russian Federal Assembly 1994–2004." *Journal of Legislative Studies* 13 (1): 121–41.

RFE/RL (Radio Free Europe/Radio Liberty). 2006. *Caucasus Report*, October 20. http://www.rferl.org/.

Rockman, Bert. 1985. "Executive-Legislative Relations and Legislative Oversight." In *Handbook of Legislative Research*, ed. Gerhard Loewenberg, S. Patterson, and M. Jewell, 519–72. Cambridge, MA: Harvard University Press.

Rundquist, Paul S., and Clay H. Wellborn. 1994. "Building Legislatures in Latin America." In *Working Papers on Comparative Legislative Studies*, ed. Lawrence D. Longley, 387–405. Lawrence, WI: Research Committee of Legislative Specialists, International Political Science Association.

Shaw, Malcolm. 1998. "Parliamentary Committees: A Global Perspective." *Journal of Legislative Studies* 4 (1): 225–51.

Simon, Maurice D., and David M. Olson. 1980. "Evolution of a Minimal Parliament: Membership and Committee." *Legislative Studies Quarterly* 5 (2): 211–32.

Sivakova, Danica. 1998. "Information and Democracy—Implications for New Democratic Parliaments: A Case Study of the National Council of the Slovak Republic." In Longley and Zajc 1998, 287–93.

van der Meer Krok-Paszkowska, Anna. 2000. *Shaping the Democratic Order: The Institutionalization of Parliament in Poland*. Leuven-Apeldoorn: Garant.

Zajc, Drago. 2007. "The Slovenian National Assembly 1992–2004." *Journal of Legislative Studies* 13 (1): 83–98.

CHAPTER 12

Separation of Powers and Legislative Oversight in Russia

Thomas F. Remington

Scholars identify three general ways in which a legislature may control the bureaucracy in a separation-of-powers system: oversight, legislation, and budget making (Huber, Shipan, and Pfahler 2001). For these to work, some conditions must be met: a certain degree of cooperation must occur between the branches in policy making (each side must be willing to bargain and compromise in order to get some policy benefits), the legislature must have some capacity to monitor the executive, and the executive needs to be willing to comply with legislative enactments. Certainly these conditions have not always applied in Russia. Especially in the early 1990s, when President Boris Yeltsin was fighting the Federal Assembly for a greater share of a dwindling pool of state power, policy was often made in the form of executive acts, such as government regulations and presidential decrees, rather than submitted to the open process of deliberation and mutual compromise.[1]

Yet a considerable amount of interbranch cooperation in law-making has taken place, even in periods of intense interbranch conflict. Since 1993, both sides have regularly preferred to compromise than to press a confrontation to the limit.[2] There has been a zone of shared agreement on policy goals between parliament and the executive even when the two branches are at odds on many issues. For example, the communists and the reformers were able to agree on legislation governing the federal judiciary and federal elections in the mid-1990s. Even though the 1993 constitution removed any direct reference to a right of legislative oversight— *kontrol'*—over the executive, forms of legislative oversight have existed in such mechanisms as parliamentary hearings, interpellations, investigations, and "government hour" (when government ministers appear before the Duma to make reports and respond to questions). Under President Vladimir Putin, the pendulum has swung equally far in the opposite direction: the Federal Assembly rarely opposes the president directly but uses its powers of agenda setting, amendment, and negotiation to achieve relatively minor legislative victories. In neither case has oversight been a particularly important instrument of power.

Oversight

The concept of oversight is best expressed by the Russian term *kontrol'*. The history of kontrol' institutions in the Russian state is long and revealing; since kontrol' was always understood as an instrument of political control over the bureaucracy, the Soviet state set up a number of different types of structures for monitoring the state bureaucracy's compliance with policy-makers' goals.[3] These were instruments by which one branch of the bureaucracy checked others. However, the history of legislative oversight is far shorter. Institutionally, legislative kontrol' over the bureaucracy is analogous to congressional oversight of the executive in the American context, where it was defined by a U.S. Senate committee as "a wide range of congressional efforts to review and control policy implementation (McCubbins and Schwartz 1984, 170)."

Although Russia's Federal Assembly lacks a *formal* right of kontrol' under the 1993 constitution, de facto oversight is exercised through several mechanisms. One is the Audit Chamber, which has a staff of about 500 people who conduct audits of state organizations. The Duma names its chair and gives it specific assignments. The Audit Chamber has investigated an extremely wide range of government organizations and state enterprises and worked assiduously to expand its powers. Under its ambitious chairman, Sergei Stepashin, it has created a network of regional branch offices, which it has been trying to build into a centralized hierarchy.[4] In the period 1995–2000, the Audit Chamber conducted some 3,000 investigations.[5] Much of the time, its reports have had little apparent effect on the bureaucracy, although often its findings are reported in the Russian press. Its 1997 investigation of the trust auctions (the "loans for shares" scheme) of 1995 found serious legal irregularities, but the procuracy refused to act. The chamber has regularly clashed with the government, and with the Finance Ministry in particular, over its right to conduct audits. It regularly complains that the government ignores its findings. The chamber does not have the power to bring legal charges, and its reports have only advisory force. But its power to expose abuses and corruption contributes to parliament's (and the president's) ability to generate political pressure on high-ranking government officials. In the spring of 2003, a series of well-publicized disclosures about the misuse of federal funds in the preparations for St. Petersburg's 300th anniversary undoubtedly weakened Governor Vladimir Yakovlev's political position and led to his removal as governor in June. By itself, the Audit Chamber has little power to improve governance, but when elements of the executive branch are receptive to its recommendations, it becomes another instrument at the disposal of parliament for political influence.[6]

The Federal Assembly also has the power to hold legislative hearings and to invite, although not to require, ministers to appear and answer questions before the Duma during government hour. Hearings do not need to be specifically associated with pieces of legislation; most Duma hearings in fact are not related to individual bills. Each year, Duma committees hold close to 100 hearings. These give committee chairs and members the opportunity to publicize problems, advertise their policy positions, attract press attention to their legislative agenda, and put pressure on the executive branch to act on particular issues. Committees also conduct seminars and roundtable discussions for similar purposes. Government hour is another opportunity to focus the spotlight on particular government officials and to publicize parliament's watchdog role.

Members of the Federal Assembly also have the right to submit interpellations (*zaprosy*) to the government (any deputy may propose one, but the motion to submit one requires majority support), to contact government officials directly, and to question government officials in the course of question hour. Often these powers are used for particularistic purposes—indeed, like other legislative powers, these powers often are used for corrupt purposes. In other cases, the Duma uses interpellations as a way of demonstrating that it is playing its proper role as the guardian of the public interest, as when the Duma unanimously passed a motion calling for an interpellation to Procurator-General Ustinov, demanding that he check into press reports of corruption in the Interior Ministry.[7] The net effect of these powers is a considerable increase in the flow of information from the executive to the legislative branch and greater pressure on the executive branch to fight corruption and inefficiency than existed in the Soviet era.

The Federal Assembly also has an implied, although again not formal, power to conduct investigations. It does this by forming special-purpose commissions to conduct wide-ranging inquiries, including, in the present convocation, a commission devoted to fighting corruption. An example is the Duma's investigation of the activity of the former atomic energy minister Evgenii Adamov. The Duma's anticorruption commission reported at the beginning of March 2001 that Adamov had skimmed huge sums from contracts with the ministry and created numerous commercial firms with them. At the end of the same month, Putin dismissed Adamov.[8] Pressure from the commission was also undoubtedly a factor leading to the fall of the powerful minister for railroads, Nikolai Aksenenko, at the beginning of 2002. In both cases, dismissal was the outcome of a lengthy subterranean bureaucratic war, in which pressure from the Duma was only one of many contributing reasons for the eventual outcome. The difference between these episodes and similar bureaucratic wars in the Soviet era is that now legislators, with an eye to the public and electoral consequences of taking sides, are opening—at least selectively—some scandals to public debate.

Thus the Federal Assembly's de facto oversight powers have expanded the flow of open information (often of a scandalous nature), but they have not greatly strengthened its capacity to check abuses in the executive or hold the executive accountable. This is because the executive usually acts in response to parliamentary pressure only when it is prepared to do so. Parliamentary hearings, investigations, and reports operate as another arena in which bureaucratic and social interests compete for influence.

Budget Control

The power of the purse is a vital domain of legislative control over the executive. The evidence suggests that in Russia, parliamentary influence over the budget has grown substantially. For example, the level of detail of the state budget law has increased every year as the government has shared more information about state revenues and expenditures with the Duma. If sheer length of the budget law is any indication at all of increased legislative capacity to monitor the state budget, then surely it is worth noting that the 2002 budget law was 50 times longer than the 1992 budget (see table 12.1). The budget law is now regularly signed each year before the budget year begins, rather than partway through it. The law also includes a far greater level of detail for individual line items. Also, the greater length of budget laws is not the product of large distributive coalitions in support of deficit spending, since the budget has been in balance since 2000.

In the Yeltsin period, passage of the annual budget law was a parody of responsible budgeting: as everyone knew they would, budget revenues invariably fell far short of projections, while planned outlays incorporated far more commitments than could ever have been honored. As Satarov and his associates observed, Yeltsin never vetoed the budget, despite the fact that powerful pressures from within and outside the government invariably managed to bypass the Finance Ministry and to win concessions from the Federal Assembly and the presidential administration (Satarov et al. 2001). The government always succeeded in persuading the Duma and Federation Council to pass the budget law by accepting some of Parliament's demands

Table 12.1. Federal Budget Laws, 1992–2002

Budget year	Date signed	No. of articles	No. of pages
1992	July 17, 1992	18	8
1993	May 14, 1993	27	19
1994	July 1, 1994	39	28
1995	Mar. 31, 1995	62	67
1996	Dec. 31, 1995	71	33
1997	Feb. 26, 1997	99	119
1998	Mar. 26, 1998	120	115
1999	Feb. 22, 1999	141	59
2000	Dec. 31, 1999	163	243
2001	Dec. 27, 2000	139	340
2002	Dec. 30, 2001	147	423

Source: 1994–2002 budget laws are from Sobranie zakonodatel'stva Rossiiskoi Federatsii. Budgets for 1992 and 1993 are from Vedomosti S"ezda Narodnykh deputatov RSFSR i Verkhovnogo Soveta RSFSR.

for increases in spending on politically influential groups and interests, despite the fact that these changes widened the projected deficits—never mind the actual deficits.

Nonetheless, over the course of the Yeltsin period, the Federal Assembly increased its ability to enforce budget discipline. As a result of the Budget Code, signed into law in 1998, Parliament significantly restricted the discretion of executive agencies at all levels of the state to use budget resources arbitrarily. It introduced a treasury system for the first time, requiring that all budget revenues be held in the state treasury. It closely regulated the use of incomes and revenues by state organizations and restricted the right of administrative authorities to deviate from spending the amounts specified by the budget law, and it provided substantial penalties for violations. Moreover, it ended the right of regional and local governments to form their own off-budget funds and required them to cut back on spending in proportion to shortfalls in revenue.[9] The Budget Code was tightened further in 2000, when the Duma adopted amendments proposed by the government that eliminated regions' right to borrow money in foreign capital markets and ended the practice of mutual write-offs of budget obligations.

Even more significant is the fact that the Federal Assembly also has expanded its control over extrabudgetary funds, after the period in the early 1990s when both executive and legislative acts created nonbudget funds freely. When Ruslan Khasbulatov and his supporters in the Russian Congress of People's Deputies were fighting with Yeltsin for supremacy, Khasbulatov frequently signed decrees creating special-purpose off-budget funds under government agencies, specifying that only he could control the use of funds from them (Satarov et al. 2001). The practice continued into the mid-1990s under the new constitution. Typically, by law or executive action, an administrative body would be created and given the right to form its own extrabudgetary account to receive and spend revenues. These revenues, in turn, would be exempt from taxation. In some cases they would include the right to conduct import and export operations without paying customs duties.[10] For instance, the press minister tried to persuade the Duma to create a "fund for support of the press," which he would control, as part of the law on state support for the media (the provision was dropped from the final version of the bill). A Liberal Democratic Party of Russia (LDPR) deputy introduced a bill "on the preservation and development of Slavic traditions," which would create a tax-exempt fund. Another deputy proposed a bill creating a special-purpose off-budget fund for the development of the Far North, another for treatment of solid wastes. Industries formed their own extrabudgetary funds authorized by the government and funded through contributions from individual enterprises (treated as part of production costs). In 1994, Gazprom's off-budget fund took in about 10 trillion rubles in revenues, or close to US$3 billion. Railroads minister Nikolai Aksenenko was accused of creating six off-budget funds, including the "fund for supporting educational institutions of the ministry," a "fund for health care," a "financial reserve fund," and the "fund for investment programs of the ministry." Only in December 2001 did a new law on the procuracy-general eliminate the procuracy's right to maintain its own off-budget "development" funds. These funds may have been legal, but they created an enormous temptation for corrupt diversion of resources for other purposes.

The use of off-budget funds by local and regional governments, ministries and other state organizations, and enterprises proliferated. The volume of resources flowing through them was staggering. By the mid-1990s the money in off-budget funds totaled close to two-thirds of the state budget.[11] Off-budget funds were not subject to budget control, often were free from tax, and were (until the introduction of the treasury system in 1998) managed in commercial banks. At a time when the economic system was shifting from one based on the administrative control of physical resources to one in which money became a financial resource, off-budget funds enabled public entities to act as if they were private interests outside of any public accountability and to provide elected officials with politically useful slush funds. Granting the right to form off-budget funds became yet another of the ways in which the executive and legislative branches competed for support during the early 1990s. Both parliamentarians and executive branch officials benefited from control of large slush funds outside any budgetary control. They deadlocked over policy measures designed to bring off-budget funds under budgetary control.

In summer 1995 a bill requiring that extrabudgetary funds be subject to budget oversight and regular audits, and maintained in the state treasury, died following heated debate in the Duma. Many deputies wanted to bring the pension fund and other social funds under the Duma's budgetary control, but the pension fund itself and deputies sympathetic to it argued that doing so would only increase the likelihood that pension resources would be diverted to other uses.[12] In the meantime, the Audit Chamber and the government's own auditors continually discovered massive abuses in the use of off-budget funds, including the highway fund, the pension fund, and other social funds, often by regional authorities.

Over time, the Federal Assembly has imposed tighter budget controls over these funds. A 1999 law established a general framework for social insurance funds, separating them from budgetary social assistance programs. The law on the one social tax passed in 2000 unified contributions into the four funds (pensions, medical, and the two social funds) and lowered the aggregate rate. This represented a significant step toward placing all the social funds under budgetary control. The next step was to increase the pension fund's control over pension spending by restricting governors' ability to treat pension funds as part of general budget resources (Putin issued a decree to this effect in September 2000, which the Constitutional Court upheld). In the future, the pension fund's control over pension contributions will be reduced through the shift away from social insurance (though a component of social insurance will remain) to a contributions and investment system consisting both of the state's pension system and private funds. With time, therefore, parliament has increased its control both over the state budget and over extrabudgetary flows of resources.

The government's ability to pass balanced budgets through the Federal Assembly since 2000 is owing to several changes in the political and economic environment; it is certainly not only, or even mainly, the consequence of increased parliamentary efficiency. The more favorable exchange rate for the ruble, higher oil and gas prices on world markets, and higher tax collections, as well as the government's ability to command a majority in the Duma that requires fewer spending concessions than in the past, all play a part. The formation of a coalition of four factions that command a stable majority provides a more efficient institutional mechanism for aggregating policy interests than did the old system of building ad hoc cross-factional coalitions for every individual piece of legislation. Now, bargaining between the government and its allied factions allows the government to win over a secure majority for the budget bill without having to spread benefits across the Duma too widely.

The government's practice in the third Duma (2000–03) was to begin negotiations with the "coalition of four" even before submitting the budget bill to the Duma.[13] For example, the Finance Ministry consulted with the leaders of the four allied factions in the summer of 2003 over the shape of the 2004 budget. Sensitive to the deputies' electoral interests, the government relaxed budget discipline somewhat and gave each of the four friendly factions the right to raise spending in one or two issue areas. For example, Unity, the Duma arm of the United Russia party, has sought to identify itself with the cause of greater defense procurement. The faction People's Deputy, which formed the People's Party, pushed the government for greater spending on budget sector employees in the regions. OVR (which originated as the Duma faction of the Fatherland-All Russia party, then subsequently merged into the United Russia party) demanded more funding for agricultural producers. The Russia's Regions group sought more spending on transportation and housing. Sympathetic to their interests, the government developed a budget with optimistic estimates for revenues in order to accommodate the deputies' interests; experts estimated that the deputies' wish list was about 85 percent fulfilled (Preobrazhenskii 2003). Close coordination between the government and its supporters in the Duma made it possible for the government to ensure solid majorities at each stage of the budget process, something that did not occur in the Yeltsin era. Budget and tax policy were subject to distributive bargains but with fewer costly side payments, because the government could concentrate its largesse on the interests of a smaller and more cohesive set of factions.

In the fourth Duma (2003–07), the pro-executive party United Russia enjoyed a commanding majority. This has spared the government the necessity of bargaining with deputies for support for its legislative agenda; large majorities are nearly always ensured. The Kremlin's absolute control over United Russia and United Russia's two-thirds majority in the Duma have resulted in a situation in which the Federal Assembly is effectively marginalized, both in policy making and oversight. If future elections bring a different alignment of forces to the Duma, however, a greater role for parliament as counterweight to the executive is possible.

Conclusions

Studies of governance often emphasize the contradictory qualities expected of institutions. Democratic institutions must be responsive but also decisive (Haggard and McCubbins 2001). Policy makers must be able to respond to public demands and urgent policy needs, but they must also be able to maintain commitments to policy in the face of resistance. Effective governance may require imposing losses on some groups in favor of benefits for the larger public good (Weaver Rockman 1993). Democratization does not necessarily improve institutional capacity; it can allow a broader range of interests to be taken into consideration in making policy and prevent special interests from capturing state power for private benefit, but does not necessarily do so. A weakened state undergoing democratization during a time of economic crisis is particularly vulnerable to capture and corruption by powerful interests that seek concentrated particularistic benefits at the public's expense. In the absence of strong, effective aggregating institutions, such as parties, opening the system to competitive elections and separation of powers may simply compound the problem of fragmented authority and multiply the arenas where organized interests can capture particularistic benefits. Giving a president in a weakened state decree-making authority allows him (or her) to buy off key players by granting them special benefits.

Considering the magnitude of Russia's state crisis in the early 1990s, the growth in institutional capacity is substantial. In contrast with the early 1990s, policy making has become much more efficient. Nearly all significant policy now is made by legislation rather than decree. Legislation passed in the late 1990s and under Putin has significantly increased budget control and reduced the level of loopholes, concessions, and grants of unaccountable power in fiscal policy. Public confidence in central institutions has risen. The system of parliamentary political factions and bicameralism have enabled the Federal Assembly to overcome its own collective dilemmas, as it was unable to do in the two interim systems of 1989–91 and 1990–93.

With greater capacity to deliberate and reach decisions has come greater capacity for oversight, lawmaking, and budget control. This capacity has grown, however, at the expense of Parliament's independence. Legislative oversight of the executive branch is effective to the degree that it serves the purposes of powerful executive actors, and bargaining between the legislative and executive branches is efficient because it narrows the range of political interests that must be satisfied in order to build reliable majorities. De facto oversight and other powers at the disposal of the Federal Assembly during the Yeltsin period often were instruments used by the political opposition in the legislature, which was unable to achieve its own agenda but sought to block the president's. During the Putin era, the same tools are used effectively by the president's allies in the legislature to achieve their political goals.

Therefore, the record of success that President Putin and his government have enjoyed in passing their legislative agenda through the Federal Assembly is partly the result of the growth of expertise and efficient institutions in parliament (such as the emergence of a stable majority coalition of four factions). But it is also the product of the growing use of administrative and police powers by the executive to silence the opposition, the rationalization of policy-making capacity in the executive, and the growth in the capacity of major business associations to aggregate the interests of their members. However, Russia has not developed a system of programmatic parties offering voters ideologically based choices over government formation and government policy. It appears that the key to effective governance is less the formal powers enjoyed by the legislature than the existence of institutions that aggregate social interests as broadly as possible and allow policy decisions to be made with as few side payments to affected private interests as possible. In democratic polities, systems of competitive parties, tied with national interest groups and mass media, perform this role. Russia remains far from establishing such institutions.

Notes

This chapter is based on research conducted under the auspices of the Project on Governance in Russia, directed by Stephen Holmes and Timothy J. Colton, with the support of the Carnegie Corporation of New York. The valuable comments of the participants in the project and the support of the Carnegie Corporation are gratefully acknowledged. See Remington (2006).

1. The Federal Assembly is a bicameral parliament consisting of an upper chamber (the Federation Council) and a lower chamber, the State Duma. The Federation Council consists of two representatives delegated by the executive and legislative branches of each of Russia's federal territorial subjects. The Duma consists of 450 popularly elected deputies. From 1993 to 2007, half the Duma's deputies were elected in single-member districts, the other half by party-list proportional representation in a single federal district. Since December 2007, all 450 Duma deputies have been elected by proportional representation.

2. Chaisty 2001; McFaul 2001; Remington 2000, 2001; Troxel 2003.

3. For early Bolshevik efforts to reconcile "workers' control" with "state control," see Remington 1982 and 1989.

4. Polit.ru, May 16, 2001.

5. Polit.ru, September 15, 2000.

6. Stepashin has sought to put the Audit Chamber under the direct authority of the president and to reduce the Duma's ability to demand investigations. In the spring of 2002, Stepashin pressed for a law that would make the body subordinate to *both* president and Parliament, while in summer 2003 he called for a change in rules that would require a vote by a majority of the Duma (rather than merely 90 votes) in order to begin an investigation. Stepashin has repeatedly expressed frustration that the government and the procuracy do not respond to Audit Chamber reports, and argues that placing the chamber under the presidential administration would increase its bureaucratic clout. The Finance Ministry has opposed Stepashin's empire-building efforts, and the legislation incorporating some of Stepashin's proposals has languished in Parliament for want of support. See Polit.ru, April 23, 2003; Radio Free Europe/Radio Liberty (RFE/RL) "Newsline," August 1, 2003.

7. Polit.ru, October 18, 2001.

8. *Segodnia*, March 3, 2001.

9. *Segodnia*, April 15, 1998.

10. *Izvestiia*, June 6, 1995.

11. *Izvestiia*, June 6, 1995.

12. *Segodnia*, June 8, 1995.

13. The Federation Council now participates informally but regularly on a number of pieces of legislation in these "zero reading" consultations between the government and the Duma, which in turn allows its members' interests to be accommodated before and during the passage of bills through the Duma. This is one reason nearly all legislation reaching the Federation Council from the Duma passes.

Bibliography

Chaisty, Paul. 2001. "Legislative Politics in Russia." In *Contemporary Russian Politics: A Reader*, ed. A. Brown, 103–20. New York: Oxford University Press.

Haggard, Stephan, and Mathew D. McCubbins, eds. 2001. *Presidents, Parliaments, and Policy*. Cambridge, U.K.: Cambridge University Press.

Huber, John D., Charles R. Shipan, and Madelaine Pfahler. 2001. "Legislatures and Statutory Control of Bureaucracy." *American Journal of Political Science* 45 (2): 330–45.

McCubbins, Mathew D., and Thomas Schwartz. 1984. "Congressional Oversight Overlooked: Police Patrols versus Fire Alarms." *American Journal of Political Science* 28 (1): 165–79.

McFaul, Michael. 2001. *Russia's Unfinished Revolution: Political Change from Gorbachev to Putin*. Ithaca, NY: Cornell University Press.

Preobrazhenskii, Ivan. 2003. "Pravitel'stvo naidet deneg dlia vsekh." Web site of the Center for Political Technologies, Politkom.ru.

Remington, Thomas F. 1982. "Institution Building in Bolshevik Russia: The Case of State *Kontrol'*." *Slavic Review* 41 (1): 91–103.

———. 1989. "The Rationalization of State Kontrol'," In *Party and Society in the Russian Civil War: Explorations in Social History*. Bloomington, IN: Indiana University Press.

———. 2000. "The Evolution of Executive-Legislative Relations in Russia since 1993." *Slavic Review* 59 (3): 499–520.

———. 2001. *The Russian Parliament: Institutional Evolution in a Transitional Regime, 1989–1999*. New Haven, CT: Yale University Press.

———. 2006. "Democratization, Separation of Powers, and State Capacity." In *The State after Communism: Governance in the New Russia*, eds. T. J. Colton and S. Holmes, 261–98. Lanham, MD: Rowman & Littlefield.

Satarov, Georgii, et al. 2001. *Epokha Yel'tsina: ocherki politicheskoi istorii*. Moscow: Vagrius.

Troxel, Tiffany A. 2003. *Parliamentary Power in Russia, 1994–2001: President vs Parliament*. New York: Palgrave MacMillan.

Weaver, R. Kent, and Bert A. Rockman, eds. 1993. *Do Institutions Matter? Government Capabilities in the United States and Abroad*. Washington, DC: Brookings Institution.

CHAPTER 13

Administrative Review and Oversight: The Experience of Westminster

Mark Shephard

Parliament has been left behind by far-reaching changes to the constitution, government and society in the past two decades. Despite recent innovations, particularly in the handling of legislation, the central question of Westminster's scrutiny of the executive has not been addressed.

(Report of the Hansard Society Commission on
Parliamentary Scrutiny, 2001)

Prior to the Labour Party's election victory in 1997, Labour's manifesto promised an "effective House of Commons" to be realized in large part through the creation of a special select committee with a remit to review procedures in light of the "need for modernization." Shortly after winning the elections, Labour established a Modernisation Committee chaired by the leader of the House of Commons and with a remit to review four key areas: the legislative process, ministerial accountability, working practices (such as sitting hours), and the style and form of proceedings. Between 1997 and 2003 the committee published 19 reports, starting with a report on the legislative process. However, to date, most of the reports have focused on the modernization of working practices and the style and form of proceedings. Reports that deal with improving the effectiveness of ministerial accountability have been notably lacking. Consequently, the view of the Hansard Society (2001), that "parliamentary reform has been one of improving the efficiency of Parliament, but not its effectiveness," appears just as valid today.

Challenges to Reforming Parliamentary Effectiveness

There are of course serious contextual hurdles to reforming the effectiveness of Parliament. The nature of, and possibilities for, administrative oversight at Westminster are largely bounded by constitutional arrangements such as the fusion of the executive and legislative branches in Parliament and the "first-past-the-post" electoral system that is conducive to a predominantly one-party majority government maintained through strong party discipline. Compounding the systemic strength of the executive in Parliament is the growth of careerism and an emphasis on the ministerial career ladder with rewards for partisan loyalty.

In turn, Parliament is primarily considered as a body that reacts to executive measures (Norton 1993; Rogers and Walters 2004). This context of a strong executive and a reactive Parliament lacking independent powers and associated alternative career structures ultimately limits how far modernization can go without "seismic constitutional change" (Rogers and Walters 2004, 369). A prime example of the salience of context as a hurdle to the realization of reform is the May 2002 defeat of the Modernisation Committee's proposal to move select committee appointment power from the party whips to a Committee of Nomination.[1] Alexandra Kelso argues that the context of partisan and patronage interests best explains why Parliament failed to make appointment to select committees a process independent of the whips' offices (Kelso 2003).

As well as context, the behavior of parliamentarians can be a factor in determining the effectiveness of Parliament in executive oversight. Philip Norton stressed the importance of attitudinal and behavioral changes occurring alongside any institutional reforms (Norton 1985, 2000): "There is no point strengthening the House of Commons if MPs are unable or unwilling to exploit the opportunities afforded by such change" (2000, 21).

However, David Judge challenged the Norton view on the basis that the normative system of the House reflects the preferences of those with the most power, and so attitudinal change and internal procedural reform will invariably fail unless key constitutional arrangements are addressed (Judge 1993, 215).

Oversight and Effectiveness in the Westminster Parliament

The primary means of oversight in the Westminster Parliament are through debates, questions, and committees (Norton 1993, 89). What follows is a discussion of key aspects of these means in the House of Commons, as well as an attempt to assess their effectiveness.

Debates

The salience of debates in the House of Commons as a means of oversight are constrained from the outset, as the government controls not only the timetable but much of the ground on which it will debate (Hansard Society 2001). However, even on its own ground, government does not dominate entirely. Rogers and Walters (2004) used the example of the 2003 government debate and vote on war with Iraq to illustrate the government's unprecedented decision to seek Parliament's approval for military action despite its being a prerogative power of the executive. In addition, Rogers and Walters argued that this decision had set a precedent that future governments may have to uphold if they wish to be seen as acting legitimately (374).

Although the government may control the timetable, Parliament has 20 Opposition Days (or 120 hours), when the opposition parties can debate and vote on a substantive motion of their choosing. Recent subjects chosen by the opposition have included advocating a referendum on the European Union (EU) constitution, and questioning the military situation in Iraq and the security of the electricity supply. Opposition Days provide a means for the opposition parties to scrutinize the actions and policies of the government; selected subjects typically reflect domains in which the opposition parties feel that the government is particularly exposed to criticism.

As to the effectiveness of Opposition Day debates, the evidence depends on who is consulted and what is measured. When the Hansard Society surveyed parliamentarians in June 2000, one of the questions they asked was "How effective are Opposition Day debates in securing information and explanation from Government?" (Hansard Society 2001, 131). Of the 179 responses they received, fewer than one in four replied that they were effective. The Hansard Society Commission concluded that the predictable defeat of opposition motions during debates, combined with the low quality of debate in general, the little public interest, and the use of the procedure to identify which members of Parliament (MPs) deserve promotion, meant that debates may no longer be suitable for today's politics (51).

However, the effectiveness of Opposition Days is hard to measure, and the conclusions of the Hansard Society Commission may be a little harsh, given the evidence. Though opposition motions are routinely defeated, they can have indirect effects, such as capturing or perpetuating media coverage and putting pressure on the government.

One example is the October 2001 Opposition Day debate deploring spin tactics in the Department of Transport, local government, and the regions. The debate focused on the call for special adviser Jo Moore to resign over an e-mail instructing colleagues to "bury" bad news in the wake of the September 11 attacks. Moore eventually resigned in February 2002 after constant media pressure and additional allegations of inappropriate behavior. Although the Opposition Day debate was not immediately or entirely instrumental in Moore's resignation, it may have played some part. Another more recent example concerns the government's April 2004 U-turn over the possibility of holding a referendum on the EU constitution.

As well as Opposition Days, other debates include half-hour adjournment debates, very occasional emergency adjournment debates, "early day motions, and since 1999, parallel sittings in Westminster Hall for debates on less contentious business, such as committee reports and adjournment debates. The half-hour adjournment debates occur at the end of each day and allow backbenchers to raise an issue with the government that typically reflects a specific constituency concern that an MP wants the relevant minister to respond to. Early day motions are rarely debated but are used by MPs to express opinions on subjects and provide governments with indicators of levels of backbench support and opposition on issues.

Parliamentary Questions

Arguably more important than debates, parliamentary questions (PQs) provide backbenchers an opportunity to call ministers to account. PQs can be written or oral and include departmental question time, interdepartmental question time, prime minister's questions (PMQs), private-notice questions (PNQs), and questions following ministerial statements.

Departmental question time lasts roughly an hour each Monday through Thursday while the Parliament is sitting. Although the government decides the departmental rota, or order of rotation, for question time, on balance, each department faces scrutiny from the Parliament approximately once every four weeks. Interdepartmental question time in the parallel chamber is a recent innovation (begun in 2003) that reflects attempts at a "joined-up government" for those issues such as crime that straddle departmental briefs.

The format of PMQs changed under Prime Minister Tony Blair from twice-weekly question periods on Tuesdays and Thursdays to one 30-minute question period on Wednesdays. While the overall duration of PMQs remains the same, and although time-wasting introductions and reiteration of replies were removed from the procedure under Blair, there is still some criticism of the change, particularly the loss of twice-weekly questioning. The report of the Commission to Strengthen Parliament (the Norton Commission) favored a return to twice-weekly question periods on Tuesdays and Thursdays, each 30 minutes. The rationale behind this recommendation is that it would help restore the importance of Thursdays as a major business day and that it would connect the prime minister more with the Parliament (Norton 2000).

Private-notice questions (PNQs) are questions of an urgent nature on key issues of national importance and are granted at the discretion of the Speaker. Once granted, ministers are given short notice to appear before Parliament and can be questioned as long as the Speaker permits. Unlike PNQs, statements by ministers are more common, are prompted by the executive, and provide the government with a chance to inform the House (preempting PNQs) on key issues that arise. However, statements by ministers are generally followed by questions, again at the discretion of the Speaker.

Again, effectiveness of questions depends on who is consulted and what is measured. Out of the various types of questions, the Hansard Society (2001, 131) found that just over half of MPs surveyed rated written questions as effective in securing information and explanation from government. By comparison, oral questions were rated as less effective—effectiveness ranged from 45 percent for ministerial statements to 43 percent for private-notice questions, to 25 percent for question time, to a low 8 percent for prime minister's questions.

One of the reasons why written questions are generally perceived as being more effective than oral questions is that, whereas oral questions perform other legislative functions such as political point scoring and tension release, written questions permit a more focused and persistent means of oversight. As an example of this distinction, Rogers and Walters (2004, 303) noted how Labour MP Tam Dalyell's determined usage of written questions led to the uncovering of misinformation during the Falkland's conflict.

Of the oral questions, PNQs and ministerial statements are regularly singled out as procedures that the government should give more time to by curtailing other, less-effective procedures such as debates.[2] Responding primarily to a different recommendation in the Procedure Committee report (2002), the government opted to reduce the period of notice for questions to ministers from 10 to three sitting days, arguing that this would encourage "more topical and relevant" questioning. The government rejected calls for extensions of departmental question time on a single subject because of time pressures. However, the government did consent to a once-a-week, hour-long session of questioning in Westminster Hall.

Since the mid-1990s, the Public Administration Select Committee (PASC) and its predecessor (Public Services Committee) have produced six reports on ministerial accountability and parliamentary questions. In their latest report, the PASC has continued to lament the evasive nature of many of the government's replies to questions: "The government's approach to answering questions has, at times, been characterised as minimising the opportunity for scrutiny of its actions through careful and skilful crafting of answers."[3]

The committee acknowledges that the publication of codes of conduct, codes for access, and guidance on answering PQs in the 1990s has increased the obligation of government to account for its actions. However, the committee criticizes the government for treating public inquiries like the Hutton Inquiry more seriously than either PQs or select committees: the government was "committed to co-operating fully" with the former but specified "information provided…as appropriate" for the PQ and committee inquiries.[4]

Of particular concern to the PASC are the quality of replies and the unanswered questions (often due to prohibitive costs, future promises of replies, or exemptions in the *Code of Access to Government Information*). In response to the concerns, the government has agreed to answer "reasonable requests" about refusals to answer questions within 20 days, and has also agreed to specify the source of any exemption in its replies.[5] However, the committee is skeptical about the government's level of commitment to its promises and has reacted by strengthening recommendations.[6]

Select Committees

More important than either debates or questions are the oversight roles that select committees have systematically performed since 1979. While acknowledging that the comparative effectiveness of the select committee system is constrained by the constitutional framework (primarily, no separation of powers), by single-party governments, and by strong party loyalties, the Liaison Committee reported that the "select committee system has been a success," and it has "provided independent scrutiny of the government."[7] Findings from the Hansard Society survey of MPs support this perspective, with 84 percent rating select committee hearings as effective in securing information and explanations from government (2001, 131).

There are several types of select committees. First, departmental select committees shadow each government department and are responsible for the detailed oversight of government and public body expenditure, administration, and policy. Second, interdepartmental select committees primarily oversee activities that cross-cut government departments, for example, the Environmental Audit Committee, the European Scrutiny Committee, the Public Accounts Committee, and the Public Administration Committee. Third are select committees that deal with the procedures and administration of the House, for example, the Liaison Committee (which largely comprises select committee chairs and considers matters relating to the work of select committees), the Procedures Committee, and the Modernisation of the House of Commons Committee.

Interest in reforming the select committee system has strengthened in recent years. Recommendations for reform have been wide-ranging (from increased resources to the establishment of independent appointment committees), and successes to date have been mixed.

One of the most contentious issues surrounding select committees is the independence of membership. In 2001, when the government attempted to remove two of its most ardent critics from select committee chair positions, the House of Commons voted against the motion and the critics were reinstated. Current selection procedures are still highly influenced by the party whips, and the composition of each committee is generally proportionate to the balance of the parties on the floor of the House of Commons. The Liaison Committee (2000), the Norton Commission (2000), and the Modernisation Committee (2002) all favored removing powers of selection from the whips. Proposing a more independent Committee of Nomination, the proposal of the Modernisation Committee, was defeated in a 2002 vote in the House of Commons.

Other recommendations for reform have met with more success. Arguably the most important government concession to select committee scrutiny has been the prime minister's agreement to be questioned by the Liaison Committee. Initially Blair had rejected a 2001 Public Administration Committee recommendation that the prime minister appear before the committee to discuss the government's Annual Report; however, in April 2002, he offered the Liaison Committee a two-hour twice-yearly questioning period on domestic and international affairs. To date, the prime minister has been questioned on a variety of subjects, including the Iraq war. Rogers and Walters (2004) perceived this as a further executive concession to Parliament that will be difficult for future prime ministers to withdraw from (Rogers and Walters 2004, 375).

A further advance for the select committee system is the 2003 recommendation to reward departmental and most interdepartmental select committee chairs with £12,500 on top of their MP salaries (Review Body on Senior Salaries 2003). One of the recommendations of the Norton Commission was that select committees should offer an alternative career path to that of ministerial office (Norton 2000). Though universally unpopular both inside and outside the House, this move toward variable parliamentary salaries is arguably an important first step in any attempt to alter the current imbalances in career incentives between the legislative and executive branches.

Another recent advance for select committees has been the creation and extension of staffing resources for the Scrutiny Unit—a House body that provides select committees with advice on expenditures and draft legislation. This development reflects the recent emphasis that both the Modernisation and the Liaison committees have placed on supporting a more systematic and less ad hoc approach to the exercise of scrutiny. In June 2002, the Liaison Committee established guidance on four objectives and 10 core tasks for departmental select committees (see box 13.1).

Box 13.1. Objectives and Tasks for Scrutiny Committees

Objective A: To examine and comment on the policy of the department.

Task 1: To examine policy proposals from the U.K. government and the European Commission in green papers, white papers, draft guidance, etc., and to inquire further where the Committee considers it appropriate.

Task 2: To identify and examine areas of emerging policy, or where existing policy is deficient, and make proposals.

Task 3: To conduct scrutiny of any published draft bill within the Committee's responsibilities.

Task 4: To examine specific output from the department expressed in documents or other decisions.

Objective B: To examine the expenditure of the department.

Task 5: To examine the expenditure plans and out-turn of the department, its agencies, and principal NDPBs (nondepartmental public bodies).

Objective C: To examine the administration of the department.

Task 6: To examine the department's Public Service Agreements, the associated targets, and the statistical measurements employed, and report if appropriate.

Task 7: To monitor the work of the department's executive agencies, NDPBs, regulators, and other associated public bodies.

Task 8: To scrutinise major appointments made by the department.

Task 9: To examine the implementation of legislation and major policy initiatives.

Objective D: To assist the House in debate and decision.

Task 10: To produce reports which are suitable for debate in the House, including Westminster Hall, or debating committees.

Source: Parliament, Liaison Committee, 2003 (HC 558), 9.

However, despite some recent advances (both through Parliament's own initiative and executive concessions), the select committee system continues to attract calls for reform, most notably in relation to providing access to papers and people and improving committee impact on the work and policies of government (Hansard Society 2004). Key hurdles to effective oversight of government departments remain, for example, lack of prime time in Parliament to consider major select committee reports, lack of power to require the attendance of ministers and civil servants, and lack of power to force them to answer questions. Rogers and Walters (2004) argued that focus on this lack of powers is unlikely to go away, but that any attempt to address them "would require a fundamental change in the relationship between government and Parliament (385)."

Administrative review and oversight by Parliament, although in flux and with some recent advancements for Parliament, remain constrained by the constitutional arrangements, one-party-majority governments, and strong partisanship that ensure that without fundamental change, the executive is invariably able to dominate.

Notes

1. Parliament, Modernisation Select Committee 2002 (HC 224).
2. Norton 2000; Hansard Society 2001; Parliament 2002 (Cm. 5628).
3. Parliament, Public Administration Select Committee (PASC), 2004 (HC 355), 5.
4. Parliament, PASC, 2004 (HC 355), 6.
5. Parliament, PASC, 2002 (HC 136), 5.
6. Parliament, PASC, 2004, (HC 355), 20.
7. Parliament, Liaison Committee, 2000 (HC 300), 2.

Bibliography

Hansard Society, Commission on Parliamentary Scrutiny. 2001. *The Challenge for Parliament: Making Government Accountable.* London: Hansard Society.

Hansard Society Conference. 2004. *The Future of Select Committees: Issues, Challenges, and Proposals for Reform.* London: Hansard Society.

Judge, David. 1993. *The Parliamentary State.* London: Sage.

Kelso, Alexandra. 2003. "Where Were the Massed Ranks of Parliamentary Reformers? 'Attitudinal' and 'Contextual' Approaches to Parliamentary Reform." *Journal of Legislative Studies* 9 (1).

Norton, Philip. 1985. *Parliament in the 1980s.* Oxford: Basil Blackwell.

———. 1993. *Does Parliament Matter?* Hemel Hempstead: Harvester Wheatsheaf.

———. 2000. *Strengthening Parliament: The Report of the Commission to Strengthen Parliament.* London: Conservative Party.

Parliament. 2002. *Government Response to the Procedure Committee Report on Parliamentary Questions (HC 622).* Cm. 5628. London: Her Majesty's Stationery Office.

———. 2003. *Pay for Select Committee Chairmen in the House of Commons, 55th Report of the Review Body on Senior Salaries.* Cm. 5673. London: HMSO.

———. HC Liaison Committee. 2000. *Shifting the Balance: Select Committees and the Executive*. First Report (Session 1999–2000). HC 300. London: HMSO.

———. HC Liaison Committee. 2003. *Annual Report for 2002*. First Report (Session 2002–03). HC 558. London: HMSO.

———. HC Modernisation Select Committee. 2002. *Select Committees*. First Report (Session 2001–02). HC 224. London: HMSO.

———. HC Procedure Committee. 2002. *Parliamentary Questions* Third Report (Session 2001–02). HC 622. London: HMSO.

———. HC Public Administration Select Committee. 2002. *Ministerial Accountability and Parliamentary Questions: The Government Response to the Ninth Report of the Committee (Session 2001–02)*. First Report (Session 2002–03). HC 136. London: HMSO.

Rogers, Robert, and Rhodri Walters. 2004. *How Parliament Works*. 5th ed. London: Pearson.

CHAPTER 14

Explaining Patterns of Oversight in Brazilian Subnational Governments

Scott W. Desposato

Latin American democracies face challenges typical of those faced by most young democracies. Governments are struggling to implement successful economic policies, especially in the context of recent downturns. Corruption continues to be a serious problem among bureaucracies and elected officials. Presidents, parties, and legislatures alike are receiving remarkably low levels of public trust. In this context, legislative oversight is especially important, yet it remains underimplemented in most of Latin America.

Interestingly, presidentialism—the current form of government for the great majority of Latin America's countries—can make these challenges even more pressing, while creating more incentives for oversight. The potential challenges of presidentialism are well known: separate and fixed mandates for executive and legislative branches lead to an increased potential for stalemate and regime breakdown. But presidentialism also may increase the quality of oversight, because conflict between branches and independent ambition can decrease the potential for collusion present in parliamentary systems.

Typically, oversight in Latin American democracies has been inadequate and driven more by scandals too large to ignore than by a constant pressure for efficiency, clean government, and good public policy. Many legislators have been co-opted into blindly supporting executives in exchange for public works for their constituencies, or even for bribes. Oversight comes only when executive corruption or failure simply cannot be ignored (that is, Collor, in Brazil), or only after executives have left office (Fujimori in Peru or Menem in Argentina).

Several types of oversight can be observed in political systems. First is the formal institutional framework that authorizes legislative oversight and provides legal authority for challenges to the executive's programs or policies. Second are the informal institutional incentives for using that authority. In large part these are driven by the preferences of the electorate and the electoral system. One example is the extent to which elections are clientelistic or programmatic (respectively, an electoral base built on candidates' distribution of personal favors versus one built on policy promises and issues, and the range between). Last is the capacity of the legislature to engage in effective oversight activities. This capacity is often endogenous to the other two variables; for example, legislators do not create capacity without incentives.

This chapter examines the impact of informal institutions on oversight by examining Brazilian state assemblies. Subnational governments are frequently overlooked in Latin American politics but are important for at least three reasons. First, the policies implemented and decisions made in subnational governments have important and direct effects on the quality of life of citizens. State governments frequently control and set agendas for the distribution of education resources, health programs, and infrastructure development. Though unlikely to affect inflation or unemployment rates, they do directly affect the lives of individuals. Second, subnational governments in Brazil directly mirror the formal institutions of the national government. The balance of power and patterns of politics are very similar to those of the national government. Hence, lessons learned from the states can directly affect conclusions about improving oversight at the national level. Finally, state governments provide a nearly ideal environment for testing the impact of nonformal institutions. They share virtually identical formal institutional rules and operate in the same broader economic and cultural framework, but they differ dramatically in political history and culture. Some states are more developed and programmatic in their politics, whereas others are much less developed and more clientelistic. The result is a mini laboratory for observing how the same institutions work in different contexts.

Institutions Shaping Legislative Oversight

Brazilian state governments are all mini presidential systems, with governors, unicameral legislatures, and state judiciaries. Elections for all state posts are held concurrently, with fixed four-year terms. All states use the same basic election procedures. Governors are elected through a runoff majority system, and state legislators are elected based on open-list proportional representation—a very personalistic and antiparty system (Ames 2001; Barkan, Ademolekun, and Zhou 2004; Carey and Shugart 1995; Mainwaring 1997). Some of these institutions are mandated from above by the national constitution. Other similarities across states are an artifact of history: when all state constitutions were rewritten following the return to democracy, a lack of technical expertise and experience led many state legislatures to essentially copy the national constitution.

Formal Institutions

Brazilian state assemblies would be characterized as formally weak by many scholars. The executive retains the exclusive capacity to introduce legislation affecting budgets and taxation, the expansion of public employment, and other administrative issues. Governors also have reasonable veto powers: partial (line item) or full vetoes, overridden only by an absolute majority of legislators.[1]

Although legislatures have limited capacity to initiate policy, they do have reasonable oversight authority, which is vested in several mechanisms. First, legislators can call state departmental heads to testify before committee meetings. In addition, at the request of a minimal number of legislators, the assembly can form a special investigative committee with some judicial authority, which can refer its findings directly to the public prosecutor.

The legislature is also directly charged with the responsibility of overseeing and evaluating the legality and efficiency of the use of state funds, the budget process, and all administration. One component of this responsibility is receiving, evaluating, and approving the annual audit of the state conducted by the *Tribunal de Contas*, a branch of the judiciary.

Finally, the legislature has the capability to directly confront the governor, overriding vetoes with an absolute majority vote. The legislature can also open impeachment proceedings and judge the governor, vice governor, and all state department heads for crimes related to their offices.

In a purely formal sense, the state legislatures are thus relatively weak in terms of policy formation. The governors' exclusive initiation powers restrict legislative opportunities for independent policy making in many areas. But the legislatures retain formal powers of oversight and are capable of challenging an incompetent or corrupt executive. However, many Brazilian state legislatures often do not aggressively engage the executive branch, primarily because they lack electoral incentives for oversight.

Clientelistic and Programmatic Politics

In purely clientelistic systems, elections are won through the delivery of personalistic goods in exchange for votes. Candidates distribute personal favors, goods and services, or even cash to build an electoral base. In purely programmatic systems, candidates make policy promises and take stances on issues in pursuit of votes. And of course there are intermediate types of systems between these two extremes, in which candidates offer local public goods, club goods, or a combination of individualistic goods and policy proposals.

The extent to which a political system is more or less programmatic shapes the incentives for legislative oversight. In clientelistic electoral markets there are few incentives for legislators to invest in legislative professionalization, party cohesion, or policy development (Desposato 2001). In programmatic electoral markets, such investments are much more likely. This argument has direct implications for oversight. In clientelistic electoral environments, oversight will be secondary to the pursuit of pork and patronage from the executive branch. In programmatic electoral markets, politicians can use oversight to further their careers.

The relationship between system type and oversight is driven by the types of goods, or benefits, politicians deliver and by voters' relative preferences for programmatic or individualistic goods. Individualist or private goods are relatively certain and immediate; public goods are delayed and uncertain.

Where elections are driven by private goods, such as cash, food, or T-shirts—or even by local public goods such as paving of roads, appeals to abstract notions of preventing corruption may have little interest for voters. Typically, voters in such environments have pressing short-term needs that trump promises of long-term changes in health care, corruption, or environment. A new hospital is worth more to a voter than a small cash payment, but that hospital might never be built, whereas the cash payment can be enjoyed immediately.

The result is that in individualistic electoral markets, legislators should focus on obtaining and delivering resources to voters. These investments of time and energy have direct electoral payoffs to politicians and welfare payoffs to voters. Other activities, including oversight, do not have any payoff to ambitious politicians. Indeed, a successful and clientelistic politician will be praised with a phrase common in Brazilian politics: *rouba mas faz*, roughly, "he steals but gets things done."

In contrast, in programmatic electoral markets, very different patterns are seen. Voters there are willing to forgo immediate low-value payoffs for longer-term, uncertain, and higher-value goods. The implication is that legislators will work on delivery of such goods—introducing legislation, professionalizing, engaging in debates and committee work, and also overseeing the executive to reduce corruption and increase efficiency. A few indicators of legislative behavior from Brazil show these patterns. Table 14.1 compares party cohesion for government and opposition parties, and shows how clientelism and poverty can degrade the potential for independent legislative action. In the poorest states, where individualistic goods are a common part of legislative elections, government parties are very cohesive, while opposition parties are clearly divided. The pattern reflects legislators' need to abandon party platforms for gubernatorially supplied pork. Government parties have high cohesion because of the congruence between party positions and the governors' positions. But instead of aggressive oversight and challenges, opposition parties split, with some legislators sticking with their party's platform and others defecting to vote with the governor in exchange for pork.

Table 14.1. Government and Opposition Average Party Cohesion, 1991–98

State	Cohesion			
	Government	Opposition	Difference	
Programmatic				
Rio Grande do Sul	.87	.93	−.06	***
Sao Paulo	.84	.87	−.03	***
Brasilia	.84	.86	−.02	—
Clientelistic				
Piauí	.94	.48	.46	***
Bahia	.98	.81	.17	*

Source: Desposato (2001).

Note: * .05, *** .01; — = not available.

Table 14.2. Estimated Veto Frequency, 1991–98

State	Legislative session	
	1991–94	1995–98
Programmatic		
Rio Grande do Sul	126	88
Sao Paulo	136	118
Brasilia	36	6
Clientelistic		
Piauí	0	0
Bahia	0	0

Source: Desposato (2001).

Table 14.2 shows another indicator of executive-legislative independence—the frequency of vetoes. The number of vetoes reflects the legislature's willingness to pass legislation opposed by the executive branch, and shows substantial variation among states. Specifically, legislatures in poorer states are much less likely to pass legislation that diverges from the governors' preferences. Again, legislators' primary goal is to deliver private and local public goods to constituents, so they delegate legislative authority to the executive branch. In contrast, in public goods states, there is evidence of significant executive-legislative conflict. Legislatures frequently pass bills opposed by the governor and sometimes overturn those vetoes. These patterns show how interbranch conflict and legislative independence are more likely to be observed in programmatic electoral environments as opposed to clientelistic states.

These patterns are corroborated by research on state budget processes. Schneider (2001) found that in more clientelistic states, legislators completely defer to the governor on budgetary matters, even though they are constitutionally charged with oversight. In one case, he found that budget committee members would call the governor's staff to ask which budget amendments they should pass! In contrast, in more ideological states, budget politics are much more controversial, with state assemblies even passing legislation over the governor's veto. None of these directly measure oversight, but all measure a key prerequisite of effective oversight: the independence of legislative politics from executive influence.

How Change Can Happen

There are three implications of how improvements in oversight may happen in young democracies, reflecting the role of institutional change, social change, and exogenous change.

Change through Formal Institutions and Capacity Building

Institutional change suggests increasing the powers afforded the legislative branch by increasing legislative power in relation to the executive branch, weakening veto overrides, or reducing presidents' decree or agenda authority. Ambition theory suggests that legislators will use increased powers to expand their authority over policy making through legislative oversight. However, such powers are often embedded in constitutions and can be changed only with difficulty.

Changing the availability of resources, however, is much easier. One change would be to increase legislatures' professional staff who have technical expertise in specific policy areas, including budgets. Evidence suggests that simply increasing information resources can have important effects on legislative oversight. For example, the state of Minas Gerais embarked on an ambitious legislative professionalization program in 1998, creating a legislative school to train deputies, hiring technical staff, and increasing publicity of legislative activity. The changes have reportedly been very successful. One deputy reported that previously the executive would simply send budget proposals to the legislature for a rubber-stamp approval. The legislators were not equipped to pore over a complex budget document. Now, however, they reported that the executive treated them with more respect, sending a team to present the budget and answer questions from legislators and their staff. Deputies directly attribute this to the increase in available professional resources.

Unfortunately, changes such as increased staff or information are difficult to implement because legislative professionalization and capacity are endogenous to existing political systems. One reason budget information resources are scarce is because legislators have previously had little use for them. Where elections are driven by individualistic benefits, technical tools for legislative oversight are not a priority. Similarly, if legislators challenge or limit the executive's behavior, they risk losing access to essential pork.

Informal Institutional Change

A second way to increase legislative oversight is by changing the informal electoral incentives of legislators as clientelism diminishes and programmatic politics becomes more common. There is some evidence that these transformations are taking place in Brazil.

One example of electoral market change is the case of Bahia. The less-developed state of Bahia is frequently characterized as a heavily clientelistic state, where vote buying is common and the delivery of local public goods is an essential part of elections. Along with this has been corruption and allegations of electoral fraud, as well as virtually no legislative oversight of the executive branch. The importance of executive-delivered pork is apparent in state deputies' thanking the governor for giving them their mandates. But the development of a petrochemical sector in the Reconcavo region of the state has led to some significant changes. Workers there have organized into labor unions, and ideological labor politicians have been elected from those regions. They have engaged the legislature aggressively with efforts to debate policy on the floor or in committee meetings, and are pushing for significant changes in the nature of executive-legislative relations. Status quo deputies acknowledge this shift, noting that, previously, debates were not even necessary, but now they are obliged to defend the government publicly.

Exogenous Change: Visionaries and Donors

A third way that legislative oversight may increase is exogenously, through the leadership of individual visionaries or through donor programs. In cases where there are no incentives for politicians to transform their system, there are opportunities for outsiders to contribute to an increase in legislative oversight. For example, Minas Gerais's professionalized state legislature largely reflects the vision of the administrative director of the legislature, a political appointee responsible for the administration of the state assembly. Deputies reported that he began to exert pressure for increased legislative expertise and technical capability, in the process founding a school to train new legislators in the legislative process and hiring additional technical staff.

Chance visionaries may never come to many political systems. An additional source of change is assistance from nongovernmental organizations and other donors. Such agencies can directly increase the short-term professionalization of a legislature through technical training for legislators and staff. They may also provide basic infrastructure—computers, networks, and archival material—to facilitate professionalization.

What remains unclear is the long-term impact of exogenous assistance for change. Certainly donor assistance is changing the political landscape of many communities (Brown, Brown, and Desposato 2002. Research suggests that the potential of donor assistance to permanently improve legislative oversight depends on the nature of the assistance and each political system.

One important determinant in whether professionalization programs are successful is institutional memory. Where resources are invested in legislators or politically appointed staff, turnover and progressive ambition may reduce the effectiveness of such programs. That is, where legislators quickly move on to other offices and take their staff with them—because of term limits or opportunity structures—training will be less effective and not retained within an institution. Where turnover is low, donor resources can be invested in individuals. Where turnover is high, donor resources will probably be effective only when invested in more permanent institutional capacity, such as starting a legislative school or even forming a research institute at the legislature's disposal.

A second determinant of success is the presence of legislators who have incentive to use their new resources. In largely clientelistic political systems, most legislators will have no incentive to use procedures to challenge the executive branch. The existence of a small but significant minority of legislators with electoral support for oversight can change everything. In a state like Bahia, 10 percent of the representatives were from an ideological workers party and would likely use technical resources to push for political reform. Where there are only one or two such deputies, however, pressure for change may be easily quelled.[2]

On all these dimensions there is room for optimism regarding Latin America, and in particular Brazilian state assemblies. A national organization of state legislatures has created a forum for exchange and dialogue, and for diffusion of oversight-enhancing reforms. Reformist pressure from federal prosecutors and judges is placing pressure on even the most isolated and backward states. And ongoing development and democratic consolidation will increase legislators' incentives for oversight activities.

Notes

1. States have some minor differences in their quorum requirements and veto powers. In addition, a handful of state governors have decree authority.

2. However, in Bahia, the governing coalition would simply leave if opposition deputies became too aggressive in their debates. The government coalition was so large that their departure would end the session because of a quorum call.

Bibliography

Ames, B. 2001. *The Deadlock of Democracy in Brazil*. Ann Arbor: University of Michigan Press.

Barkan, J. D., L. Ademolekun, and Y. Zhou. 2004. "Emerging Legislatures in Emerging African Democracies." Paper presented at the 2003 APSA meeting, Philadelphia, PA, August.

Brown, D. S., J. C. Brown, and S. W. Desposato. 2002. "Left Turn on Green? International NGOs, Civil Society, and Political Change." *Comparative Political Studies* 35 (7): 814–38.

Carey, J. M., and M. S. Shugart. 1995. "Incentives to Cultivate a Personal Vote: A Rank Ordering of Electoral Formulas." *Electoral Studies* 14 (4): 417–39.

Desposato, S. W. 2001. "Institutional Theories, Societal Realities, and Party Politics in Brazil." PhD diss., University of California, Los Angeles.

Mainwaring, S. 1997. "Mutipartism, Robust Federalism, and Presidentialism in Brazil." In *Presidentialism and Democracy in Latin America*, eds. S. Mainwaring and M. S. Shugart, 55–109. New York: Cambridge University Press.

Schaeffer, Fl, ed. 2007. *Elections for Sale: The Causes and Consequences of Vote-Buying*. Boulder, CO: Lynne Rienner.

Schneider, A. 2001. *Federalism against Markets: Local Struggles for Power and National Fiscal Adjustment in Brazil*. PhD diss., University of California, Berkeley.

CHAPTER 15

Evolving Patterns of Legislative Oversight in Indonesia

Edward Schneier

If the development of a rich civic culture is the most essential precondition of democratic consolidation, the closely related emergence of a viable legislature is a close second. Sipping from the same half-filled glass, few observers of Indonesian politics—after eight years of *reformasi*—are willing to pass definitive judgment on the state of democracy in post-Suharto Indonesia. Whatever else it may be, Don Emmerson writes, Indonesia is unpredictable. Seen as an omen of fragility, unpredictability is a potential weakness, but seen as evidence of vitality, unpredictability may be a strength.[1]

Indonesia has been slouching toward democracy through two parliamentary, one presidential, and one regional election, which have all been judged substantially free and fair (Bäk 2003, 88). It has seen the incremental but substantial rewriting of the constitution and the formal allocation of governing authority to a two-house legislature, a separately elected president, and a constitutional court with the power to patrol the boundaries between the branches of government.

A series of constitutional amendments adopted between the fall of Suharto in 1998 and the 2004 presidential election converted the system from one that defied conventional categories to a more or less straightforward presidential system. But although the formal division of powers between the legislative and executive branches is now more clearly defined, the political dynamics of the system continue to conflate legislative and executive powers. Article 20A of the 1945 constitution remains in force, stating that the People's Representative Council (*Dewan Perwakilan Rakyat*—DPR) holds the power to make laws, but at the same time providing that each bill will be discussed by the DPR and the president to reach joint agreement, and forbidding the reintroduction of bills that have not been negotiated. Thus, although the constitution does not formally grant the president veto powers, former president Megawati Sukarnoputri twice defeated bills regulating the Batam free-trade zone simply by refusing to appoint a minister to negotiate them. Lawmaking, the core

of legislative power in most presidential systems, thus remains very much a
shared process in which the president and his or her department heads play
an active role in both drafting and refining most major bills.

As if it were a parliamentary system, Indonesia's subtle blending of legislative and executive powers often makes it difficult to trace the process of legislative oversight. An elaborate program of decentralization without federalism,
moreover, has further blurred the lines of power and left few clear channels of
oversight over the growing number of decisions reached outside of Jakarta's
overview or control. And a long tradition of *musyawarah dan mufakat* (deliberation and consensus) makes it extraordinarily difficult to trace the locus of
decision making. Both in committee and on the floor of the legislature, formal
votes are rarely taken and decisions are almost always unanimous. Students
of the legislative process depend on interviews, hearsay, and echoes from the
back rooms rather than written records, and even these can be difficult to
come by. All political systems, as Slater (2004, 72) puts it, are largely driven
by backroom maneuvers, but what is striking in the Indonesian context is the
abject unwillingness of ostensibly democratic political elites to discuss even
the gist of their discussions after they reenter the public sphere. Even after
clearly well-planned discussions among party leaders, participants almost universally claim that it was only a *silaturahmi* (a friendly social call), and not a
political negotiation at all.

These informal meetings are at the core of the legislative process. In 2005
and 2006 there were a handful of nonunanimous, recorded votes in the DPR,
and there are some indications that they may become more common. In
general, however, plenary sittings never overrule and almost never modify
the work of the committees (*komisi*, or commissions, as they are known in
Indonesia). Yet just as Woodrow Wilson underestimated the powers of party
leaders when he described the United States as being governed by the standing
committees of the Congress, the primacy of Indonesia's komisi is more apparent than real. Bills that emerge from the committees reflect agreements reached
not just among committee members but also, when there are real conflicts,
among central party leaders. The committee leaders who negotiate the details
of legislation see themselves less as rivals to the party leaders than as parts of
the central leadership. One DPR committee chair explained in an interview in
2002 that the party never has to tell him what do in committee, because he sits
in the leadership meetings that would have to give those orders.

There is no doubt that many aspects of legislative oversight in Indonesia
are both hidden from public view and, by most standards at least, marginally corrupt. Political scientists tend to treat corruption as a relatively trivial
pathology that so marginally affects the general functioning of the healthy
body politic that it can safely be ignored in describing its physiology; however,
to ignore corruption in Indonesia is like pretending that the 500-pound gorilla
is not in the room. Indonesia inherited from the Dutch colonial office a deeply
ingrained tradition of corruption that was refined and expanded under both
Sukarno and Suharto. KKN (*korupsi, kolusi*, and *nepotisme*), or corruption,

collusion, and nepotism, is so deeply ingrained in the process of governing that President Suharto once described it to the president of the World Bank as something that, "in our part of the world, we call family values" (Wolfensohn 2004, xvii). This chapter, however, describes the basic structure of the Indonesian system of legislative oversight as if it were free of major pathologies. This is done for several reasons: first, because there are important instances in which KKN are not significant factors; second, because the general pathways of corruption are best understood in the context of the general structure of the regular rules; and finally, because for comparative purposes the Indonesian model is perhaps most useful if considered from both its physiological and pathological perspectives.

The Evolving Structure and Roles of the Indonesian Legislature

In the late 1940s Indonesia's terse and vague postindependence constitution lodged the fundamental powers of the state in the upper house of a nested bicameral legislature that consisted of the 500-member People's Representative Council (*Dewan Perwakilan Rakyat*—DPR) and the People's Consultative Assembly (*Majelis Permusyawaratan Rakkyat*—MPR) of roughly 1,000 members. The MPR, which met every five years to elect the president and had the power to amend the constitution, comprised the members of the DPR, its own elected representatives, five representatives from each of the 37 provinces, and representatives of various functional groups such as labor unions, professional organizations, and the military. Under the banner of *reformasi*, the MPR reduced its size to 700 members, phased out the direct representation of the military and other groups, and in 2004 finally reconstituted itself as a bicameral legislature with the DPR as the lower house and a separately elected upper house, the Regional Representative Council (*Dewan Perakilan Daerah*—DPD). Although it retains a diminished power to impeach, Indonesia's Parliament also took itself out of the process of presidential selection in favor of direct popular election.

The DPR is divided into a fairly standard list of committees, each with specific jurisdiction over a named list of executive departments. Aside from formal divisions, party cohesion cannot be measured, but party discipline is unquestionably strong. Centralized control over intraparliamentary patterns of advancement, networks of corruption, and tight limits on candidate recruitment put the leaders of most parliamentary parties virtually beyond challenge. Legislative committees (*komisi*, or commissions), tend to be relatively large with broad jurisdictions. The DPR's 11 commissions have between 35 and 55 members each, balancing party ratios roughly in proportion to those of the plenary and allocating chairmanships through negotiations among the leaders of the dominant parties.

Although the formal structure of the DPD strongly resembles that of the DPR, on which it is modeled, the upper house is smaller (124 members compared with 650) and more collegial; less partisan, with its members elected in nonpartisan elections; and considerably less powerful. The DPD's actual powers are vaguely confined to presenting laws on regional issues to the DPR, participating in discussions of the budget and other laws of regional interest, and performing oversight. Although the DPD appears in many respects similar to the German *Bundesrat* in its potential to expand its region-related legislative mandate, the constitution clearly gives the power to make laws to the DPR. The DPD's unique role is described by Stephen Sherlock (2005a) as:

> [A] quite unusual example of a second chamber because it represents an odd combination of limited powers and high legitimacy. Its role in law-making is limited to certain areas of policy, its powers are only advisory and no Bill is actually required to pass through it in order to be passed, yet at the same time it has the strong legitimacy that comes from being a fully elected chamber. This combination does not seem to be replicated anywhere in the world. (9)

Unlike the DPR, the DPD divides it leadership roles on a regional rather than partisan basis. It has four 32-member substantive committees (one member per province) and similarly composed committees on internal governance, ethics, legislation, and interinstitutional cooperation.

Cabinet-level agencies are created, modified, or abolished by an act of the legislature. Although the president is now directly elected and can in theory choose his own cabinet, President Susilo Bambang Yodohono, though at first inclined to choose his own ministers, followed the pattern established by his predecessors of putting together a cabinet consisting of ministers allocated among, and chosen in consultation with, the party leaders of the majority parties in the DPR. The parties, in what is informally known as the government party, thus have particular access to particular ministries, much as if Indonesia had a multiparty, coalition government. The implications of this pattern for legislative oversight are discussed later in this chapter.

The Tools of Oversight

Legislative oversight generally begins (and sometimes ends) with the creation, definition, and financing of a government body. Given the nature of Suharto's authoritarian New Order, the legislature sometimes played a surprisingly strong role in modifying a number of major laws, particularly in the regime's last years. Ironically, it appears that the DPR has not been more active legislatively than before the reform, and perhaps has even been less active. In strictly numeric terms, New Order parliaments averaged roughly 12 bills per session, all of them originating in the executive branch. That number tripled to an average of 36 between 1999 and 2005, but as Sherlock noted, an average of 14 of these laws were devoted to the essentially routine creation of new regional governments (Sherlock 2003, 19). Many others were statutes that were necessary to put into practice changes in government institutions mandated by constitutional amendments. The amount of unfinished business is large and growing. At one point in 2002 the backlog of pending government bills had grown to 120 (Sherlock 2003, 19), and in 2005, when only 12 of the 55 bills on the president's agenda had been passed, the number of bills pending on the calendar had reached 284 (Sherlock 2005b, 5).

This dismal legislative performance looks even bleaker given the enormous pressure for reformist legislation after more than 30 years of authoritarian rule (Rüland et al. 2005, 230). As a result, most government agencies continue to function under the rules, some of them unconstitutional, of the old New Order. To compound the problem of legislative languor, most qualitative assessments of the DPR's legislative performance are equally unfavorable. Fealy (2001) wrote:

> [M]uch expert legal opinion suggest[s] that the quality of bills passed by the DPR in the past two years has been at best variable. Many bills were drafted with little attention to detail, were vaguely worded, and, in some cases, contained clauses which contradicted other statutes.

"This lack of precision," he concluded, "provides the bureaucracy with opportunities to manipulate the interpretation of the legislation for its own purposes" (Fealy 2001, 109). Although it is unclear whether Fealy's conclusions can be applied to the 2004–09 legislative session, the tone of both scholarly and journalistic observations strongly suggests that the situation remains largely unchanged. Many key policies are developed in the form of administrative regulations rather than statutes and can be quite discriminatory in their impact. Foreign businessmen have long complained, for example, about arbitrary and, to them, unfair tax policies in which the rates are fixed not by statute but by negotiations that, together with normal patterns of corruption, contribute to a very unstable economic climate.

Budgetary Role

As in most presidential systems, the budgetary role of the DPR is largely one of modifying documents that have originated in the bureaucracy and been compiled by the president. In Indonesia, however, members of the budget committee are actually consulted at the outset of the process, when overall fiscal assumptions and projections are designed. Indeed, throughout the process of budget development, leaders of the DPR are in regular communication with the minister of finance and his or her top aides. Komisi XI, the Finance Committee, is among the most sought-after assignments in the DPR and, with 12 aides, the best staffed. Reforms adopted since 2005 have brought considerable transparency to a process that was, even by New Order standards, deeply opaque. Standard audit and accounting standards have also been adopted. But many government agencies, most notably the military, continue to be substantially funded by off-budget activities that elude legislative scrutiny. From the limited data available, it would appear that the final budget numbers adopted by the DPR seldom differ substantially from those presented in the president's original draft (Rüland 2005):

> Due to a lack of capacity and competence, parliament usually changes less than 1 per cent of the draft. Legislators complain that parliament does not have enough time to deliberate details, because the executive is pushing the legislators to agree. Therefore the DPR plays only a minor role in budgetary matters. (250)

Even the legislature's own budget is not fully available for review by the public or by DPR members (NDI 2005, 1). Staff shortages and the limited perspectives of rank-and-file committee members pretty much ensure that the questions asked by DPR members will focus far less on broad issues of monetary and fiscal policy than on narrow line items in the budget.

Interpellation

Both the DPR and, by implication at least, the DPD, have the power of interpellation (which had been abolished in 1950 and then restored in 1999). When President Abdurrahman Wahid appeared before parliament to explain his firing of two cabinet ministers in July 2000, he refused to answer any questions on the grounds that the power of interpellation was vested only in the MPR. Although the rules have since been clarified, this power has not been used. Committees quite frequently hold both formal hearings and informal meetings with cabinet members and their aides, and they have the power to subpoena witnesses (though this power is also seldom used). There are times, in the best spirit of Indonesia's tradition of consensus decision-making, when the details of legislation are actually negotiated in these sessions. More commonly, hearings become rather numbingly predictable forums for the often-tedious reading of the prepared speeches of both ministers and legislators. Attendance is low, with quorums difficult to achieve, and the poor record-keeping capacity of the legislature makes it impossible for absent members to catch up on what they miss. The lack of detailed minutes or of meeting notes and summaries can create confusion about what has been discussed in meetings and what has been agreed. Matters previously discussed can inadvertently be deliberated again at a later meeting and issues previously agreed upon are questioned again (NDI 2005, 56). This kind of repetition is helpful neither to member attendance nor to public respect for the work of the legislature.

During its 2006 session, various committees of the DPD traveled to different regions of the country to hold what were essentially oversight hearings on a variety of topics. Neither the legislators nor the witnesses were always well-prepared to make effective use of these meetings, but the very novelty of their existence drew considerable attention and holds out an interesting promise for the future. Ellis (2007) suggested that:

> The acceptance of important DPD recommendations in the 2006 annual statement of the presidential program as well as the role given to oversight in the

2006 DPD strategic plan suggest that the DPD will be able to establish a real, if limited, role for itself. (37)

For both the DPR and DPD, a continuing impediment to their oversight capability is, quite simply, competence. Fewer than half of the members of the DPR, and only a fifth of those in the DPD, have had previous legislative experience of any kind. The staff, such as it is, remains a part of the executive branch and lacks both interest in, and ability to engage in, significant oversight activities.

Ministers appear at open committee hearings, and they are usually well covered by the media. It is here that the Indonesian parliament most manifestly performs its public information function, and where individual members of the DPR can raise critical issues and have some potential for influencing policy. However, unlike hearings in the United States, which often feature a long parade of private sector witnesses, virtually all of those testifying before the DPR are from the government. The absence of lobbyists at this stage in the process is a testimony both to the weak civic culture[2] common to many former dictatorships and to the patterns of policy making developed by the DPR during the New Order period. This absence of a system of organized groups monitoring the performance of the government makes what McCubbins and Schwartz called the fire-alarm method of oversight largely inoperative (1984, 165–79). Routine police patrols of the same bureaucratic neighborhoods replace the kinds of reports on performance problems that extend the eyes and ears of the legislature far beyond the formal hearing room (McCubbins and Schwartz, 1984, 165–79). Mechanisms are not in place for linking the legislature with the relatively few viable interest groups that do exist. Indeed, the political culture discourages such links, as Mikaela Nyman (2006) noted:

> The problems in this context are twofold. First, there must be political will on behalf of the government to make the necessary legislative and procedural changes in order to create an enabling environment. Second, civil society representatives have to overcome a lingering New Order legacy in terms of an ever-present suspicion and mistrust of the government's ulterior motives. (200)

Group linkages are weak and individual legislators in Indonesia do not get the kinds of regular complaints from constituents that provide legislators with still another channel of information on the performance of government agencies (particularly in single-member-district electoral systems). Indonesian politicians arguably have little constituency or partisan self-interest to guide them in their oversight activities. The DPD, with its electoral system closely tied to regional concerns, is slowly beginning to elaborate its role as ombudsman. Yet just as its limited legislative powers restrict its ability to cumulate discrete complaints into comprehensive remedies, its lack of effective oversight tools makes its ombudsman function less effective. Moreover, the very existence of the DPD may further isolate members of the DPR from their constituents.

The degree to which casework—the handling of individual complaints about the bureaucracy—is preparatory to and is part of the process of oversight is not always direct, but there is little doubt that the accumulation of citizen grievances with regard to a particular agency or problem is a major spur to oversight, particularly in countries like the United States with single-member districts. The problem in Indonesia, rooted in the electoral system, central party control of nominations, and other factors, is that few legislators have even the most minimal ties with their constituents. Members of the DPR are limited to a staff of one, and the members with district offices can (quite literally) be counted on one hand. A poll by the International Foundation for Electoral Systems (2003) found that only 2 percent of the voters surveyed could name or had been in contact with their representatives in the DPR. The kinds of communications from constituents and interest groups that often spur investigations, hearings, direct questions to bureaucrats, and ideas for new laws are simply not there for Indonesian parliamentarians. A new political party, founded essentially in its support for an Islamic state, surprised many observers by polling close to 7 percent of the overall DPR vote. What makes it interesting in terms of constituent services is the party's assiduous efforts to organize at the grassroots level. Modeling itself on the long-outlawed Indonesian Communist Party (organizationally, not ideologically), the Justice and Prosperity Party (PKS) in effect gives its parliamentarians district offices and may force some of the older parties to do the same.

One tool of oversight that loomed large in the early post–New Order period has essentially been eliminated by the constitutional amendments that take the legislature out of the process of electing the president and weaken its powers of impeachment. Indonesia's first two *reformasi* presidents, B. J. Habibe and Abdurrahman Wahid, were forced to negotiate the compositions of their cabinets and the substance of their policies under the explicit threat of their eventual removal from office; and their successor, Megawati Sukarnoputri, finished her term under a slightly concealed gun of the same caliber. In trying to appoint a cabinet loyal to him rather than to parliament, Wahid was perfectly within his legal rights as president and was able to put party elites on the defensive for over a year, in spite of his weak position in parliament (Slater 2004, 73). Although it was not a foregone conclusion that the anti-Megawati coalition that installed Wahid could be turned into an anti-Wahid coalition that would, through impeachment, install Megawati, the deal was consummated at the cost of executive independence. What is more surprising is the persistence of some of these patterns into the operations of the presidency after the formal separation of powers and in the context of a weaker impeachment clause.

What the Indonesian legislature lacks in the traditional armory of oversight weapons, it partially makes up for in its still unique ties with the president's cabinet. The blending of legislative and executive powers that characterized the pre-*reformasi* constitution lives on for better or worse in a pattern of negotiating policy in frequent meetings between party and committee leaders and their counterparts in the relevant ministries. Even moving into the third year of Soesilo Bambang Yudhoyono's term as Indonesia's first directly elected president, the government continued to operate in ways that more closely resemble those of a multiparty cabinet system than a system of separated powers. Further research in this area is needed, as Sherlock (2005b) suggested, or more time to see how the new system evolves:

> [B]ut one of the reasons for the failure of the current DPR to produce legislation could be related to the increased difficulty of finding a common position on Bills amongst 11 different *Fraksi*. This in turn is exacerbated by the new complexity of the relationship between the DPR and the government and the tendency by many elements within the DPR to try to intervene in many decisions that are arguably the prerogative of executive government. (11)

The Special Case of the Military

Even at the height of his powers, Suharto was as much the creature of the military as he was its commander. From the Indonesian National Military's (*Tentara Nasional Indonesia*—TNI) historic role in the fight for independence to its continuing fight for the structural cohesion of the Indonesian state in East Timor, Aceh, Papua, and elsewhere, it has occupied a special place in the Indonesian state (Honna 2003):

> The reform movement sought to return the troops to the barracks, to hold leaders accountable for their human rights violations and to eliminate the military's prominent political role. Yet widespread turmoil under Indonesia's nascent civilian leadership has worked to sustain the military's political power. Political instability has conferred considerable influence in political circles on the current military elite because their cooperation is deemed indispensable in trying to maintain the integrity of a fragile and fractious nation-state. In assessing the prospects for democratic transition in the new Indonesia, the military remains of critical importance. (1)

While the TNI has by no means become the model of a civilian-controlled, incorruptible, apolitical, professional army, its current progress toward that goal could hardly have been predicted a decade ago. Partly through internal pressures from younger officers seeking a more professional military, partly through changes mandated by the MPR, and partly through a series of negotiated changes, the TNI's role relative to the post-Suharto state has been remarkably reformed. Between 1998 and 2005, the nation witnessed

- withdrawal of active military personnel from civilian posts,
- division of the armed forces and the police into separate organizations,
- the military's withdrawal from an active role in the Golkar political party,
- appointment of a civilian minister of defense,
- renunciation of the army's special role (*dwifungsi*) in political affairs,[3]
- disbandment of sociopolitical offices and definition of external defense as the military's primary function,

- reduction and elimination of the army's direct representation in parliament, and
- subordination of military courts to the Supreme Court.[4]

The military continues, however, to run both legal and illegal businesses and engage in other forms of rent-seeking activities, leaving no more than 40 percent of its budget subject to civilian control. Moreover, it is the only truly national institution in the country and has, under the banner of the war on terrorism, regained some of the powers it had seemingly renounced. Reform measures, as Mietzner puts it, scrapped the dual function without addressing the causes that had produced it (Mietzner 2006, 14). On the rare occasions when the DPR has taken steps to challenge the military, little has happened. A 2000 investigation of widely reported abuses in the military occupation of Aceh went nowhere when the committee was stonewalled by the generals called to testify; the generals denied all allegations and refused to answer the tentative questions from the poorly briefed committee members (Fealy 2001, 106). Increasingly, the military has also escaped parliamentary oversight by adapting its already strong territorial organization to the newly decentralized national budget. As Mietzner (2006) noted:

> [Decentralization] offered the armed forces increased opportunities to access the budgets of local governments at the district level, where most of the new decentralization funds were concentrated. With political parties struggling to establish a presence at the grass-roots, and legislatures and bureaucracies trying to cope with their new roles, the military stood out as the only institution with a widely connected and already tested infrastructure. (15)

Under strong external pressure, particularly from the United States, and in response to terrorist bombings in Bali, Jakarta, and elsewhere, the military has regained some of the police and intelligence powers it lost to *reformasi*, and has even been given the power to impose military rule.

Although the role of the Parliament at both the national and local levels has gained importance, this has not necessarily translated into increased civilian control over the military. For the military, in fact, resisting civilian executive control is now incomparably easier and less risky than during Suharto's time (Honna 2003, 195). Whether the legislature can exert controls of its own remains one of the general problems of oversight in the Indonesian system.

Constitutional Change and Continuing Realities

The movement that successfully challenged the New Order and democratized the structure of the Indonesian state peacefully changed the dynamic of the system in ways that not even the most optimistic student of Southeast Asian politics could have predicted. That the legislature has not used the manifest powers granted to it by *reformasi* justifies the predictions of the most pessimistic. Weak but disciplined nonideological parties, combined with the absence of a balanced and viable civic culture, widespread corruption, and an economic elite that is essentially unchanged from that which thrived under Suharto, provide little comfort to institutionalists. Moreover, as Rosser, Roesed, and Edwin (2005) noted:

> [The old New Order bureaucracy] continues to play a major role in formulating (as well as implementing) government policy. Although the parliament now exercises an effective veto over government policy, it lacks the administrative, research and technical capacity to take full advantage of its authority to draft and initiate legislation. The bureaucracy, which is much stronger in terms of its administrative, research and technical capacity, continues to play the key role in this respect. It also continues to formulate the various regulations, decrees, and other official policy decisions that allow enacted laws to be implemented. Although parliament is formally able to override these, its limited capacity means that it can do so infrequently. (66)

One could conclude that the Indonesian DPR remains essentially a pseudo-parliament (Schneier 2004). The continuing problems can be put under two headings, one institutional, one political.

The institutional barriers to effective oversight are manifest. Not only is the legislature understaffed, it is poorly staffed to the point that the most basic records of the institution are difficult to obtain. There now is an independent research and analysis unit, but it gets little use from members. Under the leadership (ironically) of President Yodohono, steps are being taken to give the secretariats of the DPR and DPD control over their own staffs (they have been part of the general civil service), but resources remain scarce. The legislature itself needs professionalization, yet the proportion of experienced legislators returning to the DPR actually declined between 1999 and 2004, and only 11 of the DPD's 124 members have had previous political experience at the national level. Of equal concern is the state of the bureaucracy. In Schneier (2004),

> [Oversight] is depicted as a means of controlling runaway bureaucracies. But while the independence of the army and police has posed continuing threats to the stability and democratization of the Indonesian polity, in many cases it is the *weakness* of the bureaucracy that makes oversight both necessary and problematic. (18)

Oversight, at its best, unearths problems of a systemic nature, problems caused by faults in the law or the process of implementation that can be remedied through changes in the law, through reorganization, or through different allocations of resources. Oversight cannot deal effectively with ad hoc bureaucracies, or with bureaucracies that are funded by corporations rather than the government, or with enforcement officials who have been paid off not to act. Although Indonesia is not a marginal state in the sense that its capacity for governance is minimal and largely symbolic,[5] many if not most of its local bureaucracies are at best intermittently connected with Jakarta. As is probably true in most emerging democracies, it is difficult to evaluate the power of the legislature without first establishing the power of the state.

Central state weakness in Indonesia has been compounded by a strong yet poorly planned process of decentralization that has made that central government far less effective, particularly in more remote areas. Bäk (2003) noted that corruption has not been contained, only spread out:

> No longer does Indonesia have one Suharto; it now has multiple Suhartos spread across the archipelago. Demands for slices of the pie, as it was, got bigger, much bigger. In fact, in one of her few year-end public appearances in December 2002, President Megawati Sukarnoputri clearly acknowledged that corruption had become even more rampant in the Reform Era than under the New Order. (81)

The case of extensive illegal logging concisely illustrates the dynamic of the process through which laws protecting national forests have been rendered nugatory by the bureaucracy's inability to enforce the law. Local coalitions of farmers and local officials, sometimes backed by outside capital, were able to generate their own norms, values, and rules, and the ability to enforce them, in contravention to the formal forestry laws (McCarthy 2002, 94). With the TNI, the police, and local governments often deeply involved in illegal logging, and able to use the profits from these operations to free themselves from dependence on government appropriations, effective oversight becomes all but impossible.

The political dynamics of the Indonesian system compound these problems and further militate against effective oversight. Extensive corruption is but a widely recognized symptom of a more fundamental political problem. The question of how effective the legislature is in performing its oversight functions is rendered void if that legislature is only the instrument of an overarching political cartel that spans the legislative and executive branches and much of the private sector as well. In a perverse way, one can argue that the Indonesian legislature (the DPR in particular) is, in terms of its leaders' goals and not those of outside observers, performing its oversight role with consummate efficiency. Rent-seeking politicians can use the threat and process of oversight to advance both their personal and political fortunes. Robison and Hadiz (2004, 104) argue that *reformasi* has been less about democratization than the old oligarchy's development of a political format that would further protect their economic ascendance and insulate them from threats, whether those threats emanate internally from within the state, or externally, from wider civil society.

By dividing up cabinet portfolios and the chairmanships of the DPR's committees, the older, established parties have created a corporatist system of subgovernments that effectively distributes the spoils and reinforces the status quo. Central legislative oversight is virtually nonexistent, but there is, in effect, a party fox in every chicken coop. With so many patronage opportunities at hand, one wonders whether even the best-intentioned party leadership could discipline its members into serving as a vocal opposition in parliament rather than quietly joining in on the take (Slater 2004, 91). It seems unlikely that the party cartel now in control faces any serious challenge. The rise of the Islamist PKS (Justice and Prosperity Party) as a specific opposition force illustrates the potential for such a challenge, but the PKS is limited in what remains a largely secular Muslim society by its sectarian core. What is an essential starting point for reform in Indonesia is the very thing that remains lacking, specifically, a disciplined and even ruthless political party driven and defined by any coherent ideological agenda for liberal reform and transparent governance. That such a party has not emerged is no surprise, given the resilience of a civil and military state apparatus enmeshed in the old structures of political capitalism (Robison and Hadiz 2004, 258).

This is not the place for an examination of the Indonesian party system and its future possibilities. What is worth speculating on here is the efficacy of oversight in emerging democracies dominated by what Katz and Mair called party cartels (1995, 6). The Indonesian case raises the broader question of whether it is always a good idea to strengthen the legislature's tools of oversight. Those who study legislatures tend generally to support them as well, connecting their performances strongly with the process of democratization. Critics of Indonesia's power-sharing formula, as Slater (2004, 64) put it, have emphasized its negative effects on government effectiveness and performance. The fact that such a coalitional arrangement stifles democratic accountability by limiting effective voter choice has gone relatively unmentioned. When parliament used its power of impeachment to prevent President Wahid from appointing an independent cabinet, it demonstrated both an ability and a willingness to exercise its powers of oversight. The ability of the 2004–09 DPR to persuade President Yodohono to adhere to the tradition of Megawati's rainbow cabinet is illustrative of its continuing ability to exercise strong powers of oversight, even with a directly elected president. Whether such oversight powers strengthen democracy, however, is not as clear.

Notes

1. Emmerson 2005. Also see the essays by Hefner and Clear 2007; Ananta, Arifin, and Suryadinata 2005, Liddle 2001, and Nguyen 2004.

2. Destroyed by Suharto, flooded by the rush of cultural streams (*aliran*), there are—outside of the church and the military—precious few organized membership groups in the country. A profusion of nongovernmental organizations, many with outside funding, sometimes gives the illusion in Jakarta of an evolving pluralism, but it is just that, an illusion.

3. *Dwifungsi* is the dual function of defending the state and helping administer it.

4. This list is adapted from Mietzner 2006, p. 60.

5. For a fuller definition of *marginal state* see Hadenius (2001), 251.

Bibliography

Ananta, Aris, Eva Nurvidya Arifin, and Leo Suryadinata. 2005. *Emerging Democracy in Indonesia*. Singapore: Institute of Southeast Asian Studies.

Bäk, Michael L. 2003. "Slouching Toward Democracy: Social Violence and Elite Failure in Indonesia." In *Indonesia Matters: Diversity, Unity, and Stability in Fragile Times*, eds. Thang D. Nguyen and Frank-Jürgen Richter, 73–89. Singapore: Times Media Private Ltd.

Ellis, Andrew. 2007. "Indonesia's Constitutional Change Revisited." In *Indonesia: Democracy and the Promise of Good Governance*, eds. Ross H. McLeod and Andrew MacIntyre, 21–40. Singapore: Institute of Southeast Asian Studies.

Emmerson, Donald K. 2005. "What Is Indonesia?" In *Indonesia: The Great Transition*, ed. John Bresnan, 7–74. Lanham, MD: Rowman and Littlefield.

Fealy, Greg. 2001. "Parties and Parliament: Serving Whose Interests?" In *Indonesia Today: Challenges of History*, eds. Grayson Lloyd and Shannon Smith, 97–111. Singapore: Institute of Southeast Asian Studies.

Hadenius, Axel. 2001. *Institutions and Democratic Citizenship*. New York: Oxford University Press.

Hefner, Robert W., and Annette Clear. 2007. In *Indonesia: Toward Democracy*, ed. Taufik Abdullah, 53–72. Singapore: Institute of Southeast Asian Studies.

Honna, Jun. 2003. *Military Politics and Democratization in Indonesia*. New York: Routledge Curzon.

IFES (International Foundation for Electoral Systems). 2003. *National Public Opinion Survey*. Jakarta: IFES.

Katz, Richard S., and Peter Mair. 1995. "Changing Models of Party Organization and Party Democracy." *Party Politics* 1 (January): 1–22.

Liddle, William R. 2001. *Crafting Indonesian Democracy*. Bandung, Indonesia: Mizan Media Utama.

McCarthy, John F. 2002. "Power and Interest on Sumatra's Rain Forest Frontier: Clientelist Coalitions, Illegal Logging and Conservation in the Alas Valley." *Journal of Southeast Asian Studies* 33 (February).

McCubbins, Matthew, and Thomas Schwartz. 1984. "Congressional Oversight Overlooked: Police Patrols Versus Fire Alarms." *American Journal of Political Science* 28 (February).

Mietzner, Marcus. 2006. *The Politics of Military Reform in Post-Suharto Indonesia: Elite Conflict, Nationalism, and Institutional Resistance*. Washington, DC: East-West Center Washington.

NDI (National Democratic Institute for International Affairs). 2005. *Towards a More Effective Indonesian House of Representatives: Options for Positive Change by Legislators*. Jakarta: NDI.

Nguyen, Thang D., ed. 2004. *The Indonesian Dream: Unity, Diversity and Democracy in Times of Distrust*. Singapore: Marshall Cavendish International.

Nyman, Mikaela. 2006. *Democratising Indonesia: The Challenge of Civil Society in the Era of Reformasi*. Copenhagen: Nordic Institute of Asian Studies.

Robison, Richard, and Vedi R. Hadiz. 2004. *Reorganising Power in Indonesia: The Politics of Oligarchy in an Age of Markets*. London: Routledge Curzon.

Rosser, Andrew, Kurnya Roesed, and Donni Edwin. 2005. "Indonesia: The Politics of Inclusion." *Journal of Contemporary Asia* 35 (March): 79–101.

Rüland, Jürgen, Clemens Jürgenmeyer, Michael H. Nelson, and Patrick Ziegenhain. 2005. *Parliaments and Political Change in Asia*. Singapore: Institute of Southeast Asian Studies.

Schneier, Edward. 2004. "Emerging Patterns of Legislative Oversight in Indonesia." Paper presented at the 2004 Annual Meeting of the Southern Political Science Association, New Orleans, LA, January 11.

Sherlock, Stephen. 2003. *Struggling to Change: The Indonesian Parliament in an Era of Reformasi*. Canberra, Australia: Center for Democratic Institutions.

———. 2005a. *Indonesia's Regional Representative Assembly: Democracy, Representation and the Regions*. Canberra, Australia: Center for Democratic Institutions.

———. 2005b. *The Legislative Process in the Indonesian Parliament (DPR): Issues, Problems and Recommendations*. Jakarta: Friedrich Naumann Stiftung.

Slater, Dan. 2004. "Indonesia's Accountability Trap: Party Cartels and Presidential Power After Democratic Transitions." *Indonesia* 78 (October): 61–92.

Wolfensohn, James D. 2004. Preface. In *The Indonesian Dream: Unity, Diversity and Democracy in Times of Distrust*, eds. Thang D. Nguyen. Singapore: Marshall Cavendish International.

CHAPTER 16

Legislative Oversight and the Israeli Committee System: Problems and Solutions

Chen Friedberg

The 19th-century English philosopher John Stuart Mill determined that the most appropriate tasks of a representative body are to oversee the government, clarify its activities to the public, compel the executive to provide full explanations and justification for its deeds, criticize it, and, in extreme cases, withdraw support (Mill 1958). One of the ways parliament can fulfill its oversight role is through its committees, which have been formed in large part to strengthen the role of the legislature and to protect democratic regimes by ensuring the existence of proper governmental and administrational order (Hazan 2001; Lees and Shaw 1979; Pelizzo and Stapenhurst 2004).

This chapter looks at parliamentary oversight by the Israeli parliament, the Knesset, through its committee system. It centers on the main structural and procedural problems that characterize the Israeli parliamentary committee system, and that impair its functioning and thereby impair the effectiveness of its oversight. These obstacles are demonstrated by examining the functioning of two committees: the State Control Committee and the Education, Culture and Sports Committee.

The Knesset and Its Oversight Role

The Knesset is a House of Representatives with 120 members elected for a four-year term. One of the functions of the Knesset is to oversee the government's ministerial cabinets, most of whose ministers and deputy ministers are also elected Knesset members. The Knesset fulfills its supervisory role in various ways:

• Every law that the government intends to enact must be approved by the Knesset, including the budget and taxation laws.

• The Knesset may also demand that the government provides additional information, either within the framework of its committee system or in the plenum, by means of debates, motions for the agenda, or parliamentary questions.

- Additional means of supervision are the state comptrolle' reports, which are presented to the Knesset, and budget monitoring.

The Parliamentary Committee System in the Knesset

The Israeli government is based on coalitions, and membership in the committees is on a parliamentary group basis. The number of Knesset members who are free to serve on committees is limited to about 80 (about one-quarter are government members who are not allowed to serve in the committees, and other functionaries like the Knesset chair deputies and the head of the opposition, who are allowed to serve in the committees but often choose not too), while possible nominations for Knesset committees can reach about 200.

There are four types of Knesset committees:

- *Permanent committees* are elected at the beginning of each Knesset term (discussed in detail below).

- *Parliamentary inquiry committees* are appointed by the plenum to deal with special issues of national importance.

- *Special committees* include two permanent committees, the Ethics Committee and the Interpretations Committee, which have a different status from that of the permanent committees.

- *Committees on particular matters* function in a similar manner to the permanent committees but are appointed for a limited period of time.

There are also subcommittees established by the permanent committees on a temporary basis to deal with specific issues that demand more intense attention.

The Knesset committees draw their power from three legal sources: Basic Law: the Knesset (1958), Basic Law: the Government (2001), and the Knesset Rules of Parliamentary Procedure.

Permanent Committees

There are 12 permanent committees. The permanent committees and their chairs are elected at the beginning of the term of each Knesset on the basis of a recommendation by the Arrangements Committee. Membership in the committees is on a parliamentary group basis. The number of members in each committee has changed over the years (usually ranging from 10 to 20 members). It should be noted that the number of Knesset committees and their size enables, at least in theory, more efficient oversight of the executive. However, committee structure and other factors often hinder the committees' ability to implement effective oversight.

Structural and procedural failures characterizing the Israeli committee system. Numerous aspects of the committee system result in their failure to provide effective oversight.

1. *Lack of overlap between committees and government ministries.* Each permanent committee is responsible for a number of, or sometimes all, governmental ministries. As committees are forced to cover a wide variety of government activities under several ministries, committee members are often unable to focus on, and gain in-depth expertise in, an area of a specific government ministry.

2. *The ability of factions to change committee members as desired.* Knesset parliamentary procedures permit parties to change their committee representatives whenever they wish. Factions do so particularly when one of their committee members expresses an opinion in opposition to the position of the faction. This turnover weakens the power of the committees and thus their oversight ability, because members who have gained expertise can be replaced by a member with no expertise.

3. *The lack of requirement for a quorum.* The Knesset parliamentary procedures do not require a quorum for debates or votes and determine that the committee chair has the power to continue committee meetings with any number of members present. The lack of requirement for a quorum impairs the decision-making ability of the committee and also damages their public image because committees may meet and vote with a small number of members present (even if it is only one member).

4. *The lack of committees' legal ability to require ministers and officials to appear before them.* The Knesset committees have the power to request (i) information regarding a government ministry's activities and (ii) that ministers and government officials appear before them. However, the committees do not have the power (except for the State Control Committee) to compel appearances of the government officials or to enforce handing over a full set of information. There are no sanctions to deal with nonappearance of officials or provision of only partial or even false information.

5. *The lack of binding status for committee conclusions.* The Knesset parliamentary procedures determine which part of the motions for the agenda are to be returned to the Knesset with the committee's conclusions. After a lengthy period of government disregard of committee conclusions, two sections were incorporated in the Knesset Rules of Parliamentary Procedure (1977, 1985), which state that the Knesset chair will transfer committee

conclusions to the relevant minister, who then is obliged to respond within three months regarding actions taken in the light of the conclusions. However, it should be noted that committee conclusions are not binding and are treated only as recommendations to the government.

6. *The public nature of committee meetings.* Knesset parliamentary procedures stated until recently that committee meetings are not open to the public unless the committee decides otherwise. Closed-door sessions may enable committees to conduct their business in a more conducive atmosphere, which may lead to a compromise across party lines and provide one condition for more efficient oversight. Starting with the 7th Knesset (1969–73) committees began opening some of their meetings to the media. Since then this trend has increased as a result of the general penetration of electronic media into the Knesset and the desire of many Knesset members to appear publicly; the trend has even been anchored in the Knesset parliamentary procedures (2007) in order to suit them to the current reality. Some have argued that this trend may weaken oversight ability by committees (Hazan 2001).

Empirical examination of two Knesset permanent committees— methodological issues.
Research Population—The two Knesset permanent committees whose oversight functions are examined are the State Control Committee and the Education, Culture and Sports Committee. Committee functioning is defined for the purpose of this chapter as a continuum, which is termed the *functioning continuum*, and appears as follows:

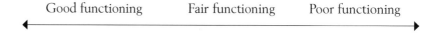

Good functioning   Fair functioning   Poor functioning

The functioning of the two committees is examined through a number of detailed parameters, which move along the functioning continuum, ranging from poor to good functioning. The research comprises qualitative content analysis from archival sources, committees' protocols, and official and internal publications.

Period of Time Examined—The period of the study covers three Knesset terms during the last three decades of the 20th century, chosen in order to identify the development of trends in parliamentary oversight over time. The examined Knessets are the 7th Knesset (1969–73), the 10th Knesset (1981–84), and the 13th Knesset (1992–96).

Definitions of Parameters—The functioning of both committees was examined by reviewing the following parameters:

1. The first parameter differs for the two committees. For the State Control Committee: Deficiencies Raised by the State Comptroller. For the

Education, Culture and Sports Committee: Sources of Information Used by Committee.

2. Simultaneous membership in a number of committees.

3. Participation of committee members in meetings.

4. Professional advisory staff.

5. Monitoring of implementation of committee's recommendations.

Sampling

The State Control Committee—The State Control Committee scrutinizes the state comptroller's reports and submits its conclusions and proposals to the Knesset plenum, which debates and approves them. It should be noted that in the 7th Knesset, the State Control Committee was a subcommittee of the Finance Committee.

Three annual reports of the state comptroller that were published during the terms of the three Knessets were examined: Annual Report 23 for 1972 (7th Knesset), Annual Report 33 for 1982 (10th Knesset), and Annual Report 44 for 1993 (13th Knesset).

Then the State Control Committee's protocols dealing with the three annual reports mentioned above were surveyed. The debates that were chosen dealt with deficiencies raised by the state comptroller in three main areas that consume more than one-third of the annual budget: Ministries of Education, Health, and Interior (one debate in the 7th Knesset, 14 debates in the 10th Knesset, and 14 debates in the 13th Knesset). Oversight activities of the State Control Committee are evaluated in this chapter according to these protocols within the chosen parameters.

The Education, Culture and Sports Committee—The Education, Culture and Sports Committee deals with the following issues: education, culture, science, the arts, broadcasting, cinema, and sports. In the first two Knessets examined (7th and 10th), a random sample of 15 committee debates was chosen. These debates were identified as having an "oversight" character (that is, debates on government plans and activities of government ministries) that resulted in conclusions tabled in the Knesset. Oversight activities of the Education, Culture and Sports Committee are evaluated according to these discussion protocols, with analysis performed according to the chosen parameters. In the 13th Knesset it was found that the committee did not draw conclusions in its plenum, therefore, no statistical evaluation of activity of the committee in that Knesset was possible.

Empirical evaluation of the two Knesset committees—findings. The extent of oversight activity of the committees was examined through five parameters.

The State Control Committee

1. Deficiencies Raised by the State Comptroller (regarding activities of the Education, Health, and Interior Ministries):

13th Knesset— committee debated most deficiencies (95%).	10th Knesset— committee debated only a portion of the deficiencies (44%).	7th Knesset— committee debated only one deficiency (4%) during one debate.
Good functioning	Fair functioning	Poor functioning

The findings indicate that the State Control Committee activity, regarding discussion on deficiencies raised by the state comptroller, improved over years. The committee debated only one deficiency (4 percent) in the 7th Knesset, whereas in the 13th Knesset it debated 95 percent of the deficiencies. However, the debate on the large number of deficiencies raised by the state comptroller does not imply better functioning of the committee in other parameters that were examined.

2. Simultaneous Membership in a Number of Committees:

Number of members who served only on State Control Committee: - 7th Knesset: 46% - 10th Knesset: 0% - 13th Knesset: 6%	Number of members who served on a second committee: 7th Knesset: 39% 10th Knesset: 44% 13th Knesset: 47%	Number of members who served on at least two other committees: 7th Knesset: 15% 10th Knesset: 56% 13th Knesset: 47%
Good functioning	Fair functioning	Poor functioning

The findings show that close to half of the committee members in both the 10th and the 13th Knessets served on at least two other committees, and the others served on a second committee.

3. Participation of Committee Members in Meetings:

The average attendance in the debates in the 7th Knesset was 62%. However, there was only one debate on one deficiency raised by the committee.	The average attendance in the debates in the 10th Knesset was 45%. There were 14 debates on deficiencies.	The average attendance in the debates in the 13th Knesset was low, at 25%. There were 14 debates on deficiencies.
Good functioning	Fair functioning	Poor functioning

The findings show that the average participation of members in the committee meetings decreased from 62 percent in the debates examined in the 7th Knesset (although, the committee debated only one deficiency and thus arguably did not fulfill its oversight role) to 44 percent in the 10th Knesset and 25 percent in the 13th Knesset.

4. Professional Advisory Staff

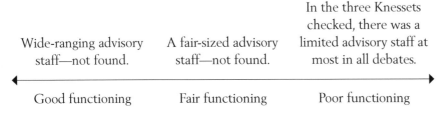

Wide-ranging advisory staff—not found.	A fair-sized advisory staff—not found.	In the three Knessets checked, there was a limited advisory staff at most in all debates.
Good functioning	Fair functioning	Poor functioning

Findings indicate there was a limited number of professional advisory staff attending and available to support the committee work in the debates checked.

5. Monitoring of Implementation of Committee's Recommendations:

The committee carried out continual monitoring activity—not found.	The committee in the 13th Knesset carried out limited monitoring activity.	The committee did not monitor implementation of its recommendations raised in three main areas in the 7th and 10th Knessets.
Good functioning	Fair functioning	Poor functioning

When it comes to committee monitoring of government implementation of its recommendations, there was a minor improvement in the 13th Knesset in comparison with the two previous ones. However, it may be said that within this parameter, all three Knessets indicated overall poor functioning. In the 7th and 10th Knessets, the committee did not debate any follow-up steps, and in the 13th Knesset it carried out only very limited monitoring activities.

6. Overall Findings
According to three parameters, there has been deterioration in committee functioning, except for the last parameter (monitoring of implementation of the committee's recommendations), which shows poor committee functioning during all three Knessets. Simultaneous membership of the State Control Committee members in at least two other committees may have hindered the quality of the committee's work and impaired its ability to apply proper oversight in the examined Knessets (particularly in the 10th and the 13th Knessets). There may be a link between membership in multiple

committees and the meager attendance of the committee meetings. Finally, even when a large number of deficiencies raised by the state comptroller were debated, there was no monitoring of the implementation of the committee's recommendations, as was mentioned above. If the committee's recommendations were not implemented, then the committee's work may have been in vain. The data show that the State Control Committee's functioning (although improved a little in one of the parameters examined) was mediocre at best and deteriorated into poor functioning in several cases over time.

The Education, Culture and Sports Committee

1. Sources of Information Used by Committee:

Use of independent sources only—not found.	In two Knessets checked there was great dependence on governmental sources (76% and 65% in the 7th and 10th, respectively).	Dependence only on governmental sources—not found.
Good functioning	Fair functioning	Poor functioning

The committee functioning during the two periods was at best mediocre, since the committee depended primarily on government sources of information (76 percent in the 7th Knesset and 65 percent in 10th Knesset).

2. Simultaneous Membership in a Number of Committees:

Number of members only on Education, Culture and Sports Committee:	Number of members who served on a second committee:	Number of members who served on at least two other committees:
7th Knesset: 32%	7th Knesset: 63%	7th Knesset: 5%
10th Knesset: 46%	10th Knesset: 27%	10th Knesset: 27%
13th Knesset: 0%	13th Knesset: 38%	13th Knesset: 62%
Good functioning	Fair functioning	Poor functioning

The findings indicate that in the second parameter, there was deterioration (particularly from the 10th Knesset to the 13th Knesset). In the 10th Knesset, almost half of the members served only on the Education, Culture and Sports Committee, while one-third of the members participated in a second committee. In the 13th Knesset, no members served exclusively on the Education, Culture and Sports Committee, and almost two-thirds of them served on at least two other committees.

3. Participation of Committee Members in Meetings:

Average attendance of committee members in debates was high (more than 50%)—not found.	In the 7th and 10th Knessets, average attendance of committee members in 30 debates checked was fair—42% and 47%, respectively.	Average attendance of committee members in all debates was low (less than 30%)— not found.
Good functioning	Fair functioning	Poor functioning

In the third parameter in the two Knessets examined, functioning was mediocre. The average participation in committee meetings was 42 percent in the 7th Knesset and 47 percent in the 10th Knesset.

4. Professional Advisory Staff:

A wide-ranging advisory staff—not found.	A fair-sized advisory staff—not found.	In the two Knessets checked there was no advisory staff present during the debate except for one legal advisor during one debate in the 10th Knesset.
Good functioning	Fair functioning	Poor functioning

Research showed a lack of independent professional advisers; therefore, the committee functioning is determined as poor.

5. Monitoring of Implementation of Committee's Recommendations:

Follow-up debates regarding implementation of most of the committee conclusions—not found.	Follow-up debates regarding implementation of some of the committee conclusions—not found.	In the 7th and 10th Knessets the Education, Culture and Sports Committee did not carry out follow-up debates on implementation of its conclusions.
Good functioning	Fair functioning	Poor functioning

In the fifth parameter, the research shows that the committee did not carry out any follow-up debates on its conclusions that were tabled in the Knesset.

6. Overall Findings

Many of the Education, Culture and Sports Committee members served on other committees during the three Knessets examined, potentially diminishing the time spent on the committee. This may be linked to the relatively low participation of committee members in the checked debates. In addition, the committee depended largely on government information and lacked independent professional staff and advisers. Finally, the lack of follow-up debates on implementation of the committee's recommendations demonstrates weak oversight ability. Lack of follow-up may mean that government does not feel pressure to implement the committee's recommendations. Overall the Education, Culture and Sports Committee's functioning deteriorated in one of the parameters examined from the 7th to the 10th Knessets, while in the other parameters it was poor to mediocre at best. During the 13th Knesset there were almost no conclusions despite the large number of matters debated, showing weak oversight ability.

Conclusions

Knesset committees suffer from structural deficiencies and a large number of procedures that impair their ability to oversee the executive. The examination of the State Control Committee and the Education, Culture and Sports Committee shows that simultaneous membership on different committees has been increasing over the years. Previous research shows this may lead to lowered attendance in the committee meetings, thus hindering oversight of the executive, which requires time, expertise, and knowledge of the supervised areas. Through the benefits of specialization, committees can scrutinize draft laws from the government more efficiently and effectively than the plenary assembly (Krehbiel 1991). When a Knesset member serving on several committees must rush from one meeting to another (most committee meetings take place in the mornings of the three working days of the Knesset), that member may not have the time nor the ability to prepare for committee meetings, or to develop expertise in the supervised areas, particularly as committees tend to oversee the activities of several, sometimes all, ministries.

How could Knesset committees' functioning be improved? The following conclusions, supported by a study of Knesset committees carried out by Hazan (2001), show that partial solutions are possible. Since the number of Knesset members will not change in the foreseeable future, and the Knesset will continue to be one of the smallest legislatures in the Western world, structural changes could alter the committees' areas of authority in order to harmonize them with the central government ministries' areas of activities. At the same time, the number of members of each committee could be decreased a little. These steps would reduce some of the difficulties, particularly the problem of simultaneous membership in a large number of committees. Knesset members who serve on fewer committees will have more time to prepare and to strengthen their knowledge and expertise on the issues covered by the committee. Furthermore, committee members should cover only activities of one or two ministries in order to further narrow down the areas covered.

To address procedural failures, political factions should be restricted from freely changing members of committees, and committees should be autonomous so their members are not constantly threatened with removal when they express opposition to the position of their party. In addition, all committees (not only the State Control Committee) should have the authority to compel public servants and other citizens to appear before them and to submit full documentation; not only that, they should have the authority to hold sanctions against those who disregard the summons. Having the power to compel individual cabinet ministers to attend a committee meeting and supply oral testimony places committees in a strong position to monitor ministries' activities. Committees can use such hearings as an opportunity to question a minister on activities and policies, and to determine how the minister's actions and attitude might differ from the politics of the coalition. Finally, in some cases committee meetings may benefit from being closed to the media and the public.

Only by increasing committee budgets and removing them from the control of government will the committees be able to provide truly independent oversight, which should be enhanced by professional staff (including external experts and research institutes). Increasing the number of professional staff available to support the work of committees is crucial. Today each committee has one to two legal advisers on staff (the Finance Committee also has an economist); however, the committee chairs still complain that this support is insufficient to meet their needs. Furthermore, improving information sources for committees will improve their functioning. The first significant step to address this issue was taken by the chair of the 15th Knesset. In 2000 he initiated a reform that established an independent information and research center to supply Knesset members with objective and practical information through research, studies, and comprehensive background documents. Today it is considered to be a very professional, fruitful center, and Knesset members benefit from its activity and praise its contributions.

The final area where significant change is possible is the ability of a committee to follow up on implementation of its recommendations. The committee, in general, must be capable of verifying government reactions to its conclusions and recommendations, and whether those recommendations were taken into consideration or not. Strong committees are not only able to monitor and amend proposed government legislation, they have the added ability to monitor and scrutinize the nonlegislative actions of individual cabinet ministers. Therefore, committee conclusions should be granted a legal status, requiring ministers to report back to committee on their subsequent actions and holding sanctions against those who do not. Only then will the chain of oversight be complete.

An improvement in the Knesset's oversight function through its parliamentary committees is possible. If reforms are undertaken, they may help turn the Knesset committees into real watchdogs that can help defend public interest, oversee government spending, and ultimately help prevent corruption.

Bibliography

Hazan, Reuven Y. 2001. *Reforming Parliamentary Committees: Israel in Comparative Perspective*. Columbus: Ohio State University Press.

Krehbiel, Keith. 1991. *Information and Legislative Organization*. Ann Arbor: University of Michigan Press.

Lees, John D., and Malcolm Shaw, eds. 1979. *Committees in Legislatures—A Comparative Analysis*. Durham, NC: Duke University Press.

Mill, John Stuart. 1958. *Considerations on Representative Government*. Jerusalem: Hebrew University Press (in Hebrew).

Pelizzo, Riccardo, and Rick Stapenhurst. 2004. "Tools for Legislative Oversight: An Empirical Investigation." World Bank Policy Research Working Paper 3388. World Bank Institute, Washington, DC.

State of Israel. 1958. *Basic Law: The Knesset* (in Hebrew).

———. 2001. *Basic Law: The Government* (in Hebrew).

State of Israel, The Knesset. 2004. *Rules of Parliamentary Procedure*. Jerusalem (in Hebrew).

———. The 7th Knesset. 1969–73. Education, Culture and Sports Committee. Protocols 12, 13, 51, 57, 59, 72, 88, 109, 111, 115, 135, 139, 155, 170, 175 (in Hebrew).

———. The 10th Knesset. 1981–84. Education, Culture and Sports Committee. Protocols 3, 15, 16, 19, 21, 22, 30, 33, 39, 55, 60, 68, 74, 103, 247 (in Hebrew).

———. The 7th Knesset. 1969–73. State Control Committee. Protocol 637 (in Hebrew).

———. The 10th Knesset. 1981–84. State Control Committee. Protocols 9, 22, 26, 126, 136, 137, 144, 160, 179A, 181, 200, 205, 206, 210, 211 (in Hebrew).

———. The 13th Knesset. 1992–96. State Control Committee. Protocols 5, 202, 203, 216, 221, 230, 240, 249, 280, 287, 308, 309, 317 (in Hebrew).

State of Israel, Office of the State Comptroller. 1972. *Annual Report No. 23*. Jerusalem. (in Hebrew).

———. 1982. *Annual Report No. 33*. Jerusalem (in Hebrew).

———. 1993. *Annual Report No. 44*. Jerusalem (in Hebrew).

CHAPTER 17

Parliamentary Oversight of Defense in South Africa

Robert J. Griffiths

South Africa's transformation from apartheid to majority rule represents a remarkable example of democratic transition and consolidation. The creation of perhaps the world's most progressive constitution combined with the establishment and strengthening of institutions supportive of democracy have been important components of this success. Among the critical issues that have had to be addressed in the context of this transformation are the reorientation of defense policy and the establishment of civilian control of the armed forces. The issues surrounding security sector reform have been particularly important because of the role of the armed forces in repressing opposition to apartheid. South Africa's role as regional hegemon and its role in regional peacekeeping and humanitarian intervention further underline the importance of security sector reform.

One of the key elements of the effort to ensure transparency and accountability in the reorientation of defense policy is the establishment of parliamentary oversight of defense policy. Because the security sector has responsibility for a critical state function, and because of the role of the military under apartheid, it is essential that Parliament ensure that the armed forces are under effective civilian control. Beyond that, Parliament can also serve as a counterweight to executive dominance of defense policy (Inter-Parliamentary Union and Geneva Centre for the Democratic Control of Armed Forces [IPU-DCAF] 2003). During apartheid, mechanisms of civilian control theoretically existed, although in practice there was little oversight of the armed forces. There were two reasons for this lack of supervision. First, national security played a paramount role during the "total strategy" era, giving the armed forces considerable influence in policy making.[1] Second, while members of Parliament had some military experience due to conscription, there was little effort to develop expertise in military affairs. Instead, the tendency was for Parliament to accept the military's assessments and recommendations.[2] As one member of the parliamentary defense committee remarked in 1996, before 1994 there were no civil-military relations to speak of; no strict oversight existed.[3] Democracy's requirements of accountability, transparency, and legitimacy necessitated the creation of institutions to ensure civilian dominance of defense policy and also opened civil-military relations and defense policy to greater parliamentary control. This involved the creation of a civilian defense department and secretariat, as well as established mechanisms for effective parliamentary oversight. The effectiveness of parliamentary oversight is influenced by a variety of institutional and practical considerations, including the nature of the electoral system, patterns of party discipline, executive-legislative relations, and the capacity of the defense committees to effectively monitor policy.

The Establishment of Parliamentary Defense Oversight

South Africa's electoral system uses a closed-list, proportional representation method. Political parties compile regional and national lists for the 400 seats in the National Assembly (NA), and representation is awarded on the basis of the party's proportion of the vote using the proportional, largest-remainder method.[4] Because the parties submit the lists of candidates and members of Parliament (MPs) do not represent specific districts, the party can impose strict discipline on its members, and there is a high likelihood that MPs will support the party's position on policy issues (Nijzink 2001). Moreover, the executive has a substantial advantage in terms of expertise, especially given the technicalities of defense policy. The technical expertise of the executive provides greater influence in formulating defense policy in contrast to the parliamentary committees, which lack support staff.

Reflecting the concern about civil-military relations and defense policy, two parliamentary committees were created to deal with defense after the 1994 elections, the Portfolio Committee and the Joint Standing Committee on Defense (JSCD). The Portfolio Committee focuses largely on legislation regarding defense. However, due to the changes required of the armed forces in South Africa, the JSCD, composed of members of both the National Assembly and the National Council of Provinces (NCOP), was established primarily to oversee the military's transformation.

The current distribution of seats on the committee breaks down in the following way: the African National Congress (ANC) holds 11 seats, while the Democratic Alliance (DA), the Inkatha Freedom Party (IFP), the Freedom Front Plus (FF+) and the Pan-Africanist Congress (PAC) each have one seat. Three of the ANC seats are alternatives; the United Democratic Movement (UDM) also has an alternate member of the committee. On the JSCD, where representation is restricted to those parties with more than 10 seats, the ANC holds 26 seats, the DA has four, and the IFP has two. Eleven of the ANC seats are alternate members.

The committees have a range of powers that include the ability to summon witnesses before them; require witnesses to give evidence or produce documents; require reports from individuals or institutions; and receive petitions, representations, or submissions from the public.[5] Under the NA rules, the Portfolio Committee must maintain oversight of "the exercise within its portfolio of national executive authority, including the implementation of legislation; any executive organ of State falling within its portfolio; any constitutional institution falling within its portfolio; any body or institution in respect of which oversight was assigned to it." It may also "monitor, investigate, enquire into, and make recommendations concerning any such executive organ of state, constitutional institution, or other body or institution, including the legislative program, budget, rationalization, restructuring, functioning, organization, structure, staff and policies of such organ of the state, institution, or other body or institution."[6]

The JSCD has responsibility for investigation and for recommendations on the budget, functioning, organization, armaments, policy, morale, and the South African National Defense Force's (SANDF) state of preparedness, as well as any other functions related to parliamentary supervision of the forces as may be prescribed by law.[7] The JSCD played an important role in reviewing the drafts and final version of the 1996 *White Paper on National Defence for the Republic of South Africa* (the Defense White Paper) and the 1998 Defense Review (DOD 1996, 1998). Its membership has been drawn largely from the ranks of party bureaucrats, and the committee has exercised considerable political clout (Frankel 2000, 118). Because of the broad mandate outlined in the Defense White Paper of 1996, the JSCD has been involved in a variety of oversight activities. It has reviewed the budget, overseen policy implementation, tried to reconcile differences that emerged between the SANDF and the Defense Secretariat, and engaged in fact-finding efforts such as after the September 1999 incident in which a black officer went on a rampage at an army base outside Blomfontein and killed seven whites before being shot dead. The JSCD's broad monitoring role was deemed necessary due to the challenges of integrating and transforming the South African armed forces.[8] Although the transformation of the South African National Defense Force is not yet complete, the Portfolio Committee has taken on most of the responsibility for committee work related to the defense sector (Cawthra 2005).

Early tensions between the defense force and the parliamentary committees have given way to greater cooperation. Initial exchanges between the defense force and parliamentary committees were strained, especially between old guard South African Defense Force officers who were unaccustomed to scrutiny by Parliament, particularly by a committee headed by ANC members of Parliament.[9] In fact, an initial request by the navy to purchase new vessels was rejected by Parliament. This came as a surprise to military officers accustomed to getting what they wanted.[10] During the development of the Defense White Paper and the 1998 Defense Review, as well as work on the Defense Act, the JSCD was actively involved and refused to rubber-stamp decisions. Their involvement in drafting policy was initially resisted and viewed as interference but it has now come to be accepted and even welcomed (Modise 2004). Despite getting off to a somewhat rocky start, parliamentary oversight is now well established, and the committees regularly request meetings with defense officials and review policy and budgets.

Certain key documents provide the basis for South Africa's defense policy and represent guidelines for parliamentary oversight. South Africa's shift to democracy prompted the minister of defense to present a draft white paper on national defense in June 1995 and to invite comments from Parliament and the public. Several subsequent drafts incorporated the comments of the various political parties, nongovernmental organizations, the defense industry, defense analysts, the SANDF, the parliamentary committees, and the public. The final draft, incorporating input from these participants, was approved by the cabinet and released in May 1996. In presenting the white paper, then–Defense Minister Joe Modise described it as reflecting "a national consensus on defense policy" (DOD 1996, "Foreword"). The white paper outlined policy on the challenges of transformation, civil-military relations, the strategic environment, budgetary issues, the role and function of the armed forces, the arms industry, and human resources issues.

In an effort to elaborate on the broad policy outlines of the white paper and in a further effort to involve the public, a defense review was undertaken in 1996. Under the auspices of a working group appointed by the minister and coordinated by the defense secretary, national consultative conferences were held in February and August of 1996 and in May of 1997. Two rounds of regional workshops were also held throughout the country in July 1996 and May 1997.[11] The defense review sought to determine the appropriate size, structure, and force design of the SANDF into the 21st century and addressed issues such as South Africa's approach to security and defense, arms control, defense posture and spending, peace operations and regional security, and deployment of the defense forces in support of the police. The review concluded that the SANDF should be primarily a defensive force under constitutional control and shaped by South African defense and national policy. Its tasks were to defend against military threats and internal threats to the constitutional order and to promote regional and international security. The SANDF was envisioned as consisting of a core force that could be expanded by calling up a part-time component when necessary. The size and design of the force was to be based on a needs-driven but cost-constrained approach to defense. Initial indications were that defense allocations would be in the neighborhood of 1.5 percent of gross domestic product (GDP) with recognition that circumstances might dictate fluctuation in that figure.[12]

The Strategic Defense Procurement Package and Parliamentary Oversight

The R 50 billion Strategic Defense Procurement Package (SDPP) announced in 1998 provides an opportunity to examine South Africa's progress in solidifying legitimacy, transparency, accountability, and parliamentary oversight of defense in light of the controversial decision to go forward with a large purchase of weapons from abroad.

During apartheid, an international arms embargo prevented Pretoria from acquiring weapons abroad. Although South Africa developed a sophisticated domestic arms industry, it could not meet all the armed forces' needs. In 1998, after a four-year debate, the government announced an R 30 billion arms procurement deal to upgrade South Africa's defense capability. The purchases included three submarines, four corvettes, 30 helicopters, 28 jet fighters, and 24 training aircraft.[13] To pay for this package, military spending was slated to increase from R 10.72 billion in fiscal year 1999/2000 to R 13.76 billion in 2000/01 and then up to R 15.27 billion the following year (*Africa Confidential* 2000). The R 3 billion increase in the defense budget between the 1999/2000 and the 2000/01 budget was due to this procurement (*Cape Times* 2000). Military spending was scheduled to rise to R 16.8 billion in 2002/03, with a further increase to R 17.8 billion in 2003/04, and by fiscal year 2006/07, defense spending rose to R 23.9 billion (Department of Defense 2007).[14]

The decision to purchase these weapons and the increased military spending provoked considerable debate. While the need to replace aging weapons was widely acknowledged, many questioned the expenditure of such a large sum. Critics argued that it was extravagant in a country that was struggling to provide housing, electricity, and other social services, while others charged that the procurement was ill-suited to South Africa's likely defense challenges (Williams 1999). Defense Department officials contended that instability in the region and the need to protect maritime resources justified the spending package (Nevin 1999). To make the purchase more palatable, a deal was negotiated that would purportedly bring some 65,000 jobs to South Africa's economy, which is desperately in need of employment opportunities. The jobs would come as a result of an industrial offset package that requires suppliers of the weapons to invest in local industry (*Mail & Guardian* 2000). Despite government approval of the package, questions remained regarding the employment benefits of the deal and irregularities in the procurement process.

The force design contained in the defense review was presented to Parliament in March 1998. While Parliament endorsed the review, it is not clear that Parliament ever actually approved the arms package. The Institute for a Democratic South Africa (IDASA) asserted that when Parliament approved the force design, it did not approve the procurement package. Instead, IDASA maintained that Parliament approved a concept of defense that was likely to change over time, was subject to parliamentary oversight, and actually represented a wish list the Defense Department realized was unrealistic given fiscal constraints (IDASA 2001). Nevertheless, the government went forward with the deal, announcing in September 1999 that the suppliers had been selected and the price of the package was placed at R 21.3 billion over eight years (IDASA 2003a). The cost subsequently rose to R 30.3 billion and by September 2000 was reported to be R 43.8 billion due to foreign exchange rate changes and contractual price escalations.[15] Estimates of the cost of the SDPP eventually rose to R 53 billion by 2003 (*Mail & Guardian* 2003).

Aside from the cost increases, questions were also raised regarding the benefits of the offsets guaranteed under the terms of the deal. These offsets required contractors to provide certain economic benefits to South Africa,

including selecting local subcontractors to provide some of the military hardware. Contractors were also required to provide nonmilitary trade and investment. The value of these offsets was initially put at R 110 billion, but this
was later reduced to R 104 billion (IDASA 2003b). These offsets were also
supposed to create the 65,000 new jobs (Nevin 2001).

There were also allegations of corruption in the awarding of the contracts.
Then Pan-Africanist Congress MP Patricia de Lille produced documents she
said came from ANC members alleging corruption, including bribes paid to
senior ANC officials and contracts for their relatives (*Africa Confidential* 2001).
Among those subsequently convicted of corruption were Tony Yengeni, then
the ANC's chief parliamentary whip and chair of the Joint Standing Committee on Defense during the contract negotiations, who obtained a discounted
Mercedes from a contractor. He was convicted of fraud and sentenced to four
years. Other high-ranking ANC officials accused of wrongdoing were the late
former defense minister Joe Modise, who signed an agreement for the purchase of submarines three days before leaving office. Modise subsequently
obtained a loan to buy shares of a company, of which he served as chairman,
that had interests in the arms industry. Shamin Shaik, who was head of arms
procurement for the Defense Department, was also alleged to have family
connections to local firms that were awarded contracts as part of the offsets
arrangement (*Time International* 2001). Shaik's brother, Durban businessman
and one-time financial adviser to former deputy president Jacob Zuma, was
also convicted of fraud and corruption. His conviction resulted in Zuma's
dismissal from his post as deputy president following Judge Hilary Squires'
characterization of the relationship between Shaik and Zuma as "generally
corrupt."[16] The combination of skepticism about the cost and benefits of the
package, as well as the allegations of corruption, ultimately triggered a series
of investigations into the arms deal.

In September 2000, the auditor general, who is constitutionally responsible
for auditing all government expenditures, submitted a report to Parliament's
Standing Committee on Public Accounts (SCOPA). SCOPA has responsibility for overseeing public expenditure of all government departments. When
SCOPA receives a report from the auditor general (AG) indicating any fiscal
irregularity, the committee must investigate. In the course of its investigation,
SCOPA has the power to call the parties involved before the committee to
account for and explain their actions.[17] The AG questioned why the approved
package was significantly more expensive than other proposals and recommended a full investigation (IDASA 2003a). SCOPA considered the AG's
report and issued its own report in October 2000, raising questions about
the cost, offsets, the selection of both contractors and subcontractors, and the
Defense Department's acquisition policies. It also called for a combined investigation involving the auditor general, the Special Investigating Unit (SIU), the
public protector, the Investigating Directorate of Serious Economic Offenses,
and any other relevant investigative bodies.[18]

A meeting was held in November 2000 of several investigative bodies, and
it was determined that the Directorate of Special Operations of the National

Prosecuting Authority, the offices of the auditor general and the public protector, and the SIU, under the direction of Judge Willem Heath, would conduct a joint investigation of the Strategic Defense Procurement Package.[19] The South African Constitutional Court subsequently ruled that a judge could not head the SIU, and Minister of Justice Penuel Maduna advised President Mbeki that the SIU under Heath should not play a role in the investigation. President Mbeki then announced that he would not grant a special proclamation authorizing the SIU to take part in the investigation (IDASA 2003a). The SIU, established by former president Nelson Mandela, had the capacity to invalidate contracts and reclaim state money if corruption was involved in the granting of contracts (Nevin 2001). The SIU reclaimed some R 314 million between 1997 and early 2001 from deals where it found evidence of corruption. Critics charged that the SIU was excluded because of its effectiveness (*Africa Confidential* 2001). This issue became the subject of considerable controversy around whether SCOPA expressly called for the inclusion of the SIU in the investigation and President Mbeki's decision not to allow the SIU permission to participate (February, J., 2004).

Acting on the recommendation of the Standing Committee on Public Accounts, the Joint Investigative Team (JIT), consisting of the public protector, the auditor general, and the Directorate of Special Operations of the National Prosecuting Authority, held its first meeting in November 2000. Prior to the meeting's commencement, the JIT was referred to a total of six parliamentary committees.[20] The joint investigation was unique because it involved the cooperation of three agencies conducting a simultaneous investigation into alleged irregularities and criminal conduct. The public nature of the investigation was also unprecedented, and as a result the JIT worked in uncharted territory. In its 2001 report, the JIT found some irregularities and shortcomings in the procurement process. There was a lack of evaluation criteria for companies submitting bids, business plans were not submitted in a timely fashion, and decisions on offset arrangements were made on an ad hoc basis. The JIT also found that the Cabinet was aware of the cost escalation in the deal and investigators were critical of the model used by the Affordability Team. In addition, the JIT found that there had been a conflict of interest related to the involvement of the Defense Department's chief of acquisitions, Shamin Shaik, whose brother had an interest in one of the foreign contractors (IDASA 2003b).

The Implications for Defense Oversight

The Strategic Defense Procurement Package provides insight into the development of transparency and accountability in defense policy and highlights the challenges of effective parliamentary oversight. Arms procurement is particularly well-suited for analysis of transparency and accountability due to the controversy generated by arms sales, their technical complexity, and the potential for corruption often associated with such lucrative transactions.

The arms package also exemplifies several problems associated with parliamentary oversight, including the role of party discipline, executive-legislative relations, and the capacity of parliamentary committees to adequately monitor the complexities of defense policy, particularly those related to arms procurement. Although the Defense White Paper and the Defense Review offered broad guidelines for defense policy, details were left out. The controversy over whether Parliament directly approved the SDPP illustrates the ability of the executive to push forward with policies it favors even in the absence of explicit legislative approval. Once the executive decision was made, strong ANC party discipline made it difficult for MPs to challenge the SDPP. Opposition parties could question the deal, and they did, but they were powerless to stop it. Moreover, a lack of both parliamentary expertise related to arms procurement and parliamentary support staff to assist MPs in making independent judgments regarding the purchase made it even less likely that Parliament would challenge the decision. This reflects a key shortcoming of parliamentary committees in new democracies—the lack of defense expertise (Nathan 2004). Although members of the South African parliamentary committees often have military backgrounds, that does not guarantee the high level of expertise required to oversee the complexities of such an arms deal.

Although the arms purchase was unique and such a decision is unlikely to come up again soon, the package demonstrates that the military retains significant influence in defense policy making, despite the fiscal constraints and competition for resources in postapartheid South Africa. The armed forces, prevented from purchasing arms from abroad during apartheid, lobbied successfully for a major upgrade in military hardware, taking advantage of an open market and a post–Cold War excess of defense production capacity in the West. The end of the international arms embargo and the decision to purchase arms from foreign suppliers required the creation of new procurement procedures. Parliamentary capacity, characterized by an unfamiliarity with the recently established procurement process and lack of technical knowledge needed to translate the approved force structure into appropriate weapons systems, combined with executive dominance of decision making and tight party discipline, hindered the ability of Parliament to effectively moderate the armed forces' push for an expensive weapons package. There was also confusion regarding whether the Parliament's approval of the Defense Review constituted approval of the arms purchase. Gaps in the oversight capacity of the defense committees on this issue are also apparent. Among the general shortcomings mentioned by MPs regarding oversight are a lack of budgetary expertise, some unwillingness to challenge the Defense Department for fear of being labeled obstructionist or undermining democracy, and the lack of overall capacity to effectively oversee defense issues.[21] In the latter case, legislative capacity building has to be emphasized through the "development of analytical and policy-interrogative skills and defense parliamentarians' understanding of the defense policy, planning, budgetary, and programming cycle" (Williams 2005, 21).

The arms deal also suggests some questions regarding the functions of independent investigative agencies, the separation of the ANC and the government, and the role of parliamentary committees. As IDASA noted, in one-party-dominant democracies, the strong party system and the close links that MPs have with the executive branch make it difficult to exercise effective oversight (IDASA 2003b). The ANC's dismissal of Andrew Feinstein, its head of the parliamentary study group on SCOPA, and his replacement by Geoff Doidge, the ANC's deputy chief whip, was seen as a reprisal for Feinstein's backing of SIU involvement in the Joint Investigative Team (*Africa Confidential* 2001). Feinstein later spoke at an IDASA seminar on parliamentary oversight and accountability and advocated close oversight of the executive and executive accountability to Parliament. He also called for SCOPA's insulation from political interference, particularly from the executive (IDASA 2003a). The February 2002 resignation of the inspector general of intelligence also raised questions of civil oversight, and in the aftermath of the SCOPA's controversial push for an investigation of the arms deal, indicated a trend toward consolidation of executive power.

Under President Mbeki parliamentary oversight has become less vigorous. The president no longer faces weekly questions from Parliament, and ministers appear before Parliament less than they did under President Mandela (*Africa Confidential* 2002). Nevertheless, parliamentary oversight has been firmly established, even if not always fully realized. The Defense Portfolio Committee and the Joint Standing Committee on Defense are capable of reviewing legislation, holding hearings, and monitoring defense policy. Also, since 1994, parliamentary rules give committees extensive powers, and most parliamentary committees conduct their meetings in public (Streek 2001). Furthermore, oversight ability is improving, and the Portfolio Committee regularly amends bills seeking to leave its mark on legislation.[22] Parliamentary influence on two other important pieces of legislation since the arms deal has yielded mixed results. The National Conventional Arms Control Act of 2002 was enacted despite concerns in Parliament regarding issues of transparency and Parliament's participation in the review of conventional arms sales. In the case of the Protection of Constitutional Democracy Against Terrorism Act of 2004, Parliament played an important role in changing the provisions of the law defining terrorist activity (February, J., 2004).

In addition, the so-called Chapter 9 institutions, which are grouped in the constitution under the heading of "State Institutions Supporting Constitutional Democracy" and include the public prosecutor and the auditor general, are functioning and, in conjunction with the National Prosecuting Authority of the judicial branch, have played an important role in the investigation of the arms deal. IDASA's evaluation of the Joint Investigative Team's report disagreed with critics who labeled the report a "white wash." IDASA (2003b) concluded that the report was in some ways "quite damning." It noted that the report was explicit about areas and departments in which controls were nonexistent and checks and balances were ignored. Furthermore, IDASA's monitoring role, and that of other organizations, demonstrates an increasingly effective and vigilant civil society.

The problems illustrated by the arms deal can be seen as partly attributable to the growing pains of a consolidating democracy. However, the ANC's dominant political position raises some concerns about transparency and accountability. Those concerns are likely to remain, given that the ANC captured of two-thirds of the vote in the 2004 elections and has a commanding advantage of 279 of the 400 National Assembly seats. The party also looks set to retain a strong majority in the 2009 elections. Perceptions of the ANC's intolerance of criticism and the centralization of power in the executive reinforce these concerns (Piombo 2004). Despite some flaws, the handling of the investigation and the public nature of the controversy over the SDPP nevertheless demonstrate significant promise for the further strengthening of South African democracy. Civil society and a lively press pushed for a full investigation of the allegations of corruption. In the process, the arms deal also provided important insights and lessons regarding parliamentary oversight of defense in South Africa.

Postscript

Additional evidence of corruption surrounding the arms deal has surfaced since the JIT report in 2001. In June 2005, Shabir Shaik, a financial adviser to Deputy President Jacob Zuma, was convicted of corruption and fraud and sentenced to 15 years in prison. Shaik's conviction resulted in Zuma's dismissal from his post and his subsequent indictment on corruption charges. The case was thrown out of court in 2006, but the court of appeals opened the door for the filing of further charges in November 2007. Charges were refiled on December 28, 2007, just a week after Zuma was elected president of the ANC. His election as head of the ANC positions him to become president after the 2009 elections. He faces trial in August 2008.

Corruption allegations have also emerged against President Mbeki, who was a member of a committee that oversaw the bidding process. Mbeki's involvement came to light during an investigation (recently dropped) in Germany of a supplier of naval vessels. British authorities have also opened an investigation of bribery allegations involving the British supplier of planes to South Africa. Chippy Shaik, former head of procurement during the arms deal and the brother of Shabir, has also been accused of accepting a US$3 million bribe in conjunction with the arms deal. Although the three members of the JIT—the auditor general, the public protector, and the national prosecuting authority—ruled out a reopening of the investigation, spokesmen for the opposition Democratic Alliance and the Independent Democrats have called for further investigation. In January 2008, the ANC's National Executive Council announced the formation of an ad hoc committee to look into the arms deal. In February 2008, Parliament's Standing Committee on Public Accounts (SCOPA) put a request from the opposition Democratic Alliance to reopen the investigation on its agenda. There is clearly potential for further parliamentary action as this scandal continues to unfold.

Notes

1. Total strategy was a policy formulated by the apartheid regime to combat what it saw as a total onslaught from communist and antiapartheid forces. See, for instance, Griffiths (1991), Grundy (1986), and Metz 1987.

2. Interviews, Defense Headquarters, Pretoria, June 1992 and July 1996.

3. Interview, Parliament, Cape Town, February 2000.

4. For a detailed explanation of South Africa's electoral system see Alvarez-Rivera (2006).

5. See *Parliament of the Republic of South Africa.* "The Work of Committees," http://www.parliament.gov.za.

6. *National Assembly Rules,* June 1999, Part 9, Rule 201, p. 50.

7. DOD (1996), chap. 3, sec. 2.

8. Interviews, Parliament, Cape Town, February 2000.

9. Interviews, Parliament, Cape Town, July 1996 and February 2000.

10. Interviews with Defense Committee staff, Cape Town, July 1996.

11. See *South African Defence Review* (DOD 1998), chap. 1.

12. DOD (1998), chap. 15, sec. 13–20.

13. Address by Minister of Defense Mosiuoa Lekota on the Occasion of the Defense Budget Vote, April 7, 2000, before the National Assembly. http://www.dod.mil.za/ministry/speeches.htm.

14. GlobalSecurity.org. 2001–2008. "South African Military Budget." http://www.globalsecurity.org/military/world/rsa/budget.htm.

15. SCOPA (Standing Committee on Public Accounts), Parliament of South Africa. 2000 (October 30). "Fourteenth Report of the Standing Committee on Public Accounts."

16. "Zuma Axed." *The Star,* June 14, 2005. http://www.iol.co.za.

17. "A Brief Introduction to SCOPA." http;//www.idasa.org.za.

18. SCOPA. 2000 (October 30). "Fourteenth Report of the Standing Committee on Public Accounts."

19. "Joint Report on the Strategic Defense Procurement Package," chap. 1, p. 7. Web site of the Office of the Auditor General of South Africa. http://www.agsa.co.za.

20. Interview, Parliament, Cape Town, July 2003.

21. Interviews, Parliament, Cape Town, February 2000.

22. Interviews, Parliament, Cape Town, July 2003.

Bibliography

Africa Confidential. 2000. "Military Manoeuvres," 41 (8): 1.

———. 2001. "Arms for Oblivion," 42 (3): 7.

———. 2002. "Watch on the Spooks," 43 (3).

Alvarez-Rivera, Manuel. 2006. "Election Resources on the Internet: The Republic of South Africa Electoral System." http://electionresources.org/za/system. Last updated June 13, 2006.

Auditor General, Republic of South Africa. *Joint Report on the Strategic Defense Procurement Package.* http://www.agsa.co.za.

Cape Times. 2000. "Business Report Budget Special," February 24, 2000.

Cawthra, Gavin. 2005. "Security Governance in South Africa." *African Security Review* 14 (3). http://www.iss.co.za/index.php?link_id=3&link_type=12&tmpl_id=3.

DOD (Department of Defense, Republic of South Africa). 1996. *White Paper on National Defence for the Republic of South Africa* (Defense White Paper). Pretoria, South Africa. http://www.dod.mil.za/documents/WhitePaperonDef/whitepaper%20on%20defence1996.pdf

———. 1998. *South African Defense Review*. Pretoria, South Africa. http://www.dod.mil.za/documents/defencereview/defence%20review1998.pdf.

———. 2007. *Annual Report FY 2006/07*. Pretoria, South Africa. http://www.dod.mil.za/.

February, Judith. 2004. "Case Study: Democracy and the South African Arms Deal." Prepared for the Anti-Corruption Strategies Programme, "Three Strikes against Graft," Gauteng, South Africa, March 15–17. http://www.iss.co.za/seminars/2004/1503graft/rsa.pdf.

Frankel, Philip. 2000. *Soldiers in a Storm: The Armed Forces in South Africa's Democratic Transition*. Boulder: Westview Press.

Griffiths, R. 1991. "The South African Military: The Dilemmas of Expanded Influence in Decision-Making," *Journal of Asian and African Studies* 26: 1–2.

Grundy, Kenneth. 1986. *The Militarization of South African Politics*, Bloomington: Indiana University Press.

IDASA. (Institute for Democracy in South Africa). 2001. "Democracy and the Arms Deal: An Interim Review." May 15, IDASA, Cape Town. http://www.idasa.org.za/.

———. 2003a. "The Arms Deal Update 2003." Research report, June 21. IDASA, Cape Town. http://www.idasa.org.za/.

———. 2003b. "Democracy and the Arms Deal: Part 3. Submission to Parliament." Research report, August 5. IDASA, Cape Town. http://www.idasa.org.za/.

IPU-DCAF (Inter-Parliamentary Union and Geneva Centre for the Democratic Control of Armed Forces). 2003. *Parliamentary Oversight of the Security Sector: Principles, Mechanisms, and Practices Handbook for Parliamentarians No. 5*. Geneva: Geneva Center for the Democratic Control of Armed Forces.

Mail & Guardian Online. 2000. "Improper Influence in Arms Deal Probed," October 31, 2000. http://www.mg.co.za.

———. 2003. "Arms Deal Cripples SANDF," March 20, 2003. http://www.mg.co.za.

Metz, Steven. 1987. "Pretoria's Total Strategy and Low-Intensity Conflict in Southern Africa," *Comparative Strategy* 6 (4): 437–69.

Modise, Thandi. 2004. "Parliamentary Oversight of the South African Department of Defense: 1994–2003." In *Guarding the Guardians: Parliamentary Oversight and Civil-Military Relations: The Challenges for SADC*, eds. Len LeRoux, Martin Rupiya, and Naison Ngoma. http://www.iss.co.za/pubs/books.

Nathan, Laurie. 2004. "Obstacles to Security Sector reform in New Democracies." *Journal of Security Sector Management* 2 (3). http://www.jofssm.org.

Nevin, Tom. 1999. "South Africa: Guns and Butter" *African Business* (January).

———. 2001. "SA's R50b Arms Deal Scandal." *African Business* (June).

Nijzink, Lia. 2001. "Opposition in the New South African Parliament." *Democratization* 8 (1): 56.

Piombo, Jessica. 2004. "Politics in a Stabilizing Democracy: South Africa's 2004 Elections." *Strategic Insights* 3 (5). http://www.ccc.nps.navy.mil/si/.

SCOPA (Standing Committee on Public Accounts), Parliament of South Africa. 2000 (October 30). "Fourteenth Report of the Standing Committee on Public Accounts."

Streek, Barry. n.d. "Watchdogs That Bark, Not Bite." *Mail & Guardian Online.* February 14. http://www.mg.co.za.

Time International. 2001. "Lethal Weapons: South Africa's Arms Deal Investigation May Uncover Corruption in the ANC," April 16, 2001, 44.

Williams, Rocklyn. 1999. "How Primary Is the Primary Function? Configuring the SANDF for African Realities." *African Security Review* 8 (6). http://www.iss.co.za/pubs/ASR.

———. 2005. "African Armed Forces and the Challenges of Security Sector Reform." *Journal of Security Sector Management* 3 (2): 1–35.

CHAPTER 18

Keeping a Watchful Eye?
Parliaments and the Politics
of Budgeting in Latin America

Carlos Santiso

Largely neglected in the first stage of economic reform, legislative budget institutions are being rediscovered in a second wave of reform in public financial management. In democratic regimes, parliament is a key player in the budget process—approving the budget and overseeing its implementation. As such, parliament must hold government to account for the manner in which it manages public funds. Policy makers, while promoting strong executive authority to ensure fiscal discipline, recognize that, left unchecked, executive discretion in the budget process can degenerate into corruption. Moreover, there is heightened awareness of the weaknesses of the institutions of "horizontal accountability" within the state, notably in presidential systems (O'Donnell 1999; Mainwaring and Welna 2003).[1]

Increasing budget transparency and anchoring fiscal responsibility are critical tasks for emerging economies seeking to strengthen fiscal governance and curb corruption. The role of parliament in the budget process and the contribution of auxiliary institutions such as audit offices and anticorruption agencies are thus being reevaluated in the broader context of strengthening accountability in public finances and the dynamics of executive-legislative relations in public budgeting (Santiso 2004a, 2005, 2006b, 2006c). It is increasingly recognized that legislative oversight of the budget by capable parliaments and external scrutiny of public accounts by credible audit offices help mitigate the risks of excessive executive discretion in public budgeting.

In light of this, international financial institutions such as the World Bank and the Inter-American Development Bank have stepped up their efforts to strengthen budget oversight institutions (Santiso 2006a, 2006d). However, in many developing countries, parliaments are weak and discredited, with limited institutional capacity or political incentives to influence the budget process. Their role in the governance of the budget is often subdued and dysfunctional, partly as a result of executive dominance, but also because of their own deficiencies. Rather than promoting accountability, they are often sources of financial mismanagement and corruption, resulting from patronage politics, pork-barrel deals, and electoral clientelism. The legacy of parliamentary indiscipline in budgetary matters has convinced policy makers and parliamentarians alike that centralizing the budget process within the executive and limiting the fiscal prerogatives of parliaments improve fiscal discipline. Indeed, parliaments' ineffectual role in public budgeting is linked to their limited role in public policy making, the general weakness of checks and balances, and the often-blurred separation of powers.

The case of Latin American countries is particularly instructive in that regard, as they combine presidential systems of government with highly centralized budgetary systems. A paradox of legislative budgeting in Latin America is that, while parliaments possess a wide range of formal budgetary powers, they often fail to exercise them effectively or responsibly. What explains this disjuncture between their formal powers and their actual role? This chapter argues that institutional arrangements and political economy considerations help in understanding why parliaments have not exploited the full scope of their budgetary powers in an effective manner. As noted above, parliaments' oversight is hampered both by technical constraints and political factors.

Against this backdrop, this chapter examines the budget role of Latin American parliaments and underscores the benefits that could be derived from a more balanced relationship between the executive and the legislature in budgetary matters. A reequilibration of budgetary powers requires parliaments to assume a more responsible role in public budgeting. Ultimately, the governance of the budget reflects a delicate balance between executive prerogatives and legislative oversight, a constant challenge for developing countries seeking to strengthen political accountability while furthering fiscal discipline.

Parliaments and Budget Governance

As Carlos Scartascini and Ernesto Stein (2004, 2) underscored, "Understanding the budget process and the incentives of the multiple agents that participate in this process is a key ingredient for any fiscal reform seeking lasting results in terms of improvements in fiscal discipline and efficiency in the use of public resources."[2] Figure 18.1 describes the political economy of the budget process, the multitude of actors and processes involved, and the accountability checks in the budget cycle.

While knowledge of the dynamics of public budgeting *within* the executive has considerably improved in recent years, budgetary institutions *beyond* the executive have received little systematic scrutiny. In most Latin American countries, the executive dominates the budget process and legislatures often act as mere rubber stamps. Latin American parliaments are typically characterized by operational, administrative, and resource problems that limit the fulfillment of their legislative, representative, and oversight responsibilities. Capacity constraints are compounded by political dysfunctions linked to

Figure 18.1. Governance of the Budget

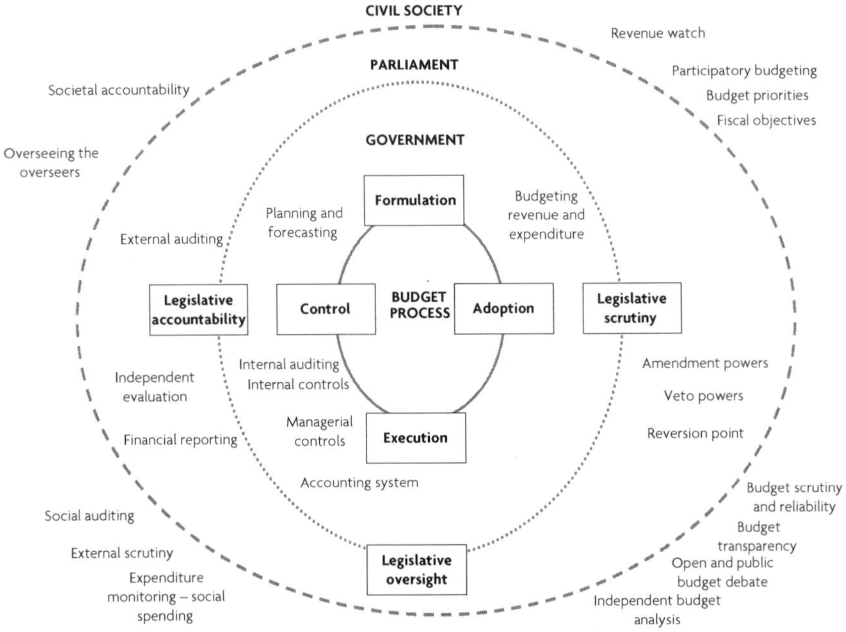

Source: Author.

the nature of political regimes and electoral systems, which severely affect the public credibility of parliaments.

These structural weaknesses affect their ability to engage with the budget process in a purposeful manner. Stein et al. (2005) constructed an index of legislative capabilities, reproduced in table 18.1, that underscores their weakness.

A number of structural constraints limit the scope of parliaments' influence over the budget, including the conditions imposed by international lenders and investors and the general inertia of the budget itself. Furthermore, the type of public spending on which parliament could potentially have the greatest influence, capital expenditure, represents only a small fraction of public expenditures, albeit sometimes, as in Brazil, it is of strategic importance for building ad hoc political coalitions. The adoption of fiscal rules and hard budget constraints further limits the margins for legislative discretion and political bargaining.

Parliaments and Financial Reform

In the early 1990s, first-generation economic reforms focused on improving transparency and efficiency in governmental financial administration *within* the executive branch, targeting finance ministries, tax authorities, and central banks. The fiscal crisis of the state forced Latin American governments to reorder their public finances and revamp their budgetary systems. For example, Argentina modernized its public finance management system

Table 18.1. Legislative Capabilities Index in Latin America (2005)

Country	Congress capabilities index
Argentina	Low
Bolivia	Medium
Brazil	High
Chile	High
Colombia	High
Costa Rica	Medium
Dominican Republic	Low
Ecuador	Medium
El Salvador	Medium
Guatemala	Low
Honduras	Low
Mexico	Medium
Nicaragua	Medium
Panama	Medium
Paraguay	Medium
Peru	Low
Uruguay	High
Venezuela, R. B. de	Medium

Source: Stein et al. (2005, 55).
Note: The Congressional Capabilities Index is constructed from eight subindexes measuring various features of parliaments' institutional capacity and political incentives, including public confidence in parliaments, the experience and specialization of parliamentarians, the strength of committees, the degree of technical expertise, or the availability of advisory support.

in 1992, with the adoption of the *Public Sector Financial and Control Systems Act* (Rodríguez and Bonvecchi 2004). Largely led from the executive, these efforts are contributing to the transformation of the budget into a credible tool of macroeconomic management, increasing the reliability of aggregate financial information and budget management systems. As a result of these reforms, significant achievements have been made in anchoring fiscal discipline (Santiso 2006a, 2006c). In recent years, however, greater attention has been directed at strengthening the institutions of public finance management *beyond* the executive, such as parliamentary budget committees, legislative budget offices, or auditor general's offices, to improve transparency, oversight, and accountability in budget management.

Benefits of Centralization

Institutional arrangements for public budgeting do matter. Recent findings on the political economy of public finance underscore that the choice of budget procedures and institutions influence fiscal performance (Alesina and Perotti 1996; Stein, Talvi, and Grisanti 1998; Alesina et al. 1999).[3] Similarly, research by Lisa Baldez and John Carey (1999) demonstrates that budgetary restraint and fiscal discipline in Chile is largely attributable to the institutional arrangements of budget policy making. Conversely, David Samuels (2002) and Jeffrey Weldon (2002) underscored the negative impact legislative politics has had on fiscal policy and budgetary processes in Brazil and Mexico, respectively.

Much of the literature argues that greater centralization of budgetary powers and procedures in the executive leads to more fiscal discipline and lower budget deficits. It posits that "hierarchical" budget systems that "concentrate power in the finance minister, vis-à-vis other ministers, and in the executive vis-à-vis congress" (Stein, Talvi, and Grisanti 1998, 3) provide stronger procedural incentives for achieving and maintaining fiscal prudence (Alesina and Perotti 1996).[4] Under these institutional arrangements, typically enshrined in the countries' constitutions or organic budget law, the central budget office of the finance ministry becomes the guardian of budgetary rectitude (Schick 2001). Alesina et al. (1999) identified three main institutional arrangements promoting greater fiscal discipline: laws that establish limits on deficits, procedural rules, and transparency.

The prevailing consensus thus warns against the dysfunctional fiscal effects of unrestrained legislative budgetary powers and favors the insulation of economic policy making within the executive branch. Centralized budgetary systems limit the powers and capacity of parliaments to influence the budget through, for example, restrictions on legislative amendment, veto, and override powers. Moreover, parliaments often voluntarily relinquish portions of their budgetary powers, delegating important prerogatives to the executive to reform taxation regimes or reallocate expenditures during the execution of the budget. As Allen Schick noted, "The legislature voluntarily yielded budgetary power to the executive because it accepted the view that parliamentarians cannot constrain their political inclination to tax less and spend more. Legislatures entrusted budgetary authority to the government because they could not trust themselves to make responsible financial decisions" (2002, 16).

Gabriel Filc and Carlos Scartascini (2006) confirmed the positive correlation between centralized budgetary systems and fiscal discipline, as shown in figure 18.2, first discerned by Stein, Talvi, and Grisanti (1998) and Alesina et al. (1999). The degree of centralization of the budgetary system is measured along three variables: numerical, procedural, and transparency rules.[5]

These views have influenced the reform of budgetary systems in the region in the course of the 1990s. Many countries have rationalized their public finance management systems. They have upgraded finance ministries, increased the independence of central banks, and strengthened the autonomy of tax agencies. The move toward more hierarchical budgetary institutions was particularly swift in Argentina under Carlos Menem (1989–99) and in Peru under Alberto Fujimori (1990–2000). Table 18.2 provides an overview of recent reforms in budgetary rules in the region, and figure 18.3 shows the acceleration of budget reforms since the mid-1990s.

The case of Chile, which has one of the most centralized budgetary systems in the region, is instructive in terms of the tensions between executive discretion and legislative prerogatives. In Chile, the centralization of budget institutions is the result of a long historical process initiated well before the

Figure 18.2. Budget Institutions and Fiscal Discipline in Latin America, 2000

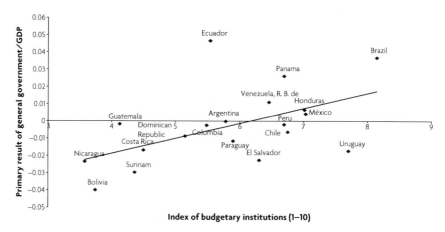

Source: Filc and Scartascini (2006).

structural reforms of the 1990s. The Revolution of 1891 originated in a deadlock over the budget in the context of recurrent conflict over the budget between the executive and the legislature during the liberal republic (1861–91), which continued during the parliamentary regime (1891–1925). The role of parliament diminished steadily after the adoption of the 1925 constitution, until the 1975 financial administration law and the 1980 constitution cemented the primacy of the president.

Risks of Centralization

Some important risks are associated with hierarchical budgetary arrangements. First, hierarchical budget arrangements tend to exacerbate executive discretion in public budgeting, especially in presidential systems, and thus impede the consolidation of the countervailing mechanisms of accountability. This, in turn, makes public finances particularly vulnerable to corruption and capture. Indeed, in Brazil, restoring the powers of parliaments in public budgeting was an integral part of the restoration of democracy in the 1980s.

Second, unconstrained and unchecked executive discretion in public budgeting undermines the credibility of the budget as an instrument of strategic planning. It hampers the consolidation of predictable budgetary processes with clear procedures and capable structures. The combination of presidents' constitutional powers, the executive's use and abuse of decree authority, the delegation of legislative budgetary powers to the executive, and the political configuration of parliaments all contribute to reinforce executive dominance.

Third, hierarchical budget institutions tend to overemphasize aggregate fiscal discipline over strategic prioritization and operational efficiency of public spending, which undermines the countries' capacity to reorient public spending toward poverty reduction and social policies (Schick 1998).

Table 18.2. Legal Framework of Budgetary Systems in Latin America, 2005

Country	Fiscal governance	Fiscal transparency			Fiscal responsibility	Fiscal accountability
	Organic budget law; organic financial administration law*	Access to public information law*	Habeas data	Law on fiscal transparency	Law on fiscal responsibility *	Law on fiscal control
Argentina	1992, 1997	** (2002)	1994	1999	1999, 2001, 2004	LAFCSP Law 24156 (1992)
Bolivia	1990 (1997)	(2004) 2005		2004		SAFCO Law 1178 (1990, 1997, 1999)
Brazil	2001		1988	2000	2000	Law 10180 (2001)
Chile	1975				***	LOAFE Decree 1263 1975
Colombia	2004	1985	1997	2003	2003	Laws 43 (1993) and 2145 (1999)
Costa Rica	2001	**				LAFPP Law 8131 (2001)
Dominican Republic	1969	2004				LOPSP (1969)
Ecuador	1977	2004	1996	2002	2002	Decree 1429 (1977, 1990)
El Salvador	1995					LOAFE Decree 516 (1995)
Guatemala	1997		1995			LOP Decree 101-97 (1997)
Honduras	1976, 2004	** (2003)			2004	LOP Decree 407-76 (1976)
Mexico	1976	2002	2002			LFSF Law (2000)
Nicaragua	2005 (1987)	2002	1995			LOCGRSCAP Decree 625 (1981, 1984, 2000) and LAFRP (2005)
Panama		2002	2002	2002	2002	
Paraguay	1999	2004	1992			LAFE Law 1535 (1999)
Peru	2004	2002	1993	1999, 2003	1999, 2003	LOSNCCGR Law 27785 (2002)
Uruguay	1999					TOCAF Decree 95 (1991, 1999)
Venezuela, R. B. de	2000, 2003		1999		2003	LOAF SP (2000) and Decrees 2621 and 2268 (2003)

Source: Author's compilation, as of December 2005.

* Joint World Bank-IMF Country Budget Law Database, complemented by Web-based research of the countries' ministries of economy and finance.

** Under consideration.

*** In 2001 Chile introduced fiscal numerical rules not enshrined in legislation but as part of a political agreement.

Figure 18.3. Reform Path of Budget Institutions in Latin America, 1990–2005

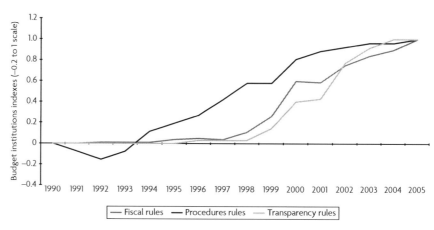

Source: Filc and Scartascini (2006).
Note: To construct the figure, the reforms were weighted in accordance with their relevance and direction and were normalized between 0 and 1.

Fourth, centralized budgetary systems are usually less transparent (Alesina et al. 1999), which makes fiscal discipline and expenditure control harder to achieve.[6] This is a particularly acute problem considering the quasi-monopoly of the executive on financial information, the limited access to budget information, and the lack of independent sources of fiscal information. By increasing the scrutiny of the budget, legislative oversight helps to redress the information asymmetries between the state and society; to open up the budget to public debate and social control; and to scrutinize economic assumptions, policy choices, and budget allocations.

For example, there is often controversy around how government estimates fiscal variables, especially tax revenues. In Argentina, the executive has tended to over- or underestimate the projected change in the gross domestic product in order to retain greater control over the execution of the budget, as it has discretionary powers over the allocation of supplementary credits or the reduction in spending (Uña et al. 2005). Similarly, in Nicaragua, the executive has often underestimated revenue estimates to exercise greater discretion over the allocation of nonbudgeted revenues. In many cases, parliament can only increase the budget if it identifies sources of additional finance. In Bolivia, it has simply invented them, augmenting revenue projections by changing the forecasted collection of tax revenues (Scartascini, Stein, and Filc 2005). These "games" in executive-legislative budget negotiations tend to undermine the integrity and reliability of fiscal information.

Parliaments and Public Budgeting

Parliaments' actual role in public budgeting may significantly differ from what their formal powers would predict. In Argentina, for example, public budgeting has been the subject of more conflict and bargaining than previously thought, through both formal processes as well as informal channels (Eaton 2002; Morgenstern and Manzetti 2003). The Brazilian parliament has traditionally been analyzed in terms of pork-barrel politics and political bargaining over budget appropriations and amendments (Samuels 2002). However, recent research suggests that the budget process is characterized by sophisticated strategic interactions, which allow the executive to discipline parliamentary groups and gather support for its policy initiatives (Pereira and Mueller 2004).

Parliaments' role remains inhibited by structural factors related both to the internal organization of parliamentary work and to the broader governance context of executive-legislative budget relations.[7] Three sets of factors are particularly determinant: the extent of parliaments' formal budgetary powers; their institutional capacities in terms of resources, structures, and procedures; and the political incentives of individual parliamentarians, as shaped by the nature of political competition, party systems, and electoral rules. Therefore, this chapter proposes to determine the actual role of Latin American parliaments in public budgeting in terms of three sets of variables: (1) their constitutional and legal powers, (2) their institutional capacities, and (3) their political incentives.

Legal Powers

Undoubtedly, in Latin American presidential regimes, legislative budgetary powers are limited. Constitutional provisions endow presidents with uncommon powers in public budgeting, in both absolute and relative terms, although important variations exist between countries. Presidents enjoy exclusive power over spending legislation, and legislatures' amendment powers are severely constrained, as shown in figure 18.4. Table 18.3 captures the main constitutional restrictions on the budgetary powers of parliaments in 17 Latin American countries.

Figure 18.4. Index of Legislative Budgeting in Latin America, 2003

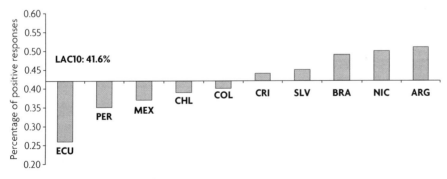

Source: Lavielle, Pérez, and Hofbauer (2003), 14–16.
Note: This index of legislative budgeting is based on survey data conducted in 2002. It measures, on a scale from 0 to 1, the degree of legislative budget authority, including (1) the extent of legislative powers to amend the executive's budget proposal, (2) the time allowed for legislative budget review, and (3) the intensity of legislative debate. The index measures the average percentage of positive responses to these three questions and was normalized between 0 and 1. LAC10 refers to the un-weighted average for the 10 countries for which data was available in 2003.

Table 18.3: Executive-Legislative Budget Relations in Latin America

	Presidential initiative	Legislative amendment powers		Executive veto	Legislative override	Reversion point				Budget reallocation authority		
		Unrestricted	Restricted (cannot increase deficit or spending)			Budget of previous year	Executive budget proposal	New proposal has to be presented	Deadlock (no expenditure can be incurred)	Executive with legislative approval	Executive without legislative approval	Legislature
Argentina	✓	✓ (a)	✓ (b)	✓	✓	✓				✓		
Bolivia	✓	✓		✓	✓		✓					✓
Brazil	✓		✓	✓	✓			✓			✓	
Chile	✓		✓	✓	✓	(c)	✓			✓		
Colombia	✓		✓	✓	✓		✓			✓		
Costa Rica	✓	✓		(d)	(d)		✓			✓		
Ecuador	✓		✓	✓	(e)	✓	✓			✓		
Guatemala	✓	✓		✓	✓							✓
Honduras	✓	✓		(d)	(d)			✓		✓		
Mexico	✓		✓ (b)	✓	✓				(f)		✓	
Panama	✓		✓	✓	✓	✓				✓		
Paraguay	✓	✓		✓	✓		✓				✓	
Peru	✓	✓ (g)	✓ (h)	✓	✓		✓				✓	
Dominican Republic	✓			✓	✓	✓				✓		
El Salvador	✓		✓	✓	✓			✓		✓		
Uruguay	✓		✓	✓	✓	✓				✓		
Venezuela, R. B. de	✓	✓ (i)		✓	✓	✓				✓		

Source: Alesina et al. (1999); Payne et al. (2002); Rodríguez and Bonvecchi (2004); Santiso (2006b); World Bank (2001).

Note: (a) Until 1992. (b) Since 1992. (c) The budget of the previous year would apply only if the executive did not present its proposal on time; otherwise the executive's proposal would apply. (d) The presidential veto does not apply to the budget. (e) Override powers are limited. (f) The location of the reversion point in Mexico is subject to controversy. (g) Until 1991. (h) Since 1993. (i) Cannot increase spending.

Nevertheless, the balance of budgetary powers between the executive and the legislative branches varies along the different phases of the budget cycle. Comparative analyses of executive-legislative budget relations in Latin America have largely focused on the earlier phases of the budget process, particularly the approval phase. Less attention has been paid to the role of parliaments in the latter stages of the budget process, in particular in the scrutiny of budget reallocations, the oversight of budget execution, and the ex post control of budget performance.

Budget Formulation

The executive has a predominant role in the formulation of the budget and the drafting of the budget bill. In all 17 countries under review in table 18.3, the executive has the exclusive right to draft the budget proposal. It is, in fact, the only branch of government with the necessary technical capacity and information base to be able to do so. The central budget offices of the finance ministries are responsible for coordinating the budget drafting process within the executive and for overseeing the budget's execution by spending agencies. The executive's control over government financial information gives it an undisputed advantage over the legislature.

In several countries, the executive has the exclusive prerogative to formulate the budget and draft fiscal legislation. In Ecuador, for example, chapter 147 of the 1998 constitution stipulates that only the president can propose bills that create, modify, or suppress taxes, or that increase public expenditure.

Budget Approval

Once agreed upon within the cabinet, the draft budget bill is submitted to parliament for consideration, review, and approval. As with any other law, the budget must be approved by parliament to enter into force. Five variables frame executive-legislative relations during the budget-approval stage: (1) the amendment powers of parliament, (2) the veto powers of the president, (3) the override powers of parliament, (4) the location of the reversion point, and (5) the general legislative process and structures, including internal rules and legislative capacities, and the timing and sequencing of the budgetary process.

The time allocated for budget review varies across countries but is generally close to the three months that international standards recommend (OECD 2002). On average, Latin American parliaments have 90 days to review and approve the budget, varying from 30 days in Mexico to 120 days in Honduras (Santiso 2006b).[8]

Few parliaments have unrestricted powers to amend the budget, and most countries place restrictions on amendment powers. Many parliaments cannot propose amendments that would increase the deficit or spending, except as it pertains to their own budget. For example, since 1992, the Argentine parliament can increase spending only if it also increases revenues. In Nicaragua, the parliament can only increase overall spending if its finds the necessary revenues to finance it. As noted earlier, this loophole, which is commonly found in Latin American budgetary systems, has often led parliaments to revise governments' revenue estimates to have greater discretion over budgetary appropriations.

Legislative amendment powers may be further limited by the executive's ability to veto the proposed amendments, either fully or partially. In a majority of countries the executive has package and line-item veto powers. In Argentina, between 1993 and 2003, the president vetoed only one annual budget law but amply vetoed specific provisions of most budget laws approved by parliament. In many cases the legislature may nevertheless insist on its amendments and override the executive's veto, if it can muster the necessary qualified majority.

The rules and procedures governing the amendment process constitute another set of determining factors. Within parliament, the budget and finance committee plays a key role in the budget process, as the main forum in which the budget bill and its amendments are discussed, negotiated, and agreed to. The capacity of parliaments to effectively engage with the budget thus often depends on the internal organization, technical capacities, and political incentives of the budget and finance committee or its equivalent.

The outcome of the budget game is conditioned by the location of the reversion point, that is, what happens if the budget is not approved by parliament by the set deadline. In Latin America the executive tends to have extraordinary leverage over the legislature, as legislative inaction does not preclude the executive proposal from being adopted. There exist four alternative scenarios: (1) the budget of the previous fiscal year remains in effect in the interim, which is the case in Argentina, Nicaragua, República Bolivariana de Venezuela, and Uruguay; (2) the executive must present a new budget proposal, as is the case in Brazil; (3) the executive's proposal automatically becomes law, as in Bolivia, Chile, Colombia, Costa Rica, Ecuador, Panama, or Peru; or (4) there is a deadlock and government cannot incur any expenditure, as in Brazil or Mexico (although there is controversy in that respect).[9] The situation of Latin America diverges from that of the rest of the world, especially Organisation for Economic Co-operation and Development (OECD) countries where interim arrangements take effect in 65.1 percent of the cases until the budget deadlock is resolved.

Budget Oversight

Constitutions and organic budget laws usually give parliaments an important role in the oversight of budget execution, the scrutiny of budget reallocations, and the ex post review of public accounts. In practice, however, legislative oversight of budget execution is limited, in terms of both monitoring compliance and evaluating performance. This situation is the result of a conjunction of factors, including the influence of informal rules and the nature of political institutions. In particular, the combination of the legislative delegation of budget authority and the recourse to executive decrees has exponentially augmented executive discretion and has allowed the executive to expand its formal prerogatives.

Argentina provides an extreme example of the excessive concentration of budgetary powers in the executive branch with little external scrutiny and legislative oversight, resulting in discretion without accountability (Santiso 2007b, 2007c). Since 1994, the Argentine parliament has delegated important budgetary powers to the executive, which is able to amend the budget during its implementation almost at will and largely unchecked using emergency decree authority (Uña et al. 2005). This practice has traditionally been sanctioned ex post facto by parliament. Since 1997, parliament has routinely allowed the executive to exempt itself from some of the disciplining restrictions of the 1992 financial administration law, including provisions of chapter 37, which stipulates that only parliament can approve major changes to the total budget envelope (Rodríguez and Bonvecchi 2004). In August 2006, parliament derogated key portions of chapter 37, giving the executive free rein to modify the budget during its execution. Parliament would approve only the overall amount of the budget and the level of indebtedness (Díaz Frers 2006). The measure was accompanied by a relaxing of the rules governing the approval of executive decrees, which are now considered automatically approved if not objected to by parliament. The bicameral committee tasked with overseeing executive decrees, which was provided for in the 1994 amendment to Argentina's constitution, has yet to be established.

Ex Post Scrutiny of the Budget

Many parliaments possess a powerful instrument to control budget execution and enforce accountability: the review of public accounts and the discharge of government. However, they seldom use this tool effectively. In theory, the annual certification of public accounts constitutes a critical moment in the fiscal year. Using the audit of public accounts by the Auditor General's Office, a specialized parliamentary committee or a subcommittee of the budget and finance committee (often called the public accounts committee) reviews the public accounts submitted by the executive's general accounting office and submits an opinion to the plenary, which decides whether or not to discharge government.

In Latin America, public accounts committees have seldom refused to discharge governments. Furthermore, the likely consequences of doing so are unclear. In Argentina, for example, this uncertainty has led to a paralysis of the certification process in the joint public accounts committee (Lamberto 2005; Uña et al. 2005). In Peru, a constitutional provision stipulates that if parliament fails to act on the public accounts reports within a certain time frame, the opinion of the public accounts committee is transmitted to the executive for adoption by decree. These dysfunctional practices neutralize the oversight prerogatives of parliaments in the later phases of the budgetary process. They are compounded by uneasy relations between parliaments' public accounts committees and auditor general's offices in most countries. Furthermore, auditor general's offices often lack political independence and technical capacities to discharge their responsibilities effectively.

Institutional Capacities

Weak institutional capacities constitute a second set of constraining factors. These relate to the organization of parliamentary work and the structures and procedures framing the budget process within parliament. Three variables are particularly important: (1) the organization of legislative committees, (2) the extent of legislative technical advisory capacity, and (3) the extent of legislative budget research capacity.

Parliamentary Committees

A first institutional constraint resides in the unconsolidated nature of the committee system. The organization of committee work often lacks the kind of institutionalization that would allow specialized committees to effectively contribute to the budget process (Saeigh 2005). At a technical level, a more rational division of responsibilities between the different committees dealing with different facets of public finance (taxation, budgeting, oversight, and control) could enhance the coherence of parliaments' impact on the budget process.

In most Latin American countries a single legislative committee, the budget and finance committee, deals with the executive's budget proposal. It is generally considered the single most important legislative committee. In Brazil, the Joint Committee on Plans, Public Budgets and Auditing (CMPOF) consists of 84 members from both houses of parliament (21 senators and 63 deputies; World Bank 202). In bicameral systems, joint legislative budget committees are not always permanent structures. In Chile, the Special Joint Budget Committee of its bicameral parliament became a permanent structure only in 2003. In addition to budget and finance committees, sectoral committees often formally or informally participate in the budget negotiations, such as in Argentina or Mexico. Public accounts committees, which have the responsibility for ex post oversight, are generally weak, especially if they function as stand-alone committees separated from the budget and finance committee.

The internal composition of committees tends to lessen incentives for effective oversight of government. In conditions of unified government, the ruling party normally chairs these committees and sets their agendas. In most cases, the composition of the budget committee is decided on a proportional basis, mirroring parliamentary majorities. This is a natural outcome of democracy and generally not a problem, as committees tend to act in a less partisan way. However, these arrangements may diminish the incentives for legislative scrutiny, which is particularly detrimental to oversight committees such as public accounts committees. These features are exacerbated in situations of dominant or single parties, such as República Bolivariana de Venezuela since 1999.[10]

Advisory and Research Capacity

A second institutional constraint relates to parliaments' limited access to technical advice and support to adequately evaluate government policy proposals, as well as the quality, timeliness, and impartiality of this advice, which tend to be limited and uneven. This is partly a consequence of the poor quality and instability of the parliamentary services. Without alternative sources of information, parliamentary committees are forced to rely on the information provided by the government, significantly constraining their ability to carry out independent reviews of budget proposals and government performance and thus their ability to engage in effective oversight.

In Latin America, budget and public accounts committees are assigned only a limited number of permanent technical advisers. The political advisers of individual parliamentarians sitting in the budget and public accounts committees carry out most of the advisory work despite the fact that they may not be budget experts and are not solely dedicated to budget issues. In Argentina and Colombia, individual parliamentarians have political advisers specializing in budgetary matters. Advisers to political parties also provide some assistance to parliamentarians in budgetary matters, either directly or indirectly through political foundations, as is the case in Chile.

Two noteworthy exceptions are Brazil and Mexico. In Brazil, a research office consisting of 35 professionals assists the Joint Committee on Plans, Public Budgets and Auditing. The lower house has an advisory organ, the Legislative Consultancy, with 245 employees, 190 of whom are specialist consultants in various areas of public policy. Similarly, the upper house has its technical support service, with 308 consultants. These individuals are full-time parliamentary employees, selected through a competitive examination and benefiting from the most generous conditions of the Brazilian civil service.

Mexico's Chamber of Deputies is assisted by the *Centro de Estudios de las Finanzas Publicas* (CEFP—Center for Public Finance Studies), established in 1998 and staffed with around 27 advisers. The CEFP provides budget information to committees, parliamentary groups, and individual deputies and maintains a library with copies of reports on finance and public debt. In Argentina, a proposal to create such an office was tabled in 2004. Furthermore, legislative research offices and parliamentary libraries exist in several countries, such as Brazil, Chile, Colombia, and Peru. Moreover, parliamentary budget offices are being established or strengthened, such as in Chile, Costa Rica, Mexico, Nicaragua, and Panama. Chile has a small bicameral budget office with a professional staff of three analysts.

Political Incentives

A third set of factors is linked to the political incentives of individual members of parliament to build the parliament's institutional capacities and use them effectively. The formal and informal rules shaping executive-legislative relations include factors such as (1) the presidential nature of political systems, (2) the modes of governance and the reliance on executive decrees, and (3) electoral rules and the nature of the party system, both in general and as it determines parliamentary politics.

Economic Governance

In Latin America, the executive's excessive reliance on executive decrees in economic policy making has detrimental effects on legislative budget oversight and government financial accountability (Santiso 2004b). Parliaments generally exercise little oversight on presidential decrees used to amend the budget or approve supplementary appropriations during the fiscal year.

The overreliance on executive decrees has become an "addiction to decrees," reflecting wider dysfunctions in fiscal governance in the region. Argentina represents an extreme case of these pathologies, which can nevertheless be found in most Latin American countries to varying degrees. In Peru, for example, between January 1994 and March 2001, parliament passed 1,152 laws or legislative resolutions, while the president issued 870 decrees, 86 percent of which were urgency decrees. Of those 748 urgency decrees, 27 percent directly amended the budget and an additional 41 percent had a clear effect on public finances (World Bank 2001).

Political Governance

The presidential structure of Latin American political regimes further exacerbates these trends. Party systems and electoral rules have a decisive impact on executive-legislative relations in public budgeting, both at a macro level (political system) and a micro level (parliamentary politics). Electoral systems affect the degree of party fragmentation (or cohesion) and volatility (or stability). They largely determine the incentives to which parliamentarians respond, which is reflected in how they behave in budgetary matters.

In Argentina, for example, members of the lower house are elected for a four-year mandate (renewable) by proportional representation on closed party lists. In the absence of open primaries at the national level, the party's leadership determines candidate nomination. The ordering of party lists, which determine the candidates' likelihood of being elected, is the result of delicate intraparty negotiations at the provincial level, at times arbitrated by internal primaries. Therefore, the Argentine political system is party centered, delivering a relatively high degree of party discipline: political parties exert considerable influence over parliamentarians and their careers.

In Brazil, however, electoral rules provide a different set of political incentives to parliamentarians. Brazilian members of the lower house are elected for a four-year term (renewable) by proportional representation at the state level, but using open party lists. Individual candidates usually have more political appeal and traction than political parties, except in a few cases such as the Workers' Party (*Partido dos Trabalhadores*—PT). Party cohesion and discipline are thus lower than in Argentina. This is reflected in the budget process, which resembles a chess game more than a football game. Presidents have to show a great deal of skill at assembling coalitions and building ad hoc alliances for passing individual reforms, often negotiating with individual parliamentarians one by one. In such contexts, pork barrel deals become a critical variable in understanding the budget process, in particular budget appropriations and their implementation (Pereira and Mueller 2004).

Other features of electoral politics have a critical influence on parliamentary budgeting and executive-legislative budget relations, such as limiting parliamentarians' terms. Party volatility, term limits (as in Mexico), and low reelection rates (as in Argentina) reduce the incentives for individual parliamentarians to invest in the parliaments' institutional and technical capacities. As their career prospects largely depend on their relationship with the governing party, their incentives to oversee the government's budget are reduced. As a result, parliamentarians are "professional politicians and amateur legislators" (Jones et al. 2000).

Moreover, high rotation rates in the budget and public accounts committees can weaken the committees' capacity to effectively engage with the budget process. Though these committees tend to be more stable than other standing committees, they are seldom stable enough to institutionalize the expertise they have accumulated. In Nicaragua and Peru, for example, committee membership rotates every year. Since these committees most often do not possess permanent advisers, technical expertise seldom becomes institutionalized. Nevertheless, in some countries, such as Chile, individual members of the budget and finance committee often have ample expertise in fiscal matters, some of them having occupied senior positions in government, including as finance minister. The high rate of reelection in the Chilean parliament also helps translate individual expertise into institutional expertise (Montecinos 2003). Hence, electoral rules that improve party coherence are likely to increase the political incentives of parliamentarians to effectively oversee the budget process.

Parliamentary Opposition

More fundamentally, the effectiveness of legislative oversight depends on the degree of competition in the political system and the relative strength of parliamentary opposition. In presidential systems, the separation of powers provides greater incentives for legislative oversight than in parliamentary systems with fused majorities (Dubrow 2002), especially in situations of divided government, where presidential and parliamentary majorities do not coincide. As Richard Messick underscored, "When the interests of a legislative majority and the executive branch coincide, the majority has little incentive to oversee the executive" (2002, 2). When the ruling coalition holds a disciplined majority position in parliament, such as in parliamentary systems and presidential systems with unified government, control can be diluted or neutralized.

The emergence of strong and assertive parliamentary oppositions in recent years has tended to reactivate legislative oversight in some countries. In Mexico, for example, the emergence of a parliamentary opposition in 1997 and the alternation in power in 2000 have led to a surge in parliament's budget activism (Weldon 2002; Gutiérrez, Lujambio, and Valadés 2001). The case of Mexico demonstrates that the emergence of a credible parliamentary opposition significantly increases the incentives of parliamentarians to oversee the budget, which, in turn, leads to steps toward strengthening their capacities for independent review of the budget (Santiso 2007b). It shows that parliaments do possess important budgetary powers but often fail to exercise them effectively until political incentives are considered to be right. The exercise of parliaments' formal budgetary powers ultimately depends on the configuration of political power.

The Mexican parliament does indeed possess extended formal de jure budgetary powers, and its authority to approve, modify, or reject both the income and expenditures pieces of the budget gives it much more authority than most of its Latin American counterparts. These powers were nevertheless neutralized for decades by the configuration of political power and the metaconstitutional powers of the president.

Government Discharge

As mentioned earlier, the impact of political systems on parliaments' role in the budget process is acutely reflected in the dysfunctions in the certification of public accounts and the discharge of government. Parliaments often lack the motivation to enforce government accountability and effectively use the instruments at their disposal.

The connection between parliamentary public accounts committees and auditor general's offices is a critical one. In Latin America, it is often dysfunctional for a variety of reasons (Santiso 2006c, 2006d, 2007a, and 2007b). In theory, the Office of the Auditor General acts as an auxiliary institution to parliaments and should provide valuable assistance to parliament in its ex post oversight of the budget by auditing government accounts. However, audit reports receive limited publicity, audit findings are largely ignored, and audit recommendations may not be followed up by parliamentary committees. Even when the public accounts committee or its equivalent takes up the auditor general's recommendations in its reports, it may not follow up on whether government has implemented these recommendations. Acknowledging these shortcomings, Latin American countries are seeking to strengthen the office of the auditor general, with varying degree of success.

Parliament's review of government's budget proposal is largely disassociated from its control of the previous budget. In Peru, for example, parliament receives the audit report on the previous year's public accounts by November 15 and must approve the following year's budget by November 30. During that short period of 15 days, the budget debate takes place in plenary, which further limits technical input into the process. In Brazil, the certification of public accounts suffers important delays within parliament, partly reflecting parliament's lack of interest in evaluating past performance (World Bank 2002).

In most Latin American countries, government discharge is largely an irrelevant autopsy. There is a "fiction of control," which is often worse than the absence of control (Santiso 2007b). Whereas the formal rules and institutions are in place to oversee government financial management, the reality is a lack of internal restraints, an absence of legislative oversight, and a weakness in public scrutiny. Often, existing checks and balances designed to constrain executive discretion are circumvented, if not subverted.

Conclusions: Politics of Public Budgeting

Parliaments have a critical role to play in the budget process and possess a range of budgetary powers that could be deployed to bring government to account for the manner in which it manages the public purse. However, parliaments' contribution is hampered by structural factors related to the executive's predominance in public budgeting as well as their own deficiencies. The evaluation of the role of parliaments in budgeting must be couched in the broader context of parliaments that are institutionally weak and largely unconsolidated.

Five main conclusions can be drawn from this review. A first issue concerns the role parliaments *should* have in the budget process. The debate over the most adequate degree of centralization of the budget is largely unresolved. More research is required to compare and contrast the effectiveness of legislative oversight of the budget in presidential and parliamentary systems. In presidential systems, this debate has nevertheless centered on the nature of executive-legislative relations in the early stages of the budget process, principally its formulation, review, and adoption. This chapter underscores that more attention should be devoted to the role of parliament in the later stages of the budget cycle, in particular the oversight of budget execution, the scrutiny of budget reallocations, and the ex post control of budget performance.

Second, modifying political incentives through reforms in electoral rules and party politics is likely to be more effective than strengthening technical capacity or financial resources. As Thomas Carothers underscored, "To build effective legislatures, mobilizing political power is more important than increasing technical skill" (1999, 181). Parliaments often lack the political incentives and institutional capacities to deploy their budgetary prerogatives effectively and responsibly. They do not necessarily lack powers or resources, but the manner in which they use them is often ineffectual. As Saeigh (2005, 36) noted, "We will not be able to empower legislatures if we do not establish the right incentives for individual legislators first." Thus, parliaments should be reformed inasmuch as they must be strengthened.

Third, parliaments cannot be strengthened in isolation. They are part of a broader system of fiscal control whose ultimate efficacy depends on the quality of interinstitutional connections and the synergies between the different components of the system. For example, the functional linkages between parliaments and audit offices are critical to strengthen fiscal transparency and enforce financial accountability. Improving transparency and accountability in public finances necessarily requires focusing on the *overall process* of fiscal control as much as on the *individual organizations* in charge of specific aspects of budget oversight.

Fourth, a key challenge of legislative budgeting is to adequately combine legislative oversight with fiscal discipline. Schick summarized the critical tension to be resolved: "As legislatures enhance their budget role, one of the challenges facing budget architects will be to balance the impulse for independence with the need to be fiscally responsible. The future of legislative-governmental relations will be strongly influenced by the manner in which this balance is maintained" (2002, 14).

Fifth, parliaments can make a decisive contribution to the governance of the budget by demanding greater transparency in public finance management. In Chile, for example, parliament has successfully pressed government to disclose more fiscal and budgetary information, requesting regular financial reports and performance evaluations. Several countries, such as Brazil, Chile, Mexico, and Peru, have been able to introduce piecemeal reforms that have gradually strengthened transparency and accountability in budgetary systems. The adoption of freedom of information and fiscal responsibility legislation in many countries is a step in the right direction.

Achieving these qualitative changes will require transforming institutional attitudes in executive-legislative budget relations, from a predominantly confrontational and adversarial relationship to a more cooperative and constructive approach. This paradigm shift should be built on the recognition that building legislative fiscal capacity is not only about restraining government, lengthening budget execution, or sanctioning financial mismanagement. It is about improving financial accountability, stimulating budget efficiency, and promoting fiscal responsibility. As Schick underscored, "The legislature's new role in budgeting cannot come from government's weakness … The legislature's role must be defined more in terms of policy, accountability, and performance, and less in terms of control and restriction" (2002, 17).

Notes

1. *Horizontal accountability* is defined as "the existence of state agencies that are legally enabled and empowered, and factually willing and able, to take actions that span from routine oversight to criminal sanctions or impeachment in relation to actions or omissions by other agents or agencies of the state that may be qualified as unlawful" (O'Donnell 1999, 38).

2. The governance of the budget can be defined as encompassing the interests and incentives of individuals and institutions governing the formulation, approval, execution, and oversight of the budget. On the politics of the budget in developed countries, see Wildavsky and Caiden 2000; Schick 2002.

3. Nevertheless, empirical studies and cross-country statistical analyses of budgetary institutions tend to focus on the formal rules shaping the interaction of the different actors. However, budgetary practices differ substantially from formal budgetary rules.

4. Hierarchical budget arrangements are those that "limit the role of the legislature in expanding the size of the budget and the deficit, and attribute a strong role to a single individual, typically the treasury minister, in the budget negotiations within the government, limiting the prerogatives of the spending ministries" (Alesina et al. 1999, 255).

5. The proxy indicator used for fiscal discipline is the general government primary balance for the 2000–02 period. The index of budgetary institutions is composed of three subindexes measuring (1) fiscal rules, including the existence and hierarchy of numerical rules that restrict total expenditure, the deficit or borrowing, the utilization of medium-term fiscal frameworks, restrictions on borrowing by subnational

governments, and the existence of stabilization funds; (2) procedural rules, including the power of the finance ministry over the line ministries in the preparation stage, the power of the executive over the legislature in the approval stage, and the power of the finance ministry through cash management during the execution stage; and (3) transparency rules, including extent to which the budget covers the totality of state outlays and the availability of this information, emphasizing the enactment of transparency laws. The general index is constructed on a weighted average of the subindexes in line with the quantity of subjects they cover.

6. Proponents of hierarchical budget institutions acknowledge the value of transparent processes to ensure fiscal prudence, although they do not necessarily link the hierarchical system to a strengthening of legislative oversight.

7. A series of factors condition parliaments' actual role in the budget process, including whether they are legally empowered to intervene in the budget process, whether they are endowed with the required institutional and technical capacities, whether their members possess the necessary individual and political incentives, and whether the broader governance environment is favorable, in particular the nature of political competition and the balance of political power.

8. In Peru, for example, the executive must submit the draft budget bill by August 30, and parliament must approve it by November 30, and in Mexico the federal government must submit its proposal by November 15, and parliament has until December 31 to approve the final budget. In Argentina, the executive must submit the budget proposal by September 15, and parliament has until its recess on November 30 to approve it before the beginning of the fiscal year. In Nicaragua, the budget proposal is introduced by October 15 to be approved by December 15 each year. Bicameral systems, where both chambers need to approve the budget, are not necessarily given more time to consider the budget.

9. On Brazil, see Samuels (2002) and Figueiredo (2003). On Mexico, see Gutiérrez, Lujambio, and Valadés (2001) and Sour, Ortega, and Sebastián (2003, 2004).

10. By contrast, in around two-thirds of Commonwealth countries, which tend to have Westminster-style parliamentary systems, the chair of the public accounts committee is a senior opposition member (McGee 2002).

Bibliography

Alesina, Alberto, Ricardo Hausmann, Rudolf Hommes, and Ernesto Stein. 1999. "Budget Institutions and Fiscal Performance in Latin America." OCE Working Paper 394, Office of the Chief Economist, Inter-American Development Bank, Washington, DC.

Alesina, Alberto, and Roberto Perotti. 1996. "Budget Institutions and Budget Deficits." NBER Working Paper No. 5556, National Bureau of Economic Research, Cambridge, MA.

Baldez, Lisa, and John Carey. 1999. "Presidential Agenda Control and Spending Policy: Lessons from General Pinochet's Constitution." *American Journal of Political Science* 43 (1): 29–55.

Carothers, Thomas. 1999. *Aiding Democracy Abroad: The Learning Curve.* Washington, DC: Carnegie Endowment for International Peace.

Díaz Frers, Luciana. 2006. *El debate sobre los superpoderes.* Buenos Aires, Argentina: Centro de Implementación de Políticas Públicas para el Crecimiento y la Equidad, CIPPEC Documentos de Políticas Públicas.

Dorotinsky, William, and Yasuhiko Matsuda. 2002. Reforma de la gestión financiera en América Latina: Una perspectiva institucional" *Reforma y Democracia* 23: 141–66.

Dubrow, Geoff. 2002. "Systems of Governance and Parliamentary Accountability" In *Parliamentary Accountability and Good Governance*, 23–30, Washington, DC: Parliamentary Centre and World Bank Institute.

Eaton, Kent. 2002. "Fiscal Policy Making in the Argentine Legislature." In Morgenstern and Nacif 2002, 287–314.

Figueiredo, Argelina. 2003. "The Role of Congress as an Agency of Horizontal Accountability: Lessons from the Brazilian Experience." In Mainwaring and Welna 2003, 170–98.

Filc, Gabriel, and Carlos Scartascini. 2006. "Budgetary Institutions." In *The State of State Reform in Latin America*, ed. Eduardo Lora, Stanford, CA: Stanford University Press.

Gutiérrez, Gerónomo, Alonso Lujambio, and Diego Valadés. 2001. *El proceso presupuestario y las relaciones entre los órganos del poder*. Mexico, DF: Instituto de Investigaciones Jurídicas.

Jones, Mark, Sebastian Saiegh, Pablo Spiller, and Mariano Tommasi. 2000. "Professional Politicians, Amateur Legislators: The Argentine Congress in the 20th Century." CEDI Working Document 45, Centro Estudios para el Desarrollo, Buenos Aires, Argentina.

Lamberto, Oscar, ed. 2005. *La Cuenta de inversión*. Buenos Aires, Argentina: Comisión Parlamentaria Mixta Revisora de Cuentas de la Nación.

Lavielle, Briseida, Mariana Pérez, and Helena Hofbauer. 2003. *Latin America Index of Budget Transparency*. Washington, DC: International Budget Project.

Mainwaring, Scott, and Christopher Welna, eds. 2003. *Democratic Accountability in Latin America*. Oxford, U.K.: Oxford University Press.

McGee, David. 2002. *The Overseers: Public Accounts Committees and Public Spending*. London: Commonwealth Parliamentary Association and Pluto Press.

Messick, Richard. 2002. "Strengthening Legislatures: Implications from Industrial Countries." PREM Note 63, World Bank, Washington, DC.

Montecinos, Verónica. 2003. "Economic Policy-Making and Parliamentary Accountability in Chile." Paper 11, United Nations Research Institute for Social Development, Geneva.

Morgenstern, Scott, and Luigi Manzetti. 2003. "Legislative Oversight: Interests and Institutions in the United States and Argentina." In Mainwaring and Welna 2003, 132–69.

Morgenstern, Scott, and Benito Nacif, eds. 2002. *Legislative Politics in Latin America*. Cambridge, U.K.: Cambridge University Press.

O'Donnell, Guillermo. 1999. "Horizontal Accountability and New Polyarchies." In *The Self-Restraining State*, ed. Schedler et al., 29–52, Boulder and London: Lynne Rienner Publishers.

OECD. 2002. "OECD Best Practices for Budget Transparency." *OECD Journal on Budgeting* 1 (3): 7–14.

Payne, Mark, Daniel Zovatto, Fernando Carillo Flórez, and Andrés Allamand Zavala. 2002. *Democracies in Development: Politics and Reform in Latin America*. Washington, DC: Inter-American Development Bank.

Pereira, Carlos, and Bernardo Mueller. 2004. "The Cost of Governing: Strategic Behavior of the President and Legislators in Brazil's Budgetary Process." *Comparative Political Studies* 37 (7): 781–815.

Rodríguez, Jesús, and Alejandro Bonvecchi. 2004. "El papel del poder legislativo en el proceso presupuestario: La experiencia argentina." Macroeconomy of Development Working Paper Series 32, United Nations Economic Commission for Latin America and the Caribbean (ECLAC), Santiago, Chile.

Saeigh, Sebastian. 2005. "The Role of Legislatures in the Policymaking Process." Unpublished background paper for the Inter-American Development Bank's 2006 *Report on Economic and Social Progress in Latin America.*

Samuels, David. 2002. "Progressive Ambition, Federalism and Pork-barreling in Brazil." In Morgenstern and Nacif 2002, 315–40.

Santiso, Carlos. 2004a. "Legislatures and Budget Oversight in Latin America: Strengthening Public Finance Accountability in Emerging Economies." *OECD Journal on Budgeting* 4 (2): 47–77.

———. 2004b. "Re-forming the State: Governance Institutions and the Credibility of Economic Policy." *International Public Management Journal* 7 (2): 271–98.

———. 2005. "Budget Institutions and Fiscal Responsibility: Parliaments and the Political Economy of the Budget Process." Working Paper No. 37253, World Bank Institute, Washington, DC,

———. 2006a. "Banking on Accountability? Strengthening Budget Oversight and Public Sector Auditing in Emerging Economies." *Journal of Public Budgeting and Finance* 26 (2): 66–100.

———. 2006b. "El día que me quiera: Parlamentos y presupuestos en América latina." In *Cada cual; ¿atiende su juego? El rol del Congreso en el presupuesto nacional de Argentina,* ed. Miguel Braun, Luciana Frers, and Gerardo Uña. Buenos Aires, Argentina: Centro de Implementación de Políticas Públicas para el Crecimiento y la Equidad.

———. 2006c. "'Pour le meilleur ou pour le pire? Le rôle du parlement dans le processus budgétaire dans les pays en développement." *Revue française d'administration publique* 117: 149–85.

———. 2006d. "Combattre la corruption et améliorer la gouvernance financière: Les institutions financières internationales et le renforcement du contrôle budgétaire dans les pays en développement." *Revue française d'administration publique* 119: 459–92.

———. 2007a. "Auditing, Accountability and Anticorruption: How Relevant Are Autonomous Audit Agencies?" In *Global Corruption Report 2007,* 358–62. Berlin: Transparency International.

———. 2007b. "Eyes Wide Shut? The Politics of Autonomous Audit Agencies in Emerging Economies." CIPPEC Working Paper, Centro de Implementación de Políticas Públicas para el Crecimiento y la Equidad, Buenos Aires, Argentina.

———. 2007c. "Eyes Wide Shut? Reforming and Defusing Checks and Balances in Argentina." *Public Administration and Development* 28 (1): 67–84.

Scartascini, Carlos, and Ernesto Stein. 2004. *The Bolivian Budget: A Year-Long Bargaining Process.* Washington, DC: IDB.

Scartascini, Carlos, Ernesto Stein, and Gabriel Filc. 2005. "El rol del legislativo en el proceso presupuestario: Un análisis comparativo." Presentation at the XVII Regional Seminar on Fiscal Policy of the ECLAC, Santiago, Chile, January 24–27.

Schick, Allen. 1998. *A Contemporary Approach to Public Expenditure Management.* Washington, DC: World Bank Institute.

———. 2001. "The Changing Role of the Central Budget Office." *OECD Journal on Budgeting* 1 (1): 9–26.

———. 2002. "Can National Legislatures Regain an Effective Voice in Budget Policy?" *OECD Journal on Budgeting* 1 (3): 15–42.

Sour, Laura, Irma Ortega, and Sergio San Sebastián. 2003. *Política presupuestaria durante la transición a la democracia en México: 1997-2003*. Mexico, DF: Centro de Investigación y Docencia Económica.

———. 2004 *¿Quién tiene la última palabra sobre el gasto público en México?* Mexico, DF: Centro de Investigación y Docencia Económica.

Stein, Ernesto, Erneto Talvi, and Alejandro Grisanti. 1998. "Institutional Arrangements and Fiscal Performance: The Latin American Experience." OCE Working Paper 367, Office of the Chief Economist, Inter-American Development Bank, Washington, DC.

Stein, Ernesto, Mariano Tommasi, Koldo Echebarría, Eduardo Lora, and Mark Payne, eds. 2005. *The Politics of Policies: Economic and Social Progress in Latin America*. Washington, DC: Inter-American Development Bank.

Uña, Gerardo, Gisell Cogliandro, Nicolás Bertello, and Juan Labaqui. 2005. *El Congreso y el Presupuesto Nacional: Desempeño y Condicionantes de su Rol en el Proceso Presupuestario*. Buenos Aires, Argentina: Fundación Konrad Adenauer.

Weldon, Jeffrey. 2002. "Legislative Delegation and the Budget Process in Mexico." In Morgenstern and Nacif 2002, 377–412.

Wildavsky, Aaron, and Noemi Caiden. 2000. *The New Politics of the Budgetary Process*. 4th ed. New York: Addison Wesley.

World Bank. 2001. "Peru: Institutional and Governance Review" Report 22637-PE, World Bank, Washington, DC.

———. 2002. *Brazil Country Financial Accountability Assessment*. Washington, DC: World Bank.

CHAPTER 19

Does the Parliament Make a Difference? The Role of the Italian Parliament in Financial Policy

Carolyn Forestiere and Riccardo Pelizzo

As noted in previous chapters, legislatures in presidential systems are generally more involved in the *preparation* of the budget than legislatures in either parliamentary or semipresidential systems. The picture, however, is very different when one looks at legislatures' *oversight* of the budget. Legislatures in parliamentary systems are generally more involved in the examination and final approval of the budget than are legislatures in presidential and semipresidential systems.[1] In light of these considerations, it should not be terribly surprising to find that the executive is more likely to be held accountable to the legislature for its spending in parliamentary systems than in presidential systems.

This seems to imply that legislatures in parliamentary systems have considerable power to influence and shape the budget. In reality, however, their power is often remarkably inferior to what the list of formal powers suggests. Each parliament's ability to examine, amend, modify, confirm, and approve the budget is constrained by both institutional and political factors. On the institutional side, in many countries parliament's ability to alter the government's budget is subject to extensive procedural limits.[2] For example, in the United Kingdom, Parliament can amend tax proposals but cannot increase spending (OECD 1998, 76). In Germany, parliamentarians' ability to modify the budget is constrained by budget regulations as well as by the expenses generated by current legislation.[3] On the other hand, in some countries, such as Belgium and Canada, there are no institutional limits on parliament's ability to amend the budget. Although such conditions might imply extensive legislative participation, there are fairly obvious political limits to such potential interference. Significant modification of the executive's budget, particularly in Westminster-style parliaments, could imply a loss of confidence of the parliamentary majority and would, in all likelihood, initiate or exacerbate a government crisis.

The examples above demonstrate that the preparation, choice, and implementation of the budget are influenced by both institutional and political conditions. But which are more important? What predictions of legislative activity can be made? This chapter attempts to answer these questions by outlining the institutional and party system theories that explain parliaments' ability to shape the budget and by testing these theories on changes to the national budget in the Italian Parliament. The Italian Parliament is an excellent preliminary case study for the theory that institutional and political conditions influence parliament's ability to modify the national budget for two reasons. On the institutional side, the Italian Parliament has a complex array of procedural opportunities within the legislature, which may encourage extensive parliamentary activity during the amendment and the approval of the budget. On the political side, Italy has experienced undisciplined parties (and coalitions) and government instability (Pelizzo and Cooper 2002), both of which have led to general legislative ineffectiveness (Pelizzo and Babones 2001). Furthermore, and most important, there have been extensive changes to both the institutional design and the political climate of the Italian Parliament over the past 20 years. As a result, with a quasi-experimental design, one can gauge if there was any change in legislative activity after the institutional or political changes occurred. This analysis can be done using original data that measure the difference between the government's proposed budget and Parliament's final law each year. Positive findings would compel one to conclude preliminarily that institutions and political conditions matter significantly for Parliament's real ability to modify a national budget.

Institutional Theories

In virtually all parliamentary systems, the executive fully controls budgetary politics. Parliament's role is purposively restricted. Because the executive is paramount in setting the national budget, the comparative literature on budgeting reflects the importance of executive institutions (Alesina and Perotti 1999). This literature emphasizes the collective action problems within the executive for reaching decisions.

Literature investigating the role of the legislature in budgetary politics has also emerged. These studies argue that a parliament's ability to shape the budget is deeply affected by institutional factors. Institutions in this context refer to the "rules of the game," that is, the procedural and structural mechanisms that actors use to influence policy outcomes (North 1990).

For example, Krafchik and Wehner (1998) argued that the impact a legislature can have on the budget depends on the formal design of amendment powers, on the scope of conferred powers, and on the role of committees.[4] Poterba and Hagen (1999) also considered the effect of a broad array of legislative institutions on fiscal policy. The more that institutions allow a greater number of actors to influence budgetary politics, the more difficult it is to bring budget deficits under control. For example, budgetary institutions include procedures such as the timing of voting or amendments procedures (Alesina and Perotti 1999). These procedures create iterative collective action problems in which individual legislators from the government and opposition continually find incentives to defect from austerity agreements and secure particular benefits for narrow constituencies. This occurs at the expense of collective fiscal austerity.

When procedurally permitted, legislatures may serve to alter an executive's original budget proposal. Each country's institutional opportunities thus affect the incentive structures that individual legislators can manipulate.[5] The availability of these types of procedures empowers the legislature. Though often minor, this influence should be understood. Parliaments are not universally impotent, especially in the presence of particular types of party systems that are conducive to shifting majorities.

Party System Theories

A parliament's ability to shape, alter, and modify the national budget is also affected by political factors. Most theories concerning the party system generally argue that legislatures naturally defer to executive proposals simply because parliaments and governments are "fused": as the government must maintain majority support in the legislature in order to survive, the legislative majority tends to support government proposals, especially important ones.[6] According to Laver and Shepsle (1996):

> In terms of practical politics, however, a cabinet in which the government parties control a majority of seats in parliament can summon up a legislative majority whenever it cares to do so, provided party discipline holds firm. Thus a majority government with disciplined parties can comprehensively dominate any legislature once it has been installed in office. This in turn means that the legislature cannot in practice pass laws constraining the government. (57)

Despite the power of this parsimonious argument, there are still significant exceptions to this rule. Laver and Shepsle themselves defined the conditions under which parliaments would engage in activities to challenge their governments: "When party discipline breaks down and dissident members of a government party join forces with the opposition to pass legislation on some particular issue," it is possible for the parliament to impose "its will on a majority executive" (Laver and Shepsle 1996, 40).

A corollary of such political theories thus suggests that it is particularly difficult for governments always to control their legislative majorities and keep them together when the parliamentary party system is highly fragmented and when there are profound ideological divisions in the legislature. Therefore one can expect that parliamentary influence is affected not only by the institutional opportunities in parliament, but by the party system as well.

The Italian Parliament

The Italian Parliament provides a perfect setting to test the institutional and party system theories because there have been major revisions to the institutional design and to the party system over the past 20 years. These changes may have had an effect on parliamentarians' abilities to influence financial legislation. The institutional revisions include the removal of the secret vote (1988), a revision of the Parliament's decentralized agenda-setting process (1990), and the reduction of preference votes in the electoral system (1991). In addition, the electoral system has changed (1993), which may have led to a different configuration of political parties in the party system.

Institutional Factors

This section describes how the abolition of the secret vote, the reform of parliamentary agenda setting, and electoral reform contributed to the transformation of the Italian Parliament's role in the budget process.

The secret vote. Until 1988, the standing orders of the Italian Parliament allowed secret voting. No official record was kept on how each member of Parliament (MP) voted; only the number and names of those present and voting were recorded and counted. Though the government should have had enough support to pass its bills, the government was often defeated (and embarrassingly so) on many bills, including important proposals, during the first 40 years of the republic.

However, because no official vote was recorded, party whips could not find out who was responsible for the government's defeat, and thus no sanctions could be imposed on the *franchi tiratori*, the MPs who defected from the party line in secret votes. This problem often stalemated the executive and caused numerous governments to collapse. Ironically, these stalemates occurred even during times of oversized government, when the government should have been able to garner enough support from its parliamentary majority to pass its bills.

Because this problem threatened Italian political stability, reform legislation passed in 1988 abolished the provision of secret voting, except for very special circumstances, such as votes of no confidence. The open vote (*il voto palese*) is now required for the great majority of bills. The use of the secret vote was important for the empowerment of the Parliament before 1988 because party members were able to defect without sanction from party leaders. Government party MPs especially could introduce amendments and modify the budget to provide benefits to their constituents, rather than unilaterally supporting the government on financial legislation.

Parliamentary agenda setting. In 1971, the Italian Parliament passed reforms to implement a unique agenda-setting formula that extended veto power to a leader from each parliamentary group during the determination of the legislative agenda and calendar (Leonardi, Nanetti, and Pasquino 1978; della Sala 1988, 1998; Cotta 1994). Setting the parliamentary agenda is an important tool to manipulate public policy (Doering 2001; Tsebelis 2002). For example, in 1986 the government suffered a significant setback when the order of voting for the Financial Bill was discussed. The minister of the treasury wanted to vote on the total spending amount in Article 1 *first* in order to set an upper cap for spending, but the opposition argued that it preferred to vote on other articles first and on Article 1 *last*. The opposition clearly did not want to limit the amount of money Parliament could commit to spending, and knew that it could, through subsequent amendments, raise the overall amount as long as the ceiling was not already set. The crucial point is that the agenda-setting process in the Italian Parliament prohibited the government from imposing a timetable that was unattractive to the opposition. As a result, the government was defeated, and the Finance Law was passed over two months late. Della Sala (1988) argued:

> The important point about this discussion on what seems to be a technical point is that it highlights the fact that the government has few guarantees over the fate of its program once it reaches Parliament … The government was defeated over an issue it saw as crucial for achieving its objectives primarily because it had few levers which it could pull once the bill reached Parliament. (121)

Because of persistent problems with the agenda, additional reforms were passed in 1990 to strengthen the president of the chamber, who currently has the ability to impose an agenda when a unanimous vote does not pass.

Preference votes. Another significant institutional factor empowering Parliament was Italy's electoral system. Until 1993, when it was reformed by the laws 276/93 and 277/93, the Italian electoral system was a proportional representation (PR) system. This system was coupled with preference voting, which allowed voters to express their preference for specific candidates. Voters could express up to three or four such preferences until 1991, when, in the wake of a national referendum, the number of preferences that voters could express was reduced to only one. The PR system with single preference (*preferenza unica*) was used only in the 1992 elections, as the electoral system was further revised from PR to a mixed electoral system in 1993. But before 1991, preference voting affected the political behavior of voters as well as that of the elected officials.

The allocation of seats among the various parties depended on parties' electoral fortunes. Parties with a larger share of the vote would be entitled to larger shares of parliamentary seats. The allocation of seats among the candidates of a given party depended on the candidates' ability to receive more preference votes than their fellow party members. This is important because it gave individual MPs strong incentives to secure constituency benefits, to gain popularity and name recognition. The more benefits an MP managed to secure for her potential voters, the more preference votes an MP could expect to receive in the next election. Because of the preference vote, opposition members knew that engaging in collaborative activities with members of other parties could result in increased constituency benefits for all MPs.

Party System Factors

In addition to producing strong incentives for individual MPs to secure constituency benefits, the pre-1993 PR electoral system also produced a highly fragmented and ideologically polarized party system. In the 1990s, the average number of effective parties in the Italian Parliament was 7.3, the second highest among Western European democracies. For this time period, only Belgium had a slightly higher number of parties.[7] In addition, the extent of ideological polarization among Italian parties was among the highest in Western Europe.[8] The extensive fragmentation and polarization of the party system (Farneti 1985; Sartori 1976) produced undisciplined parliaments. Because of fragmentation, bargaining costs within parliament were quite high. Individual defection from party mandates and shifting coalitions among individuals and parties were not uncommon.

In addition, the presence of extreme ideological polarization led to two phenomena. First, Italian MPs learned to logroll particularistic policies that often spent government funds unchecked. These laws were notoriously referred to as the *leggine* (small laws; di Palma 1977). One clear indication of this trend is the number of individual spending proposals introduced in Parliament each year. The number of items for expenditures greatly exceeded the number of items concerning revenues. Because encompassing collective decisions were difficult to reach, Italian MPs learned to use decision rules in the Parliament for policy benefits in their own constituencies. Second, fragmentation meant that parliamentary majorities are often formed among ideologically dissimilar parties. Bills had to reflect a variety of interests before receiving majority support. Otherwise they faced intense scrutiny in Parliament.

How have these processes changed in the wake of the institutional reform and changes to the political landscape? First, with the removal of the secret vote in 1988, the passage of reforms in 1990 to allow the president of the chamber to impose a parliamentary agenda, and the introduction of the single preference 1991, the system of incentives was dramatically transformed. In addition, it is possible that the restructuring of the electoral system in 1993 altered the party system as well. If it is true that the institutional mechanisms that permit extensive policy influence have been removed, and if the party system is no longer as fragmented or polarized as before, then the benefits of defecting from government-party unity should decline. Therefore, a steady decline of parliamentary influence starting in 1988 should be apparent.

Data Analysis

Ordinary least squares regressions are used to test whether the institutional and/or party system changes have influenced Parliament's ability to amend the government's budget. The dependent variable is the percentage difference between the government's proposed bill and the Parliament's approved law for the spending side of both in the budget. Superficially, these data indicate quite clearly that the Italian Parliament has not always been a rubber-stamp parliament on financial policy. Instead, at times the Italian Parliament has been an important actor in the determination of spending priorities (see table 19.1).

Several independent variables are used, based on the theories elaborated above, to explain differing levels of parliamentary interference in spending priorities in Italy. First, the measure of legislative institutions tracks the changes to the institutional design of the Italian Parliament over the past 20 years.[9] Second, to measure party system attributes, the analysis includes both legislative polarization and legislative fragmentation. Legislative polarization is measured as the sum of the seats held by the most left-wing and the most right-wing parties. For most years, the two most extreme parties were the Italian Communist Party and the neofascist Italian Social Movement, often comprising at least 30 percent of the total seat share. The larger the seat share of extremist parties, the more polarized the Parliament. The percentage of the seat share for extreme parties changed, however, after international events dampened the appeal of the Communist Party, domestic scandals shook the major parties, and the electoral system changed from proportional representation to a mixed majoritarian formula. These changes may have also influenced the number of effective parties (Taagepera 1989).

Table 19.1. Italian Budget Laws for 1982 to 2001

For year	Proposed by government (billion lire)	Passed by parliament (billion lire)	Percent difference
1982	135460	164087	17
1983	172772	203510	15
1984	227077	242321	6
1985	274163	297597	8
1986	280900	334543	16
1987	311432	358997	13
1988	368360	414814	11
1989	388562	406271	4
1990	456202	445655	−2
1991	498505	509594	2
1992	541967	559556	3
1993	612696	588981	−4
1994	563208	549658	−2
1995	611073	611390	0
1996	647486	637007	−2
1997	633348	642245	1
1998	634393	653414	3
1999	658278	672500	2
2000	673282	679779	1
2001	700646	725944	3

Source: Chamber of Deputies.

The results of the regression analyses are presented in table 19.2. When one regresses the percentage change between the budget proposed by the government and the budget approved by the Parliament against polarization, one finds, as expected, that the Parliament's ability to modify the budget increases as polarization increases. Polarization by itself explains more than 45 percent of the variance in the Parliament's ability to alter the budget. This is because more dispersed points of view need accommodation in order to reach consensus in Parliament. But when one regresses the percentage change between the proposed budget and the approved budget against fragmentation, one finds, in contrast to what party system theory claims, that the Parliament's ability to change the government budget *declines* as fragmentation increases. This anomaly could very well be explained by the fact that when a parliament is too fragmented it becomes increasingly difficult to form any alternate majority that can change the status quo.

Next, when one regresses the percentage change between the government budget and the budget approved by the Parliament one finds that institutional change largely explains the Italian Parliament's ability to modify the budget. In fact, institutional change accounts for 64 percent of the variance in the Parliament's power to alter the government budget. And finally, when all the independent variables are entered into the model, one finds that while institutional change remains a fairly strong and significant determinant of the Parliament's ability to change the government budget, the influence of both polarization and fragmentation becomes insignificant. This suggests that the institutional variable trumps the power of the party system. Based on this finding, one can preliminarily conclude that parliamentary institutions, at least in the Italian context, are more important than the party system in explaining the extensive amount of parliamentary influence in the determination of spending priorities.

Table 19.2. Regression Analyses

| Dependent variable | Intercept | Independent variables (sig.) | | | R-squared |
		Polarization	Fragmentation	Institutional change	
Percentage change between proposed budget and passed budget	−8.593 (.027)	.494 (.001)			.464
	24.259 (.000)		−3.777 (.001)		.497
	−.187 (.884)			3.886 (.000)	.640
	−7.400 (.623)	.027 (.902)	1.075 (.615)	4.629 (.033)	.645

Source: Authors' calculations.
Note: Polarization and fragmentation are calculated by the authors on the basis of the electoral results; percentage change between proposed and passed budget is measured as indicated in table 19.1.

Conclusions

Clearly, more testing is required, both within the Italian context and comparatively, to determine the power of institutions and the party system in explaining how and when parliaments would be expected to influence national budgets. Based on the results of this analysis, which uses novel data to gauge the difference between the first and last drafts of budget legislation, institutions explain more of the variation in parliamentary influence. This tentative finding could be, however, spurious. Institutional reform took place *before* the party system changed, and thus the effect noted may not be absolute. It is entirely possible that had the reforms proceeded in the reverse (changing the electoral system before changing the procedural mechanisms), the party system variables would have explained more than the institutional ones. More testing in other contexts would confirm the power of the independent variables. At the very least, this analysis has served to demonstrate that these variables do explain part of parliamentary influence in the budget. Comparatively, one would not expect parliaments to be rubber stamps at all. The specific rules in parliament and the number and ideological bent of parties combine to provide incentives for parliaments to deviate from what is considered standard parliamentary behavior, in which parliaments unilaterally support their governments during the passage of the national budget.

Notes

1. On these and related issues, see Pelizzo and Stapenhurst 2004a; an abridged version of the paper can also be found in Pelizzo, Olson, and Stapenhurst 2004; see also Pelizzo and Stapenhurst 2004b.

2. For comparative data concerning the passage of the budget in parliament, see Herman 1976; International Centre for Parliamentary Documentation of the Inter-parliamentary Union 1986, 1091–1122. Updated information can be found in OECD 1998. PUMA/SBO (98)4, unclassified, pp. 1–80.

3. OECD 1998, 37. See also Wehner 2001, 57–78.

4. There are three main types of conferred powers: unrestricted, restricted, and balanced budget.

5. This point should not be overstated, however. In virtually all legislatures, changes to the executive's budget are often minor. But the point remains that in some countries, the government's budget may not always be passed as presented.

6. According to Laver and Shepsle (1996), "The role of the legislature is much more that of controlling the fate of government than it is of implementing policy directly" (57).

7. The higher number of effective parties in Belgium must be qualified by the fact that many Belgian parties operate in pairs to reflect differences in region and language.

8. Polarization is measured as the percentage of support for the extreme left- and extreme right-wing parties. In Italy these are the Italian Communist Party (PCI) and the neofascist Italian Social Movement (MSI).

9. The institutions variable is measured as follows: Value of 3 for 1982–88 to measure the presence of secret voting, the inclusive agenda-setting process,

and the use of three or four preference votes (depending on the district) in the electoral system. Value of 2 for 1988–90 to measure the presence of the inclusive agenda-setting process and the use of three or four preference votes in the electoral system. Value of 1 for 1991–92 to measure the use of only one preference vote in the electoral system. Value of 0 after 1993, when the electoral system changed from pure proportional representation with preference votes to a mixed system with no preference votes.

Bibliography

Alesina, Alberto, and Roberto Perotti. 1999. "Budget Deficits and Budget Institutions." In *Fiscal Institutions and Fiscal Performance*, eds. James M. Poterba and Juergen von Hagen. Chicago: University of Chicago Press.

Cotta, Maurizio. 1994. "The Rise and Fall of the 'Centrality' of the Italian Parliament: Transformations of the Executive-Legislative Subsystem after the Second World War." In *Parliaments in the Modern World: Changing Institutions*, eds. G. W. Copeland and S. C. Patterson. Ann Arbor: University of Michigan Press.

Doering, Herbert. 2001. "Parliamentary Agenda Control and Legislative Outcomes in Western Europe." *Legislative Studies Quarterly* 26 (1): 145–65.

della Sala, Vincent. 1988. "The Italian Budgetary Process: Political and Institutional Constraints." *West European Politics* 11 (3): 110–25.

———. 1998. "The Italian Parliament: Chambers in a Crumbling House?" In *Parliaments and Governments in Western Europe*, ed. P. Norton. London: Frank Cass.

di Palma, Giuseppe. 1977. *Surviving Without Governing: The Italian Parties in Parliament*. Berkeley: University of California Press.

Farneti, Paolo. 1985. *The Italian Party System*. New York: St. Martin's Press.

Herman, Valentine (in collaboration with Françoise Mendel). 1976. *Parliaments of the World. A Reference Compendium*: New York: De Gruyter.

International Centre for Parliamentary Documentation of the Inter-Parliamentary Union. 1986. *Parliaments of the World. A Reference Compendium*: Aldershot: Gower.

Krafchik, Warren, and Joachim Wehner. 1998. "The Role of Parliament in the Budgetary Process." *The South African Journal of Economics* 66 (4): 512–41.

Laver, Michael, and Kenneth Shepsle. 1996. *Making and Breaking Governments: Cabinets and Legislatures in Parliamentary Democracies*. Cambridge, U.K.: Cambridge University Press.

Leonardi, Robert, Raffaella Nanetti, and Gianfranco Pasquino. 1978. "Institutionalization of Parliament and Parliamentarization of Parties in Italy." *Legislative Studies Quarterly* 3 (1): 161–86.

North, Douglass. 1990. *Institutions, Institutional Change and Economic Performance*. Cambridge, U.K.: Cambridge University Press.

OECD (Organisation for Economic Co-Operation and Development). 1998. Role of Legislature. 19th Meeting of Senior Budget Officials, Paris, May 25–26, PUMA/SBO (98) 4, unclassified, 1–80.

Pelizzo, Riccardo, and Salvatore J. Babones. 2001. "Determinants of Legislative Effectiveness: The Italian Case." *Quaderni di Scienza Politica* 8 (2): 301–23.

Pelizzo, Riccardo, and Joseph Cooper. 2002. "Stability in Parliamentary Regimes: The Italian Case." *Legislative Studies Quarterly* 27 (2): 163–90.

Pelizzo, Riccardo, David Olson, and Rick Stapenhurst, eds. 2004. "Trends in Legislative Oversight." Working Paper Series on Contemporary Issues in Parliamentary Development, World Bank Institute, Washington, DC.

Pelizzo, Riccardo, and Rick Stapenhurst. 2004a. "Legislatures and Oversight: A Note." *Quaderni di Scienza Politica* 11 (1): 175–88.

———. 2004b. "Tools for Legislative Oversight: An Empirical Investigation." Policy Research Working Paper No. 3388, World Bank, Washington, DC.

Poterba, James M., and Juergen von Hagen, eds. 1999. *Fiscal Institutions and Fiscal Performance.* Chicago: University of Chicago Press.

Sartori, Giovanni. 1976. *Parties and Party Systems: A Framework for Analysis.* Cambridge, U.K.: Cambridge University Press.

Taagepera, Rein. 1989. *Seats and Votes: The Effects and Determinants of Electoral Systems.* New Haven: Yale University Press.

Tsebelis, George. 2002. *Veto Players: How Political Institutions Work.* New York: Russell Sage Foundation.

Wehner, Joachim. 2001. "Reconciling Accountability and Fiscal Prudence. A Case Study of the Budgetary Role and Impact of the German Parliament." *Journal of Legislative Studies* 7 (2): 57–78.

CHAPTER 20

Legislative Budgeting in the Czech Republic

Zdenka Mansfeldová and Petra Rakušanová

In the Czech Republic the procedure of approving the state budget differs from the general legislative process. The negotiation of the state budget is governed by rules defined in the Rules of Procedure of the Chamber of Deputies.[1] The budget negotiation process proceeds according to the Rule of Procedure (Part 13), as follows. Upon elaboration of the budget by the Ministry of Finance together with bodies responsible for individual chapters and negotiations within the government, the cabinet submits a draft act on the state budget to the Speaker of the Chamber of Deputies no later than three months before the start of a new budget year (by September 30 of the previous year). Amendments to the draft act may be submitted until 15 days prior to the session of the Chamber of Deputies at which the first reading is to take place.

Procedures for Approving the State Budget

The Speaker assigns the draft act on the state budget to the Budget Committee for discussion. After the draft act is assigned to the Budget Committee, the first reading takes place at a session of the Chamber of Deputies. There, deputies engage in a general parliamentary debate on the basic aspects of the budget, such as the revenues and expenditures; the balance, and settlement of the balance; the general relationship to the budgets of the higher territorial administrative units and municipalities; and the scope of powers assigned to executive bodies. If the draft act is not approved, the chamber recommends that the cabinet redraft the bill, and sets a date for the new draft to be submitted. If the Chamber of Deputies approves the basic aspects of the budget, it is not possible to change them later during the negotiation. A draft of the state budget is debated independently and cannot be contingent upon a proposal for the adoption or amendment of another act (Kolář, Pecháček, and Syllová 2002, 188).

If the Chamber of Deputies approves the basic information in the draft act on the state budget, individual chapters are then assigned to committees. Committees are assigned a deadline (the minimum period is 30 days) and are obligated to discuss the individual chapters of the draft act on the state budget they have been given by that deadline. Committees may propose changes only to those chapters of the state budget that they have been assigned to discuss.

The Budget Committee debates the committees' resolutions and opposing views on individual chapters of the draft bill in the presence of rapporteurs, and adopts a resolution. During the second reading, the draft act on the state budget is introduced by the submitting party. The Budget Committee's rapporteur speaks after the submitting party. During the detailed parliamentary debate, amendments and other proposals are submitted. From a political perspective, the comment phase is the most important because it is in this phase that individual deputies (who, for example, did not have a chance to directly participate in the preparation of the draft act) try to secure funds for their constituencies.

The third reading of the draft act on the state budget may start no earlier than 48 hours after the second reading has been completed. During the parliamentary debate, corrections of legislative mistakes or mistakes of a technical nature, corrections of grammatical mistakes, and proposals to repeat the second reading are the only items that may be proposed. At the conclusion of the third reading, the Chamber of Deputies votes on the submitted amendments and decides whether it will express agreement with the draft act.

Changes in the Rules of Procedure

Until the adoption of the new Rules of Procedure in mid-1995, the draft act (the whole budget) was discussed by the Budget Committee and also by a number of other committees, after which a joint report was submitted. This procedure offered more opportunity for lobbying, and it was easier for a lay opinion to defeat a professional opinion, as each committee had only one vote and the special Budget and Economy Committees formed a minority (of the usual four to five committees involved). An amendment to the Rules of Procedure resulted in the Budget Committee obtaining more competencies. Currently, it is very difficult for a deputy to secure any funds for his or her own constituency, because a deputy is expected to specify how the proposed expenditure will be paid for, that is, what other expenditures should be cut in order to obtain money for that specific purpose.

Bargaining Process

The most important stage of the bargaining process is the first reading, which is meant to give a clear outline of the total amount of the mandatory expenditures (that is, expenditures explicitly required by law); the total expenditures and revenues; the balance of the state budget; and the budgets of municipalities. The Budget Committee must seek to preserve a balance between revenues and expenditures. After subtracting the mandatory expenditures, a mere 15 percent of the total funds allocated for expenditures remain; it is necessary to come to an agreement on which sphere (for example, education, science, or health care) will be emphasized. This percentage is further reduced when one considers ongoing investment projects of the government that cannot be abandoned or unwritten, plus EU and NATO obligations (percentages that are given for certain chapters of the budget, such as education, science, defense, and so forth). This means that all the media publicity around the budget actually concerns only a small number of items debated in the Parliament.

This may be the place to mention that the first round of putting together particular expenditures takes place at the ministries. This is why the ministries seem to be in a much better position to advance particular interests, as this environment is much less transparent compared with Parliament. Thus, the Chamber of Deputies is only the second step in lobbying. (For further insights on lobbying process see Kabele and Linek 2004.)

The growing percentage of mandatory and quasi-mandatory expenditures and expenditure programs that have already been launched limit the flexibility of the public budget expenditures in the short term.[2] Currently the disproportionate increase in mandatory expenditures, which significantly exceed the speed of growth of tax income revenues, is the essential problem of the fiscal policy of the cabinet, and the subject of harsh criticism from the opposition.

Political Negotiations of the Draft of the State Budget

The draft act on the state budget is approved by the plenary of the Chamber of Deputies. The negotiation is ideologically divided from the very beginning of the process, and therefore the debate and voting on the state budget is always a key issue for parliamentary party groups. Considerable party discipline is required in the vote, and voting at variance with the decision adopted by a parliamentary party group may have very unpleasant consequences for individual deputies, especially if the cabinet has a very narrow margin in the Chamber of Deputies. This has been a major problem since 1996 (see annex tables). The reason for the relatively low party unity (Rice's Index of Party Cohesion: about 80 units) lies in the size of the voting coalitions that approve individual bills: the large majorities mean the parliamentary party groups do not have to act with absolute unity. This system results in lowering the transaction costs political parties would otherwise have to expend to ensure that their bills are approved by narrow-margin majorities, for example, the vote on the state budget at the beginning of 1997, when the cabinet had a narrow majority (Mansfeldová 1997, 2002). Two ČSSD deputies who did not vote according to the approved party line were expelled from the party. One of them joined the right-wing Civic Democratic Party soon afterward.

Deputies: Attitudes and Voting

The approval of the budget is generally one of the key tasks of the Parliament, and, as can be gleaned from table 20.1, it is one of the most important activities according to the deputies. In addition to the explicitly formulated control of the cabinet, the highest importance is still attached to the adoption of the state budget, which is one of the means by which the cabinet can be indirectly controlled (Reytt 2000; Soltéz 1995).

If one compares the scores of each activity in time as well as in individual functional terms, it can be said that the approval of the state budget is rated among the highest by the deputies. While the score for other activities tend to change over time, the trend for the approval of the state budget remains stable. This is also in accordance with the perception of the committees described later in the text.

An analysis of voting in the Chamber of Deputies (tables 20.2–20.5) also shows that voting on the state budget is one of the key political issues that is usually decided strictly along party lines. Data on the voting were available for nine state budgets, starting with 1995; a more detailed analysis of voting will be possible in five years. Older records were not available.

The data contained in tables 20.2–20.5 illustrate what percentage of each parliamentary party group voted in favor of a submitted budget, and which abstained or did not participate (often allowing the budget to be adopted). The data prove the great party discipline in voting on the state budget. Sometimes the budget is not adopted on the first attempt, as was the case with the 2000 budget, where only the deputies of the minority government of the Social Democratic Party voted for the budget. Right-wing deputies voted against it, and the Communists (KSČM) abstained from voting. As a result, the government operated on a provisional budget. The budget had to be renegotiated at the beginning of 2000, at which time the opposition parties reached an agreement and the budget was approved (see table 20.4).

Table 20.1. Deputies' Perception of Importance of Individual Activities of the Parliament, 1993 to 2003

Activities	1993	1996	1998	2000	2003
Legislative activities	4.78	4.50	4.67	4.97	4.72
Control of the government	4.61	4.22	3.94	4.64	4.27
Consideration and evaluation of proposals submitted by various social groups	3.22	2.83	3.00	3.74	3.17
Approval of the state budget	4.78	4.72	4.72	4.95	4.80
Processing of petitions and comments of citizens	3.39	1.56	3.22	3.86	3.37
Preparation of the EU accession	n/a	n/a	4.22	4.61	4.06

Source: Institute of Sociology, Academy of Science of the Czech Republic (SOÚ AV ČR).
Note: Respondents were offered a 5-point scale, where 1 is least important and 5 is most important; n/a indicates that the option was not asked in the survey at the given time.

Table 20.2. Voting on the State Budgets in the 1st Electoral Term
(percent)

	ČMSS (ČMUS)	ČSSD	KDS	KDU-ČSL	KSČM	LB	LSNS	LSU	ODA	ODS	SPR-RSČ
1995	0	11	100	100	0	0	100	0	94	100	0
1996	31	0	100	100	0	0	100	n/a	100	98	0

Source: Archive of Chamber of Deputies, Parliament of the Czech Republic.
Note: During the term the ruling coalition consisted of the following parties: ODS, KDS, KDU-ČSL, and ODA. An n/a means the party was not present in the Chamber.

Table 20.3. Voting on the State Budgets on the 2nd Electoral Term
(percent)

	ČSSD	KDU-ČSL	KSČM	ODA	ODS	SPR-RSČ
1997	3	100	0	100	99	0
1998	0	100	0	100	100	0

Source: Archive of Chamber of Deputies, Parliament of the Czech Republic.
Note: During the term the ruling coalition consisted of the following parties: ODS, KDU-ČSL, and ODA. When the cabinet resigned at the end of 1997, the 1998 budget had already been approved.

Table 20.4. Voting on the State Budgets in the 3rd Electoral Term
(percent)

	ČSSD	KDU-ČSL	KSČM	ODS	US
1999	97	90	100	0	0
2000	100	0	0	88	0
2001	93	5	0	90	0
2002	96	0	0	98	0

Source: Archive of Chamber of Deputies, Parliament of the Czech Republic.
Note: During the term the Czech Republic had a minority social-democratic cabinet (ČSSD), which was able to stay in power thanks to the Opposition Agreement concluded with the strongest opposition party, ODS.

Table 20.5. Voting on the State Budgets in the 4th Electoral Term
(percent)

	ČSSD	KDU-ČSL	KSČM	ODS	US
2003	100	100	0	0	90
2004	100	0	0	100	100

Source: Archive of Chamber of Deputies, Parliament of the Czech Republic.
Note: A coalition cabinet with a narrow majority in the Parliament is in power in the Czech Republic, consisting of ČSSD, KDU-ČSL, and US.

The Budget Committee

Legislative and supervisory activities in each session of Parliament are carried out in parliamentary committees. In these committees, major decisions are made on a majority of draft acts. With the exception of legislation, the most important task of the committees is to review the functioning of the cabinet.

This task is the natural consequence of a system of government in which
the administration is directly and continuously responsible to the Parliament.
Committees are the main practical working instrument through which these
responsibilities are carried out.

The Budget Committee is crucial for the negotiation of the budget (called
the Budget and Control Committee until the transformation of the Czech
National Council into the Chamber of Deputies of the Parliament of the
Czech Republic on January 1, 1993). It is also one of the most prestigious and
busiest committees of the Chamber of Deputies (see table 20.6).

The prestige of a committee tends to be matched by the prestige of individual activities of the Parliament. With the exception of the first term, the
Budget Committee is perceived as having the highest prestige. This is mir-
rored in the peopling of the committee with nominees tending to have high
levels of professional skills. The members of the Budget Committee also tend
to have a high probability of reelection. In addition, when they are reelected,
they usually rejoin the Budget Committee.

It is worth noting that the topic of this committee is considered purely a
men's issue. During the monitored period there was not a single woman on
the committee. The responsibilities of the Budget Committee extend much
beyond merely debating the state budget and individual budget chapters. The

**Table 20.6. Committees according to Their Prestige in the Chamber of
Deputies of the Czech Republic**
(percent)

	1st Term		2nd Term	3rd Term	4th Term
Committee	1993	1996	1998	2000	2003
Constitutional Committee	91.9	88.7	63.9	60.9	40.2
Budget Committee	61.0	89.4	84.1	89.4	91.1
Economic Committee	60.3	41.5	42.7	49.7	49.7
Foreign Affairs Committee	26.5	21.3	27.4	20.7	25.4
Committee for Defense and Security	11.8	16.3	28.0	25.1	17.2
Committee for Social Policy and Health Care	8.1	12.0	22.3	15.1	10.1
Committee for Science, Education, Culture, Youth, and Sports	5.1	7.0	4.5	2.8	5.9
Petition Committee	3.7	2.8	0.6	1.7	3.6
Agricultural Committee	2.9	7.7	9.6	5.0	11.8
Committee for Public Administration, Regional Development, and Environment	2.2	1.4	7.6	18.4	16.6
Committee for European Integration	*	*	*	5.0	4.1
Mandate and Immunity Committee	1.5	4.2	2.5	3.4	2.4
Election Committee	*	*	*	*	1.2

Source: Parliamentary DICe, Institute of Sociology, Academy of Science of the Czech Republic (SOÚ AV ČR).
* During these years the committee did not exist.

committee receives regular reports on the management of the Czech Republic (quarterly, and a summary report for the whole year); the withdrawal of funds from the state budget; reports on the monetary policy (ČNB) and management of the Czech National Bank (ČNB); reports on the results of activities and the use of budget funds in individual years; and reports from the Ministry of Finance on the management of the Czech Republic.

The Budget Committee can establish subcommittees to perform its supervisory responsibilities, and these subcommittees can focus professionally on specific issues in a more concentrated way. It is up to the Budget Committee to decide on the number and types of subcommittees it will establish. For example, during almost all terms there was an Audit Subcommittee.

The Budget Committee debates any and all changes during the course of the year that occur with respect to events funded by the state budget, transfers of funds in chapters of individual ministries, and so forth. Because the deficit of the state budget is currently growing,[3] deputies strive to play a more active role early on, including in the budget preparation phase. An example of this is a bill submitted by a deputy for a constitutional act on budget discipline; however, this bill was defeated in the first reading.

Supreme Audit Office

According to the Constitution, Article 97, an independent institution—the Supreme Audit Office (SAO)—must audit national property management and implementation of the state budget. The president and vice president of the SAO are appointed by the president of the Czech Republic at the recommendation of the Chamber of Deputies. The Chamber of Deputies, and specifically the Budget Committee, initiates the tasks of the SAO; the cooperation has been very good so far, and there is mutual understanding and agreement. The SAO has a duty to submit a summary report of its activities, a report of its economic activities, and its budget to the Chamber of Deputies. The latter approves these documents at the suggestion of the Budget Committee and following consultations with the SAO. The Ministry of Finance is obligated to adopt the budgets of the Chamber of Deputies, Senate, and SAO, as suggested by Parliament.

The Audit Subcommittee of the Budget Committee has selectively dealt with some findings of the SAO. It also has at its disposal detailed records of audits and has the right to call the respective minister. There are many SAO findings; therefore the Audit Subcommittee can opt to choose only those cases that it deems to be particularly significant. Because it has access to the necessary documents, such as records of audit, the Audit Subcommittee is able to study a particular case in depth. Then, on the basis of its own proceedings, the Audit Subcommittee informs the Budget Committee, which in turn considers how to deal with the findings.

The Chamber of Deputies of the Parliament approves the budget and the report of the activities of the National Property Fund. The activity of the fund is then checked by the SAO, and its reports are submitted to the Chamber of

Deputies. The Export Bank also submits reports of its activities, reports of its economic activities, and its budget to the Chamber of Deputies. (The Export Bank was established by the state and gets state subsidies but generates revenues to cover its costs.) The cabinet is also obligated to submit a closing state account to the Chamber of Deputies.

If one examines the options available to the Parliament, especially the agenda discussed by the Economic Committee, the Budget Committee, and the Audit Subcommittee, one sees that control exists primarily in the acquisition of information. Parliament can act mostly ex post facto by establishing inquiry committees to examine a suspicious case. After the 1996 elections, when a balance between the right-of-center and left-of-center forces was achieved, it was possible for the opposition parties to gain more efficient control, although it was a disjointed opposition.[4] This can be seen as progress in developing democratic mechanisms, and one can even see a great effort by the Parliament to monitor the cabinet, for example, by setting up parliamentary inquiry committees.

Trends, Indicators, and Explanatory Factors

According to the activities of the Budget Committee since 1990 (see table 20.7), legislative activity related to the state budget, especially in the legislative phase, appears to be on the rise.

The Budget Committee, as well as other committees, has adopted a growing number of resolutions related to the state budget that concern not only the drawing up of the budget but also its control. As for the opportunity of individual deputies to influence the preparation of the state budget, the situation has not changed much: deputies of the ruling parties have a greater chance to formally and informally influence the budget. Conversely, opposition deputies take greater advantage of parliamentary hearings. Furthermore,

Table 20.7. Activity of the Budget Committee over Five Terms, 1990–2004

Term	1990–92	1992–96	1996–98	1998–2002	2002 to election	Following 2002 election	2003	2004
Number of members	17–18	17–20	20	21	21	21	21	21
Number of committee meetings	65	78	36	59	24	8	14	16
Number of adopted resolutions	398	627	318	560	324	116	196	176

Source: Archive of the Chamber of Deputies, Parliament of the Czech Republic.
Note: The election took place on July 17, 2002.

lobbyists tend to influence the process through the deputies of the ruling parties because it is deemed more efficient.

The cabinet is responsible to the Chamber of Deputies for meeting the state budget obligations. After the elapse of six months, the cabinet submits a semiannual report to the Chamber of Deputies in which it assesses the development of the economy and the fulfillment of the Act on the State Budget. The Budget Committee again plays a key role. The Chamber of Deputies approves the Closing State Account; the Budget Committee debates individual chapters of the Closing State Account.

Control Functions of the Budget Committee

As stated above, the Budget Committee may establish various subcommittees to perform its supervisory functions. In the third term these were the Subcommittee for Capital and Financial Markets and the Audit Subcommittee; in the fourth term (2002–06) the Subcommittee for the Financial Management of Territorial Self-Administration and for the Utilisation of European Funds was established in addition to the Audit Subcommittee.

During the process of decentralization, which is part of the European integration process (based on which a wide range of decision-making powers were transferred in 2001 from the central to the district level), the Parliament has strengthened its supervisory function. If one understands the Audit Subcommittee as the control mechanism of the Parliament against the cabinet, then the Subcommittee for the Financial Management of Territorial Self-Administration and for the Utilisation of Funds of the European Union is an attempt to partially control the financial flows between supranational (EU funds) and subnational levels (districts; Rakušanová 2003).

In the process of consolidating democracy in the Czech Republic, the Parliament has become functionally embedded in the constitutional system, deputies have become more professional, the professional backup support has improved, and the functions of the Parliament have crystallized. Table 20.8 shows more-or-less balanced budgets between 1992 and 1996, but starting in 1997 shows an increase in the state budget deficit. In 2000 and 2001 the budget deficits were higher than planned, approximately 31 percent and 36 percent, respectively. This deficit is primarily due to actual revenues being lower than planned revenues.

It should be noted that over the past few years the cabinet has started an artificial reduction of the state budget deficit using extrabudgetary revenues, especially privatization funds (by selling large state enterprises). In the Parliament, the opposition in particular has strongly criticized these nonsystemic measures. The cabinet has promised to cover some of the budget expenditures by using the National Fund (EU funds) to a much greater extent after the EU accession in May 1, 2004; however, it struggles to do so. In 2007 the inability to draft a satisfactory scheme for the transfer of the EU funds, as required by the EU, resulted in forced resignation of the Minister of Education Dana Kuchtova (Green Party).

Table 20.8. Fulfillment of the State Budget between 1991 and 2003

Year	1991	1992	1993	1994	1995	1996	1997	1998	1999	2000	2001	2002	2003	2004
Earnings total (billion CZK)														
Budget	241.0	249.9	342.2	385.3	446.2	497.6	519.6	547.2	581.3	592.2	636.2	693.4	686.1	754.1
Reality	225.3	251.4	258	390.5	440	482.8	509	537.4	567.3	586.2	626.2	705.0	699.7	559.3 till 9/30/04
Spending total (billion CZK)														
Budget	239.9	255.9	342.2	385.3	437.0	497.6	519.6	547.2	612.4	627.3	685.2	755.7	817.8	869.1
Reality	240.1	253.1	356.9	380.1	432.7	484.4	524.7	566.7	596.9	632.3	693.9	750.8	808.7	599.9 till 9/30/04
Surplus/deficit (billion CZK)														
Budget	1.1	–6	0	0	9.3	0	0	0	–31	–35.2	–49.0	–62.3	–131.7	–115.1
Reality	–14.8	–1.7	1.1	10.5	7.2	–1.6	–15.7	–29.3	–29.6	–46.1	–67.7	–45.7	–109.1	–113.1 till 9/30/04
Duration of parliamentary proceeding	1 day	2 days	2 days	3 mo.	1 mo.	3 mo.	3 mo.	3 mo.	4 mo.	6 mo.	3 mo.	3 mo.	3 mo.	2 mo. till 12/3/04

Sources: Ministry of Finance of the Czech Republic, Parliamentary Documentation and Information Center, Institute of Sociology, Academy of Science of the Czech Republic (SOÚ AV ČR).

Today, one can see a great structural reform of public finances. More than a mere modification, these reforms should result in a restructuring of the state budget as such, especially changes in welfare, pension, tax, and health care spending. The main objective of the reform is to transform the state budget from being a fiscal policy tool into a public management tool, that is, a performance-driven model based on defined goals and benchmarks, on negotiation, and on a system of contracts and agreements.

Conclusion

An analysis of parliamentary activities in the Czech Republic in terms of the budget shows that during the process of transformation and of democracy consolidation, the functions of the Parliament with respect to the state budget have undergone great changes. In this process, the professionalization of deputies in general, and members of the Budget Committee in particular, has been crucial. At the beginning of the 1990s, the Budget Committee, like Parliament as a whole, was composed of people without any previous experience of high-level politics. Only rarely did a deputy have an economic background. In the first meeting of the committee it was proposed that appointments to the committee take into account professional background. This proposal was rejected, and it was agreed to distribute posts in the Budget Committee to all political parties equally. Gradually, however, deputies have become more professional and have learned how to obtain information, how to work with it, and how to evaluate it critically. Today, the Budget Committee is considered the most prestigious and most influential parliamentary body.

The problem with the role of the Parliament in the budget process lies primarily in the need for large coalitions in voting and in the large transaction costs associated with party cohesion, that is, in the political party landscape rather than in Parliament's institutional capacity. Generally, there has been an increase in party discipline in voting on the budget. On the other hand, individual deputies are proposing a growing number of changes.

The Parliament is aware that its legitimacy may be eroded in the context of European integration; therefore, to counter this threat, it is strengthening its auditing functions. This also pertains to the Budget Committee, which has focused on the subnational and supranational levels, the management of territorial self-administrations, and the use of European Union funds.

Annex Table 20.1. The Composition of the Government and Its Support in the Parliament

Cabinet created	Governing party or parties	Parliamentary seats (%)
June 1990—Federal government	9 OF, 4 VPN, 2 KDH, 1 independent	65.0
June 1990—Czech government	10 OF, 2 KDU-ČSL, 1 HSD-SMS, 8 independent	84.0
June 1992—Czech government	11 ODS, 4 KDU-ČSL, 2 ODA, 2 KDS	56.0
July 1992—Temporary federal government	4 ODS, 4 HZDS, 1 KDU-ČSL, 1 without party affiliation	52.7
June 1996—Czech government	8 ODS, 4 KDU-ČSL, 4 ODA	49.5
January 1998—Semicaretaker govt.	3 KDU-ČSL, 4 US-former ODS, 3 ODA, 7 without party affiliation	31.0
August 1998—Czech government	18 ČSSD, 1 without party affiliation	37.0
July 2002—Czech government	11 ČSSD, 3 KDU-ČSL, 3 DEU	50.5

Source: Parliamentary Documentation and Information Center, Institute of Sociology AS CR.

Annex Table 20.2. Names of Political Parties in English and Czech and Their Czech Abbreviations

Abbreviation	Name of the party in English	Name of the party in Czech	Political orientation
ČMSS/ ČMUS	Czech-Moravian Centre Party /Bohemian and Moravian Union of the Centre	Českomoravská strana středu/ Českomoravská unie středu	Center
ČSSD	Czech Social Democratic Party	Česká strana sociálně demokratická	Left-wing
DEU	Democratic Union	Demokratická unie	Right-wing
KDU – ČSL	Christian Democratic Union/Czechoslovak People´s Party	Křest'ansko demokratická unie/ Československá strana lidová	Center
KDS	Christian Democratic Party	Křest'ansko demokratická strana	Right-wing
KSČM	Communist Party of Bohemia and Moravia	Komunistická strana Čech a Moravy	Left-wing
LB	Left Block	Levý blok	Left-wing
LSNS	National Socialist Liberal Party	Liberální strana národně sociální	Left-wing
LSU	Liberal-Social Union	Liberal-Social Union	Left-wing
ODA	Civic Democratic Alliance	Občanská demokratická aliance	Right-wing
ODS	Civic Democratic Party	Občanská demokratická strana	Right-wing
SPR – RSČ	Association for the Republic – Republican Party of Czechoslovakia	Sdružení pro republiku – Republikánská strana Československa	Right-wing
US	Freedom Union	Unie svobody	Right-wing
SZ	Green Party	Strana zelenych	Center

Source: Parliamentary Documentation and Information Center, Institute of Sociology AS CR; authors.

Notes

Paper prepared for the Southern Political Science Association Annual Meeting, January 6–8, 2005, New Orleans, USA, K–10/B–9 Roundtable: The Role of Parliaments in the Budget Process. The study is based on results of the GA AV CR Project No. S7028003, "Information and Documentation Centre on the Parliaments of Central Europe," and Project No. 1J 004/04–DP1, "Political and Legal Institutional Framework of the Czech Republic and Its Changes in the Context of the Accession to the EU."

1. The Parliament of the Czech Republic has two chambers: the Chamber of Deputies, with 200 deputies, and the Senate, with 81 senators.

2. Act on the 2004 Budget, http://www.psp.cz/.

3. On December 3, 2003, the Chamber of Deputies passed a draft of the 2004 state budget with 98 votes of the coalition deputies. The budget is expected to have a deficit of CZK 115 billion, revenues of CZK 754 billion, and expenditures of CZK 869 billion. The state budget deficit continues to grow.

Development of the State Budget Deficit
(billion CZK)

Year	1996	1997	1998	1999	2000	2001	2002	2003	2004
Deficit	−5.4	−17.4	−25.6	−34.8	−51.8	−66.7	−45.9	−111.3	−115.1

Source: Minister of Finance, quoted in "The Cabinet Can Have a Breather, The Budget Passed." Právo, December 4, 2003, p. 1.

4. In addition to Social Democrats, it consisted of Communists and Republicans, parties that could be defined as lacking coalition potential, which weakened the influence of the opposition.

Bibliography

Czech Republic. 1997. *Human Development Report.* United Nations Development Programme (UNDP) Project. Prague: Research Institute for Labour and Social Affairs.

Czech Republic. 1999. *Human Development Report.* UNDP Project. Prague: Research Institute for Labour and Social Affairs.

Czech Republic. 2000. *Regular report from the Commission on the Czech Republic's progress towards accession,* November 8 COM (2002) 700 final.

Kabele, J., and L. Linek, 2004. *Decision-making of the Czech Cabinet, EU Accession and Legislative Planning between 1998 and 2004.* Paper prepared for the ECPR Joint Sessions of Workshops, Workshop No. 10: The Process of Decision-Making in Cabinets in Central-Eastern and Southern Europe. Uppsala, Sweden, April 13–18, 2004.

Kolář, Petr, Štěpán Pecháček, and Jindřiška Syllová. 2002. Parlament České republiky 1993–2001 (*Parliament of the Czech Republic 1993–2001*). Praha: Linde.

Mansfeldová, Zdenka. 1997. "Sociální partnerství v České republice (*Social Partnership in the Czech Republic*)." In Reprezentace zájmů v politickém systému České republiky (*Interest Representation in the Political System of the Czech Republic*), ed. L. Brokl, 99–150. Praha: SLON.

———. 2002. *Economic Policy-Making and Parliamentary Accountability in Czech Republic.* Geneva: United Nations Research Institute for Social Development. http://www.unrisd.org.

Ost, David. 1993. "The Politics of Interests in Post-Communist Eastern Europe." *Theory and Society* 22: 453–86.

Rakušanová, P. 2003. "Role of Central European Parliaments in the Process of European Integration." Paper presented at the 19th IPSA World Congress, Durban, South Africa, June 29–July 4, 2003, Research Committee of Legislative Specialists' panel Internationalization of Parliaments—Parliaments in the Process of Globalization.

Reytt, Tomáš, 2000. Role centrálních bank v demokratických systémech (The Role of Central Banks in Democratic Systems). *Politologická revue* 6 (2): 3–28.

Soltéz, I. 1995. *Controlling the Government by the Parliament.* In *Democratization and Europeanization in Hungary: The First Parliament (1990–1994),* ed. Attila Ágh and Sándor Kurtán, 43–64. Budapest: Hungarian Centre for Democracy Studies.

CHAPTER 21

Budget Accountability and Legislative Oversight in Transition: The Case of Post-Suharto Indonesia

Vishnu Juwono and Sebastian Eckardt

Since the downfall of President Suharto in the late 1990s, Indonesia has made remarkable progress in democratizing its political system. In the wake of these reforms the parliament has become more independent from the formerly very strong executive and has gained substantial powers to scrutinize and react to initiatives and policies proposed by the executive. Among others reforms, the parliament now holds stronger powers with regard to the preparation of the state budget and oversight of its execution.

These reforms have caused unprecedented changes in the way the state budget is formulated in Indonesia. Ideally, the governance of the budget reflects the delicate balance between executive power and legislative oversight. The realignment of democratic checks and balances in the budget process is a complex process intertwined with other aspects of the full political system: the establishment of representative structures, the electoral system, and the establishment of a functioning multiparty system. How these checks and balances work in practice depends on the effective powers of elected representatives in relation to the executive branch, including the power to appoint and remove executives (through votes of no confidence, impeachment, and so forth); the power to compel information from the executive branch (for example, require reports and audits); the power of the purse; a functioning committee system capable of knowledgeably monitoring and assessing executive branch behavior; and the incentive structure for elected representatives to fulfill their mandates.

This chapter examines the institutional framework and the evolving role of the parliament, particularly of the lower house (*Dewan Perwakilan Rakyat—* DPR) in the budget process in post-Suharto Indonesia. The focus is on exploring systemic issues and developing an understanding of how the institutional framework affects the general political dynamics and mechanics in the budget process and thereby shapes executive and legislative relationships in the budgetary realm.

Democratization and the Evolving Political Role of Indonesia's Parliament Post-Suharto

During the three decades of President Suharto's rule, political power was heavily concentrated in the executive. Constitutionally the People's Consultative Committee (*Majelis Permusyawaratan Rakyat*—MPR)[1] was the highest state institution in the country, responsible for nominating and appointing the president. In practice, however, the president effectively controlled MPR decision making through an intricate system, monopolizing political power in his hands.

Political activity and political parties were restricted—in 1973 Suharto forced the then nine opposition parties to amalgamate into two groups, the United Development Party (PPP) and the Indonesia Democratic Party (PDI)— and the Joint Secretariat of Functional Groups (Golkar) was given a central role in rallying popular support for the New Order in carefully staged national legislative elections.[2] The PPP and PDI were prohibited from organizing and mobilizing at the grass-roots level between election campaigns, and Golkar was the only organization with roots down to the village level, since government officials at the village level were all members of Golkar. Not surprisingly, Golkar dominated the electoral process throughout the New Order period.[3]

The effect of these arrangements was to concentrate political power within the presidency with strong support from Golkar, the bureaucracy, and the military, effectively blurring the separation of powers to favor executive control over state affairs. This also applied to budgetary decision making. De jure legislative budget powers were enshrined in Article 23 of the 1945 constitution, which stipulates, "In establishing state revenue and expenditure, the DPR shall have a stronger position than the government." However, the New Order's DPR never questioned or amended the government's budget proposals. President Suharto demanded that politicians and legislators comply with his so-called national consensus decisions.

The New Order system was unraveled in the particularly eventful and politically volatile environment triggered by Suharto's downfall in 1998. Changes in the political system marked Indonesia's rapid transition to a more democratic system (Schneier 2005, 4), among them several related to the budget process:

• In 1999, the first constitutional amendment gave the DPR "authority to enact Laws," introduced an annual session in the MPR, and established an ad hoc committee on constitutional amendments.

• In 2000, the MPR passed the second constitutional amendment, reinstating the role of the DPR in approving the budget, legislative oversight, and authority to legislate.

• In 2001, the third constitutional amendment formalized conditions to impeach the president and further strengthened the legislative authorities to perform checks and balances by having a right to choose, among others, general election commission (KPU), Supreme Audit Board (BPK), and Judicial Commission (KY) members.

- In 2002, a fourth constitutional amendment clarified technical provisions related to the separation of powers (between judicial, legislative, and executive branches); abolished military, police, and other executive appointees in the MPR; and stipulated a two-round system for the presidential election.

The constitutional amendments and subsequent legislation substantially augmented parliamentary powers in relation to the executive (Sherlock 2007a, 23) For example, the DPR can initiate the impeachment of the president (with the consent of the Constitutional Court and the MPR).[4] The DPR also has the sole authority to enact state legislation, including the annual state budget, which is promulgated as a law.[5]

In step with the strengthened horizontal accountability between the executive and legislature, vertical accountability of members of parliament to the electorate was also strengthened. Among the first laws passed by the newly empowered DPR were the three political laws on political parties, general elections, and the formation of the legislature. These laws moved the DPR from a highly controlled political arrangement with restricted access to electoral competition to an arrangement whereby public offices, including seats in the parliament, have become subject to increasing competition and contestability. This has led to sweeping changes in the composition of the legislature, breaking the previous one-party dominance by Golkar. However, with upward of 15 parties represented in the parliament (since 2004), the electoral outcomes have also resulted in a particularly fragmented political landscape. In both 1999 and 2004 none of the competing parties obtained a sufficient majority to be able to pass legislation on their own. The electoral outcomes have affected the political dynamics that shape legislative decision making and its relationship to the executive. The fact that none of the larger parties (see table 21.1) controls a sufficient majority to pass legislation[6] necessitates political maneuvering in order to build support for

Table 21.1. Top 10 Political Parties in the 1999 and 2004 General Elections

1999			2004		
Party	Votes (%)	Seats (%)	Party	Votes (%)	Seats (%)
PDI-P	33.74	33.12	Golkar	21.58	23.27
Golkar	22.44	25.97	PDI-P	18.53	19.82
PKB	12.61	11.04	PKB	10.57	9.45
PPP	10.71	12.55	PPP	8.15	10.55
PAN	7.12	7.36	PD	7.45	10.36
PBB	1.94	2.81	PKS	7.34	8.18
PK	1.36	1.52	PAN	6.44	9.45
PKP	1.01	0.87	PBB	2.62	2.00
PNU	0.64	1.08	PBR	2.44	2.36
PDI	0.62	0.43	PDS	2.13	2.18

Source: Ananta, Arifin, and Suryadinata 2005, 14, 22.

particular initiatives. In addition, most parties compete on religious, ideological, or personal, rather than policy platforms, making it difficult to form stable coalitions.[7]

The DPR continues to face structural and performance weaknesses that prevent it from fully exercising its democratic governance role, including weak internal capacity, limited effectiveness of institutions of political-interest mediation, and a volatile and fragmented party system. News reports and analysis frequently point out the low legislative performance of the DPR, including the quantity and the quality of legislation. In 2005, just 12 laws were passed, and only four were among the 55 expected new laws projected by the National Legislation Program (*Prolegnas*).[8] Besides poor performance, concerns about corruption, waste, and abuse represent another set of problems for the DPR in terms of its public relations and perceived legitimacy. This has resulted in broad public distrust in the parliament as an institution, as witnessed by the low ranking it received in the Global Corruption Barometer 2006 by Transparency International, where it shared the lowest rank with the police and the judiciary (it received a score of 4.2, with a score of 5 being extremely corrupt and 1 being not at all corrupt).[9]

Internal Organization of the DPR

As many observers and legislators confirm, the comparatively poor performance of the DPR is largely a result of its low level of institutional capacity. Structural weaknesses, management and human resource problems, and budget constraints are the major problems in this legislature, which for so long was not expected to function as an autonomous branch of government. Arguably, it will take some time until the DPR adjusts to its new role and becomes a modern and effective legislature ready to face the challenges of democratic government—to fulfill its constitutional functions, legislate efficiently, plan the state budget, and provide effective government oversight.

The internal organization of the DPR includes house leadership, an overlapping system of party factions, sectoral commissions, and cross-sectoral committees. All have some influence on the role of the DPR in the budget process and in oversight in general. The leadership of the DPR plays the role of spokesperson on behalf of the DPR and acts as a coordinator for various DPR meetings. However, the leadership's role is largely symbolic when the DPR interacts with other state institutions or with another country's institutions or officials. Internally, the leadership is critical within the current framework of legislative decision making. Unlike most parliaments, the DPR's decision making follows a complicated system of consensus building rather than majority votes (applied if there is a deadlock). DPR leadership and commission leadership play an important role in ensuring that consensus is reached.

Furthermore, to facilitate more streamlined decision making, parties are organized into factions. Factions are groups of DPR members based on the configuration of political parties' number of seat in the DPR, and every DPR member must be associated with one faction. Each faction is required to have at least 13 DPR members from the same political party.[10] Consequently, a party that has fewer than 13 members in the DPR has to join another party to form one faction that meets the threshold number of DPR members. The leader is determined through intraparty decision making or agreement between parties. A political party will channel its political initiatives through the faction governed by the DPR's rules of procedure. Each faction is proportionally represented within commissions, standing committees, special committees, and other DPR instruments of power. The DPR currently has 10 factions. The factions, rather than the parties, are typically the basis for representation in the DPR's sectoral commissions and cross-sectoral committees. Though the factions formally represent the key structure of party organization within the parliament, incentives for effective consensus building between parties remain weak.

The DPR is organized into a system of sectoral commissions that carry out scrutiny of respective ministries and executive agencies. Every member of the DPR must be a member of at least one commission. There are currently 11 commissions, which are aligned to the portfolio ministries in the executive. The commissions are the principal working units within the DPR that are used to discuss in detail and amend draft bills. According to one assessment (Sherlock 2003):

> The commission is powerful because: they have an ability to reject, delay or facilitate bills and determine their content; DPR can exercise both formal authority and practical power through this instrument over the President, Ministers and government agencies; it [is] also often used as an instrument to shape public opinions by having a potential to embarrass government officials through hearings; and by having a big influence to determine appointments of high state official positions can influence the actual execution of government policy. (12)

The leadership of each commission (one chair and three vice chairs) plays an influential role both within the commission and while representing the commission in other bodies in the DPR (Sherlock 2007, 16). The leadership can schedule meetings and hearings and determines the agenda. Furthermore, the leadership can decide the compositions of subcommission and the commission's representation in the Budget Commission. The commission leadership regularly meets with the leadership of the house and with the Consensus Committee on the introduction and scheduling of the new bills.

In addition, a number of cross-sectoral committees are designed to help streamline decision making and facilitate consensus building among DPR factions. Among the most powerful is the Consensus Committee (*Bamus*). The Consensus Committee has several functions: determining the agenda for each annual session (including prioritization of draft bills and the time frame for enactment); providing advice to the DPR leadership; and consulting and coordinating with other institutions (government, MPR, DPD) in the context of the constitution.[11] The Consensus Committee plays a critical role in the internal procedures of the DPR. According to Sherlock, (2007a) "The power of the committee comes from the fact that it is the gatekeeper for the entry of bills and requests for inquiries" (14). Moreover, during recess, the leadership, after consulting with the leadership of factions, can call the Consensus Committee to make organizational decisions on behalf of the DPR. Another cross-sectoral committee is the legislative body which was established to ensure that the DPR fulfills its legislative role.[12] Initially the legislation body was limited to dealing with the administrative process and technical aspects of legislation and less with the substantive aspects of bills. Following the 2001 revisions in the DPR's rules of procedure, its authority became broader and now encompasses the substance of bills. The body is also responsible for drafting the legislation plan, which outlines priority legislation for each year. The body therefore has a critical impact on the overall legislative agenda.[13]

Finally, there is the Budget Commission, which is a key player in the budgetary decision-making process. The committee works on the budget with its counterpart in the government—usually coordinating with the coordinating minister for economic affairs, the minister of finance, and the minister of national development planning. In 2005–06 the Budget Commission consisted of 83 members who represented about 10 parties and 28 regional constituencies. Members are drawn from all of the other sectoral commissions. The leadership of the Budget Commission consists of one chair and three deputy chairs chosen from and by the commission members during a meeting led by the DPR leadership. The specific role of the Budget Commission is discussed in more detail below.

Parliament and the Budget Process

The institution of appropriate checks and balances, particularly with regard to budgetary decisions, are important pillars of sound governance systems. As discussed above, the process of rapid democratic transition restored parliament's substantial powers in what was previously a closed budgetary system. Since then the evolving nature of interventions by the DPR has been a striking feature of the budgetary process. The constitution and subsequent legislation established a strong parliamentary role in the budget process. As is typical for presidential systems, the DPR enjoys broad scope to revise the budget, make its own revenue and spending decisions, and monitor and discipline the discretionary power of the executive.

Some observers and large parts of public opinion in Indonesia share the view that the extension of legislative powers may have gone too far, in particular because, unlike other presidential systems, the Indonesian presidency does not have a formal veto power over legislation passed by the parliament. Indeed, once approved by the DPR and submitted to the president, bills have to be signed by the president within 30 days or they automatically become laws.[14] However, although there is no formal veto power on the part of the executive, the constitution requires that "each bill [be] discussed by the DPR and the President to reach joint agreement." Therefore, the authority to enact legislation, including the annual budget law, is shared between parliament and the president (Sherlock 2007a).

The Regulatory Framework

The institutional framework of the budget process, including the role, responsibilities, and authorities of the DPR, are set out in Law 17/2003 on state finances. The legislative powers pertain to ex ante deliberation, approval of the executive budget proposal, and ex post oversight of the budget's implementation. With regard to the budget preparation process, the DPR is involved in three stages. First, in May the executive submits the government work plan (RKP) and fiscal framework to the parliament. The deliberation and adoption of these documents results in reaching agreement on fiscal priorities and the macroeconomic framework underlying the budget. They are the basis for the setting of the indicative budget ceilings for programs and ministries by the directorate general of the budget, which are used in drafting the annual ministerial work plans and budgets.[15]

Second, during June and August, preliminary discussions of the annual work plans of ministries and agencies take place directly between sectoral parliamentary commissions and their corresponding spending ministries.[16] This provision of the law has resulted in an increase in the number and length of parliamentary hearings and interventions.

Finally, in August the government formally submits the draft budget law to parliament for debate (Law 17/2003 on state finances, Art.15). The president presents the state budget bill to the plenary session, and then deliberations of the detailed ministerial work plans and budgets (submitted to DPR as an annex to the draft state budget bill) take place at the commission level. The leadership of the Budget Commission reports to the DPR plenary session on the results of the first round of deliberations. The factions then deliver their final opinion, and the budget bill is enacted by October (or at the least two months before the budget year starts) to leave sufficient time for the executive to prepare budget implementation documents.

Once the budget is passed, the DPR has the right and responsibility to engage in oversight with regard to both financial compliance and achievement of results. The DPR has a number of means at its disposal to engage in ex post oversight. Perhaps most important, the DPR Budget Commission oversees and approves the midyear budget revision. In addition, Law 17/2003 on state finances requires the president to deliver an annual accountability report outlining the achievements and performance of the government, and sectoral commissions have the right to summon portfolio ministries to report on progress in implementing programs. The Supreme Audit Board's audit report is also submitted to the DPR for parliamentary review. So far, however, the DPR seems to invest primarily in budget formulation, paying much less attention to ex post oversight. Despite the disclaimer issued by the supreme auditor for five consecutive years on the executive's financial reports, little follow-up has taken place from the parliament's side. As such, the role of the parliament as the institution with public responsibility for financial oversight has not yet been effectively established.

Figure 21.1. Responsibilities in the Public Expenditure Management Cycle

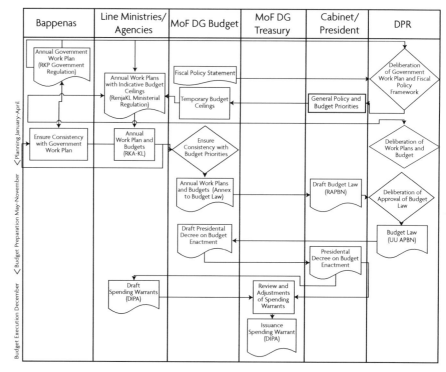

Sources: Public Expenditure Review 2007, National Development Agency (Bappenas), World Bank staff. Government Regulation Number 21 on Budget Submission Documents (RKA-KL).

Box 21.1. The Role of the House of Regional Representatives (DPD) in the Budget Process

In 2004 Indonesia established the Dewan Perwakilan Daerah (DPD)—Indonesia's House of Regional Representatives (upper house). The function of the DPD is to represent regional aspirations in the national political process. Its members are directly elected with four representatives for each province. While the powers of the DPD are limited, the constitution mandates the DPD with the authority to:

1. Propose bills to the DPR related to regional autonomy; central and regional relations; formation, enlargement, and merger of regions; management of natural resources and other economic resources; and bills related to the financial balance between the centre and the regions.
2. Participate in the discussion of bills related to the matters in paragraph 1 above, as well as provide advice to the DPR on bills on the state budget and bills related to taxation, education, and religion.

(continued)

Box 21.1. (*continued*)

3. Oversee the implementation of laws related to the matters in paragraphs 1 and 2 above, as well as submit the results of such oversight to the DPR in the form of material for its further consideration.[17]

With regard to the budget process, the powers of the DPD are limited to an advisory role. The DPR has the sole responsibility for passing the budget bill and for overseeing the implementation of it by government. The DPD has the authority only to render advice to the DPR on the state budget bills, in particular on matters that affect regions, such as the allocation of intergovernmental transfers. Moreover the DPR does not have a constitutional obligation to act on issues raised by the DPD. Similarly, the DPD has the authority to oversee budget implementation, but it is up to the DPR to take action on the results of DPD investigations.

The DPD has nevertheless shown a desire to play a strong role in the budget process and has sought outside assistance to build its capacity to do so effectively.[18] For example, the Budget Commission (Commission IV) of the DPD scrutinized the government's 2007 budget proposals, held a series of public hearings in western, central, and eastern Indonesia, and prepared a written report for the Ministry of Finance (MoF). The report, which contained 32 recommendations, was launched in a special public event well covered by over 40 representatives of the national media. In a separate address to the DPD, the president of Indonesia[19] acknowledged five recommendations by the report.

The main recommendations of the Budget Commission's report were about macroeconomic policy direction, fiscal policy (in particular, fiscal equalization between the center and the regions), budget priorities, problems regarding the budget implementation, and intergovernmental relations between central and regional government. In preparing the report, the commission used data and information from the public hearings, the Department of Finance, the State Planning Agency (Badan Perencanaan Pembanguan), regional governments, and leading nongovernmental organizations and think tanks. In addition, the final (published) version of the report was the result of a participatory process designed to involve the entire DPD. Two earlier drafts were debated at a ad-hoc commission (PAH) IV meeting and received input from all 32 members. Once approved, the final draft was circulated to all 128 members of the DPD, who were given five working days to review it and request modifications before it was debated in the plenary and approved unanimously (Datta, Handayani, and Sirait 2006).

Ellis (2007) noted that "the acceptance of DPD recommendations ... as well as the role given to oversight in the 2006 DPD strategic plan, suggest that the DPD will be able to establish a real, if limited, role for itself."

The Evolving Nature of Legislative Engagement—Some Preliminary Observations

The scrutiny and approval of the draft annual budget by parliament are essential features of the budget approval and implementation process in any well-functioning democracy. Since the first free elections were held in Indonesia in 1999, executive-legislative relations are still evolving, and both branches of government need to adjust to the new institutional environment. While the transition is arguably far from complete, a number of interrelated features stand out in the way this relationship is shaped by the political setting and institutional context.

First, under the current framework the legislative amendment powers are virtually unlimited.[20] Law 17/2003 provides that "the DPR may table amendments regarding the amount of the receipts and spending specified in the budget bill" (Article 15). The parliament has made use of this authority, and has repeatedly increased the revenue projections proposed by the executive in order to boost annual spending. For example, during deliberation of the assumptions underlying the draft 2007 budget, the aggregate *indicative* spending ceiling of Rp 230 trillion was revised up by parliament to Rp 256 trillion. Further upward revisions were made to spending after the draft state budget (ABPN) was submitted to parliament in mid-August 2006. In the current fiscal environment with buoyant revenues, this has not compromised the executive focus on fiscal consolidation and debt reduction. However, unlimited amendment rights do entail the risk of rising deficits in particular should fiscal conditions tighten.[21] In a more restrictive budgetary environment, parliamentarians may choose to raise the deficit to avoid spending cuts. Many countries have chosen to impose fiscal rules that are binding for both the executive and legislature, to curtail such risks. In Indonesia, safeguards are included in Law 17/2003, Article 12, along with subsequent implementing regulations that set the maximum deficit at 3 percent GDP (gross domestic product) and set maximum cumulative debt at 60 percent of GDP.

Second, the current budget deliberation process, and the resulting appropriations structure embodied in the budget law and annexes, allow for legislative involvement at a rather detailed level. The practice of submitting full ministerial work plans and budgets to the DPR for deliberation is one of the reasons for this focus on details. Article 15 of Law 17/2003 on state finances stipulates that budget appropriations of the DPR are to be classified by organizational units, functions, programs, activities, and types of expenditure. There are currently about 130 programs, with 19,945 spending units (*satker*) detailed by location, each of which has a detailed line item budget. Reportedly the DPR can, and routinely does, change the specific line items in expenditure appropriations proposed in the executive budget proposals.

This detailed appropriations approach is not atypical in presidential systems. John Huber and Charles Shipan (2002) noted that the more pronounced separation of powers and resulting policy conflicts between the legislature and the executive in presidential systems create incentives for a detailed rather than a flexible approach to legislation in general, and to budget appropriations in particular. In addition, the detailed legislative involvement creates opportunities for members of parliament to follow political inclinations to use budget decisions to serve their constituencies (which may be defined by geographic regions or by other shared interests), for example, through targeted spending in certain regions.[22] Individual members have also allegedly misused their authority over detailed spending items, to extract rents (see box 21.2).

These detailed deliberations not only consume considerable time and resources on the part of both the executive and the legislature, but they also presumably impair the quality of legislative engagement. Although the parliament as an institution has a strong interest in ensuring that overall spending priorities are reflected in the budget and that fiscal stability is maintained, the attention of individual members to detailed line items may distract from the focus on those more aggregate variables in the budget. Changing the current appropriation structure is politically challenging, given the enshrined vested interests in the current approach. Indonesia is pursuing an ambitious program

---

Box 21.2. Budget for Sale: The Role of Budget Brokers

Allegedly, the legislative involvement in the budget process, while designed to ensure representation of broad societal interests, has been partly captured by vested interests. Reports by the highly respected news magazine *Tempo* uncovered practices of budget "brokering" in the DPR. Brokers typically are staff or close associates working for DPR or even the DPR member himself or herself that help to seal specific deals when it comes to budget approvals by the DPR Budget Commission. They usually receive a commission based on the contract value.

For example, one case in budget year 2005 shows that budget requests by regional government for the postdisaster rehabilitation and reconstruction program under the Department of Housing and Regional Infrastructure, which were funded under supplemental finance, were more likely to be approved if there was a budget broker involved. According to *Tempo* investigations, the "fee" to get a proposal approved in the DPR is about 4 percent of the project's total value. Those whose budget exceeds the original amount that was requested are charged an even higher commission. The supplemental budget is particularly prone to such corrupt activities, since regional governments can award contracts without competitive bidding processes. Potential project contractors in collusion with regional governments are loyal "customers" of budget brokers. However, the practice does not seem to be limited to supplemental finance. Other reports describe similar practices in the DPR authorization of intergovernmental transfers, including most prominently the special allocation funds (DAK), which are largely allocated by a rather discretionary process involving the DPR Budget Commission. According to *Tempo* reports, budget approvals for specific DAK grants are brokered at a 15 percent fee.

Sources: Tempo (2005a, 2005b).

to modernize its public financial management system to underpin more transparent, accountable, and efficient resource allocation decision-making processes and sustainable fiscal policies. These reforms include a move toward results-based budgeting and the institution of a medium-term perspective in fiscal policies. In introducing a performance-oriented budget system, a first essential step is to simplify the budget appropriation structure. In other countries, this has usually been done by introducing to parliament a budget in which there are only a few budget programs (or outputs) per ministry. Politically, this would require the DPR to agree to such changes, trading off detailed controls against potential strengthened results and accountability on the part of the executive.

Third, the internal deliberation and approval process in the parliament is not sufficiently centralized. Jürgen von Hagen (2005) emphasized the importance of centralization of budgetary decisions within legislatures to ensure a disciplined approach to budget deliberations. For example, the U.S. Budget Enforcement Act passed in the 1990s reformed congressional procedures to enforce discipline in congressional budget approval. In Indonesia, some observers have remarked that internal parliamentary procedures are still evolving. For example, Sherlock (2003) observed that the large number of members on each commission (averaging more than 60), the failure of commissions to reach quorums because of nonattendance, multiple agendas for members, unfocused commission meetings, difficulties in reaching decisions, and the poor quality of discussion, debate, and questioning in commissions all contribute to a rather ineffective legislative process.

With regard to the deliberation of the budget, the Budget Commission is the key committee. The Budget Commission's main role is to coordinate the review and approval of draft budgets and budget accountability reports. It is the main counterpart of the Ministry of Finance and plays a key role in advising the plenary session on the overall budget package. However, budget requests for each ministry currently must be approved by the sectoral commission responsible for oversight of that ministry, and sectoral commissions do not always complete their examinations of detailed budgets prior to the end-October adoption by the DPR of the overall budget. In this case, the respective parts of the budget are blocked, and the budget cannot be implemented—that is, spending cannot take place—until the relevant parliamentary commission approves it. For example, for the 2007 budget, the commission responsible for agriculture had not approved the detailed budget for the Ministry of Agriculture by mid-February 2007.

Moreover, the fragmentation of the party system and feeble party discipline impose only weak incentives on individual members to comply with collective interests. With 24 political parties represented in the DPR (in 2007) and with several factions represented on parliament's 11 commissions, reaching binding consensus is often difficult. Indeed, the fragmented membership and competing interests represented in the DPR, combined with the detailed approach to appropriations, has made it difficult for the DPR to come to a consistent position in its deliberation with the executive.

Given its substantial responsibility and the complexity of the issues at stake, the parliament needs to build adequate capacity to enable informed judgment and decision making. Some countries have institutionalized a non-partisan budget office to provide impartial assistance to the parliament in preparing budget scenarios.[23] Although the Budget Commission has recruited several technical staff to assist in its analytical work, when it is compared with some other countries with presidential systems of government, the technical support to the DPR is still rather limited.

Conclusion

The political reforms that followed President Suharto's downfall in 1998 triggered grand constitutional changes in the way the Indonesian state operates and is held accountable. As in all modern democracies, representative government structures were established (1) to provide institutional channels for aggregating the preferences of individuals and groups in a society and (2) to ensure that these preferences are reflected in policy decisions. This has entailed the institutionalization of the legislative power of the purse, which arguably is one of the key features of any modern democratic system.

The realignment of democratic checks and balances in the budgetary process is a complex process that is directly affected by the broader constitutional design and political system. Typical for presidential systems, the DPR enjoys broad scope to revise the budget and make its own revenue and spending decisions and to monitor and discipline the discretionary power of the executive. Arguably, the extension of legislative powers is not without potential for conflict, in particular because, unlike other presidential systems, the Indonesian presidency does not have a formal veto power over legislation, including the budget bill, passed by the parliament to countercheck legislative powers. Though this has in the past years not resulted in major policy conflicts over the budget, neither the executive nor the legislature seems to be fully satisfied with executive-legislative interactions in the budgetary realm.

The excessively detailed legislative involvement in the current budget preparation process, and the resulting appropriations structure embodied in the budget law and annexes, has profoundly affected the quality of legislative interventions. These detailed deliberations not only consume considerable time and resources on the part of both the executive and legislative, but the attention of individual members to detailed line items may distract from the focus on more aggregate spending priorities in the budget. Changing the current appropriations structure is politically challenging and would require the DPR to agree to such changes, trading off detailed control against strengthened results and accountability on the part of the executive.

Second, internal deliberation seems insufficiently centralized. A review is under way by the DPR examining its own internal operating arrangements for budget review, decision-making, and approval. Operating procedures should aim to ensure that all parliamentary commissions, including sectoral commissions, have focused, informed, and timely discussions relating to the annual budget law.

Finally, the DPR needs to develop its capacity to meaningfully review and approve executive proposals. Although the Budget Commission has recruited a few technical staff members to assist in its analytical work, technical support to the DPR is still limited. Going forward, the DPR may wish to consider the establishment of an independent parliamentary budget office.

Annex: DPR Sectoral Commissions and Their Government Working Counterparts

Commission	Subject	Government department and/or state/government agencies
I	Defense, international affairs, information	Ministry of Foreign Affairs, Ministry of Defense, Ministry of Communication and Information, National Defense Institute, National Intelligence Agency
II	Home affairs, regional autonomy, state apparatus, land issues	Ministry of Home Affairs, State Ministry of Administrative Reform, National Land Agency, State Secretary, Cabinet Secretary, National Civil Service Agency
III	Laws and regulations, human rights, security	Ministry of Laws and Human Rights, Attorney General, National Police, Corruption Eradication Commission, Judicial Commission
IV	Agriculture, forestry, fisheries, sea foods	Ministry of Agriculture, Ministry of Forestry, Ministry of Sea and Fisheries, Logistic Affairs Agency, National Maritime Agency
V	Transportation, telecommunication, public works, people housing, rural development, underdeveloped regions	Ministry of Public Works, Ministry of Transportation, Ministry of People Housing, State Ministry of Less-Developed Region
VI	Industry, trade, cooperatives/small and medium enterprise, state-owned enterprise, investment, national standardization	Ministry of Industry, Ministry of Trade, State Ministry of Cooperatives and Small and Medium Enterprises, State Ministry of State-Owned Enterprise, Investment Coordinator Body
VII	Energy, mining, research and technology, environment	Ministry of Energy, Natural Resource and Mineral, State Ministry of Research and Technology, State Ministry of Environment
VIII	Religion, social issues, women's empowerment	Ministry of Religion, Ministry of Social Affairs, State Ministry of Women Empowerment
IX	Demography, health, labor, transmigration	Ministry of Health, Ministry of Labor and Transmigration
X	Education, youth, sport, tourism, art and culture	Ministry of Education, State Ministry of Youth and Sport, State Ministry of Culture and Tourism
XI	Finance, national planning, nonbanking financial institution	Ministry of Finance, State Ministry of National Development Planning, Central Bank of Indonesia

Source: Center for Law and Policy Study (PSHK)'s Web site on Indonesia Parliament (http://www.Parlemenen.net) and DPR official Web site (http://www.dpr.go.id).

Notes

The authors work as governance adviser and public financial management specialist, respectively, at the World Bank Jakarta. The views expressed in this paper are those of the authors only and should not be attributed to the World Bank. The authors would like to thank Soekarno Wirokartono, Frank Feulner, Stephen Sherlock, Rick Stapenhurst, and Lisa von Trapp for comments on earlier versions of this chapter.

1. During Suharto's reign (1968–98), the MPR also established the broad outlines of state policy (GBHN) meant to be the general principles to guide activities of all state organs, including the DPR (lower house), in the succeeding period. The MPR was composed of DPR members, regional and civil society group representatives, and active military officers.

2. Designed to bring diverse social groups into a harmonious organization based on "consensus," by 1969 Golkar had a membership of some 270 associations representing civil servants, workers, students, women, intellectuals, and other groups.

3. In the general elections of 1971, 1977, and 1982, Golkar won 62.8, 62.1, and 64.3 percent of the popular vote, respectively (King 2003).

4. Formally, there must be proof of legal misconduct on the part of the president for an impeachment to be legitimate. If the Constitutional Court rules that this is the case, the DPR may submit the motion to the MPR (consisting of 128 DPD (upper house) members and 550 DPR members), and two-thirds of the MPR must approved the initiative (Sherlock 2007a, 7) In practice, the only time a president was impeached was in 2001, when political differences with the DPR eventually forced President Wahid out of office. At that time the impeachment rights were less restricted than under the more recent third constitutional amendment.

5. It is important to note that the constitutional amendments of the late 1990s followed the state architecture of the pre-Suharto period and initially instituted a parliamentary system whereby the president and vice president were chosen in indirect elections by the parliament. This only changed with the revision of the regulatory framework, namely by Law 31/2002 on political parties, Law 12/2003 on general elections, and Law 22/2003, which stipulated direct elections for the presidency. The first direct presidential elections were held in 2004.

6. An early indication of the importance of politicking was the presidential election in the MPR Although the PDI-P party controlled one-third of the parliamentary seats, it did not succeed in the elections for the presidency. Megawati Sukarnoputri lost in the presidential election in MPR against Abdurrahman Wahid (Gus Dur) from the PKB party, who brilliantly maneuvered to obtain support from the so-called middle axis grouping.

7. It should be noted that the Indonesian party system has been delineated along broad ideological demarcations of Islamic and nationalistic parties.

8. The National Legislation Program consists of a list of priority legislation for the DPR.

9. The Global Corruption Barometer 1996 by Transparency International reflects the findings of a survey of 59,661 people in 62 low-, middle-, and high-income countries. To see the full report go to Transparency International. http://www.transparency.org/policy_research/surveys_indices/gcb/2006.

10. From the DPR's official Web site, "Fraksi/Faction" by Division of Public Information. http://www.dpr.go.id.

11. Pasaribu, Reny Rawasita. *DPR's Instruments of Power*. In Center for Law and Policy Study (PSHK), on Indonesia parliamentary Web site at http://www.parlemen.net.

12. There is a restriction that members of the legislative body cannot come from leadership of commissions or members of the domestic affairs committee or the Inter-Parliamentary Cooperation Committee.

13. Article 16 in Law 10/2004 on crafting laws and regulations.

14. DPR Standing Orders, Chapter 17, Art. 123, on the enactment of law.

15. Law 17/2003 on State Finances (Art. 13); Law 25/2004 on the National Development Planning System (Art. 25) and Law 17/2003 on State Finances (Art. 12) on state finance stipulate that budget formulation should be based on the government's work plan.

16. Law 17/2003 on state finances, Art. 14.

17. Art. 22D, of the 1945 constitution of the Republic of Indonesia (author's translation). Passage taken from Sherlock (2005).

18. International Institute for Democracy and Electoral Assistance (IDEA), the World Bank Institute, and the Australian Senate are among some of those supporting capacity building of the DPD.

19. Another sign that the DPD may be gaining influence in this area, the *Jakarta Post* reported that "Wednesday's session settles an argument between DPD and the House. The DPD had wanted a separate session to hear the President's annual budget speech … the House wanted to hold a joint session." "SBY [Susilo Bambang Yudhuyono] Speech to Highlight Regions." *Jakarta Post*, August 23, 2006.

20. Again, this is a typical feature of presidential systems. For example, the U.S. Congress has unrestricted budget amendment powers. However, under the 1974 Congressional Budget Act, a budget resolution, laying out fiscal aggregates expected to be respected, is adopted by congressional budget committees prior to adoption of the annual federal Appropriation Acts by Congress.

21. For example, for the 2006 budget, the Budget Commission worked on an assumption of a *central* government deficit target of a maximum of 1.2 percent of GDP.

22. Pork-barrel spending by representatives of geographically divided constituencies has been treated widely for the U.S. case, both theoretically as well as empirically. Weingast, Shepsle, and Johnson (1981) provide a comprehensive treatise and show that individual members have an interest in spending programs with regionally targeted benefits that are nationally funded.

23. For example, in the United States, the Congressional Budget Office (CBO) assists the Congress, especially the House and Senate Budget Committees, by preparing reports and analyses. In accordance with the CBO's mandate to provide objective and impartial analysis, the CBO's reports contain no policy recommendations.

Bibliography

Ananta, Aris, Evi Nurfidya Arifin, and Leo Suryadinata. 2005. *Emerging Democracy in Indonesia*. Singapore: Institute for Southeast Asian Studies (ISEAS).

Datta, Indraneel, Aprilliana Handayani, and Ningrum Sirait. 2006. "Design and Launch of Indonesia's DPD RI's Recommendations Report on the 2007 State Budget." Washington, DC: World Bank Institute.

Ellis, Andrew. 2007. "Indonesia's Constitutional Change Revisited." In *Indonesia: Democracy and the Promise of Good Governance*, ed. Ross H. McLeod and Andrew MacIntyre. Singapore: ISEAS.

Huber, John, and Charles Shipan. 2002. *Deliberative Discretion: The Institutional Foundations of Bureaucratic Autonomy*. Cambridge, UK: Cambridge University Press.

IFES (International Foundation for Electoral Systems). 2003. *Some Questions About the Electoral System for the 2004 Indonesian General Elections Answered*. Jakarta: IFES.

King, Dwight Y. 2003. *Half Hearted Reform—Electoral Institutions and the Struggle for Democracy in Indonesia*. Westport, CT and London: Praeger.

Schneier, Edward. 2005. *The Role of Constitution-Building Process in Democratization: Case Study Indonesia*. Stockholm: International IDEA (Institute for Democracy and Electoral Assistance).

Sherlock, Stephen. 2003. *Struggling to Change: The Indonesian Parliament in an Era of Reformasi: A Report in the Structure and Operation of Dewan Perwakilan Rakyat (DPR)*. Canberra: Center for Democratic Institutions.

———. 2005. "The Role and Future of the Indonesian House of Regional Representatives (DPD): The Experience of Other Second Chambers." Report prepared for the World Bank Institute, Washington, DC.

———. 2007a. *The Indonesia Parliament after Two Elections: What Has Really Changed?* Canberra: Center for Democratic Institutions.

———. 2007b. "Parliamentary Indicators Indonesia: DPR (House of Representatives) and DPD (House of Regional Representatives)." Report prepared for the World Bank Institute, Washington, DC.

Tempo. 2005a. "Budget Brokers Uncovered in Senayan." (English ed.) 03/VI/September 20–26.

Tempo. 2005b. "The House's Mercenary Middlemen." (English ed.) 02/VI/September 13–19.

von Hagen, Jürgen. 2005. "Budgeting Institutions and Public Spending," In *Fiscal Management*. ed. A. A. Shah. Washington, DC: World Bank.

Weingast, Barry R., Kenneth A. Shepsle, and Christopher Johnson. 1981. "The Political Economy of Benefits and Costs: A Neo-Classical Approach to Distributive Politics." *Journal of Political Economy* 89 (41).

CHAPTER 22

Establishment of Uganda's Parliamentary Budget Office and the Parliamentary Budget Committee

Hon. Beatrice Birungi Kiraso

Uganda's Parliamentary Budget Office (PBO) was established by an act of Parliament on February 27, 2001. It came into effect on July 1, 2001, when the president assented to the bill. The objective of the act was to "Provide for and Regulate the Budgetary Processes for Systematic and Efficient Budgetary Processes and other Matters Connected therewith.

The bill was moved as a private member's bill initiated by the chairpersons of the then Committee on Finance, Planning and Economic Development and the Committee on National Economy, Beatrice Kiraso and Isaac Musumba, respectively. The bill was scrutinized and amended by the Committee on Finance, Planning and Economic Development so that it clearly proscribed responsibilities and deadlines for the various stakeholders' participation in the budget making and execution process.

Prior to the enactment of the Budget Act, Parliament did not play an active role in the budget formulation process; however, Parliament would approve the budget as required by Articles 155 and 156 of the 1995 Constitution of the Republic of Uganda.

It was through participation in parliamentary capacity-building seminars and conferences that the chairs began to see the need for Parliament to play a more active role in the entire budget process. It became apparent that Parliament was a mere "rubber stamp" and that information provided to Parliament on budget-related matters was inadequate. Parliamentarians were kept ignorant on issues such as local resource revenue, foreign inflows in the form of budget support or project financing, national expenditure priority areas, and macroeconomic statistics.

Parliamentarians agreed in principle that as the people's representatives, if they were to be more accountable and effective in their oversight role, the budget was one of the most important tools through which they could exert influence on the economic and social development policies of the country. The executive branch, on the other hand, was resistant to increasing parliamentary participation and to providing more and better information. For this reason, the bill faced strong opposition.

Whereas bills typically take an average of three weeks between the first and second reading, the Budget Bill took about eight months from the time it was first introduced to the time it was passed. Article 93 of the Uganda constitution dictates that Parliament shall not introduce a motion (including an amendment) that would impose a charge on the Consolidated Fund. The Budget Office and Budget Committee that were included in the Budget Bill required extra funding and therefore imposed a charge on the Consolidated Fund. The government used this as a convenient excuse to reject the bill. After several months of negotiation between government (led by the Ministry of Finance) and Parliament (led by the two committee chairs), the government agreed to reintroduce the bill as a government bill. However, this failed to materialize, as the government was clearly not in favor of Parliament scrutinizing the budget. Parliament's demands to increase budget scrutiny were described as interference in the work of the executive and as an abuse of the separation of powers provided for in the constitution.

Following about two months of lobbying other members and sensitizing them to the need for Parliament to increase scrutiny of the budget, consensus grew among members of Parliament (MPs), and it was agreed that, Article 93 of the constitution notwithstanding, the private member's bill should be reintroduced and that, whether government was agreeable or not, Parliament would pass it. After all, the constitution clearly states that if, for one reason or another the president refuses to assent to a bill but Parliament by majority decides, it shall automatically become law.

The bill was reintroduced by Hon. Isaac Musumba, chair of the Committee on National Economy, and committed to the Committee of Finance, Planning and Economic Development chaired by Hon. Beatrice Kiraso. The two committees worked together to finalize the bill, which was allowed by the Speaker to be read for the second time and then passed by overwhelming majority in February 2001.

The Structure of the Parliament of Uganda and the New Budget Committee

Until September 2005 when the Ugandan constitution was amended to open up to political pluralism, Uganda was governed under a "movement" system, whereby leaders were elected on individual merit. Therefore there was no government or opposition side in Parliament, and there was no majority or minority. It was easier for MPs to support a position favorable to Parliament against the executive if it benefited or strengthened Parliament as an institution. Government was in a weaker position to whip members to its side. As with most Parliaments around the world, the Ugandan Parliament elected from among its members a Speaker and Deputy Speaker; they too are nonpartisan. It is presumed, therefore, that the Speaker and Deputy Speaker are also elected on merit in terms of their qualifications, competence, and ability to serve the interests of Parliament.

Although there were a few individuals in Parliament who considered themselves as opposition—largely because they preferred a multiparty system to the movement system—the majority of Parliament acted in a nonpartisan, independent, and objective manner. This scenario allowed Parliament to look objectively at the need to have a Budget Act and to hold government more accountable to Parliament as far as budget preparation and execution were concerned.

In addition, as with most parliaments, for efficient discharge of its functions, Parliament operates through committees. These committees, which draft reports for debate and adoption by the whole House, do most of the detailed work. The Rules of Procedure of the Parliament of Uganda provide for standing committees, which deal with cross-cutting issues (for example, Public Accounts, Rules and Privileges of Parliament, Approval of Presidential Appointments); sessional committees, which oversee the various ministries and sectors of government; and ad hoc or select committees. Standing committees' membership lasts for the life of that Parliament, that is, five years; sessional committees are constituted in every session, which is one year. It is these sessional committees under the Budget Act that scrutinize individual ministries' budgets and report to the Budget Committee. (MPs cannot belong to more than one standing committee or more than one sessional committee, but they can serve on one of each at the same time.)

The Budget Act provides for a Budget Committee, which is a standing committee. What distinguishes it from other committees is that, whereas other committees are created by the Rules of Procedure, the Budget Committee is created by an act of Parliament. Another important aspect of the Budget Committee is that all chairs of other committees (standing and sessional) are ex officio members of the Budget Committee. This makes it easier for committee members to receive reports from other committees on budget-related matters. Ex officio membership also gives the Budget Committee a broader and more comprehensive picture of the national budget as well as government programs and activities being carried out in the various sectors. The major functions carried out by the Budget Committee are prescribed in the Budget Act, Section 19(1)–(2).

The Parliamentary Budget Office

Sections 20 and 21 of the Budget Act set up the Parliamentary Budget Office (PBO). The office is headed by a director and comprises economists with expertise in macroeconomics, data analysis, fiscal policy, and tax policy. The initial structure provided for 11 posts, but because of the high demand for the services of the PBO, it has been enlarged to provide for more than 20 experts. With the new political system, it is expected that the demand on the Budget Office will increase, and there will be a need to fill any posts left vacant as a result of budget constraints. The structure of the PBO is attached as annex 1.

Government's resistance to the Budget Act and the resulting Budget
Office and Budget Committee continued even after the law was passed. By
this time Parliament had also passed the Administration of Parliament Act,
which allowed it to manage its own budget, with the Ministry of Finance
releasing funds required by Parliament based on approved activities. However, the excuse of budget constraints affected the immediate setting up and
running of the PBO. After the 2001 general elections, the 7th Parliament
came into being; Hon. Kiraso, who had initiated the Budget Bill during the
6th Parliament was elected the first chair of the Budget Committee. The urgent need to carry out their work became very apparent. The chair sought
assistance from U.S. Agency for International Development (USAID), which
at that time had an ongoing capacity-building program for the Parliament.
The special request for assistance in setting up the PBO was also shared with
other donor agencies. USAID, the U.K. Department for International Development (DFID), the German Agency for Technical Cooperation (GTZ), the
European Union (EU), the World Bank, and the North American Aerospace
Defense Command (NORAD) all contributed assistance in form of furniture,
computers and software, filing cabinets, and other office equipment, as well
as the initial allowances for the officers. Within one year the Parliamentary
Commission was in a position to advertise posts and embark on recruitment
of the PBO officers.

Later, the Parliamentary Commission insisted that any support to any
department or section of the parliamentary service should be channeled to
the common basket, and that the budget officers would be accommodated
in the existing employment structure. Therefore they could not benefit from
additional funding outside the Parliament's budget. Because of the heavy
workload, some officers refused to accept the salary Parliament was offering
and opted to leave. All in all, however, the PBO attracted high-caliber personnel from other organizations and later could afford to take on fresh graduates
and train them. Organizations from which the initial personnel were attracted
included the Ministry of Finance (Budget Department), Uganda Revenue
Authority, the Central Bank, and the Uganda Bureau of Statistics.

The PBO has been (and continues to be) nonpartisan, objective, and highly
committed to its functions provided for under Section 21 of the Budget Act.
The level of interaction with the parliamentary committees, the quality of
the analysis of information, and the periodic (normally quarterly) budget performance reports have become better each year. Among the regular analysis
that the PBO carries out are local revenue, foreign inflows, expenditure, and
economic indicators, as described below.

Local Revenue

The Uganda Revenue Authority is required to submit monthly performance
reports to the Budget Committee and the Budget Office. The Budget Office
analyzes this information and reports on it to the Budget Committee. The
reports identify whether the revenue collections are on target, if the targets

were correct or could have been better made, if there are shortfalls or overperformance, and possible reasons for shortfalls.

If the Budget Committee finds that there is something critical that requires further analysis, it notifies the sessional Committee on Finance, Planning and Economic Development, which oversees the Ministry of Finance, under which the Uganda Revenue Authority falls. The Budget Office's tax policy expert will then work together with the sessional committee to prepare a report and recommendations for the whole house.

The PBO has proposed to Parliament different ways in which the tax base could be widened, for example, introduction of property tax, which the Uganda Revenue Authority has attempted to implement since the 2004/05 budget. The PBO has also identified possible areas where reduction in taxes could trigger increased consumption and therefore more revenue. It has also proposed tax education methods to enhance tax administration.

Foreign Inflows

Section 13 of the Budget Act requires the president to present information on the total indebtedness of the state to Parliament during the presentation of the annual budget.

The Budget Office, on behalf of Parliament, scrutinizes these presentations and reports to the Budget Committee, pointing out issues that require the attention and discussion of Parliament. Article 159(1) of the constitution allows government to borrow from any source, but Article 159(2) gives the authority to approve any loan or guarantee to Parliament. Until recently, up to about 50 percent of the national budget was externally funded, although the percentage has been reduced to about 42 percent in the 2004/05 financial year. Any departure from budgeted disbursements of foreign funds would distort the budget. The PBO monitors and reports on such disbursements from both multilateral and bilateral donors in order to point out possible shortfalls that would require government to reprioritize its expenditures.

The PBO has greatly improved the relevant committee's capacity to understand the loan agreements between the government and the donors, and Parliament no longer passes loans automatically. Parliament is now in a position to question or even request government to renegotiate provisions that are found to be unfavorable.

Expenditure

Section 6 of the Budget Act requires each minister to submit a policy statement to Parliament by June 30 in each financial year. The statement is expected to reflect, among other things, the funds appropriated for that ministry for that financial year and to describe how much was actually released and what it was used for.

The PBO then reconciles the shortfalls (or in some ministries the supplementary funds) with the total budget performance, and if there are discrepancies, it brings this to the notice of the Budget Committee. The PBO has also developed modules—which are still simple—that committees use to monitor the performance of the sectors they oversee. Whereas ministries are by law required to submit annual policy statements, the PBO has been producing quarterly budget performance reports, based on information collected from the treasury, as well as from all the sectors. This has enabled Parliament to follow the general budget performance and particular sector performance throughout the year.

Economic Indicators

The PBO at any given time is able to give an independent report (independent of the executive) on the performance of the economy. Since the PBO was established, Parliament has been able to follow the implications of macroeconomic policies, receive independent information on poverty trends, and verify figures given by government on economic growth. Parliament is now able to debate, from an informed position, the socioeconomic trends and, as is required by the Budget Act Section 2, analyze programs and policy issues that affect the national budget and economy and, where necessary, recommend alternative approaches to government.

On issues that are budget and economy related, at the close of each financial year the PBO produces a record of Parliament's recommendation to government, and government is expected to respond, showing where they have not complied, and give Parliament the reasons for noncompliance. This procedure has greatly improved the quality of Parliament's oversight role, and it has enhanced government's accountability and consequently the accountability of members of Parliament to their constituents.

The Budget Cycle

The Uganda Budget, under Article 155(1) of the constitution, is prepared and laid before Parliament no later than the 15th day before the commencement of the financial year. The financial year commences July 1. Article 155 also requires the president to request the preparation of the following, to be presented to Parliament:

- Fiscal and monetary programs and plans for economic and social development covering periods exceeding one year.
- Estimates of revenue and expenditure covering periods exceeding one year.

Parliament, in return, is expected to debate and approve the budget. Before the budget is passed, the constitution allows the president to authorize issuance of money from the Consolidated Fund account to meet expenditures necessary to carry out the services of government for up to four months. This authorization is also endorsed by Parliament and constitutes approximately one-third of the total budget for that financial year.

Prior to passage of the Budget Act, Parliament would receive the budget when it was presented on or about June 15 in each financial year. Committees would then look at the policy statements of their relevant ministries and present reports to the full Parliament, which would pass the budget by the end of October. Meanwhile, government spent funds appropriated as vote-on-account. In 2001, when the Budget Act came into force, Parliament began participating more in the process by setting the expenditure priorities both for the following financial year and for the three years to follow. The priority setting for the three years indicates government programs with medium-term expenditure frameworks, which in turn are drawn from the long-term plan, the Poverty Eradication Action Plan.

Among the most important changes that demonstrate greater participation of Parliament with the assistance of the PBO are the following:

1. Whereas prior to 2001 Parliament would receive the budget figures at the time that the budget was read, the Budget Act, Section 4(2), now requires the president (represented by the Ministry of Finance) to request the preparation of the indicative, preliminary revenue and expenditure framework of government for the next financial year, to be submitted and laid before Parliament by April 1 in each financial year. The indicative figures are then committed by the Speaker to the Budget Committee and all sessional committees. Sessional committees consider, discuss, and review the indicative allocations and prepare reports, which are submitted to the Budget Committee by April 25. When sessional committees are reviewing the indicative allocations, an economist from the PBO is attached to each committee to give guidance and assist in pointing out areas of importance or discrepancy with earlier approved policies.

Sessional Committees are then able to agree or disagree with the activities and programs for which funds have been allocated in that year's budget or to recommend reallocations (within the ceilings given to the respective sectors).

At the Budget Committee level, where all chairs of other committees participate, the 10 sessional committees' reports are reviewed and recommendations are adopted or rejected, normally by consensus. It is at this level that reallocations across sectors are proposed to government. All these recommendations, proposals, and advice on policy issues are contained in one comprehensive report, which the Budget Committee, again with the assistance of the PBO, prepares and submits to the Speaker. The Speaker must then forward it to the president no later than May 15. The period between this submission and the final budget (about one month) allows the executive to incorporate Parliament's recommendations and wishes in the budget. If the executive has strong reservations about some recommendations, this one month offers an opportunity for the two arms of government to discuss and come up with commonly agreed-upon positions.

2. The constitution requires that the president submit to Parliament fiscal and monetary programs as well as estimates of revenue and expenditure for periods exceeding one year. In practice, the president only submitted one-year programs and budget estimates. With the coming into force of the Budget

Act, the practice changed, as the act, specifically in Section 4(1), emphasizes this constitutional requirement. Therefore Parliament now has received not only annual estimates but also estimates for the three consecutive years. The Budget Committee, with the assistance of expert scrutiny for the PBO, then reports to Parliament, pointing out any inconsistencies, policy changes and their justification (or lack of it), and revenue and expenditure projections for the following three years. MPs are now able to inform their constituents more authoritatively on government programs with a clearer indication of when they will be implemented.

3. Policy statements, which used to be submitted any time before the budget was passed, are now submitted by June 30 (Budget Act Section 1). This gives sessional committees enough time to scrutinize them and report to Parliament as part of the appropriation exercise. Again, an official from the PBO is attached to each sessional committee as they scrutinize the policy statements. Section 6(2) requires that these policy statements reflect value of money and extent of achievement of targeted objectives. The standardization of the policy statement was done by the PBO together with the Ministry of Finance and approved by the Budget Committee.

4. It was recognized that there were pieces of legislation that, when passed during a financial year, distort the budget, such as bills and motions whose implementation would require amounts of funds not previously budgeted for. The Budget Act Section 10 now requires that every bill introduced in Parliament be accompanied by its indicative financial implications, if any. The certificate of financial implications is tabled together with the bill on its first reading and is committed to the relevant sessional committee along with the bill. Committees seek the expertise of the PBO to verify the accuracy of these certificates and advise on the implications on the budget for that financial year. Parliament is now able to defer bills to another financial year after accommodating their implications in the MTEF (the medium-term expenditure framework).

5. Section 11 of the Budget Act mandates that Parliament analyze programs and policy issues that affect the national budget and economy and, where necessary, recommend alternative approaches to the government. Parliament would not be able to do this without the assistance of the PBO, which prepares economic performance reports on a quarterly basis. As already mentioned, these include revenue-related as well as expenditure-related issues.

6. The constitution provides for supplementary expenditure over and above what Parliament has appropriated. Before the Budget Act came into force, these expenditures could be as high as 20 percent of the initial budget. This distortion is addressed in Section 12 of the Budget Act. The PBO helps the Budget Committee analyze the figures to ensure that the supplementary expenditure is within the 3 percent allowed by law. The PBO is also in constant touch with the various ministries to ensure that budget execution is as approved by Parliament. Parliament is now able to receive reports on reallocations both

within and across ministries or departments. Such timely information allows Parliament to keep track of budget discipline.

7. The reports from the president on the total indebtedness of the state are scrutinized by the PBO. A more simplified and easier-to-understand analysis is then prepared for the Budget Committee, which in turn presents a report to Parliament. The Uganda Parliamentary Budget Office, in doing all the above, carries out its important functions, namely:

- Providing economic forecasts
- Formulating baseline estimates
- Assisting in analyzing the National Budget
- Helping Parliament analyze the MTEF

The PBO has also been a key actor in identifying alternative policy approaches and has presented such modules, particularly on taxation, to the relevant committees. The nonpartisan and professional nature of the unit has enabled it to perform the above functions to the satisfaction of Parliament as well as the executive. The executive branch now recognizes and appreciates that Parliament is able to deal with budget issues on an equal footing.

The Successes

With the assistance of the PBO, the budget process has been demystified. What was earlier overlooked as a specialized, difficult, and even boring area—dealing with figures—has now become accessible, interesting, and easier to understand. Budget discussions are livelier, both inside and outside Parliament.

The strict measures prescribed in the Budget Act on how to deal with the budget have assisted in making budget formulation and execution more transparent. Since all Parliament committee meetings are open to the press and the public, budget-related issues are now understood by most of the population.

The participation of MPs as people's representatives has enhanced the creditability of the budget. There is more ownership. Other stakeholders such as civil society organizations and the donor community, though not addressed specifically in the act, are able to interact with the committees during the budget discussion stage. In fact, interest groups like manufacturers, exporters, farmers, and so forth that are affected by tax measures are accommodated by Parliament, which has a better understating of the issues they face.

The deadlines in the Budget Act have improved the discipline in preparation as well as execution of the budget. Though at first there was resistance from the executive, now the players appreciate their roles, those of others, and the time frames. Government compliance has improved, and accountability has been promoted.

Parliament is able to respond rapidly to problems because of the better flow of information and greater scrutiny. Government is more alert and mindful of making mistakes in implementing the budget. Donors seem to have more confidence in the process than ever before, and this manifests itself when Parliament is included among the stakeholders to be continuously consulted.

Parliament is now able to participate and contribute during public expenditure review meetings and formulation of poverty reduction programs. All in all, the ownership between the executive and Parliament was greatly improved by the Budget Act.

Challenges

In performing its duties outlined above, the PBO has faced a number of challenges. Key among them are the following:

1. Information. Before the Parliamentary Commission insisted on having all funds that go to Parliament as basket funds, the Budget Committee and the PBO had worked out the costing of having information technology connectivity to the key centers where budget-related information could be accessed by the PBO more easily and quickly. This has not happened, since Parliament itself has other requirements apart from strengthening the Budget Office. The PBO therefore relies on information provided by other centers, for example, the Ministry of Finance, the Bank of Uganda, and the Uganda Bureau of Statistics and has no way of cross-checking the information it receives. There are times when the information furnished to the PBO has been inaccurate, inadequate, and sometimes not timely.

2. Establishment structure. Since the structure was revised to provide for more officers in the PBO, some posts have remained vacant because of budget constraints. The existing officers therefore are faced with a very heavy workload, and they work long hours, especially during the budget scrutiny period.

3. Cooperation. Though cooperation with government sectors has generally improved, some ministries either deliberately, or out of incompetence, do not furnish the PBO with the information it requires to assist Parliament with comprehensive reports. The prime minister (leader of government business) has been particularly cooperative insofar as compelling ministries to provide information, but some still do not comply.

4. Discrimination and bureaucracy. Surprisingly, the PBO suffers to some extent from discrimination from the administration of Parliament under the Parliamentary Commission. There is a general feeling among other officers that the PBO is a "superdepartment" because it has better facilities, including offices, office equipment, and vehicles. These facilities were provided by donors to support the establishment of the PBO. Some donor agencies have continued to directly fund the PBO outside the general budget of Parliament, a practice that did not satisfy the Parliamentary Commission.

The bureaucracy in the administration of Parliament sometimes causes delays in the PBO's work. The time spent between the requisitioning and the release of funds for office accessories (even small ones including paper, toner, fuel, and so forth) bogs down the PBO's work.

5. Demands from members of Parliament. Most MPs have shown little interest in reading reports containing a lot of figures. The PBO puts in a lot of work, but only a few MPs take advantage of it. At the same time, they continuously demand information, which has often already been provided to them, and some even expect information to be collected for them for individual projects. The PBO sometimes finds itself overwhelmed with individual MPs' demands. Although the requests for information are required to go through the Budget Committee or the clerk, some MPs do not follow this procedure.

6. Lessons for other parliaments. Legislatures in different counties are at different levels in terms of participation in the budget formulation process. The need for as much participation as possible cannot be overemphasized, as the budget is the single most important tool through which economic and social policy can be influenced. With more participation, parliaments will be in a better position to play their three basic roles: representation, lawmaking, and oversight.

The executive branch in most governments will not support parliaments' increased participation in budget formulation. This means that parliaments, especially in Africa and other transition economies, should initiate their own legislation that will ensure that they are able to participate fully and in a meaningful way.

Parliaments can benefit by sharing experiences and assisting in building capacity in other parliaments to make them more effective and to ensure better public policies and more prudent management of public resources. Parliaments may need to be assisted with funds, personnel, and initial office equipment, as well as capacity building to use mechanisms such as private member's bills and lobbying skills to bring on board colleagues and nongovernmental bodies, including civil society organizations that support more transparent budgeting.

Uganda's Budget Act and the subsequent establishment of the Parliamentary Budget Office, its successes, and the challenges it has faced offer many useful lessons for other parliaments.

Annex: Parliamentary Budget Office (PBO) Initial Structure

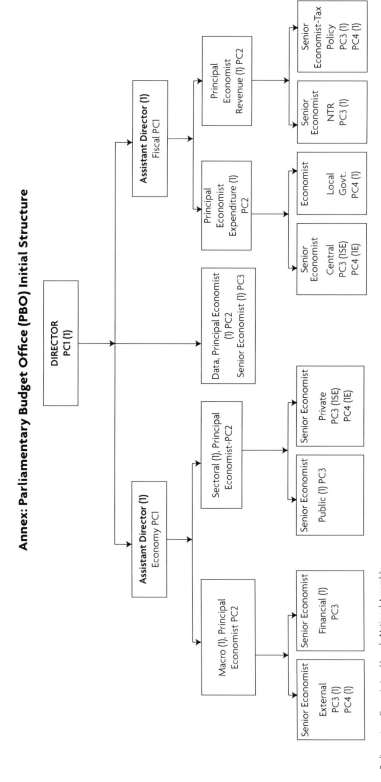

Source: Parliamentary Commission, Uganda National Assembly.

CONCLUSIONS

Legislatures and Administration in Oversight and Budgets: Constraints, Means, and Executives

David M. Olson

The rich array of chapters in this book stems from two sources: researchers, to understand how legislatures work, and professionals who provide democracy-strengthening assistance, to help legislatures work. To know and to do are the twin impulses found in each chapter. Each set of authors, perhaps for different immediate objectives, at the end ask: What do we now understand about legislatures in their oversight and budgeting activities?

Oversight as Concept

The more the terms *oversight* or *scrutiny* are used in democracy-building efforts, the more enthusiastic their advocacy but the more vague their meaning. Several of the chapters in this book note sources that, for example, explicitly include the legislative function within the terms *oversight* and *scrutiny*, thus broadly including all activities of a legislature rather than only some.

The distinction between oversight and scrutiny and the other activities of legislatures might be based on the concept of the policy cycle, differentiating successive stages of policy development, beginning with definition of the policy problems, alternative designs, debate and enactment (predominantly a task of legislation), and evaluation of policy implementation (predominantly a task of oversight). But the cycle is an endless loop, so that problems encountered in the initial policy enactment can lead to revisions in both subsequent policy and administration (Olson and Mezey 1991, 17–20).

At least four problems inhere in developing a limited and workable definition of legislative oversight. First, the policy implications of oversight are potentially important (and deserve more research than reported in this book), but the policy consequences of oversight need to be clearly distinguished from the oversight function itself. Precisely because of possible policy consequences, beginning systems of oversight expressly define the tasks of oversight mechanisms—such as the Public Accounts Committees established in Westminster systems more than a century ago—as limited to an examination of honesty and efficiency in administration, rather than of the desirability or even effectiveness of the policy itself (Bradshaw and Pring 1981, 332, 358).

Second, a more difficult problem in defining the concept of oversight is to distinguish oversight from the selection and dismissal of political executives. The vote of no confidence in parliamentary systems and impeachment in presidential systems are the possible ultimate consequences of, and perhaps motivations for, legislatures' adverse reviews of executives. But most policy choices and implementation problems are more mundane practical questions, ordinarily not leading to the highly visible and potent issues of who occupies political power (Oleszek 1996, 300–04).

Third, budgeting is a task that cuts across the distinction expressed in the first problem, that of policy and administration. The efficiency and honesty emphasis of oversight examines the expenditure side of budgeting, in the narrow terms of numbers in financial ledgers. "Accounts" is a good description of the PAC responsibility. The legislative activities of budgeting and oversight also raise questions about broader terms, especially accountability (Jacobs, chap. 4, in this book).

Budgeting itself has a set of discrete stages in an endless policy cycle (Santiso, chap. 18) and can become a full-time task of both a legislature's committees and professional staff units, as illustrated by several of the chapters in this book (Anderson, chap. 9; Johnson and Stapenhurst, chap. 10; Juwono and Eckardt, chap. 21; Stapenhurst, chap. 3). Budgeting, including revenues as well as expenditures, is both an object of oversight and a means of oversight in any other policy sector.

One important respect in which budgeting differs from most other parliamentary decisions is the calendar-based necessity for a state budget decision. If parliament has not acted by a certain date, specified budget decisions are automatically activated (Dorotinsky, chap. 7). In pursuit of this same objective, changes by parliament in the proposed budget are subject to severe limitations (Mansfeldová and Rakušanová, chap. 20; Wehner, chap. 5).

A fourth problem is the divergent use of the English language terms *scrutiny* and *oversight*. In Westminster systems, *scrutiny* has a broad meaning, referring to all executive-legislature relations, while *oversight*, stemming from the American separation-of-powers system, is mainly limited to the review of policy implementation. These English language differences are illustrated by the chapters in this book. Many of the chapters in this book address oversight as a daily and routine executive-legislature interaction, avoiding the first two problems discussed above. Budgeting, however, is directly considered in the chapters of part 2 in the same manner as oversight.

The chapters, written at various times, with different data, and for different purposes, are not the product of a single encompassing research design. As a result, the generalizations in this concluding summary emerge from, but have not been systematically tested by, the collection of chapters as a whole. The conclusions begin by summarizing the outer constraints within which legislatures exist and function in their review and examination of the conduct of administration. Second, it considers the means used by legislatures for oversight purposes. Finally, it considers time, contexts, and executives as both enabling and limiting considerations in examinations of parliaments' oversight function.

Constitution and Power Distribution

In stable political systems, the constitution and the party system are fairly constant over time, whereas in new political systems, both the constitution and electoral system are themselves in flux. In stable systems, both executives and legislators work within those two major constraints; by contrast, in new systems they are in the process of being defined as part of the wider political struggle. Several of the chapters report on cross-national surveys that show the distribution of constitutional and formal executive and legislative features at any one time, chapters on single legislatures show how these constraints function in specific settings over time.

The distribution of several selected oversight tools among 47 countries varies with their constitutional structure (more so in parliamentary systems than in presidential), and there is some indication of differences in budgeting in relation to broad differences in constitutional systems as well (Pelizzo and Stapenhurst, chap. 1, and Barraclough and Dorotinsky, chap. 6).

More specific executive-legislative relationships are explored in the review of budgeting powers and practices of 43 countries (Wehner, chap. 5). Of three summary indexes, two combine executive and legislative features—on budget powers and on budget information. Only one of the three indexes is confined to organization and procedures internal to the legislature. The low correlation among the three indexes suggests that each country develops its own configuration of authority, structures, and procedures.

Though the broad constitutional structure of executive-legislative relationships is not related to the three budget indexes, one formal constitutional feature, federalism, is related positively to all three, which is also expressed in the form of legislative bicameralism (Barraclough and Dorotinsky, chap. 6). In addition, the degree of one-party control of the executive and parliament is consistently related, negatively, to each of the three measures of legislative budgetary capability—a theme that is emphasized in several chapters on parliaments.

The many legislatures in Latin America, although they share broad constitutional design features, illustrate the diverse ways in which specific legislatures work in practice. They also illustrate how variations in executive control and party systems relate to variations in how legislatures function in the budget process (Santiso, chap. 18).

In every legislature included in this book, the party system (number and sizes of parties) and the internal unity of the parliamentary party group are major considerations. If an executive is the dominant leader in a one-party government with a clear majority in parliament, the parliament has little possibility of exercising either independent oversight or independent judgment on policy. However, at the opposite extreme, with a highly fragmented party system and with noncohesive parliamentary parties, the executive is also likely the dominant figure in parliamentary life. If the Russian Federation illustrates the first condition (Remington, chap. 12), Indonesia (Schneier, chap. 15, and Juwono and Eckardt, chap. 21) illustrates the opposite. In a two-party system, as often found in Westminster systems, the single majority government is also the dominant power, if only for a decade or so (Shephard, chap. 13, and Pelizzo and Stapenhurst, chap. 8).

In a multiparty system (three to seven parties), and consequently with either minority or multiparty coalition governments, parliaments typically have a greater possibility to think and act independently of the government in legislation, oversight, and budgeting (Mezey 1991). Among the chapters of this book, Italy (Forestiere and Pelizzo, chap. 19), Israel (Friedberg, chap. 16), and the Czech Republic (Mansfeldová and Rakušanová, chap. 20) are examples. Mexico illustrates how one-party systems and legislative passivity can slowly become a more competitive electoral system with increased legislative independence from the executive (Santiso, chap. 18).

Similar considerations of government support or opposition affect the extent and direction of oversight activity in more established legislatures as well. A member of the U.S. Congress observed, for example, "We are of the same political party as the President, and, of course, we do not want to do anything to embarrass him unless there is something absolutely wrong." (Ogul 1977, 216). In Westminster systems with strong government party control over parliament, the practice of having a member of the opposition party chair the Public Accounts Committee is a way to preserve parliamentary autonomy in the oversight function (Bradshaw and Pring 1981, 331–34).

Nevertheless, Westminster-derived parliaments tend to cluster as a distinctive set. While they tend to resemble one another on the three budget indexes (Wehner, chap. 5), the chairpersons of Commonwealth PACs have different views about the importance of political parties and about the effectiveness of their own efforts (Pelizzo and Stapenhurst, chap. 8). The contemporary British House of Commons seems to have the same experiences and evaluations (Shephard, chap. 13).

Organization, Procedures, and Members of Parliaments

Even a small parliament, much less a large one of hundreds of members, requires organization and procedures to get work done. Committees are the major organizational device for legislation, budgeting, and oversight activities, while parliamentary party groups are more concerned with the organization and uses of power. Rules prescribe the procedures by which the organizational units of a legislature interact with one another and also with the executive (Olson 1994, 31–32; Olson and Norton 2007, 177–78).

Legislative committees, the functional equivalent of administrative agencies, are discussed in almost all of the chapters in this book. Westminster parliaments feature the Public Accounts Committee, a unique committee dedicated to budget review (Beetham 2006; McGee 2002; Pelizzo and Stapenhurst, chap. 8). Most other legislatures have a committee system defined by jurisdiction over specified policies and related administrative agencies, and also a committee responsible for the state budget. That is, the formal committee structure of most legislatures more resembles the American and continental European patterns than the British patterns.

The jurisdictions of committees in parliament are far more stable than the structure of ministries in government. Whereas ministries are reorganized and redistributed, not only after an election but also during an electoral term, the structure of parliamentary committees remains relatively stable from one term to the next. Committee members often serve longer on a committee than does a minister in the government (Olson and Norton 2007).

But precisely how committees are organized, the scope of their powers, and the extent of their support staff vary greatly (Crowther and Olson 2002; Hazan 2001). The Israeli committees function apparently only sporadically and not very effectively (Friedberg, chap. 16). The Czech Republic's Budget Committee, by contrast, is both active and informed, and has become the most prestigious committee in parliament (Mansfeldová and Rakušanová, chap. 20).

The members of committees also differ greatly. Although the Czech Republic's Budget Committee members, over the almost two decades of their existence, have become increasingly well qualified for the tasks of the committee, the members of Israeli committees, by contrast, do not often attend and are replaced by alternates. In Brazilian federal states, members are in legislatures to seek more attractive positions elsewhere (Desposato, chap. 14). In Indonesia (Schneier, chap. 15) and South Africa (Griffiths, chap. 17), the members of a powerful committee are themselves important figures both in the party and economy outside parliament; it is their external capabilities that give power and influence to their parliamentary committee, rather than the reverse.

Incumbency of members is an important attribute of parliaments and their committees. In new parliaments, the common phenomenon of high member turnover limits the opportunity for either personal learning or institutional memory. But chamber incumbency may not translate into committee incumbency for either members or chairpersons (Santiso, chap. 18; Crowther and Olson 2002, 178–80).

For both budgeting and oversight, legislators are dependent upon staff. Although some committees discussed in this book are developing a small staff, and some parliaments are developing a budget office, an external national audit office is a more common resource, as in the Czech Republic, Poland, South Africa, and Great Britain and other Westminster cases. A clear majority of legislatures, however, have no budget analysis office (Barraclough and Dorotinsky, chap. 6; Johnson and Stapenhurst, chap. 10). Either providing staff to a new budget committee or creating a new budget office has been a slow and also difficult task in both Indonesia and Uganda (Juwono and Eckardt, chap. 21; Kiraso, chap. 22).

All of the above structures and practices are defined through the rules, or standing orders, of the legislature. The rules or orders, in turn, are developed through interparty negotiations and change over time (Barker and Levine 1999; Olson and Norton 2007, 174–75).

Rules and procedures regulate the circumstances under which government budget proposals are transmitted to parliament, as well as how the committees work on the budget in both authorization and oversight stages. Though internal rules can be defined by executive decree and constitution in some postcommunist and Latin American parliaments (Olson, chap. 11; Santiso, chap. 18), the rules are internal parliamentary decisions in both the Czech Republic and Italy.

The viability and importance of the parliament itself, and thus of its members, as well as its internal structure and procedures, can be vitiated by an executive in command of a dominant party. Though the Duma has a committee system, it is superseded by informal negotiations between the executive and the members of parliament, as is also suggested for Indonesia. Under these circumstances, the lack of oversight is part of the broader pattern of executive leadership of the dominant party and thus of parliament. In a Westminster parliamentary system, however, both the structure and the rules are subject to the preferences of the prime minister supported by a cohesive majority.

Contexts, Time, and Executives

Every parliament discussed in this book has been characterized as undergoing change. Many are new bodies in newly democratized political systems, and often in newly created sovereign nations undergoing dramatic change induced by necessity—but with no clear choices, only paradoxes (Olson 1997).

Among the former Warsaw Pact countries, the Czech Republic (Mansfeldová and Rakušanová, chap. 20) has become a democracy with a parliamentary system of governance, while the Russian Duma has become increasingly dominated by the Russian president (Remington, chap. 12). South Africa (Griffiths, chap. 17) has recently emerged from the apartheid regime, and Indonesia from military rule (Schneier, chap. 15; Juwono and Eckardt, chap. 21), and Brazil and Latin America generally (Desposato, chap. 14, and Santiso, chap. 18, respectively), have experienced several cycles of military and civilian rule over the past several decades. Only the United Kingdom (Shephard, chap. 13), Italy (Forestiere and Pelizzo, chap. 19), and Israel (Friedberg, chap. 16), in this set of studies, are continuous democracies.

As a type of political system, the "hybrid," with a presidentially dominated legislature, raises questions about the viability of legislatures as capable and independent bodies (Diamond 2002). Public dispute centers on neither the content nor administration of public policy, but on the struggle for power in the state. The struggle for power between parliament and president is waged through both elections and the ensuing government formation negotiations. Once in office, disputes concentrate on the legitimacy and legality of the government in power and allegations of unlawful suppression of the opposition. The opposition itself is often fragmented, with defections to and from the government. Usually ineffectual in parliament, the opposition often resorts to boycotts on the floor and demonstrations in the street. In hybrid states, the legislature's main preoccupation is with the elemental and generic task of government formation within the broader struggle over the constitutional shape of the state. Oversight is beyond both the concerns and capabilities of the legislature (Khmelko, Pigenko, and Wise 2007).

The practice of limited but detailed oversight, though often found inadequate in stable democracies (Shephard, chap. 13), can encourage the beginning of independent activity by legislatures in executive-dominated one-party states (Blondel 1973). The case of Poland illustrates how, within a communist political system, structures and procedures centering on oversight can be developed and survive as useful instruments in a new democratic system (Olson, chap. 11). Perhaps the century-long experience of the British Parliament provides a template for more contemporary developments: the originally limited Public Accounts Committee has slowly expanded its functions and increased its scope of activity.

In all of the parliaments included in this book, there is a profound sense of inadequacy in dealing with their government's executive branches. Both members of parliament, as in Uganda (Kiraso, chap. 22), and PAC chairs (Pelizzo and Stapenhurst, chap. 8) are dissatisfied. Parliaments' desire to develop the means to obtain information about administration policy and to require executives to make desired changes reflects their dissatisfaction with the more general circumstance of being subject to executive power buttressed by party control.

The experiences of postauthoritarian legislatures featured in this book suggest at least three considerations for understanding the conditions under which active and democratic institutions develop: time, societal and cultural context, and the executive.

Though the breakdown of authoritarian systems—a democratic "outer" transition—may occur quickly, the institutions and practices of democratic self-governance—the "inner" transitions—develop slowly. Many inner transformations are needed to fulfill the aspirations of the political system's outer transition. The analogy of the "founding moment" has to be measured in decades. Time can also act as a leavening agent within authoritarian regimes, as in both Poland (Olson, chap. 11) and Brazil (Power 2004). Over time, legislators can learn and legislatures can develop structures and practices that increase their autonomy from dominant executives (Baaklini and Pojo do Rego 1991; Olson 1995).

As examples of societal context, the Czech Republic and Poland provide evidence of rapid change toward parliamentary capability, whereas, at a relatively earlier stage of both national and parliamentary development, Indonesia, Uganda, and many other states face difficulties that are all too apparent. These examples illustrate the broader considerations of society, economy, and culture within which both parliaments and executives function. Stable democracies and functioning parliaments, as well as their opposites, may be very different in very different settings. They also develop in different ways and at different speeds. Each has its own history; for example, not only does the communist legacy of postcommunist states have important consequences for current behavior, but their precommunist historical inheritance does as well.

Both considerations of social context and of developmental time suggest cautions for attempts to help new democracies and newly active legislatures achieve their potential, as well as for retrospective assessments of the impact of such institutional assistance (Schultz 2004).

Executive powers have been a part of every chapter in this book. While concentrating on legislatures, chapters have also referred to prime ministers, presidents, and other types of government executives. Oversight and budgeting are examples of the broader and pervasive executive-legislative relationship. Both entities require equal analysis to assess the interactive dynamic between them and the changes in that dynamic over time. If newly democratized parliaments continue practices from the authoritarian past, perhaps executives and their administrative functions do as well. If the impetus to this book is to understand parliaments, one of its conclusions is that the need to understand executives is equally important.

Bibliography

Baaklini, Abdo I., and Antonio Carlos Pojo do Rego. 1991. "Congress and the Development of a Computer Industry Policy in Brazil." In Olson and Mezey 1991, 130–59.

Barker, Fiona, and Stephen Levine. 1999. "The Individual Parliamentary Member and Institutional Change: The Changing Role of the New Zealand Member of Parliament." *Journal of Legislative Studies* 5 (3/4): 105–30.

Beetham, David. 2006. *Parliament and Democracy in the Twenty-First Century: A Guide to Good Practice.* Geneva: Inter-Parliamentary Union.

Blondel, Jan. 1973. *Comparative Legislatures.* Englewood Cliffs, NJ: Prentice-Hall.

Bradshaw, Kenneth, and David Pring. 1981. *Parliament and Congress.* Rev. ed. London: Quartet Books.

Crowther, William E., and David M. Olson. 2002. "Committee Systems in New Democratic Parliaments: Comparative Institutionalization." In *Committees in Post-Communist Democratic Parliaments: Comparative Institutionalization,* ed. David M. Olson and William E. Crowther, 171–206. Columbus: Ohio State University Press.

Diamond, Larry. 2002. "Thinking About Hybrid Regimes." *Journal of Democracy* 13 (2): 21–35.

Hazan, Reuven. 2001. *Reforming Parliamentary Committees.* Columbus: Ohio State University Press.

Khmelko, Irina S., Vladimir A. Pigenko, and Charles R. Wise. 2007. "Assessing Committee Roles in a Developing Legislature: The Case of the Ukrainian Parliament." *Journal of Legislative Studies* 13 (2): 210–34.

McGee, David G. 2002. *The Overseers: Public Accounts Committees and Public Spending.* London: Commonwealth Parliamentary Association, with Pluto Press.

Mezey, Michael L. 1991. "Parliaments and Public Policy: An Assessment." In Olson and Mezey 1991, 201–14.

Ogul, Morris. 1977. "Congressional Oversight: Structures and Incentives." In *Congress Reconsidered*, ed. Lawrence C. Dodd and Bruce I. Oppenheimer, 207–21. New York: Praeger.

Oleszek, Walter J. 1996. *Congressional Procedures and the Policy Process*. 4th ed. Washington, DC: CQ Press.

Olson, David M. 1994. *Democratic Legislative Institutions: A Comparative View.* Armonk, NY: M. E. Sharpe.

———. 1995. "Organizational Dilemmas of Postcommunist Assemblies." *East European Constitutional Review* 4 (2): 56–60.

———. 1997. "The Paradoxes of Institutional Development: The New Democratic Parliaments of Central Europe." *International Political Science Review* 18 (4): 401–16.

Olson, David M., and Michael L. Mezey, eds. 1991. *Legislatures in the Policy Process: The Dilemmas of Economic Policy.* Cambridge, U.K.: Cambridge University Press.

Olson, David M., and Philip Norton. 2007. "Post-Communist and Post-Soviet Parliaments: Divergent Paths from Transition." *Journal of Legislative Studies* 13 (1): 164–96.

Power, Timothy J. 2004. "Time and Legislative Development in New Democracies: Is Executive Dominance Always Irreversible?" In *Trends in Parliamentary Oversight*, ed. Riccardo Pelizzo, Rick Stapenhurst, and David Olson, 47–54. Washington DC: World Bank Institute.

Schultz, Keith. 2004. "Measuring the Impact of Donor Funded Legislative Strengthening Programs on Legislative Oversight Performance." In *Trends in Parliamentary Oversight*, ed. Riccardo Pelizzo, Rick Stapenhurst, and David Olson, 55–58. Washington, DC: World Bank Institute.

Index

Boxes, figures, and tables are indicated by b, f, and t, respectively.

oversight capacity of parliaments, 244–245

political economy, 244, 257, 258–260

recent reforms, 247

risks of centralization, 248–250, 255

role of auditor general, 260

role of parliaments, 250–251, 261, 262

strategies for improving, 261–262

transparency in, 262

See also specific country

Budget process oversight

access to information for, 56, 83, 86, 256–257

accounting strategies for, 75–77

accrual-based accounting, 68, 74

attitudes of legislators in Czech Republic, 282

auditing systems, 57–58

benefits of transparency, 259

"beyond budgets" movement, 73

budget cycle, 52

capacity building for, 61–63

classification of legislative roles in, 141–142

committee capacity for, 82–83, 85, 256

committees for. *See* Committees, budget oversight; Public Accounts Committees

conceptual and historical evolution, 51–52, 71, 84–85

confidence convention, 83

control process modeling, 69–72

in Czech Republic, 279–280, 282–289

defense procurement oversight in South Africa, 232–235

definition, 324

definition of budget, 94 n.2

drafting stage. *See* Drafting stage of budget

ex ante, 53–57

executive flexibility during implementation, 82, 85

executive veto power and, 83–84

ex post, 57–60

form of democratic governance and, 57, 267

in Indonesia, 205–206, 293, 298–299, 301, 302–306

ineffective parliaments, 243–244

institutional capacity, 81, 90–91

institutional determinants of parliament's power, 267–269, 274, 275

in Italy, 269–275

legislative activism in, 54, 131

measures of centralization, 247

multiperiod evaluations, 75–76

objectives, 51, 61, 69, 71–72

outcomes evaluation in, 75

Parliamentary agenda setting in, 270–271

participants, 52

performance monitoring, 304

political context of accounting practice, 67–69, 274, 275

political determinants of parliament's power, 267–268, 269, 272

political will for, 61–62

power to amend budget, 56, 81, 90, 251, 253–254, 302

public role, 52, 54–55, 60

purpose of budgets, 69

rationale, 243

rationale for centralized budgetary system, 246–248

resources for, 61, 86, 256–257

risks of centralization of budgetary arrangements, 248–250

in Russia, 176–179

salient issues, 3–4

secret voting in parliament and, 270

significance of, in legislative oversight, 3

significance of variances in, 69, 75

in state governments of Brazil, 195

structures and procedures for, 52, 79

technical complexity, 67

time allotted for scrutiny, 82, 85, 253, 263 n.8, 317

transfer pricing approach, 73–74

trends in budget process, 53, 286–287

See also Budget governance in Latin America; Drafting stage of budget; Failure to pass budget; Index of legislative budget institutions; Parliamentary Budget Office, Uganda's

C

Caiden, N., 80

California Legislative Analyst's Office, 142–144, 153–154

Canada, budget process, 88, 112

Capacity building

donor assistance for, 199

legislative strengthening, 61–63

strategies for increasing legislative oversight in Brazil, 197–200

visionary leadership for, 199

Capacity for oversight

actual oversight versus, oversight effectiveness and, 35–40, 44

in budget process, 81, 90–91

clientelistic and programmatic politics and, 198–199

determinants of, 21

determinants of oversight effectiveness, 31

expertise for military procurement oversight, 236

gross national income and, 9, 15–18, 21, 34

in Indonesia, 202, 211–212

information resources to increase, 198

in post-Soviet states, 168–169, 173–174,
180–181
in post-Suharto Indonesia, 201–202,
209–211, 293, 294–296, 305
risk of capture and corruption, 180
role of legislative oversight, 2, 117–118
social contexts, 329–330
sources of legislative power, 173
stability of forms, 117, 127 n.2
trends, 117
See also Liberal democracies; Parliamentary
democracies; Presidential and
semipresidential democracies
Denmark, budget process, 89
Developing countries, budget process, 53
Doidge, Geoff, 237
Donor assistance
for oversight capacity-building, 199
Drafting stage of budget
baseline estimate preparation, 133, 153
committee capacity, 106–107
in Czech Republic, 280–281
debate on ceilings, 100, 104–105
determinants of legislative involvement,
3–4, 109
determinants of legislature's influence,
55–56
determinants of legislature's role, 105
economic forecasting in, 133, 153
form of democracy and differences in, 55,
106, 107, 108–109
form of democratic governance and, 101,
102, 103, 104
good practices, 99–100
as judgmental process, 72–73
in Latin America, 253
long-term analyses, 135
medium-term analyses, 133–134
national income and, 101, 102, 103,
104, 107
political power relationships and, 56, 108
power of legislature, 105
prebudget statements, 100–104, 105
public hearings, 107
research capacity and information access,
56, 83, 105–106, 131, 154
specialized committees for, 56–57
timelines, 100, 101–102
transparency in, 109, 152
zero-based budgeting, 73
See also Independent analytic unit for
budget preparation

E

Edward III, King, 52
Edwin, Donni, 211
Effectiveness of oversight efforts
actual versus potential oversight and,
35–40, 44

determinants of, 25, 31
differences among oversight tools in
democracy promotion, 29, 30,
40–43, 44–45
executive–parliament power relations
and, 328–329
nonpartisanship as factor in, 42, 45 n.3
parliament structure and procedures and,
326–328
public accounts committees, 59
research needs, 21–22
scope of investigative focus and, 44
urgent versus normal questioning, 40–42
Ellis, Andrew, 206–207
Ethiopia, 63
Ex ante oversight
definition, 13
role of legislature, 118
tools, 13
See also Budget process oversight
Executive branch
budget drafting process, 108
budget power in Latin America,
251–253, 258
budget responsibilities and authority, 52,
83–84
effect of independent analytic unit for
budget preparation on power of,
152
flexibility during budget implementation,
82, 85
Latin American budget governance,
243–244, 245–246
legislative branch relations in clientelistic
and programmatic states, 197
rationale for centralized budgetary
system, 246–248
risks of centralized budget arrangements,
248–250
See also Presidential and semipresidential
democracies
Ex post oversight
definition, 13
Latin American budgets, 255
role of legislature, 118
tools, 13

F

Failure to pass budget, 4
interim spending, 85, 111, 112, 113, 114
in Latin America, 254
outcomes in OECD and non-OECD
countries, 84–85, 112–113
political costs, 111
possible responses, 111–112
in presidential versus parliamentary
systems, 113–114
as variable in index of legislative budget
institutions, 81–82

Wehner, Joachim, 54, 55
Westminster-style parliaments, 4, 55, 71,
        83, 326
Wildavsky, A. B., 80
World Bank, 2, 54

Y

Yakovlev, Vladimir, 174

Yeltsin, Boris, 173, 176
Yodohono, Susilo Bambang,
        204, 213

Z

Zambia, budget process, 56
Zuma, Jacob, 238